SOCIAL PRINCIPLES AND ECONOMIC LIFE

SOCIAL PRINCIPLES
AND
ECONOMIC LIFE

REV. JOHN F. CRONIN, S.S., Ph.D.

ASSISTANT DIRECTOR, DEPARTMENT OF SOCIAL ACTION
NATIONAL CATHOLIC WELFARE CONFERENCE

THE BRUCE PUBLISHING COMPANY
MILWAUKEE

NIHIL OBSTAT:

EDMUND KURTH
Censor deputatus

IMPRIMATUR:

✠ PATRICK A. O'BOYLE
Archbishop of Washington
February 11, 1959

The nihil obstat and imprimatur are official declarations that a book or pamphlet is free of doctrinal or moral error. No implication is contained therein that those who have granted the nihil obstat and the imprimatur agree with the content, opinions, or statements expressed.

Library of Congress Catalog Card Number: 59–10753

(3/62)

To My Mother

PREFACE

THIS book was intended as a condensation and revision of the author's earlier work, *Catholic Social Principles*, published in 1950. The process of condensation, however, proceeded to a point where only about half of the original text remained. In the revision, there was more new and rewritten material than holdovers from the earlier text. Even in the passages embodying papal and other authoritative quotations, there were substantial deletions and replacements with fresh and more pertinent material. Under the circumstances, the only way to avoid total confusion among teachers and those who used the earlier work as a reference text was to change its name. The change in title did not imply any difference in purpose. But the type of problems faced in American economic life and the emphasis in papal statements in the 1950's were sufficiently different to warrant a fresh approach within the old framework.

Like its predecessor, this book offers an explanation of Catholic social principles in the light of American economic life. The social teaching of the Church is basically a mixture of ethics, moral theology, and prudent judgment as applied to the field of social economics. It is called Catholic because of its immediate source. But its principles are so founded in human nature that men of all creeds can readily see its truth and wisdom. While it has been presented authoritatively by various statements of recent popes, its roots go back to the inspired words of Holy Writ.

The primary sources used are the social writings and addresses of Popes Leo XIII, Pius X, Benedict XV, Pius XI, Pius XII, and John XXIII. Occasional reference is made to other authoritative documents. But the papal statements cited crystallize and apply to modern conditions, social principles developed from scriptural teachings and natural law. In presenting Catholic social teaching, textual excerpts from authoritative sources are reprinted in each chapter. This practice gives the reader convenient opportunity to study the documents which are being explained and applied. Each set of excerpts is then explained in the light of general ethical and moral principles. Where useful, background material is supplied. This is sometimes necessary where the full meaning of writings destined for the entire world may not be immediately evident in terms of our language and customs. Moreover, there are many important points where the encyclicals are either silent or not conclusive. In these cases moralists often differ in their views. On controversial questions, different points of view are presented and references given for further study. Moreover, the best available experts have been consulted. In this way, a distinction is made between what is clear or generally agreed upon and what is still the subject of serious discussion.

The ethical commentary is accompanied by an application of principles to current American economic conditions. Economic application is especially needed as a service to the great body of Catholics, clergy and laity, who are already familiar with the broad principles of social ethics. Unfortunately, these principles are not easily applied in the complex world of economic life. In many cases, it is even difficult to learn the facts to which principles pertain. Even when the facts are known, there may be disputes as to the relevant economic laws governing the situation. Yet, unless moral norms are applied properly, they remain abstract and indefinite. We have not hesitated in other fields, such as medical ethics, to face delicate issues in applying principles. There is even greater need in the social field for concrete application, since the popes, dealing with world-wide problems, must necessarily speak in general terms. But time and again they have urged Catholic social scientists to apply principles to the problems of their day and age.

Practical application is likewise needed if our teachings are to be honored by the non-Catholic world. Too often Catholics are secretly apologetic about their social teachings. They act as if they were an *arcana disciplina*, truths too sacred to be bandied about. Such diffidence is largely unwarranted. On the contrary, when our principles are presented in language and context familiar to Americans, they usually meet with enthusiastic acceptance.

In presenting our social ethics, the order of treatment involves a progression from general principles to fields of more limited application. There are three main parts to the present book. In the first, the social problem is outlined in relation to the broad bases of human nature. The general social teachings of the Church are given. Judgment is passed upon other social philosophies prevalent in the modern world. In the second part, the focus is narrowed to special fields, such as capital, labor, wages, family, property problems, and the state. Finally, in the third part, there are considered other vital social institutions and problems, such as international economic life, race problems, and rural life. The concluding chapter relates social principles to social action.

Two major bibliographical changes were made in this book. First, references to articles in *Social Order* were included in the chapter readings. Without prejudice to other good periodicals, it appears that *Social Order* has been ideal for amplifying and updating material on the development and application of Catholic social principles. Second, the Appendix reading lists are more closely integrated with the order of treatment in the text. This will facilitate consultation for the purpose of further study.

The earlier version of this book appealed equally to two classes of readers. First, it was widely used by Catholic clergy and laity interested in social problems and social action. Several features of the present edition should make for even broader interest in this group. The effort to condense the volume by omitting items no longer of substantial interest has permitted the inclusion of new features. These include the more important principles dealing with family, racial, political, and international problems.

In addition to general use as a source and reference book, the first version was widely adopted as a textbook by many colleges and universities. Many teachers were consulted on the present revision. Their suggestions resulted in the tighter writing of the chapters retained from the earlier version, as well as the inclusion of new material. This should make for easier classroom use.

All these features make the present version quite different from its predecessor. It is hoped that these efforts will inspire new generations of American Catholics to seek to restore all things in Christ, that our society may be inspired by justice and charity.

REV. JOHN F. CRONIN, S.S.

ACKNOWLEDGMENTS

THE author wishes to thank again those who so kindly assisted in the preparation of *Catholic Social Principles*, the predecessor of this book. Those aiding in this present version include Rev. Edmund J. Kurth, who offered helpful suggestions while acting as ecclesiastical censor; Rev. Edward Duff, S.J., and his colleagues in *Social Order*, Reverends Leo C. Brown, S.J., Joseph M. Becker, S.J., Mortimer H. Gavin, S.J., and John L. Thomas, S.J. This able combination of economic and social talent was a great aid to the author. Individual chapters were read by Rev. James H. Brennan, S.S., Dr. Michael P. Fogarty, Rev. Oswald von Nell-Breuning, S.J., Rev. James J. Vizzard, S.J., and Miss Agnes Waldron.

Appreciation is also extended to the Most Rev. Patrick A. O'Boyle, Episcopal Chairman of the Department of Social Action; Rt. Rev. Msgr. Paul Tanner, General Secretary of the N.C.W.C.; and Very Rev. Msgr. George G. Higgins, Director of the Department of Social Action. They were all willing to consider this work "in the line of duty," even though it meant the author's bearing less than a normal share of departmental work. Msgr. Higgins in addition was kind enough to read proofs.

The editors of *The Pope Speaks* graciously allowed quotations from their valuable periodical. Mr. Eugene Willging, director of the Mullen Library at Catholic University, extended full use of the facilities of the Library.

Miss Mary O'Leary had the fortitude to survive under the burden of typing and pasting numerous versions of the manuscript, as well as helping with the proofs and index.

To all, the author expresses a heartfelt "Thank You."

AUTHORITATIVE REFERENCES

THE following list names the major documents used as authoritative sources in the text. They are listed in chronological order in each main heading. After each document, a key is given which indicates the source used for the text cited. Where possible, English translations or originals were used. Where there was a discrepancy in dates between the translation and the original in *Discorsi e Radiomessagi*, the date given in the original was used. Numbers in parentheses after each reference indicate the chapters in which the document was cited. If citations are found in practically every chapter, this is noted by the use of *passim* instead of chapter numbers.

Pope Leo XIII

Quod Apostolici Muneris, December 28, 1878 (Husslein) (V)
Diuturnum Illud, June 29, 1881 (Husslein) (XIII)
Immortale Dei, November 1, 1885 (Husslein) (IV, XIII)
Libertas Praestantissimum, June 20, 1888 (Husslein) (XIII)
Rerum Novarum, May 15, 1891 (N.C.W.C.) (*passim*)
In the Midst of Solicitudes, February 16, 1892 (G.E.L.) (XIII)
Graves de Communi, January 18, 1901 (Husslein) (II, VIII, XVII)
Letter to Italian Bishops, December 8, 1902 (A.S.S.) (XVII)

St. Pius X

Il Fermo Proposito, June 11, 1905 (P.Pe.) (P.P.) (VII, XVII)

Pope Benedict XV

Letter to Bishop of Bergamo, March 11, 1920 (C.L.) (XVII)

Pope Pius XI

Ubi Arcano, December 23, 1922 (Husslein) (II, XIV)
Casti Connubii, December 31, 1930 (Husslein) (X, XI, XIII)
Quadragesimo Anno, May 15, 1931 (N.C.W.C.) (*passim*)
Non Abbiamo Bisogno, June 29, 1931 (Husslein) (V)
Caritate Christi Compulsi, May 3, 1932 (Husslein) (I, III, XIV, XVII)
Ad Catholici Sacerdotii, December 20, 1935 (Husslein) (XVII)
Mit Brennender Sorge, March 14, 1937 (Husslein) (III)
Atheistic Communism, March 19, 1937 (N.C.W.C.) (*passim*)
Firmissimam Constantiam, March 28, 1937 (Husslein) (XVII)

Pope Pius XII
1939–1946

Summi Pontificatus, October 20, 1939 (P.P.) (IV, V, XIII, XIV, XV, XVII)
Sertum Laetitiae, November 1, 1939 (P.P. and N.C.) (IV, IX, XV)
La Solennità della Pentecoste, June 1, 1941 (P.P.) (II, III, IV, IX, XIV, XVI)
Nell' Alba, December 24, 1941 (P.P.) (I, III, XIV)
Christmas Broadcast, 1942 (P.P.) (III, IX, XII, XIII, XIV)
To Italian Workers, June 13, 1943 (C.M.) (XI)
Mystici Corporis, June 29, 1943 (N.C.) (XV)
Radio Address, September 1, 1944 (C.M.) (I, III, XII)
Christmas Message, 1944 (XIII)
To Italian Workers, March 11, 1945 (C.M.) (VII)
To College of Cardinals, June 2, 1945 (C.M.) (V, XIV)
To the Holy Roman Rota, Oct. 2, 1945 (D.R.) (V)
On Women's Duties, October 21, 1945 (C.M.) (I, V, XI)
To Members of Italian Electric Industry, January 24, 1946 (D.R.) (IX)
To Negro Publishers, May 27, 1946 (Osservatore Romano) (XV)
To Italian Farmers, November 15, 1946 (N.C.R.L.C.) (XVI)

1947–1949

To Members of Rinascita Cristiana, January 22, 1947 (C.M.) (II)
To Sacred College of Cardinals, June 2, 1947 (C.M.) (II)
To American Delegates, International Labor Organization, July 16, 1947 (C.M.) (III)
Letter to Semaines Sociales, July 18, 1947 (C.M.) (VII, X, XVII)
To International Union of Leagues of Catholic Women, September 12, 1947 (N.C.) (XIII)
To Congress of International Exchange, March 7, 1948 (C.M.) (XIV)
To International Institute for the Unification of Private Rights, May 20, 1948 (D.R.) (XII)
To Sacred College of Cardinals, June 2, 1948 (C.M.) (X, XVII)
To Christian Association of Italian Workers, June 29, 1948 (C.M.) (IX)
To Young Men, September 12, 1948 (C.M.) (II)
On Public Finance, October 2, 1948 (C.M.) (XII)
To Representatives of Fiat Automobile Plant, October 31, 1948 (C.M.) (III)
Christmas Message, 1948 (C.M.) (XIV, XVII)
To Catholic Employers, May 7, 1949 (C.M.) (IV, VII, VIII, XIII)
To Women of Italian Catholic Action, July 24, 1949 (C.M.) (XI)
Letter to Semaines Sociales, July, 1949 (N.C.) (II)
To German Catholics, September 4, 1949 (C.M.) (IX)
To Belgian Workers, September 11, 1949 (C.M.) (IX)
To International Union of Family Organizations, September 20, 1949 (D.R.) (X)

1950–1952

Social Function of Banking, April 25, 1950 (C.M.) (X)
Address to International Congresses for Social Study and Social Action, June 3, 1950 (C.M.) (III, VIII, XI, XIII)

To Congress on Private Law, July 15, 1950 (C.M.) (XIII)
Humani Generis, August 12, 1950 (N.C.) (II)
Christmas Message, 1950 (N.C.) (XI)
To Spanish Employers and Workers, March 11, 1951 (D.R.) (X, XII)
To International Catholic Congress on Rural Problems, July 2, 1951 (C.M.) (XVI)
To World Congress on the Lay Apostolate, October 14, 1951 (N.C.) (XVII)
To Italian Catholic Employers, January 31, 1952 (N.C.) (III)
To Belgian Pilgrims, April 12, 1952 (D.R.) (XV)
To Delegates of Italian Catholic Action, July 16, 1952 (N.C.) (XV)
To Members of Pax Christi, September 13, 1952 (N.C.) (XVII)
To Austrian Catholics, September 14, 1952 (C.M.) (I, VIII)
Christmas Message, 1952 (C.M.) (I, III, VIII, IX, X, XI, XIII, XIV)
On Centenary of St. Thomas the Apostle, December 31, 1952 (D.R.) (IV)

1953–1955

To Italian Catholic Workers Association, May 14, 1953 (N.C.) (III, XI, XVII)
To International Federation of Agricultural Producers, June 10, 1953 (N.C.) (XVI)
To Autonomous Institute of Popular Housing, November 21, 1953 (N.C.) (XI)
To Italian Catholic Jurists, December 6, 1953 (N.C.) (XIV)
To United Nations Food and Agriculture Organization, December 8, 1953 (N.C.) (XIV)
Letter to Semaines Sociales, July 14, 1954 (T.P.S.) (XIII)
To Delegates to International Foundry Congress, September 28, 1954 (T.P.S.) (V)
To Cardinals, Archbishops, and Bishops of Rome, November 2, 1954 (T.P.S.) (II)
To Spanish Workers, November 12, 1954 (T.P.S.) (X)
To Administrative Council of the International Labor Organization, November 19, 1954 (T.P.S.) (IX)
Christmas Message, 1954 (T.P.S.) (II)
To the Italian National Federation of Farmers, May 18, 1955 (T.P.S.) (II, XVI)
To Christian Employers' Association of Italy, June 5, 1955 (T.P.S.) (XIII)
To Delegates of World Petroleum Congress, June 10, 1955 (T.P.S.) (VIII)
To Railroad Workers of Rome, June 26, 1955 (T.P.S.) (IX)
Christmas Message, 1955 (T.P.S.) (V, VI, IX)

1956–1958

To International Conference on Human Relations in Industry, February 4, 1956 (T.P.S.) (VIII)
To the Italian Federation of Commerce, February 17, 1956 (T.P.S.) (V, VIII, XI, XIII)
To Members of the Vatican Diplomatic Corps, March 4, 1956 (T.P.S.) (III)
To the Society for the Construction of Waterworks, April 13, 1956 (T.P.S.) (XIII)

To *Spanish Social Week*, May, 1956 (A.A.S.) (IV)
To the *Apostolate of the Sea*, September 7, 1956 (D.R.) (XV)
To the *International Association of Economists*, September 9, 1956 (T.P.S.) (X)
Radio Address to *International Congress of Catholic Doctors*, September 11, 1956 (T.P.S.) (III)
To *International Association for Financial and Fiscal Law*, October 2, 1956 (T.P.S.) (XII)
Radio Address to the *Federation of Italian Women*, October 14, 1956 (T.P.S.) (XI)
To the *International Institute on the Middle Classes*, October 25, 1956 (T.P.S.) (IV, XII)
To *Pilgrimage of Working People from the City of Terni*, November 18, 1956 (T.P.S.) (II)
Christmas Message, 1956 (T.P.S.) (II, III)
To *Christian Union of Executives and Businessmen*, March 7, 1957 (T.P.S.) (X, XIII)
To *Assembly of the International Movement of Catholic Intellectuals*, April 27, 1957 (T.P.S.) (II, XIV, XVII)
To *"Stations de Plein Air" Movement*, May 3, 1957 (T.P.S.) (XI)
To *Christian Associations of Italian Workers*, June 7, 1957 (T.P.S.) (IX, X, XII)
To *Atlantic Treaty Association*, June 27, 1957 (T.P.S.) (XIV)
Problems of Rural Life, September 18, 1957 (T.P.S.) (XVI)
To *World Union of Catholic Women's Organizations*, September 29, 1957 (T.P.S.) (XVII)
Aspects of Automation, October 23, 1957 (T.P.S.) (III, X)
Christmas Message, 1957 (T.P.S.) (I, XVII)
To *Directors of Chemical Products Organizations*, January 10, 1958 (T.P.S.) (IX)
To the *Associations of Large Families of Rome and Italy*, January 20, 1958 (T.P.S.) (XIV)
Easter Message, April 6, 1958 (N.C.) (XVII)
To *French Government Officials*, April 13, 1958 (N.C.) (XIV)
To *National Society for Aid to Orphans*, April 29, 1958 (N.C.) (I)
To *Italian Workers*, May 1, 1958 (N.C.) (IV)
To *Italian Federation of Middlemen and Business Agents*, June 22, 1958 (N.C.) (II)
To *Catholic World Health Congress*, July 27, 1958 (N.C.) (XIV)
To *Delegates of the Hematological Congress*, September 5, 1958 (XV)

Pope John XXIII

To *Members of U.N. Housing Committee*, November 14, 1958 (N.C.) (X)
To *Italian Catholic Jurists*, December 11, 1958 (N.C.) (XIII)
Christmas Message, 1958 (N.C.) (III, XV)

American Hierarchy

Pastoral Letter, 1919 (H.) (IV, VII)
Bishops' Statement, 1933 (V)

The Church and Social Order, 1940 (H.) (II, IV, IX, X, XII)
Essentials of a Good Peace, 1943 (H.) (XV)
Secularism, 1947 (H.) (XVII)
The Christian in Action, 1948 (H.) (VII)
The Christian Family, 1949 (H.) (X)
God's Law: Measure of Man's Conduct, 1951 (H.) (XIII)
Discrimination and the Christian Conscience, 1958 (N.C.) (XV)

Other Authorities

Summa Theologiae, St. Thomas Aquinas (IV)
Peace in Industry, Australian Hierarchy, 1947 (A.N.S.C.A.), (IX)
Socialization, Australian Hierarchy, 1948 (C.M.) (XII)
Pastoral Letter, French Cardinals, September 8, 1949 (C.M.) (V)
Pastoral Letter, Hierarchy of Quebec, February, 1950 (S.E.) (IX, X)
Morality in Public Life, Australian Hierarchy, 1950 (C.M.) (II, IX)
Standard of Living, Australian Hierarchy, 1954 (C.M.) (X)
The Church in the Modern World, French Hierarchy, June, 1954 (N.C.)
    (VI)
Race Relations, South African Hierarchy, June, 1952, and July, 1957 (C.M.)
    (XV)
On Right-to-Work Law, Bishops of State of Ohio, March 20, 1958 (N.C.)
    (IX)
Code of Social Principles, 1952 English translation of 1948 French revision
    (Oxford: Catholic Social Guild) (II, III, IV, VII, IX, X, XI, XII,
    XIII, XIV, XVI)

Key

A.A.S.: Acta Apostolicae Sedis (Rome: Typographia Vaticana, 1909–)
A.S.S.: Acta Sanctae Sedis (Rome: Typographia Vaticana, 1878–1908)
A.N.S.C.A.: Australian National Secretariat of Catholic Action (Melbourne,
    Australia)
C.C.: Le Canoniste Contemporain
C.L.: Ryan, J. A., and Husslein, J., The Church and Labor (New York: Mac-
    millan, 1920)
C.M.: Catholic Mind
D.R.: Discorsi e Radiomessagi di sua Santità Pio XII (Rome: Tipographia
    Poliglotta Vaticana, 1939–1959)
G.E.L.: Great Encyclical Letters of Pope Leo XIII (New York: Benziger,
    1903)
H.: Huebner, R. M., Our Bishops Speak (Milwaukee: Bruce, 1952)
Husslein: Husslein, J. (ed.), Social Wellsprings (Milwaukee: Bruce, 1940–
    1942)
N.C.R.L.C.: "The Pope Speaks on Rural Life" (Des Moines: National Cath-
    olic Rural Life Conference, 1948)
N.C.W.C.: National Catholic Welfare Conference
P.P.: Koenig, H. (ed.), Principles for Peace (Milwaukee: Bruce, 1943)
P.Pe.: The Pope and the People (London: Catholic Truth Society, 1937)
S.E.: Service extérieur d'éducation sociale, Quebec
T.P.S.: The Pope Speaks (3622 12th Street, N.E., Washington 17, D. C.)

See also Sister M. Claudia Carlen, I.H.M., *A Guide to the Encyclicals of the Roman Pontiffs* (New York: H. W. Wilson, 1939), *Guide to the Documents of Pius XII* (Westminster, Md.: Newman, 1951), and *Dictionary of Papal Pronouncements* (New York: Kenedy, 1958). These books list original sources, translations, and important commentaries in connection with major pontifical documents.

CONTENTS

PART III. SOCIAL PRINCIPLES AND SELECTED SOCIAL AND POLITICAL PROBLEMS

Part I

THE CHRISTIAN SOCIAL ORDER

Chapter I

THE SOCIAL QUESTION

SOCIAL AND ECONOMIC EXPLOITATION

Leo XIII, Rerum Novarum

6. After the old trade guilds had been destroyed in the last century, and no protection was substituted in their place, and when public institutions and legislation had cast off traditional religious teaching, it gradually came about that the present age handed over the workers, each alone and defenseless, to the inhumanity of employers and the unbridled greed of competitors. A devouring usury, although often condemned by the Church, but practiced nevertheless under another form by avaricious and grasping men, has increased the evil; and in addition the whole process of production as well as trade in every kind of goods has been brought almost entirely under the power of a few, so that a very few rich and exceedingly rich men have laid a yoke almost of slavery on the unnumbered masses of nonowning workers.

66. For the violence of public disorder has divided cities into two classes of citizens, with an immense gulf lying between them. On the one side is a faction exceedingly powerful because exceedingly rich. Since it alone has under its control every kind of work and business, it diverts to its own advantage and interest all production sources of wealth and exerts no little power in the administration itself of the state. On the other side are the needy and helpless masses, with minds inflamed and always ready for disorder.

Pius XI, Quadragesimo Anno

3. For toward the close of the nineteenth century, the new kind of economic life that had arisen and the new developments of industry had gone to the point in most countries that human society was clearly becoming divided more and more into two classes. One class, very small in number, was enjoying almost all the advantages which modern inventions so abundantly provided; the other, embracing the huge multitude of working people, oppressed by wretched poverty, was vainly seeking escape from the straits wherein it stood.

5. The same feeling those many Catholics, both priests and laymen, shared, whom a truly wonderful charity had long spurred on to relieve the unmerited poverty of the nonowning workers, and who could in no way convince themselves that so enormous and unjust an inequality in

3

the distribution of this world's goods truly conforms to the designs of the all-wise Creator.

54. Property, that is, "capital," has undoubtedly long been able to appropriate too much to itself. Whatever was produced, whatever returns accrued, capital claimed for itself, hardly leaving to the worker enough to restore and renew his strength. For the doctrine was preached that all accumulation of capital falls by an absolutely insuperable economic law to the rich, and that by the same law the workers are given over and bound to perpetual want, to the scantiest of livelihoods. It is true, indeed, that things have not always and everywhere corresponded with this sort of teaching of the so-called Manchesterian Liberals; yet it cannot be denied that economic-social institutions have moved steadily in that direction. That these false ideas, these erroneous suppositions, have been vigorously assailed, and not by those alone who through them were being deprived of their innate right to obtain better conditions, will surprise no one.

59. But since manufacturing and industry have so rapidly pervaded and occupied countless regions, not only in the countries called new, but also in the realms of the Far East that have been civilized from antiquity, the number of the nonowning working poor has increased enormously and their groans cry to God from the earth. Added to them is the huge army of rural wage workers, pushed to the lowest level of existence and deprived of all hope of ever acquiring "some property in land," and, therefore, permanently bound to the status of nonowning worker unless suitable and effective remedies are applied.

60. Yet while it is true that the status of nonowning worker is to be carefully distinguished from pauperism, nevertheless the immense multitude of the nonowning workers on the one hand and the enormous riches of certain very wealthy men on the other establish an unanswerable argument that the riches which are so abundantly produced in our age of "industrialism," as it is called, are not rightly distributed and equitably made available to the various classes of the people.

62. All these things which Our Predecessor has not only suggested but clearly and openly proclaimed, We emphasize with renewed insistence in Our present Encyclical; and unless utmost efforts are made without delay to put them into effect, let no one persuade himself that public order, peace, and the tranquillity of human society can be effectively defended against agitators of revolution.

105. . . . it is obvious that not only is wealth concentrated in our times but an immense power and despotic economic dictatorship is consolidated in the hands of a few, who often are not owners but only the trustees and managing directors of invested funds which they administer according to their own arbitrary will and pleasure.

109. Free competition has destroyed itself; economic dictatorship has supplanted the free market; unbridled ambition for power has likewise succeeded greed for gain; all economic life has become tragically hard, inexorable, and cruel. To these are to be added the grave evils that have resulted from an intermingling and shameful confusion of the functions and duties of public authority with those of the economic sphere — such as, one of the worst, the virtual degradation of the majesty of the state, which, although it ought to sit on high like a queen and supreme arbitress, free from all partiality and

intent upon the one common good and justice, is become a slave, surrendered and delivered to the passions and greed of men.

132. Hence arises that unquenchable thirst for riches and temporal goods, which has at all times impelled men to break God's laws and trample upon the rights of their neighbors, but which, on account of the present system of economic life, is laying far more snares for human frailty. Since the instability of economic life, and especially of its structure, exacts of those engaged in it most intense and unceasing effort, some have become so hardened to the stings of conscience as to hold that they are allowed, in any manner whatsoever, to increase their profits and use means, fair or foul, to protect their hard-won wealth against sudden changes of fortune. The easy gains that a market unregulated by law opens to everybody attracts large numbers to buying and selling goods, and they, their one aim being to make quick profits with the least expenditure of work, raise or lower prices by their uncontrolled business dealings so rapidly according to their own caprice and greed that they nullify the wisest forecasts of producers. The laws passed to promote corporate business, while dividing and limiting the risk of business, have given occasion to the most sordid license. For We observe that consciences are little affected by this reduced obligation of accountability; that furthermore, by hiding under the shelter of a joint name, the worst of injustices and frauds are perpetuated; and that, too, directors of business companies, forgetful of their trust, betray the rights of those whose savings they have undertaken to administer. Lastly, We

must not omit to mention those crafty men who, wholly unconcerned about any honest usefulness of their work, do not scruple to stimulate the baser human desires and, when they are aroused, use them for their own profit.

135. With the rulers of economic life abandoning the right road, it was easy for the rank and file of workers everywhere to rush headlong also into the same chasm; and all the more so, because very many managements treated their workers like mere tools, with no concern at all for their souls, without indeed even the least thought of spiritual things. Truly the mind shudders at the thought of the grave dangers to which the morals of workers (particularly younger workers) and the modesty of girls and women are exposed in modern factories; when we recall how often the present economic scheme, and particularly the shameful housing conditions, create obstacles to the family bond and normal family life; when we remember how many obstacles are put in the way of the proper observance of Sundays and Holy Days; and when we reflect upon the universal weakening of that truly Christian sense through which even rude and unlettered men were wont to value higher things, and upon its substitution by the single preoccupation of getting in any way whatsoever one's daily bread. And thus bodily labor, which Divine Providence decreed to be performed, even after original sin, for the good at once of man's body and soul, is being everywhere changed into an instrument of perversion; for dead matter comes forth from the factory ennobled, while men there are corrupted and degraded.

Pius XI, On Atheistic Communism

47. But when on the one hand we see thousands of the needy, victims of real misery for various reasons beyond their control, and on the other so many round them who spend huge sums of money on useless things and frivolous amusement, We cannot fail to remark with sorrow not only that justice is poorly observed, but that the precept of charity also is not sufficiently appreciated, is not a vital thing in daily life.

Pius XI, Caritate Christi Compulsi

3. From greed arises mutual distrust, that casts a blight on all human dealings; from greed arises hateful envy, which makes a man consider the advantages of another as losses to himself; from greed arises narrow individualism, which orders and subordinates everything to its own advantages without taking account of others, on the contrary cruelly trampling underfoot all rights of others. Hence the disorder and inequality from which result the accumulation of the wealth of nations in the hands of a small group of individuals who manipulate the market of the world at their own caprice, to the immense harm of the masses. . . .

28. In place of moral laws, which disappear together with the loss of faith in God, brute force is imposed, tramping on every right. Old-time fidelity and honesty of conduct and mutual relations, extolled so much even by the orators and poets of paganism, now give place to speculation in one's own affairs, as in those of others, without reference to conscience.

Pius XII, Nell' Alba, Christmas, 1941

1748. For the human spirit, overwhelmed in the confusion of this moral abyss, by its alienation from God and Christian practices, no other course remained but that of turning all its thoughts, purposes, and enterprises and every evaluation of men's possessions, actions, and labor and directing them to the material world, striving and sweating with might and main to spread out in space, to surpass all previous accomplishments in the attainment of riches and power, to engage in a competition of speed, to produce in greater quantity and quality everything that material advancement and progress seemed to require. These very symptoms appear in politics as an unlimited demand for expansion and political influence without regard to moral standards. In economic life they are represented by the predominance of mammoth concerns and trusts. In the social sphere it is the agglomeration of huge populations in cities and in the districts dominated by industry and trade, an agglomeration that is accompanied by the complete uprooting of the masses who have lost their standards of life, home, work, love, and hatred. By this new conception of thought and life, all ideas of social life have been impregnated with a purely mechanico-materialistic character.

1749. With the increasing lack of restraint, outward compulsion and domination founded purely on power seemed to prevail over the forces of order, which established the relations of law and charity in their natural and supernatural foundations as they had been laid down by God. To the detriment of human dignity and personality as well as society, the conception makes headway that it is might which creates right. Thus private property is being abused on the one hand as a means of exploitation; on the other hand, as a reason for envy, revolt, and hatred. The situation ensuing therefrom is being exploited by a struggle of interests which is being waged without any restraint.

Pius XII, Radio Address, September 1, 1944

We see the small and medium holdings diminish and lose their value in human society, and constrained to join in a conflict ever more difficult and without hope of success.

On the one side, We see immense riches dominating public and private economic life and often even civil life; on the other, the countless number of those who, deprived of every direct or indirect security of their own livelihood, take no further interest in the true and higher values of the spirit, abandon their aspiration to genuine freedom and throw themselves at the feet of any political party, slaves to whoever promises them in some way bread and security; and experience shows of what tyranny, under such circumstances, human nature is capable even in our times.

Pius XII, On Women's Duties, October 21, 1945

. . . can a woman . . . hope for her real well-being from a regime dominated by capitalism? . . . You know its characteristic signs and you yourselves are bearing its burden: excessive concentration of population in cities; the constant, all-absorbing increase of big industries; the difficult and precarious state of others, notably those of artisans and agricultural workers; and the disturbing increase in unemployment.

THE SOCIAL PROBLEM TODAY

Pius XII, To Austrian Catholics, September 14, 1952

Today the Church looks back upon the first phase of modern social dispute. At its center stood the problem of the workingman: the distress of the proletariat and the task of lifting this class of society, exposed defenselessly to the caprices of economic ups and downs, to a status of dignity equal to that enjoyed by the other classes, and of endowing it with clearly defined rights. This task has been solved — at any rate in its essentials — and the Catholic world has honestly and effectively contributed to its solution. Even if in certain groups of countries the realization of this problem and action came very late at the eleventh hour, the social principles and directives stated by the successors of St. Peter during the past sixty years have, on the whole, become common property of Catholic thought and action.

If the signs of the times are not misleading, then the questions and task coming to the fore in the second phase of the social dispute, which we have probably already entered, are of a different nature. We shall now point out two of them:

The overcoming of the class struggle through an organic co-ordination of employer and employee, for class struggle can never be a goal of Catholic social ethics. The Church is always aware of its duties toward all classes and layers of the people.

In the second place, the protection of the individual and of the family against the vortex which threatens to draw them into an all-embracing socialization, at the end of which looms the very real nightmare of "Leviathan." The Church will conduct this fight to the utmost, because the highest things are at stake: human dignity and the salvation of the soul.

Pius XII, Christmas Message, 1952

Modern industry has unquestionably had beneficial results, but the problem which arises today is this: will a world in which the only economic form to find acceptance is a vast productive system be equally fitted to exert a happy influence upon society in general and upon the three fundamental institutions of society in particular?

We must answer that the impersonal character of such a world is contrary to the fundamentally personal nature of those institutions which the Creator has given to human society. In fact, marriage and the family, the state, and private property tend of their very nature to form man as a person, to protect and render him capable of contributing through his own voluntary co-operation and personal responsibility to the similarly personal life and development of human relations. The creative wisdom of God is therefore alien to that system of impersonal unity which strikes at the human person, who is origin and end of society, and in the depths of His being an image of his God.

*   *   *

Here may be recognized the origin and source of that phenomenon which is submerging modern man under its tide of anguish: his "depersonalization." In large measure his identity and name have been taken from him; in many of the more important activities of life he has been reduced to a mere material object of society, while society itself has been transformed into an impersonal system and into a cold organization of force.

Pius XII, Christmas Message, 1957

Why else is there such great indifference to other people's right to life, so much disregard for human values, such a lowering of the tone of genuine civilization, if not for the reason that stress on material progress has upset the balance and harmony of man as a whole, and has deprived him of his feeling for those concepts and values, by developing him in one direction only?

*   *   *

Technical progress, on the other hand, when it imprisons man within its own narrow confines, cuts him off from the rest of the universe, especially the world of the spiritual and of the inner man, and forms him according to its own characteristics, the most noteworthy of which are superficiality and instability. The way this kind of deformation comes about is no secret to anyone who is aware of man's tendency to accept false judgments and errors as long as they hold out the promise of an easier life.

Take for example the questionable substitution of values that has taken place as a result of the wonderful progress made in the speed of machines. The "speed-crazy" man is attracted by this progress and easily carries his high regard for speed over to things whose proper development and value do not depend on rapid change, but rather on stability and fidelity to traditions. As a result, his life is like a reed shaken by the wind; it is unproductive of any lasting results and incapable of supporting himself and others.

A very similar situation arises from the remarkable increase in the powers of our senses which has been brought about by incredible modern instruments of research which permit man to see, hear, and measure every creature, every movement, every change in almost every corner of the universe.

The "all-seeing" man is so overjoyed with this great increase in his power and so totally absorbed in the use of his senses that he is led, without realizing it, to give less attention to using that completely spiritual power that enables him to see into the heart of things: his intellect. As a result, his power to produce and develop the true ideas which are the very substance of life grows weaker and weaker.

In the same way, the wonderful increase in the number of ways to use external energy is tending more and more each day to enclose human life within the limits of a mechanical system that does everything by itself and on its own. As a consequence it cuts down on the number of incentives which primarily forced man to develop his own personal energy.

Pius XII, To the National Society for Aid to Orphans, April 29, 1958

To Christianity, as an idea, as a sentiment and furthermore as a readiness to action, may be justly ascribed the merit of a determining cause of social progress, above all however that of having kept the thirst for social justice within the bounds of natural rights, preserving it from excesses and open upheavals of equally unjust attitudes.

YOUNGER readers of the preceding quotations may be astonished at the strength and even violence of papal language in condemning social and economic abuses. Fortunately, most of such readers have had no direct experience of the extreme evils cited. Nonetheless, there are two valid reasons for citing these passages and for beginning with a study of what is called the "social question." The first reason is the old adage that history is man's greatest teacher. When we understand the historical reasons for certain laws and institutions, we can better realize their purpose in modern society.

A second reason for careful reading of the strong indictments of social abuses is the tragic fact that many still persist in various parts of the world today. A Roman Jesuit, one of the world's great social scientists, remarked in a private conversation: "It is most difficult for the Holy

Father to address the world on social and economic problems. He confronts a world that lives partly in the times of Pope Leo XIII, partly in the times of Pope Pius XI, and yet a world that has seen the exuberant prosperity of such nations as the United States and West Germany."

Many areas of Asia, Africa, and Latin America are indeed blighted by the evils cited by Pope Leo XIII. Extreme poverty lives almost side by side with fabulous wealth. Other parts of the world, including some European nations, have progressed little since the days of *Quadragesimo Anno*. By contrast, more prosperous nations hope to see the day when poverty and destitution can be abolished within their borders. These sharp differences in economic life are by no means unrelated to the bitter political clashes that have bedeviled the world during the 1950's.

Even to understand American economic society, and its place in world affairs, it is useful and even necessary to seek a wider historical perspective. With this in mind, we begin by discussing a civilization that in many ways reflected Christian morality. We refer to medieval society, so often favorably commented upon by the popes. Next we study the breakdown of this society and the advent of modern industrialism, with its many social problems. Finally, we try to pinpoint the social problem in the United States today.

A Christian Social Order. Medieval society in Europe is important to the Christian social scientist mainly because religious ideals permeated the *institutions* of that society. There is a substantial difference between moral principles as accepted by individuals, and these same principles embedded in social institutions. Individual moral conduct reflects the opportunities and moral strength of the persons concerned. But when right principles are enmeshed in the very fiber of society, through its laws, customs, and institutions, those who are morally weak or even evil face powerful compulsions to conform to accepted standards.

The term institutions might well be explained here, since it recurs frequently in the chapters to follow. An institution is a stable and deep-rooted pattern of human conduct. It is stronger and more fundamental than custom. The family, private property, and the prevailing code of business ethics can be described as institutions. By contrast, the practice of teen-age single dating would rather be called a custom, since fortunately it is not yet entrenched as a permanent feature of our society.

It is important that social institutions direct men toward goals consonant with the moral law. Otherwise it becomes extraordinarily difficult for men of good will to fight the pressures engendered by faulty social institutions. Catholics who feel that the social problem can be solved in the confessional alone, or in religion classes, or by pious practices, or by good personal leadership are misreading the lessons of history and sociology.

Insofar as the social question springs from human greed and avarice, from pride of life and lust for power, it will always be with us. Man, hurt in intellect and weakened in will, is prone to evil as well as good. There will always be selfish men, ambitious for power and material success, whatever the means used to accomplish their ends. But men do not act in a social vacuum. The sanctions of society have a strong impact upon the wills of individuals. Hence it is of compelling importance to study how social climate helps or hinders the influence of Christian principles upon economic life.

In medieval times, as today, the Church formulated a moral code for social life. But the influence of the Church upon society was far greater in the Middle Ages. Its teachings about justice, political life, property, the social virtues, avarice, and usury were often as effective in the market-place as would be a Supreme Court decision in the United States today. Good men were encouraged and evil men constrained by the body of principles laid down by theologians and canonists.

Church influence is best seen in such institutions as feudalism and the guild system, and in its teachings on the just price, usury, and property.

Feudalism is often treated in modern writings as the equivalent of slavery. But contemporary documents emphasize the fact that the serf, while in a status of dependence, had rights as well as duties. He was bound to the land, but he could not be expelled from it. There was effective machinery to protect his rights. In contrast to the anarchy of the Dark Ages, feudal society represented an advance toward the ideal of full freedom and human dignity. "All powerful custom determined every man's rights and obligations. This fact alone was enough to prevent the pitiless severity to which the free exercise of economic supremacy gives rise under the spur of profit."[1]

Medieval guilds were legally recognized organizations that both repre-

---

[1] H. Pirenne, *Economic and Social History of Medieval Europe* (New York: Harcourt, 1937), p. 64. Many historians hold that the power of law and custom, involving the consent of the governed, made medieval society democratic in a real sense. For an extensive documentation from non-Catholic sources, see R. W. and A. J. Carlyle, *A History of Medieval Political Teaching in the West* (New York: Putnam, 1903–1936). See also R. H. Tawney, *Religion and the Rise of Capitalism* (New York: Harcourt, 1926), and A. Fanfani, *Catholicism, Protestantism, and Capitalism* (New York: Sheed, 1936).

sented and regulated industrial and commercial activity. They aimed to protect the rights of both workers and employers, while safeguarding the consumer. To do this, they established standards of quality, training of apprentices, and fair prices. These guilds deteriorated starting with the fourteenth century. They became monopolistic and oppressive. But at their best periods they did apply moral concepts to economic society.

The ethical norm determining the conduct of the guilds was the common good, an expression of which was the just price. Basically this involved equality in exchange. The price of an article must conform to its true value, as determined by public authority or common estimate. It would be immoral for either a buyer or seller to exploit a monopoly position in order to lower or raise the price. The price should not be so low as to impoverish workers, artisans, or merchants; nor should it be so high as to deprive the poor of the necessities of life. The significant point is that this ethical norm was accepted by the commercial and industrial community and institutionalized in the guilds.[2]

Ethics also entered into the sphere of finance. The condemnation of usury was bound to affect economic life. While a return from rent and partnership was permitted, pure interest was considered an unjust exaction. Many of the considerations which enter into the modern interest rate, such as a charge for the risk of loss, were allowed, but a fee for the use of money as such was outlawed. The basic reason for this was that money, in contrast to real property, was considered unproductive. Hence a charge for its use was an exploitation of another's needs, not a participation in a productive venture. The influence of Church teaching on usury was so great that, even in the late Middle Ages, the powerful Antwerp Bourse and the House of Fugger sent couriers to Rome for moral rulings on their transactions.

Above all these particular practices was a concept of property. Private ownership was considered to be in accord with the nature of man. Private property is a normal expression of man's right of ownership. But property should be used in such a way as to promote the common interest of all. Right laws and customs would lead to such a happy situation that the advantages of both private and common ownership would be preserved. Moreover, actual ownership would be diffused, since possession of property is an important distinction between the slave and the free man. The property owner has resources which minister to his

---

[2] The best English treatment of medieval ethical ideas is contained in G. A. O'Brien, *Essay on Mediaeval Economic Teaching* (New York: Longmans, 1920).

freedom. Moreover, the social virtues, such as liberality, should guide the individual in the use of his property.[3]

Thus there emerges a picture of a theocentric society, with economic life governed by moral obligations embodied in social institutions. At its peak, this society combined a large measure of justice with economic stability. Yet it was not adverse to progress, as is testified by the great growth of commerce and industry during the medieval period. Such a society offers a striking contrast to modern notions, in that economic life was then strictly subordinate to cultural, moral, and religious considerations.

THE RISE OF THE SOCIAL PROBLEM

The system was to fail, although not from any inherent weakness in the approach. A combination of events served to sharpen man's acquisitive instincts, at the very time that a decline in religious fervor and observance was taking place. The fearful catastrophe of the Black Death (1347) in itself would have been sufficient to disrupt even the most stable of societies. Not only did it depopulate much of Europe, but its impact was hardest upon the leaders of society who ministered to the sick and dying.

Religious fervor declined for other reasons as well. Many abuses grew within the Church. Schisms and heresies became more common. Even the papacy itself had unworthy members, while the period of exile at Avignon (1309–1377) was weakening and disruptive. These trends culminated in the Protestant Revolt. The influence of the Church upon society declined as it engaged in a terrific struggle for internal reform and the return of its lost members. It could be said that, from the sixteenth until the mid-nineteenth century, the Church was preoccupied with the hard core of doctrinal orthodoxy and moral reform.

The newly formed Protestant churches, after an uncertain beginning, were to turn away from the ideal of organized social morality. Both Luther and Calvin accepted much of the economic morality of the Church. But the branches springing from Lutheranism were to carry religious individualism to its logical conclusion. With religious belief left largely to personal conscience and private interpretation of Scripture, there was little chance for a widely accepted social morality to be imposed on the institutions of society. At the same time, the Calvinist root

---

[3] See W. J. McDonald, *The Social Value of Property According to Saint Thomas Aquinas* (Washington: Catholic University, 1939).

of Protestantism was to develop the concept of "calling." The sign of predestination to heaven was God's blessing upon one's "vocation." In the minds of many, this led to an equation of material success and divine approval.[4]

As the influence of religious and moral sanctions lessened, other factors were to offer positive stimulus to business enterprise. Among these was the revival of commerce which began with the Crusades. Commerce expanded until the quest for supplies and markets led to the discoveries of New-World colonial opportunities in the fifteenth and sixteenth centuries. The growth of merchant power in turn brought about a clash between the medieval city and the feudal nobility. This struggle gradually developed into the broader contests which led to modern nationalism. An alliance between merchant groups and ambitious lords favored the consolidation of national power, particularly in France and England. These new states then used every means to stimulate economic growth as an instrument for political power. By the seventeenth century, France under Louis XIV was even to impose a form of statism upon business, in order to regulate it in the interest of national strength.

While commerce expanded, both of its own momentum and as a result of state encouragement, businessmen were growing restive under government controls. They turned eagerly to the theories formulated by the great pioneer economists of the eighteenth century. These theories are now known as *laissez-faire* individualism. It was held that economic life was regulated by its own natural laws, which should not be subject to interference by the state or any other group. These laws are based on the human desire to maximize pleasure and minimize pain. Man is considered basically selfish in his economic pursuits. But, by the benevolent designs of Providence, man's selfishness actually leads to the greatest common good. In the struggle for survival, each man produces to the best of his ability. The sum of such efforts is maximum production at the highest quality possible. Hence, the good of all is served. Any interference with this process, through state or private intervention, only leads to decreased production and increased misery. Free competition must be the sole guiding rule of economic life.

Transition to Modern Times. By the eighteenth century, the social institutions of earlier ages, embodying a moral and religious code in their

---

[4] This point is treated in detail by Tawney and Fanfani, cited earlier. See also E. Troeltsch, *The Social Teaching of the Christian Churches* (London: Allen & Unwin, 1949). For current Protestant views, see E. Duff, *The Social Thought of the World Council of Churches* (New York: Association Press, 1956).

THE SOCIAL QUESTION   **15**

practices, were largely gone. Their ideological base was destroyed as a result of the factors noted above. Moreover, the very process of commercial and industrial growth and change was important in breaking up social organizations founded under different conditions. Great movements of population, the subdivision of labor as a result of new processes, and the enlargement of the market necessarily outmoded the guilds and their customs. Even if society had not changed in its moral and ethical framework, economic developments would have called for profound modification of existing institutions. By the eighteenth century, however, the temper of society was such that earlier organizations were destroyed without being replaced. As a result, the masses of workers in the newly expanded cities became a proletariat, a formless group without internal coherence, security, or direction in economic life.

The policy of freedom was to lead to an enormous expansion of commerce and industry. But the price paid in terms of human suffering was indeed great. Speculative orgies led to periodic depressions that caused prolonged unemployment and intensive suffering. Poor families sent children to work even at such early ages as five or six. A seventeen-hour day was not uncommon. In English coal mines, women were harnessed to the carts to pull up coal, since the tunnels were too narrow to permit the use of animals. During the early part of the nineteenth century, Negro slaves in the agricultural United States were often better treated than "free" workers in the great industrial and commercial nations.

Conditions in the United States never reached the levels of degradation that were all too common in Europe. The safety valve of the frontier, with its vista of virgin lands and unlimited opportunity, prevented the worst forms of exploitation. Yet, during the nineteenth century, we too were plagued with panics and unemployment, slums, long hours of work, child labor, exploitation of workers and savage repression of unions, the victimization of the farmer, and sharp contrasts between wealth and poverty. These conditions persisted into the present century, although living standards gradually improved. The worst evils of exploitation were slowly disappearing as a result of legislation and unionization. Nevertheless, comprehensive social reform here was not achieved until the 1929 depression led to the New Deal legislation of 1933–1938.[5]

The rise of the social problem produced strong reactions, especially in Europe. Two patterns particularly were to emerge. One was a socialist

---

[5] For reference material, see M. Josephson, *The Robber Barons* (New York: Harcourt, 1934), and F. L. Allen, *The Lords of Creation* (New York: Harper, 1935).

trend that reached its ideological peak with the writings of Karl Marx
and Nicolai Lenin and its practical expression in the communist movement that flowed from the Russian revolution of 1917. The other current
was the movement toward Christian social reform, starting in Germany
and France early in the nineteenth century and culminating in the great
social writings of Leo XIII, Pius XI, and Pius XII. These writings deeply
influenced the Christian Democratic parties that governed much of
Western Europe after World War II.

The citing of socialist and Christian movements should not detract
from the achievements of many, not formally connected with either camp,
who sponsored labor organization and social legislation during the past
century. Yet socialism and Christianity were the leading ideological
forces of the time. Those who acted independently of such movements were nevertheless powerfully influenced by the ferment of thought
they engendered.[6]

These reactions to the social evils attendant upon the Industrial
Revolution brought about far-reaching reforms. In the United States,
at least, the crude exploitation of earlier days is now exceptional, directed
largely against Negroes and the Spanish-speaking, who are still unable
to achieve their full rights. Such measures as fiscal and monetary reforms,
unemployment compensation, guaranteed wages, farm price supports, and
heavy government spending have lessened the likelihood that a severe
and prolonged depression may occur. Living standards have climbed to
historic highs. As a result of these and other changes, the question arises:
Does the United States have a social problem in the form outlined in
papal writings? Can we rightly say that papal strictures upon economic
society do not apply to current conditions here? To answer these questions, it may be useful to examine our contemporary economic life in the
light of Christian teachings.

THE SOCIAL PROBLEM TODAY

Since the present chapter has stressed so strongly the philosophy and
moral principles behind a given period of history, it is only logical to
begin our inquiry at this level. The New Deal reforms of the 1930's

---

[6] See P. T. Moon, *The Labor Problem and the Social Catholic Movement in France*
(New York: Macmillan, 1921), and M. P. Fogarty, *Christian Democracy in Western
Europe, 1820–1953* (Notre Dame: University of Notre Dame Press, 1957). In the
present century, the persistent effort of socialists to secure legislation benefiting the
worker explains the political strength of this movement in Western Europe. Catholics
were less active in this regard before World War II.

were, in general, imposed by law upon an unwilling business community. In the interval the viewpoint of the business world has changed considerably. Thus, regulation of the securities' markets and the banking community is now regarded as inevitable in the light of the abuses of earlier years. Social security is not now questioned; indeed, it is often supplemented by industrial pensions and other "fringe benefits" in labor-union contracts. Government aid to farmers seems to be accepted in principle, although there are disputes over particular programs. Labor's right to organize is generally recognized, even when it is denied in practice in some areas.

It is difficult to generalize about a nation as large and diverse as the United States. Yet the preponderance of evidence indicates that most Americans now accept the idea that government has the right and duty to prevent economic abuses, on the part of either business or labor, that detract from the general welfare. Businessmen, with a minority in opposition, feel that they have definite obligations toward the community, their workers, stockholders, and customers. The idea that profit is the only motivating force in business does not seem to prevail today. In other words, the competitive individualism of the postmedieval period is no longer the dominant factor in our society.

The question often arises, however, as to the depth of the change. Many contend that individualism persists in a different form. They cite as examples the alleged group individualism that is said to manifest itself in great concentrations aiming at economic and political power and at influencing public opinion. To give concrete examples: business has been charged with price-fixing in an effort to secure unreasonable profits; organized labor is said to secure high wages for its members at the expense of other elements in the community; and farmers are blamed for demanding price-support programs that pile up ever increasing surpluses of unneeded commodities. All these groups are alleged to be seeking to dominate government, particularly the federal government, so as to secure special favors for their members.

Closely related to the charges just made is the claim that there is an excessive concentration of power in modern society. Individuals and small groups are losing out. Giant aggregations in industry, commerce, finance, labor, and farming are becoming ever more powerful. Political power is being increasingly centralized in Washington, in spite of professed efforts to reverse the trend. As a result, many contend, the organization is everything, the individual is nothing.

In this connection, the student should read carefully the papal Christmas messages of 1952 and 1957, or at least the excerpts cited at the head of this chapter. Pope Pius XII was worried over the "depersonalization" of modern society, its excessively mechanical character. We seem to have lost the ability to distinguish between ends and means, seeking ever increasing supplies of goods and gadgets — more than we need — as ends good in themselves, not merely as means to secure higher goals. We lose sight of the individual and the family, and private property as their economic supports, as the real goals of social and economic achievement.[7]

While general living standards in the United States have increased sharply, particularly since 1945, problems still persist. It is not certain that we can control inflation without slowing economic growth and causing deflation and unemployment. Moreover, prosperity is uneven. Many men are practicing "moonlighting," or the holding of two jobs, in the effort to keep afloat. The number of married women workers, including mothers of young children, has mounted at an appalling rate. Thousands of families receive incomes inadequate by any reasonable standard. In all probability, the bulk of these families are members of minority groups or are marginal farmers. At the other extreme, many feel that the cult of constantly increasing living standards is making our society too materialistic and pleasure mad.

More specific evils may be found in some segments of our society. Some business firms turn out shoddy goods or offer poor services. A particular complaint is the high cost of servicing complicated products, such as an automobile or television set, and the conviction that some service firms are exploiting the public by gross overcharges. Another abuse that often affects the poorer groups is the charging of high interest rates on installment sales. Some contracts are written in such a way as to keep the unwary in debt, even after an article has been repossessed. False and deceptive advertising, particularly over the radio, often misleads those who can least afford the loss. One hidden factor in costs is the rather prevalent practice of commercial bribery and corruption.

Many families still cannot afford housing suitable for their needs. Slums and urban blight plague many areas, in spite of many excellent redevelopment programs. Race discrimination is often involved here, and in

---

[7] See J. K. Galbraith, *The Affluent Society* (Boston: Houghton Mifflin, 1958) for an economic analysis often parallel to papal pronouncements on this subject.

business hiring policies as well. Another hiring practice that causes severe hardship is unwillingness to hire workers over forty.

Organized labor is no longer a weakling needing every help it can get. It has become rich and powerful. An important part of the labor movement has been plagued with corruption, racketeering, and autocracy. Less publicized, but possibly more dangerous in the long run, is the immense economic power achieved by some unions. A union monopoly of transportation, for example, can paralyze a nation almost overnight.

These evils are noted, not in any way to belittle the great achievements of the American economy, but only to point out that the work of social reform is a continuing task. Our living standards are unquestionably high. The pattern of income distribution has greatly improved. The percentage of the extremely rich or extremely poor has been declining, as more and more Americans move into the "middle class."

But the ultimate test of a society is not its distribution of wealth, important as that may be. The real test is the prevalence of justice and charity in relationships among men. We must ask: Does a given social pattern contribute to family life and minister to human dignity? Poverty, fraud, and injustice point up the urgency of reforming society according to Christian principles. But the absence or the minimizing of these abuses does not mean that we can become complacent and feel that the social teaching of the Church has no relevance in our country.

In 1959, Nikita Khrushchev boasted that Soviet living standards would soon excel those of the United States. If his boast were to be fulfilled, it would still be unimportant. So long as communism persisted in the U.S.S.R., its people would still be slaves, even if well-fed and well-housed slaves. Material prosperity is not the ultimate goal of society. It can be a good, and its absence can be an evil, but it is not the highest good even in the temporal order. This thought should serve as a necessary background to any discussion of Christian social principles.

READINGS*

J. Messner, Social Ethics, pp. 249–280.
B. W. Dempsey, The Functional Economy, Chaps. 5, 6, 7, 24.
Economic Growth in the United States: Its Past and Future (Research and Policy Committee of the Committee for Economic Development, 1958).

---

* For further readings, see List No. 1 in the Appendix. Publishers, dates of publication, and descriptive data on books listed above may also be found in the Appendix.

G. A. O'Brien, *Essay on Mediaeval Economic Teaching.*
A. Fanfani, *Catholicism, Protestantism, and Capitalism.*
R. H. Tawney, *Religion and the Rise of Capitalism.*
E. Troeltsch, *The Social Teaching of the Christian Churches.*
H. Johnston, *Business Ethics,* Chap. 6.
M. E. Walsh and P. H. Furfey, *Social Problems and Social Action,* Chap. 3.
Social Order: Paul W. Facey, S.J., "Current Social Problems," June, 1950; Paul V. Kennedy, S.J., "*Civitas Humana,*" May, 1951; Edward Duff, S.J., "The Conduct of Life," April, 1952; Francis J. Corley, S.J., "Leisure and Work," April, 1952; "Christian Humanism," May-June, 1953; Christopher Dawson, "Christian Culture," April, 1954; Francis J. Corley, S.J., "Individualism Reconsidered," November, 1954; Philip J. Land, S.J., "People of Plenty," May, 1955; Lawrence Moran, "The Myth of Machine-Made Leisure," November, 1957; William F. Kennedy, "Facing Our Economic Problems," September, 1958.

Chapter II

THE CHURCH AND THE SOCIAL PROBLEM

Leo XIII, Graves de Communi

10. For it is the opinion of some, which is caught up by the masses, that the social question, as they call it, is merely economic. The precise opposite is the truth. It is first of all moral and religious, and for that reason its solution is to be expected mainly from the moral law and the pronouncements of religion.

Leo XIII, Rerum Novarum

24. We approach the subject with confidence and surely by Our right, for the question under consideration is certainly one for which no satisfactory solution will be found unless religion and the Church have been called upon to aid.

25. Assuredly, a question as formidable as this requires the attention and effort of others as well, namely, the heads of the state, employers and the rich, and finally, those in whose behalf efforts are being made, the workers themselves. Yet without hesitation We affirm that if the Church is disregarded, human striving will be in vain. Manifestly, it is the Church which draws from the Gospel the teachings through which the struggle can be composed entirely or, after its bitterness is removed, can certainly become more tempered.

42. But it must not be supposed that the Church so concentrates her energies on caring for souls as to overlook the things which pertain to mortal and earthly life. As regards the nonowning workers specifically, she desires and strives that they rise from their most wretched state and enjoy better conditions.

Pius XI, Ubi Arcano

60. For, although from her divine mission the Church is directly concerned with the spiritual and not with the temporal, still, as all these things aid one another and are closely intertwined, the Church fosters the temporal prosperity of individuals and society as effectively almost as if she had been instituted for that purpose alone.

Pius XI, Quadragesimo Anno

41. Yet before proceeding to explain these matters, that principle which Leo XIII so clearly established must be laid down at the outset here,

namely, that there resides in Us the right and duty to pronounce with supreme authority upon social and economic matters. Certainly the Church was not given the commission to guide men to an only fleeting and perishable happiness but to that which is eternal. Indeed "the Church holds that it is unlawful for her to mix without cause in these temporal concerns"; however, she can in no wise renounce the duty God entrusted to her to interpose her authority, not of course in matters of technique for which she is neither suitably equipped nor endowed by office, but in all things that are connected with the moral law. For as to these, the deposit of truth that God committed to Us and the grave duty of disseminating and interpreting the whole moral law, and of urging it in season and out of season, bring under and subject to Our supreme jurisdiction not only the social order but economic activities themselves.

42. Even though economics and moral science employ each its own principles in its own sphere, it is, nevertheless, an error to say that the economic and moral orders are so distinct from and alien to each other that the former depends in no way on the latter. Certainly the laws of economics, as they are termed, being based on the very nature of material things and on the capacities of the human body and mind, determine the limits of what productive human ef-

fort cannot, and of what it can attain in the economic field and by what means. Yet it is reason itself that clearly shows, on the basis of the individual and social nature of things and of men, the purpose which God ordained for all economic life.

43. But it is only the moral law which, just as it commands us to seek our supreme and last end in the whole scheme of our activity, so likewise commands us to seek directly in each kind of activity those purposes which we know that nature, or rather God the Author of nature, established for that kind of action, and in orderly relationship to subordinate such immediate purposes to our supreme and last end. If we faithfully observe this law, then it will follow that the particular purposes, both individual and social, that are sought in the economic field will fall in their proper place in the universal order of purposes, and We, in ascending through them, as it were by steps, shall attain the final end of all things, that is God, to Himself and to us, the supreme and inexhaustible Good.

130. Yet it is not rash by any means to say that the whole scheme of social and economic life is now such as to put in the way of vast numbers of mankind most serious obstacles which prevent them from caring for the one thing necessary; namely, their eternal salvation.

Pius XI, On Atheistic Communism

34. The Church does not separate a proper regard for temporal welfare from solicitude for the eternal. If she subordinates the former to the latter according to the words of her divine Founder, "Seek ye first the Kingdom of God and His justice, and all these things shall be added unto you," she

is nevertheless so far from being unconcerned with human affairs, so far from hindering civil progress and material advancement, that she actually fosters and promotes them in the most sensible and efficacious manner. Thus even in the sphere of social economics, although the Church has never proposed a definite technical system, since this is not her field, she has nevertheless clearly outlined the guiding principles which, while susceptible of varied concrete applications according to the diversified conditions of times and places and peoples, indicate the safe way of securing the happy progress of society.

Pius XII, La Solennità della Pentecoste, June 1, 1941

1676. It is . . . the indisputable competence of the Church, on that side of the social order where it meets and enters into contact with the moral order, to decide whether the bases of a given social system are in accord with the unchangeable order which God, our Creator and Redeemer, has shown us through the natural law and Revelation . . . the Church, guardian of the supernatural Christian Order in which nature and grace converge, must form the consciences even of those who are called upon to find solutions for the problems and the duties imposed by social life. Upon the form given to society, whether conforming or not to the divine law, depends and emerges the good or ill of souls, depends the decision whether men, all called to be revived by the grace of Christ, do actually in the detailed course of their life breathe the healthy vivifying atmosphere of truth and moral virtue or the disease-laden and often fatal air of error and corruption. Before such a thought and such an anticipation, how could the Church, loving Mother that she is, solicitous for the welfare of her children, remain an indifferent onlooker in their danger, remain silent or feign not to see or take cognizance of social conditions which, whether one wills it or not, make difficult or practically impossible a Christian life? . . .

Pius XII, To Members of Rinascita Cristiana, January 22, 1947

This task of the Church is indeed arduous, but they are simply unwitting deserters or dupes who, in deference to a misguided supernaturalism, would confine the Church to the "strictly religious" field, as they say, whereas by so doing they are but playing into the hands of their enemies.

Pius XII, To Sacred College of Cardinals, June 2, 1947

By disposition of Divine Providence, the Catholic Church has formulated and promulgated its social doctrine. She points out the path to be followed, and no hope of achieving temporal gain, or fear of losing possessions, or of appearing less in harmony with modern civilization, or less national or social, could authorize true Christians to deviate even a hair's breadth from this path.

Pius XII, To Young Men, September 12, 1948

The social question, beloved sons, is undoubtedly an economic question also, but even more than that it is a question which concerns the ordered regulation of human society. And, in its deepest sense, it is a moral and therefore a religious question. As such, it may be summed up thus: have men — from the individual to the people, and right through to the community of peoples — the moral strength to create such public conditions that in the life of society there will not be any individuals or any peoples who are merely objects, that is to say, deprived of all right and exposed to exploitation by others, but all instead will be subjects, that is, having a legitimate share in the forma-tion of the social order and able, according to their art or profession, to live happily and tranquilly with sufficient means of support, protected effectively against the violence of an egoistic economy, in freedom defined by the general welfare, and with full human dignity, each respecting his neighbor as he respects himself? Will humanity be capable of generating and possessing the moral strength to realize such a social order?

Pius XII, Letter to Semaines Sociales, 1949

There can be no incompatibility between a realism, healthfully nourished by facts, statistics, and economic laws, and a social order quite legitimately imbued with aspirations for more justice and humanity. These two aspects of the same problem are complementary; to them can be applied the words of the Gospel, *Haec oportuit facere et illa non omittere.*

Pius XII, Humani Generis, August 12, 1950

20. Nor must it be thought that what is expounded in Encyclical Letters does not of itself demand consent, since in writing such Letters the Popes do not exercise the supreme power of their Teaching Authority. For these matters are taught with the ordinary teaching authority, of which it is true to say: "He who heareth you, heareth me"; and generally what is expounded and inculcated in Encyclical Letters already for other reasons appertains to Catholic doctrine. But if the Supreme Pontiffs in their official documents purposely pass judgment on a matter up to that time under dispute, it is obvious that that matter, according to the mind and will of the same Pontiffs, cannot be any longer considered a question open to discussion among theologians.

Pius XII, To Cardinals, Archbishops, and Bishops of Rome, November 2, 1954

Therefore, when it is a question of instructions and propositions which the properly constituted shepherds (i.e., the Roman Pontiff for the whole Church, and the Bishops for the faithful entrusted to them) publish on matters within the natural law, the faithful must not invoke that saying (which is wont to be employed with respect to opinions of individuals): "the strength of the authority is no more than the strength of the arguments." Hence, even though to someone, certain declarations of the Church may not seem proved by the arguments put forward, his obligation to obey still remains.

Pius XII, Christmas Message, 1954

. . . if there are — as there actually are — relations of cause and effect between the moral world and the economic world, they must be so ordered that primacy be assigned to the former, that is, the moral world which must authoritatively permeate with its spirit the social economy. Once this scale of values has been established and its actual exercise permitted, economics will, insofar as it is able, consolidate the moral world and confirm the spiritual postulates and forces of peace.

Pius XII, To the Italian National Federation of Farmers, May 18, 1955

Indeed, it is not enough to have just principles nor to apply them to the limited circle of one's personal life. On the contrary, it is necessary to spread them within one's environment, to make them of advantage to others also, and to show clearly the worth and the strength of the national interest.

Pius XII, To a Pilgrimage of Working People From the City of Terni, November 18, 1956

Meanwhile We remind all whom it concerns that even though . . . economic problems must be met and solved in accordance with the laws of production, distribution, circulation, and consumption of goods in their relation to the social order, it is equally certain that these same laws can be formulated and applied with human understanding and Christian charity. We must not lose sight of the fact that, by introducing the principles of ethics into our investigation of economic facts, we do no violence to the economy, but rather contribute effectively to the correct solution of the problems that it poses and confronts.

Pius XII, Christmas Message, 1956

Efforts at correction have been made through large-scale institutional reforms, often too broad in scope, or based on false principles; but the reform of institutions is not as urgent as that of conduct.

Pius XII, To Assembly of the International Movement of Catholic Intellectuals, April 25, 1957

Without by any means forgetting that his goal is to contribute to his neighbor's salvation, the Christian must be ever mindful that the establishment of God's Kingdom in men's hearts and in social institutions very often requires a minimum of human development, a simple demand of reason to which a man normally assents even if he does not have the grace of faith.

For this reason, the Christian will always be ready to work for the relief of every material distress and for the development of some common basis of knowledge. In a word, he will be diligent to achieve the betterment of the poor and the disinherited. And in this way he will be certain of fulfilling a great obligation placed on him by collective charity, that of clearing the way to a worthy life for many men and of thereby making their co-operation in common effort easier. All this will lead men to a better state of life, enabling them to look higher, to welcome the Light and embrace the only Truth which can make them free (John 8, 32).

Pius XII, To Italian Federation of Middlemen and Business Agents, June 22, 1958

When, for instance, one says "business is business," a norm is adopted which, if considered as an absolute and universal principle, must be included among the maxims that no Christian conscience could accept, for that which applies to every human activity equally applies to economic operations. They must be subject to divine, natural, and positive laws.

The Church and Social Order

18. Who can deny the close relationship between economic injustice and a long train of evils, physical, social, and moral? Unfair wages due to greed for excessive profits and insecurity due to false and immoral economic principles lead directly to undernourishment, bad housing, inadequate clothing, and indirectly to irregular family relations, child delinquency, and crime. Excessively long hours in some industrial areas and in some industrial processes create danger to life and limb, impair the health of workingmen, and impoverish whole families through infection, disease, and premature death. Because human beings and not animated machines toil in industry, therefore the Church cannot abdicate her right and duty to speak out in defense of the rights of human personality nor fail to declare uncompromisingly the moral obligations of industrial and economic life.

The Australian Hierarchy, Morality in Public Life, September, 1950

The power of organized bodies in the modern world is so immense that there is no man or woman whose personal life is not intimately affected by the policies they formulate.

Organizations, in themselves, are inanimate. Dead things do not make policies. Policies are made by men, the men who lead the organizations, the men who elect them or who passively allow them to lead.

With such immense consequences following upon their policies and their actions, it is intolerable that members should permit their organizations to base their policies on lying, on dishonesty, on fraud, on greed, or on the lust for power.

Above all, it is intolerable that those Christians who, in either capacity, compose these organizations, should follow two moral codes — one, in their personal life, which does not permit lying or dishonesty or fraud or greed, and another, in their public life, which regards all of these things as lawful instruments of policy.

For the Christian, sin is sin whether it is committed in the course of private or public life. And although the gravity of the sin committed in the formulation of many public policies will vary with the degree of knowledge, with the position of responsibility and with the motives of the person concerned, and also with the effects of his wrongdoing, no sin is ever palliated by the consideration that it is committed not for private gain, but for public policy.

Code of Social Principles

10. Economic science observes, describes and directs the human relationships of joint labor, exchange and distribution, which necessarily arise as soon as man desires to be master over matter and to satisfy his needs. It is at once descriptive and normative; it describes phenomena; it lays down the order which should be applied for better management in the material field of life, in the successive human acts of joint labor and exchange.

11. Between economics and ethics there are necessary relations and a true co-ordination. For the human relationships treated of in political economy, between landlords and tenants, employers and workers, tax-collectors and tax-payers, sellers and buyers, producers and consumers, are subject to the control of moral conscience.

89. Economic laws relate to human acts. These laws are discovered through the study of psychology and history and the observation of facts. Economic laws can produce certain evil or unjust consequences according to the conditions under which they are allowed to operate. A surplus of goods or services, for instance, results in their depreciation. It is therefore often necessary to provide by suitable organization for the working of this or that economic law. Monetary inflation has unavoidable results; but inflation itself can be avoided.

91. Since economic phenomena relate to human affairs, the interpretation which is put upon them calls for an exact knowledge of human nature and of imponderable factors in the psychological and moral order which react upon human activities; it depends upon a multitude of other than statistical data. Into this work of interpretation necessarily enter metaphysical ideas regarding human nature, its origin, its destiny, the relative values of men, and their mutual relations.

The Catholic economist must seek these ideas in Christian philosophy, if he wishes to remain logical with himself.

92. Besides, the Church herself has here both the competence and the right to intervene, certainly not in the technical sphere, but in all that touches the moral law. For, if it is true that the Church has received the mission to lead mankind to eternal happiness, she can never forget that economic activity must be subject to the moral law and that the temporal end is subordinate to the eternal.

POPE PIUS XI made clear that "the body of truth that God committed to Us, and the grave duty of disseminating and interpreting the whole moral law . . . bring under and subject to Our supreme jurisdiction not only the social order but economic activities themselves."[1] This assertion of authority over economic life has astonished many persons, including some within the Catholic Church. This is the more true because the divorce of religion from social life, noted in the preceding chapter, has often been taken for granted in modern times. To correct any misconceptions on this point, it is important to state clearly why the Church speaks on social and economic matters, the authority of this teaching, how it should be interpreted, and how moral pronouncements are to be applied to everyday life.

RIGHT AND DUTY TO INTERVENE

The Church stresses two areas in which moral law affects economic life. The first concerns the consciences of individuals as they participate daily in their chosen fields of activity. This we may term personal morality. The second area involves the moral effects of social conditions: the implications of the laws, customs, and institutions of economic life. These affect individuals because they are members of various groups, such as labor unions, corporations, or trade associations. It also affects them in their capacity as citizens. We may call this social morality.

Among good men, there are likely to be few who question the right of the Church to pronounce on matters of *personal morals*. They accept the idea that justice, charity, and similar obligations apply universally. Theft in the course of business is just as much a violation of justice as it is in the case of a thief who steals a purse. Of course, there are businessmen who have double standards. They accept such axioms as: "Let the buyer beware" or "All's fair in business." But it is doubtful that really sincere merchants stifle their consciences with such axioms.

Social morality is another matter. Persons who may be eminently fair in their direct dealings with others may act quite differently as members of a corporation, a labor union, or a political party. Even when they may not sanction sins of commission by such groups, they may be blind to sins of omission. Group individualism, mentioned earlier, seems to justify indifference toward their social responsibilities. Because of this confused state of many consciences, it is advisable to spell out in more detail the morality of human actions in the economic sphere.

Personal Morality. Theologians note three factors that influence the morality of our actions: the object sought, the motives of the doer, and

---

[1] Quadragesimo Anno, No. 41.

the circumstances under which we act. Each of these factors should be considered in any economic decision.

Certain economic problems involve a purely objective morality. Thus, a promotion venture which is permeated with fraud is dishonest of its very nature. The same is true if economic force is used to compel another to do something wrong. Abuse of a monopoly position by the charging of clearly exploitive prices is contrary to the virtue of justice. Stealing does not become right, merely because it is accomplished in the course of large-scale business transactions. On the other side of the picture, certain business practices can be called morally good by their nature. Thus the inventor who markets a new process that will create useful employment renders a service to society. The industrialist who gives an example of fine human relations in his plant is acting according to sound ethics.

In other cases, motives will influence the morality of a transaction. While good motives will never make right out of wrong, it is possible to do something morally good or neutral for unsound motives. It is not wrong in itself to amass wealth, but greed and avarice are sinful. The acquisition of economic power may be a normal result of shrewd and successful business operations, but it may also be the product of pride and disordered ambition. A labor leader may often be morally justified in calling a strike, yet it is not inconceivable that personal pique or like unworthy motives may enter into his decision. Thus, he could be guilty through unethical motives.

Finally, circumstances and especially the impact upon others enter into the morality of business operations. Actions may not be judged in isolation. A factory which gives out obnoxious fumes might legitimately be constructed in a remote region. If the same factory were constructed in a residential neighborhood, it would lower property values and make homes useless for living purposes. Again, factory waste dumped into a river could ruin its drinking and recreational values. An industrial process that would poison the workers in the plant would be wrong. A pace of operations that would burn out a worker's energy in a few years would do him an injustice. Thus, the moral nature of a transaction may not be judged in the abstract. The total picture must be considered, particularly the social effect of a given operation.

The fact that morally wrong practices often prevail in the economic world indicates that not everyone has a right conscience about such matters, or that many fail to live up to their known obligations. The production and sale of shoddy goods, cheating in the servicing of appliances, or the failure of workers to do a good job even when well paid, all are too common to allow us to be complacent. So far as Catholics are concerned, there is room for more sermons on these topics, better religious teaching in the schools, and more realistic texts in ethics and moral theology.

Social Morality. The religious teaching that we are "our brother's keeper" applies in a much broader area than personal contacts with workers, employers, or customers. It extends also to the social effects of decisions made by impersonal economic groups. Actions by labor unions, corporations, political pressure groups or legislatures must be judged by their impact upon the general welfare. It is wrong to seek group interests when this causes grave harm to the community as a whole. The common good of all must be the supreme norm to be used in judging the social effects of individual and group decisions. Undoubtedly most religious persons accept this principle as a general statement. Yet, it is often evaded through self-deception, omission, or sheer inertia.

One method of flouting the general welfare is the practice of clothing selfish actions in the guise of disinterested public service. To illustrate, corporations rarely complain that their own profits are excessive. Unions may demand substantial wage increases in times of inflation so as to keep up with living costs. When conditions are reversed, they want additional increases in order to stimulate business as a result of increased purchasing power. Likewise, farm groups and political parties seem to find a parallel between their desires and the general good. It is difficult to avoid the conclusion that many public appeals to the common good are mere rationalizations of decisions adopted primarily for group interests.

Again, few conscientious persons escape the stings of conscience when they participate, however remotely, in really selfish and antisocial actions. But many fail through omission, even though they might balk at directly committing an unjust or selfish deed. An example would be indifference toward the root causes of such problems as poverty or racial discrimination in a community. People who contribute to charity drives, in order to take care of some of the effects of destitution, slum living, or discrimination against minorities, may never dream that they have an obligation to seek the prevention or the radical cure of such evils. Many who are concerned about poverty at home remain indifferent to the sufferings of millions in remoter areas of the world.

Custom and inertia also explain slowness in seeking basic reforms. The fact that conditions have prevailed over centuries make many accept them as inevitable or even natural. They fail to realize that certain evils tend to be self-perpetuating, unless outside help is given. Thus, malnutrition and disease cause low living standards in many areas of the world. Low standards in turn make it impossible to secure needed food and medicines. Again, when a minority group is denied equal opportunity in education, housing, and job prospects, it is bound to be culturally submerged. These very cultural differences are then used as an excuse for further discrimination.

Why the Church Intervenes. From the viewpoint of the Church, there is a double obligation, affecting both the material and the spiritual welfare of our neighbors, that applies in these cases. First, there is the direct duty to seek the material welfare of our fellow man. We are obliged to feed the hungry and clothe the naked. And the best form of help, as Moses Maimonides once said, is helping people to help themselves. Second, there is the fact that, so far as we know, adverse social conditions contribute to the loss of souls. Pope Pius XII said that some conditions make "difficult or practically impossible a Christian life."[2] These are strong words, but hundreds of serious thinkers, from Aristotle to the present-day moralists, have stated that there is a form of poverty that hinders the practice of virtue. The Gospel ideal of poverty involves detachment from material things. But the grinding destitution of many persons causes them to be almost exclusively preoccupied with the material.

One does not need to be a materialist or a determinist to hold that external conditions often affect human behavior. Children in slums, for example, are less likely than middle-class children to have a good home life. In the former situation, both parents may be working and hence unable to give adequate time to the guidance of their children. Housing may be so poor that the streets are more attractive than home for play and relaxation. Yet, on the streets children not only meet bad companions, but they also suffer many rebuffs that can engender in them antisocial attitudes. These facts may explain the high correlation between slum living and delinquency.

Nor is the Church indifferent to the broader consequences of social injustice. Much of the appeal of communism throughout the world is based on its program to cure social ills. We grant that this program is deceptive. But the embracing of communism by a nation is a process not

---

[2] *Supra*, p. 23.

easily reversed. Once its adherents have taken power, they use force to maintain themselves.

The bitter fact is that, when given the choice between freedom and bread, many will sacrifice freedom. Political freedom is often an empty phrase to the man on the park bench, without a job or assurance that he will eat. Desperate men can always convince themselves that things will be different in their country, just as today French or Italian communists (in the lower ranks) try to reconcile communism with love of country and of Church. In the face of such a menace, can anyone say that the Church should confine itself to worship and keep out of the market place? Under these conditions, indifference to the social problem would be inviting a persecution so drastic that millions may apostatize rather than face it. Nor should it be said that we must fight this evil with spiritual weapons only. Not only is the social question a moral question, and hence a problem for the Church, but the exclusively spiritual approach to any material problem is of doubtful doctrinal orthodoxy. We do not seek to cure epidemics by prayer alone; we use our God-given intelligence to discover causes and remedies. We should be no less zealous in facing the social problem.

To summarize, the Church has the right to discuss social problems because they are at the same time moral problems. It has the duty to enter this field, because its teaching mission includes the moral law as well as dogmas of faith. This duty is reinforced by the urgency of modern problems. Failure to solve them may lead to the loss of souls, the more so if it brings about the totalitarian state. This much established, it is important to define the precise scope and nature of intervention by the Church.

HOW SOCIAL TEACHINGS APPLY TO ECONOMIC LIFE

Moral Law and Economic Life. When the Church teaches on social questions, it deals with moral, not technical issues. It is not the function of the Church, as such, to choose, for example, between Keynesian and classical economics. It does not usually pronounce upon interest theories or techniques for computing national income. It may incidentally raise these issues, if moral factors intervene. But normally the Church treats of direct moral considerations such as those affecting man, the family, the state, property, and God's purpose in economic life.

The fact that ethical and value judgments are interposed in economic matters does not mean that the Church questions the validity of economic law. On the contrary, there is no disposition to deny the soundness of physical and economic laws. If a poor country is afflicted with a famine, no amount of preaching about proper living standards will prevent hardship, unless aid from without is forthcoming. Should incomes be increased in a nation that cannot increase production, then inflation is a necessary result, barring unusual fiscal or control measures. The laws implied in these examples are based on either the nature of material things or valid generalizations about human behavior.

But human foresight can change the conditions under which physical and economic laws operate. Famine can often be prevented by good irrigation systems. It can be alleviated by generous contributions from wealthier nations. Inflation can be forestalled either by preventing an increase of a nation's money supply or by provisions to expand production. In such ways, laws, policies, and programs do affect the working of economic law.

In applying moral principles to economic life, we must avoid two extremes. One is the determinism of those who claim that economic laws are so absolute that any interference with them is fatal. Modern nations have shown considerable ability to control their economies. Even nations dedicated to a relatively free economy, such as Germany and the United States, employ fiscal and monetary controls to prevent inflation and deflation. In reality, there is no such thing as a purely economic system. All economic theories involve certain assumptions about human nature. Some are merely more explicit than others in stating these assumptions.

The other extreme is the voluntarism that states, in effect, that what is morally desirable can be easily achieved by men of good will. The fallacy of this approach can be proved by many examples. One instance is the phenomenon of serious business depressions. A major depression is a serious matter. No one can be sure of profiting from it; most people lose heavily as a result. But only in recent years have we had much success in controlling such tragic events. Even now there is not complete agreement as to the causes of a depression or the means to prevent or cure a slump. The fact that a slump is tragic for all is no guarantee that we can find proper remedies for it. Hence when the Church teaches the moral desirability of certain objectives, such as a family living wage, it has raised a problem, not solved it. It is up to men of good will, using proper economic means, to achieve the end pointed out by moral teaching.

How Church Teaching Is Determined. Before we discuss problems connected with the application of moral law, it is well to understand clearly just how one knows the moral teaching of the Church on economic matters. Clearly, as in all other matters of faith, the first source is the See of St. Peter. The popes have the right and duty to teach with authority on matters of faith or morals. Even when they are not pronouncing infallibly, they speak with clear authority. Catholics must give their assent, at the very least in terms of religious obedience, to the Vicar of Christ. Bishops likewise teach with authority in their own dioceses. Clergy and faithful must obey them, unless the Holy See directs otherwise in special cases. In addition, the common teaching of the Fathers and theologians of the Church must be accepted, unless higher authority decides otherwise.

In accepting the teaching authority of the Church, we must be careful to interpret correctly what is taught and how it is taught. For example, a papal encyclical might exhort the faithful to follow a given practice as most useful. Such is the case, for example, when Pope Pius XI advocated profit-sharing.[3] It is obvious from the context that this is neither a doctrinal teaching nor a disciplinary command. It is an exhortation demanding prudent and filial consideration, but it is not meant to command the faithful. But in other matters, such as the condemnation of communism, the pope is peremptory and decisive. No Catholic could disregard this position and advocate communism as defined by the pope.

Again, any papal document must be interpreted in accord with the customary norms used by theologians. They use the context to determine the solemnity and universality of any teaching. This is an intricate process, since the external form of certain pronouncements may offer no indication of their universality. Solemn encyclicals may contain passages that are merely counsels, not commands. Occasional discourses to pilgrims, particularly in the pontificate of Pope Pius XII, often contain broad doctrinal declarations. By contrast, some of his world-wide discourses, such as Christmas or Easter messages, may deal extensively with localized problems, as for example, the European Common Market.

There may be changes of emphasis as conditions warrant. Thus, in the citations given in this chapter are passages stressing both institutional and moral reforms. Either, cited out of context, could be used to favor an excessive stress upon one or another approach to social reform. Actually, papal teaching insists upon both aspects, although there is an under-

---

[3] *Quadragesimo Anno*, No. 65.

standable tendency to stress the method that at any given time may be neglected in broad areas.

The context used in judging papal documents must also take account of the full historical situation that prompted the document. Many political statements of Pope Leo XIII relate to nineteenth-century problems. He was concerned with certain abuses in newly formed democratic regimes. But his successors would be far more likely to emphasize the virtues of democracy and the evils of centralized power, especially when it is totalitarian. Again, Pope Pius XI excoriated the economic system of his day for many evils. To apply every word literally to the present economic situation of the United States or West Germany would be a stultifying misapplication of the pope's meaning. On the other hand, there are areas of Europe, Latin America, Asia, and Africa where the strong language of *Quadragesimo Anno* is literally applicable today.[4]

All these observations are but aids in the direction of one goal: understanding what the popes taught and how they taught it. Thus we distinguish between matters of faith and those statements that are pastoral counsels. We differentiate between eternal truths based on revelation or natural law and judgments tied to specific changing historical events. With intelligence, sincerity, and good faith, it should not be too difficult to obtain a clear and consistent idea of the Church's teaching on great social matters. It is true that there have been controversies among Catholics as to both the content and the application of Catholic social teaching. Many of these controversies, however, need never have occurred. They were often the product of strongly partisan disputes, in which one side or another sought to use some papal statement to vindicate its position. Too often the statement in question was used out of context, or at least without reference to its historical background. By contrast, those who humbly seek to learn the entirety of the Church's social teaching should at least attain reasonable certainty and clarity in regard to the content of such teaching. Problems of application, of course, are more difficult, as will be noted presently.

Application of Moral Principles. Once it is clear what the popes teach and how they teach it — as a matter of divine faith, or natural law, or

---

[4] It is taken for granted in these pages that intelligent Catholics no longer make the mistake of assuming that Church teaching on social matters is not to be considered binding doctrine. The passages from *Humani Generis* and the 1954 address to the Roman clergy, cited above, should make the position of the Church abundantly clear. For further development of this idea, see *Catholic Social Principles*, pp. 55–61.

merely a prudential recommendation — the next step is to apply it to practical economic life. We repeat here that the Church teaches morals, not economics. Yet this moral teaching, to be fruitful, must be applied. It cannot be left in the abstract. Like other moral teachings of the Church, its application is often difficult. We cannot merely tell the faithful: "This is the law," any more than we can assume that the Ten Commandments can be readily applied in utmost detail by anyone of good will. Volumes of moral theology have been written to guide pastors of souls in applying these commandments. Centuries of thought have gone into these applications. We need equal diligence in developing the full implications of Catholic social teaching.

A common fallacy to be avoided is the confusion between the moral teaching of the Church and an individual writer's application of this doctrine to concrete affairs. The writer may understand perfectly the teaching of the Church. But he could be wholly wrong in application because of a faulty understanding of economic life. For example, a theologian might advocate compulsory arbitration of all labor disputes, on the grounds that the Church is opposed to class strife. The fallacy here lies in the choice of means to prevent disputes from developing into strikes. Experience has shown that arbitration of differences about wages and other economic issues involves a degree of outside control of a firm that, in effect, leads to socialism. Socialism, of course, is likewise condemned by the Church. This example shows the necessity of economic insight, as well as theological competence, by those who would make moral pronouncements on current social issues.

Consequently, it is best, when applying Church teaching to a concrete problem, explicitly to separate moral principles from historical and economic presuppositions used in making the final prudential judgment. Thus listeners or readers will not confuse the authoritative teaching of the Church with the fallible, even though expert, judgments of the specialist who is applying such truths. Thus, the writer could state why a controversial question is a moral problem and what moral principles apply. He could then give a factual analysis of the relevant economic and social factors. Finally, he could present his conclusion as to the proper policy in a given set of circumstances.

These points should not deter the laity, or the clergy who are not specialists, from endeavoring to apply justice and charity to everyday problems. Ideally such persons should seek advice from those expert in both economics and Church social teaching. Should this prove to be

impractical at any time, it is better to act according to the spirit of the
Church, as understood at the time, than to be guided by secularist axioms.
God's blessing will not be denied to such men of good will.

Finally, it is well to remember that the bulk of Church social teaching
is based on natural law rather than on divine revelation. This means
that, in an overwhelming number of cases, these truths can be defended
on the basis of human reason alone, without appeal to authority. This
point is particularly relevant when one is discussing social morality with
non-Catholics. If they are willing to accept natural-law teachings on man
and society, they should not quarrel with the social teaching of the
Church. Actually a large number of distinguished non-Catholic scholars,
both in Europe and the United States, have openly professed their admiration for papal social teachings. Thus, the Catholic in business, labor,
or politics need not feel that he will be considered rash when he promotes policies based on Christian social principles. On the contrary, many
men of good will may rally to his cause and support well-considered applications of universally acknowledged truths.

READINGS*

J. C. Ford and G. Kelly, Contemporary Moral Theology, Chaps. 1–3.
J. Messner, Social Ethics, pp. 697–947.
G. Clune, Christian Social Reorganization, pp. 3–6, 226–267.
J. Villain, S.J., L'Enseignement social de l'Église, Vol. I, pp. 15–34, 46–80.
B. W. Dempsey, The Functional Economy, Chaps. 1, 4, 23.
O. von Nell-Breuning, Reorganization of Social Economy, pp. 79–89.
R. Kothen, L'Enseignement social de l'Église, pp. 128–140.
H. Johnston, Business Ethics, Chaps. 1–2.
M. E. Walsh and P. H. Furfey, Social Problems and Social Action, Chaps. 1–2.
Social Order: Roberto Saboia de Medeiros, S.J., "Social Attitudes of the
    Brazilian Hierarchy," January, 1951; Joachìn Azpiazu, S.J., "Social Attitudes
    of the Spanish Hierarchy," February, 1951; Frank Maher, "Social Attitudes
    of the Australian Hierarchy," March, 1951; Jean Villain, S.J., "Social At-
    titudes of the French Hierarchy," June, 1951; Rev. Dr. Dominic Pillen,
    O.F.M., "Social Attitudes of the Dutch Hierarchy," September, 1951;
    Wilfrid Parsons, S.J., "Social Thought of the American Hierarchy," June,
    1952; John Doebels, "Pius' Basic Social Addresses," November, 1952; Jean
    Hulliger, "Social Thought of the Canadian Hierarchy," September, 1955;
    Philip S. Land, S.J., "Practical Wisdom and Social Order," November,
    1955; Paul A. Montavon, "Ethics and Social Sciences," January, 1958.

* For further readings, consult List No. 2 in the Appendix.

Chapter III

MAN AND ECONOMIC LIFE

THE NATURE OF MAN

Leo XIII, Rerum Novarum

57. No one may with impunity outrage the dignity of man, which God Himself treats with great reverence, nor impede his course to that level of perfection which accords with eternal life in heaven. Nay, more, in this connection a man cannot even by his own free choice allow himself to be treated in a way inconsistent with his nature, and suffer his soul to be enslaved; for there is no question here of rights belonging to man, but of duties owed to God, which are to be religiously observed.

Pius XI, On Atheistic Communism

27. Man has a spiritual and immortal soul. He is a person, marvelously endowed by his Creator with gifts of body and mind. He is a true "microcosm," as the ancients said, a world in miniature, with a value far surpassing that of the vast inanimate cosmos. God alone is his last end, in this life and the next. By sanctifying grace he is raised to the dignity of a son of God, and incorporated into the Kingdom of God in the Mystical Body of Christ. In consequence he has been endowed by God with many and varied prerogatives: the right to life, to bodily integrity, to the necessary means of existence; the right to tend toward his ultimate goal in the path marked out for him by God; the right of association and the right to possess and use property.

Pius XII, Christmas Broadcast, 1942

1831. The origin and the primary scope of social life is the conservation, development, and perfection of the human person, helping him to realize accurately the demands and values of religion and culture set by the Creator for every man and for all mankind, both as a whole and in its natural ramifications. A social teaching or a social reconstruction program which denies or prescinds from this internal essential relation to God of everything that regards man, is on a false course; and while it builds up with one hand, it prepares with the other the materials which sooner or later will undermine and destroy the whole fabric. And when it disregards the respect due to the human person and to the life which is proper to that person, and gives no thought to it in its organization, in legislative and executive activity, then instead of serving society, it harms it; instead of encouraging and stimulating social thought, instead of realizing its hopes and expectations, it strips it of all real value and reduces it to an utilitarian formula which is openly rejected by constantly increasing groups.

1832. If social life implies intrinsic unity, it does not, at the same time, exclude differences which are founded in fact and nature. When we hold fast to God, the Supreme Controller of all that relates to man, then the similarities no less than the differences of men find their allotted place in the fixed order of being, of values, and hence also of morality.

1844. First: He who would have the star of peace shine out and stand over society should co-operate, for his part, in giving back to the human person the dignity given to it by God from the very beginning; should oppose the excessive herding of men, as if they were a mass without a soul; their economic, social, political, in-

tellectual, and moral inconsistency; their dearth of solid principles and strong convictions, their surfeit of instinctive sensible excitement and their fickleness.

1845. He should favor, by every lawful means, in every sphere of life, social institutions in which a full personal responsibility is assured and guaranteed both in the earthly and the eternal order of things.

1847. Second: He who would have the star of peace shine out and stand over society should reject every form of materialism which sees in the people only a herd of individuals who, divided and without any internal cohesion, are considered as a mass to be lorded over and treated arbitrarily; he should strive to understand society as an intrinsic unity, which has grown up and matured under the guidance of Providence, a unity which — within the bounds assigned to it and according to its own peculiar gifts — tends, with the collaboration of the various classes and professions, toward the eternal and ever new aims of culture and religion.

Pius XII, To Italian Catholic Workers' Association, May 14, 1953

When true human dignity and the transcendent destiny of all men are really lived day by day, then also industry will acquire that close unity of interest in the work which the Rerum Novarum desires. Then employers will treat their workers con-

siderately both in word and deed; they will help them in their work, and, no matter how insignificant it may seem, they will show esteem for it; they will try to give each one the job that is best suited to his capabilities and to his sense of responsibility.

Pius XII, Radio Address to International Congress of Catholic Doctors, September 11, 1956

The individual is not only anterior to society by reason of his origin; he is superior to it in virtue of his destiny as well. Society, to the formation and development of which individuals are ordered, is merely the universal

means intended by nature to bring people into contact with one another.

The relation here of part to whole is entirely different from that which exists in the physical body. When man is born into society, he is already provided with independent rights by the Creator; he carries on his activity by giving and receiving, and through his collaboration with other men he creates values and obtains results which, by himself, he could not effect nor even, as an individual, transmit. These new values show that society has its own pre-eminence and dignity; but this does not bring about a change in the relation We pointed out above because these higher values (society itself, for instance), are in their turn put in relation by nature to the individual and to people in general.

Pius XII, Address to Representatives of Fiat Automotive Plant, October 31, 1948

The Church does not promise that absolute equality which others are proclaiming because she knows that life in human society always and of necessity produces a whole range of degrees and differences in physical and mental traits, in inward dispositions and inclinations, in occupations and in responsibilities. But at the same time she assures you full equality in human dignity, as also in the Heart of Him who calls unto Himself all those who labor and are heavily burdened, and invites them to take upon themselves His yoke and find peace and rest for their souls; for His yoke is sweet and His burden light (cf. Matt. 11, 28–30).

Leo XIII, Rerum Novarum

26. There are truly very great and very many natural differences among men. Neither the talents, nor the skill, nor the health, nor the capacities of all are the same, and unequal fortune follows of itself upon necessary inequality in respect to these endowments.

Code of Social Principles

2. It is not true that the individual is self-sufficient. No one, however gifted, can maintain his existence or perfect his mind and heart save in that society in which he is called to live. His God-given faculties ordain that he live in society and they can only develop by virtue of his so doing.

3. If individualism exaggerates individual rights, other systems, on the contrary, overrate collective rights. . . . They make absolute such relative values as classless society, society, the race, the nation, or the State.

Between these extremes, Christian philosophy affirms both the outstanding dignity of the human person and the necessity of society for his complete development.

4. In the legal order, individualism betrays itself in a radical subjectivism which attributes absolute independence to the human person and unconditional value to individual rights. The political constitutions of the nineteenth century have fallen more than once into this extreme.

5. Conversely, Positivist Sociology betrays itself in the legal order by a radical objectivism. It claims that society is a reality higher than and prior to its members, so that the latter have no rights but such as social solidarity may require. Such

objectivism ends by disregarding the personality of man and in denying the rights that flow from human nature. It makes society the end, man the means.

6. In the same way, Communism and the totalitarian systems ignore the real value and the transcendental destiny of the human person and only allow him, in view of society, such rights as the latter deigns to grant him.

MAN IN SOCIETY

The Social Nature of Man

Pius XI, Mit Brennender Sorge

35. Real common good ultimately takes its measure from man's nature, which balances personal rights and social obligations, and from the purpose of society, established for the benefit of human nature. Society was intended by the Creator for the full development of individual possibilities, and for the social benefits which, by a give-and-take process, everyone can claim for his own sake and that of others. Higher and more general values, which the collectivity alone can provide, also derive from the Creator for the good of man, and for his full development, natural and supernatural, and the realization of his perfection. To neglect this order is to shake the pillars on which society rests, and to compromise social tranquillity, security, and existence.

Pius XI, On Atheistic Communism

29. But God has likewise destined man for civil society according to the dictates of his very nature. In the plan of the Creator, society is a natural means which man can and must use to reach his destined end. Society is for man and not vice versa. This must not be understood in the sense of liberalistic individualism, which subordinates society to the selfish use of the individual; but only in the sense that by means of an organic union with society and by mutual collaboration the attainment of earthly happiness is placed within the reach of all. In a further sense it is society which affords the opportunities for the development of all the individual and social gifts bestowed on human nature. These natural gifts have a value surpassing the immediate interests of the moment, for in society they reflect the divine perfection, which would not be true were man to live alone. But on final analysis, even in this latter function society is made for man, that he may recognize this reflection of God's perfection, and refer it in praise and adoration to the Creator. Only man, the human person, and not society in any form is endowed with reason and a morally free will.

34. Thus authority is reconciled with liberty, the dignity of the individual with that of the state, the human personality of the subject with the divine delegation of the superior; and in this way a balance is struck between the due dependence and well-ordered love of a man for himself, his family and country, and his love of other families and other peoples, founded on the love of God, the Father of all, their first principle and last end.

Pius XII, To American Delegates to the International Labor Organization, July 16, 1947

... any organization for improving the condition of the workingman will be a mechanism without soul and hence without life and fecundity, unless its charter proclaims and effectively prescribes first, respect for the human person in all men, no matter what their social position; secondly, acknowledgement of the solidarity of all people in forming the human family, created by the loving omnipotence of God; thirdly, the imperative demand on society to place the common good above personal gain, the service of each for all. When the spirit of man is reformed and stabilized according to these truths, the condition of the workingman will be improved. No power of the state will reform the spirit of man. That is the sacred office of religion. And the state whose foundations rest on morality and religion will be the surest protector and defender of the workingman.

Pius XII, Christmas Message, 1956

On the contrary, religion and the reality of the past teach that the social structures, such as matrimony and family, the community and professional groups, social union in personal property, are essential cells which secure man's freedom and, along with it, his function in history. Hence they cannot be tampered with, and their essence cannot be the subject of arbitrary revision.

Private and Public Societies

Leo XIII, Rerum Novarum

71. The end of civil society concerns absolutely all members of this society, since the end of civil society is centered in the common good, in which latter, one and all in due proportion have a right to participate. Wherefore, this society is called public because through it "men share with one another in establishing a commonwealth." On the other hand, societies which are formed, so to speak, within its bosom are considered private and are such because their immediate object is private advantage appertaining to those alone who are thus associated together. "Now a private society is one which is formed to carry out some private business, as when two or three enter into association for the purpose of engaging together in trade."

72. Although private societies exist within the state and are, as it were, so many parts of it, still it is not within the authority of the state universally and per se to forbid them to exist as such. For man is permitted by a right of nature to form private societies; the state, on the other hand, has been instituted to protect and not to destroy natural right, and if it should forbid its citizens to enter into associations, it would clearly do something contradictory to itself, because both the state itself and private associations are begotten of one and the same principle, namely, that men are by nature inclined to associate.

Pius XI, Quadragesimo Anno

37. Leo's learned treatment and vigorous defense of the natural right to form associations began, furthermore, to find ready application to other associations also and not alone to those of the workers. Hence no small part of the credit must, it seems, be given to this same Encyclical of Leo for the fact that among farmers and others of the middle class most useful associations of this kind are seen flourishing to a notable degree and increasing day by day, as well as other institutions of a similar nature in which spiritual development and economic benefit are happily combined.

Code of Social Principles

7. According to the Christian philosophy, there exists between the human person and society a correlation and interdependence ordained by nature because of man's destiny.

8. As the common good of society is a human good, determined ultimately by man's nature and destiny, society may never defraud man of his fundamental personal rights. It can only regulate their exercise in accordance with the demands of the common good, which must never go against true human good.

THE PURPOSE OF ECONOMIC LIFE

Pius XI, Caritate Christi Compulsi

30. No leader in public economy, no power of organization will ever be able to bring social conditions to a peaceful solution, unless first in the very field of economics there triumphs moral law based on God and conscience. This is the underlying value of every value in the political life as well as in the economic life of nations; this is the soundest "rate of exchange." If it is kept steady, all the rest will be stable, being guaranteed by the immutable and eternal law of God.

Pius XI, Quadragesimo Anno*

75. The various occupations will combine and coalesce into, as it were, a single body and like members of the body mutually aid and complete one another. For then only will the social economy be rightly established and attain its purposes when all and each are supplied with all the goods that the wealth and resources of nature, technical achievement, and the social organization of economic life can furnish. And these goods ought indeed to be enough both to meet the demands of necessity and decent comfort and to advance people to that happier and fuller condition of life which, when it is wisely cared for, is not only no hindrance to virtue but helps it greatly.

110. Since the present system of economy is founded chiefly upon ownership and labor, the principles of right reason, that is, of Christian

* See also Nos. 42–43 cited in Chapter II, page 22.

social philosophy, must be kept in mind regarding ownership and labor and their association together, and must be put into actual practice. First, so as to avoid the reefs of individualism and collectivism, the two-fold character, that is individual and social, both of capital or ownership and of work or labor must be given due and rightful weight. Relations of one to the other must be made to conform to the laws of strictest justice — commutative justice as it is called — with the support, however, of Christian charity. Free competition, kept within definite and due limits, and still more economic dictatorship, must be effectively brought under public authority in these matters which pertain to the latter's function.

Pius XII, La Solennità della Pentecoste, June 1, 1941

1685. Likewise the national economy, as it is the product of the men who work together in the community of the state, has no other end than to secure without interruption the material conditions in which the individual life of the citizens may fully develop. Where this is secured in a permanent way, a people will be, in a true sense, economically rich because the general well-being, and consequently the personal right of all to the use of worldly goods, is thus actuated in conformity with the purpose willed by the Creator.

1686. From this, beloved children, it will be easy for you to conclude that the economic riches of a people do not properly consist in the abundance of goods, measured according to a purely and solely material calculation of their worth, but in the fact that such an abundance represents and offers really and effectively the material basis sufficient for the proper personal development of its members.

Pius XII, Nell' Alba, Christmas, 1941

1751. Nobody should think that by indicting the materialism of the nineteenth and twentieth centuries We intend to blame technical progress. No. We do not indict what fundamentally is a gift of God; for, as the Lord God makes wheat to grow from earth and soil, thus, when He created the world, He hid for us in the depth of the earth treasures, metals and precious stones, so that they may be mined by man for his needs, for his works, and for his progress. The Church, the mother of so many European universities, attracts today, as she always did, the most prominent scientists; but she is well aware that man can use every good entrusted to him, even the freedom of will, either for good or for evil. Thus the spirit and the direction in which technical progress has been used has now resulted in science having to expiate its own errors. Science has been misused for destruction, and, in fact, today it destroys the very buildings that it yesterday proudly erected.

Pius XII, Christmas Broadcast, 1942

1851. Those who are familiar with the great Encyclicals of Our Predecessors and Our Own previous messages know well that the Church does not hesitate to draw the practical conclusions which are derived from the moral nobility of work, and to give them all the support of her authority. These exigencies include, besides a just wage which covers the needs of the worker and his family, the conservation and perfection of a social order which will make possible an assured, even if modest, private property for all classes of society, which will promote higher education for the children of the working class who are especially endowed with intelligence and good will, will promote the care and the practice of the social spirit in one's immediate neighborhood, in the district, the province, the people, and the nation, a spirit which, by smoothing over friction arising from privileges or class interests, removes from the workers the sense of isolation through the assuring experience of a genuinely human, and fraternally Christian, solidarity.

Pius XII, Radio Address, September 1, 1944

Technical progress does not determine economic life as a fatal and necessary factor. It has indeed too often yielded timidly to the demands of rapacious, selfish plans calculated to accumulate capital indefinitely; why should it not then yield also to the necessity of maintaining and ensuring private property for all, that cornerstone of social order? Even technical progress, as a social factor, should not prevail over the general good, but should rather be directed and subordinated to it.

Pius XII, To Catholic International Congresses for Social Study and Social Action, June 3, 1950

In the domain of social economy the duty pressing for attention is the judicious adjustment of production to consumption on the basis of human needs and human dignity.

Pius XII, To the Italian Catholic Association of Employers, January 31, 1952

The great misery of the social order is that it is not deeply Christian nor really human, but only technical and economic. It is not built on what should be its basis and the solid foundation of its unity — the common character of men by their nature and by being sons of God through the grace of divine adoption.

Pius XII, Christmas Message, 1952

Human society is not a machine, and must not be made such, not even in the economic field. Rather one must always work with the native endowment of the human person and the individuating characteristics of nations as a natural and basic point of departure in striving to attain the end of the economic order, which is to insure a stable sufficiency of goods and material services, directed in their turn at improving moral, cultural, and religious conditions.

Pius XII, To Members of the Vatican Diplomatic Corps, March 4, 1956

The Church, on the other hand, has never lost sight of man's real needs and has dedicated herself to the mission of preserving the true stability of his existence. She knows that man's temporal destiny finds its sanction and fulfillment only in eternity. Without in any way denying the achievements of science and technology, she keeps them in their proper place and gives them their true meaning. They must serve man without upsetting the balance of all the relationships which make up the plan of his life — family, property, profession, community, and state.

To base the security and stability of human life only on an increasing quantity of material goods is to forget that man is primarily a spirit created in God's image. He is a being re-sponsible for his actions and his destiny and capable of ruling himself. He finds in these facts his highest dignity. It is right to defend this freedom against outside restraints, against the threat of social systems which paralyze it and make it illusory.

But the very person who wages this battle must realize that economics and technology are useful and even necessary forces so long as they are subservient to higher spiritual needs. They become harmful and dangerous only when they are given undue predominance and the dignity, so to speak, of ends in themselves. It is the task of the Church to assure respect for this system of values and to subordinate the elements of material progress to truly spiritual goals.

Pius XII, Aspects of Automation, October 23, 1957*

Provided that man learns how to dominate his instincts and make good use of the ample means for developing his intellectual and spiritual life, there is nothing to fear from material progress.

But should man yield to the temptation of a life of greater ease filled with more and more sensual pleasures, he will gain nothing from it except another kind of slavery and a certain moral decadence.

We hope to the contrary that the most profound needs of the soul will find their satisfaction in the greater amount of leisure time available because of modern machines.

John XXIII, Christmas Message, 1958

Here enters the principle, familiar to believers, that the good service of God and of His justice is also favor-able to the advantage of the civil community of peoples and of nations.

SINCE the Church considers the social question to be also a moral question, and since it reacts to this challenge by detailed moral teachings, it is pertinent to consider now the basic moral principles that affect

---

* Other material on the purpose of economic life can be found in quotations cited in Chapter XVI, pp. 342–343, namely, the 1946 and 1955 discourses *To Italian Farmers.*

economic life. The present chapter treats of the nature of man, society, and economic life. These realities, subject to the scrutiny of right reason, give us the fundamental basis for an economic ethic. In the following chapter the same problem is examined in terms of human conduct: the virtues that impel us to live morally and rationally in economic society. From these two processes of inquiry, the reader acquires the bedrock principles used in later chapters as we pass judgments first upon the major economic philosophies of our day (Chapters V–VII) and then the controlling institutions of American society (Chapters VIII–XVII).

THE NATURE OF MAN

Under God, man is the center of the universe. Man has an inner dignity, based on his nature, origin, and destiny, which all must respect. This nature is the immediate source of rights and duties. It confers upon man an aura of sacredness which is not shared by the animals of the field or by purely material things.

But man does not live alone. To realize fully his powers and aspirations, he must live in the society of his fellow man. This fact, to a degree, modifies the rights and duties which spring from the nature of the individual. It also adds new rights and duties.

Such in a nutshell is the foundation of Catholic social theory. The detailed spelling out of man's prerogatives and obligations is but an amplifying of these fundamental principles. Time and again, the great encyclicals of recent popes have come back to this bedrock upon which a sound social order must rest.

The Dignity of Man. The dignity of man springs from his nature. It is not conferred by society, nor is it merely a product of law or custom. Certain rights are inalienable. They may not be abridged or taken away by any man. Long before the Christian era, sound philosophers reached this conclusion, however imperfectly. Man has a soul. He has reason and free will. This spiritual nature raises him above the animal kingdom, and even higher above lifeless matter. Man is thus lord of the universe. Lesser things are made to serve his needs. He may use them in accordance with the law of his nature and nature's God.

In addition, Christian revelation teaches us of an even higher status of man. We know that man is destined, provided he is worthy, for an immortal life with God. Even in this world, the Christian in the state of grace shares in the life of God. He is "an adopted son of God," "a temple of the Holy Spirit," "a brother of Christ," and may be "a member of the mystical body of Christ." This special and gratuitous solicitude of God toward the creature made in His image and likeness confers a unique dignity upon every man. Christ teaches that what is done to the least of the little ones is done to Him.

Even among those who do not accept the full Christian revelation, there is often a traditional respect for the dignity of man. In most of the world, human life is held to be sacred. The taking of life, or even the doing of violence to the human person, is considered a crime. Men will risk their own lives to avoid even the involuntary killing of another. Thus, when an automobile driver sees a child dart into the street in front of him, he applies the brakes and swerves at the risk of fatal injury to himself. When a person falls overboard from a ship, an effort is made to rescue him, though this may involve great danger to the seamen concerned. In such circumstances, there is no calculation of cost or of the relative talents and achievements of the individuals in danger.

A great portion of Christian social ethics could be derived from this one principle of man's worth. It could be the basis of a philosophy of labor. The right to work at a decent wage, the right to fair and just treatment, and many similar rights follow from the dignity of man. Man is more than a machine or a commodity.

Because of man's nature, the great modern heresy of statism stands condemned. Any system which holds that man's rights are conferred by the state, and that they may be modified or taken away at the whim of a despot, is unnatural and grossly immoral. Communism is wrong, not primarily because of its economic tenets, but because it makes men slaves of the state. National socialism and fascism were wrong, not in the first place because of their wars of aggression, but because they made man a tool in the hands of a dictator. Wherever the state arrogates to itself supreme power, disregarding the law of God and man's inalienable rights, it is a monstrosity contrary to all reason.

The evil roots of statism are many. But in the United States, we should particularly note the influence of Auguste Comte and his philosophy of positivism. His sociology holds that the state is antecedent to man and is the source of man's rights. We are fortunate indeed to have escaped the full implications of this theory. But we should not ignore the fact that this system is taught and accepted in many American universities. It has infected our intellectual world with an empiricism and experimentalism which denies the idea of natural rights and basic moral principles. This fact undoubtedly explains in part the sympathy of some intellectuals toward collectivism and communism. With others, it leads to secularism and pragmatism. Thus, we have a rapidly shifting society, based on expediency, not principle.

A sound social philosophy also repudiates materialism. Man has a spiritual soul, and this is the source of human nobility. A concentration upon material achievement, to the detriment of the spiritual, is a perversion of right order. The material world is to be the servant of man, not his master. Economic life is not an end in itself; it must be subordinated to higher and nobler laws. Here again, we Americans must be vigilant in regard to our values. We have achieved such wonders of material progress that we are prone to exaggerate its importance. The cultivation of the mind and the soul is, after all, man's greatest boast.

More controversial is the assertion made by some that modern industrialism, with its assembly-line techniques, does violence to the dignity of man. It is held that repetitive labor is degrading, whereas creative and responsible labor is ennobling. But this type of work has always existed. The hoe-and-stick form of agriculture is certainly as monotonous as the assembly line. We should try, however, to make the surroundings of work help, rather than hinder, the development of man's personality.

The Rights of Man. Upon man's nature there are founded certain inalienable rights. A right is generally defined as an inviolable moral power which a person has to do something, or to have, acquire, or dispose of something. A duty is a moral obligation of doing or not doing something. Rights and duties are interconnected. One man's right imposes upon another the duty of respecting his prerogatives. Nevertheless, rights and duties may conflict in practice. Hence there is vital need for classifying rights and determining their relative priorities.

One method of evaluating rights is in terms of their origin. Thus, some rights spring directly from nature, whereas others are conferred by law or by man. The rights to live and to marry are natural; the right to a government job may derive from law; and the right to use another's house may come from a contract made between men. These examples also illustrate the priority of rights. Those rooted directly in human nature are fundamental and may not be abrogated by law or by agreement among men. On the other hand, just laws, enacted in the interest of the common welfare, take precedence over private contracts. Divine law is higher than the law of man. Of man's natural rights, those involving directly the spiritual side of his nature would be more vital than those connected with his physical well-being. Hence it would not be sound to treat all rights equally, not distinguishing between the higher and the lower.

A second basis for evaluation is the relative necessity of rights for their intended purpose. Thus, the right to possess property is closely connected with the natural right to live. But not all property ministers equally to the right to live. The meager stock of food and clothing of the very poor is more necessary for them than the millions possessed by a wealthy man. In the one case, the goods described are needed for the welfare of the human person. In the second instance, many of the possessions are superfluous in terms of survival. The urgency of a right deepens as it goes closer to its source and justification.

A final classification pertinent here concerns the relative priority of community rights in contrast to individual rights. Here Catholic thinking takes a turn which may surprise many. The common good has precedence over individual rights *in the same sphere*. Even with the most fundamental rights, this is true. An illustration of this point is war, in which individuals risk their lives for the welfare of the nation and the lives and liberties of others. At first glance, this point might seem to be a concession to statism. However, when the term "common good" is correctly defined, the apparent conflict will vanish. The more detailed explanations given in subsequent chapters will make this point clear.

Confusion in regard to rights and duties can be avoided when the universe is considered in relation to the master plan of the Creator. There are two profound philosophical truths in particular which should not be overlooked in discussing the foundations of social ethics. First, the world is purposive. All nature strives toward determined ends. Man, however, seeks the ends of his being consciously and freely. Second, reality is pluralistic, with gradations of being and consequently of value. Spiritual being is of a higher nature than material; living being is "more real" than nonliving being. While every grade of being tends to seek its own ends, it is at the same time subordinate to higher forms of reality. Thus, animals serve man and nonliving matter is assimilated and often transformed by living beings. In man the needs of the body are subsidiary to those of the soul.

When metaphysics is applied to the field of ethics, we have a sound basis for a distinction among various types of rights. Thus, rights essential for the basic ends of man's existence are more important than and have priority over nonessential rights, even of a higher order. For example, a man should not risk his life to protect a work of art from vandals. His right to one type of cultural perfection, though higher in nature than the right to bodily survival, is relatively nonessential, whereas the latter is essential. On the other hand, among rights equally necessary for the ends of man's nature, the higher would take precedence over the lower. In times of persecution, men rightly die rather than apostatize from their religious faith. Essential values of the spirit are more important than bodily survival.

In line with this reasoning, the economic order exists to minister to the human person. When economic institutions become perverted, so that essential ends of man's nature are not adequately realized, a change in economic life is morally justified. This point is fundamental to the present study.

These general principles will take on life and vigor when they are applied to concrete problems. Indeed, most of the field of social ethics is concerned with the classifying of relative rights and duties. Delicate balances must be struck between conflicting rights in the same sphere and in different spheres. The basic dignity of the individual must be interpreted in the light of his duties to society. Then a clear picture will emerge of a social order, conformable to man's nature, as seen in terms of sound reason and divine revelation. At the same time, it is necessary to sound a warning that the application of general principles to concrete problems is not always easy. While the principles are unchanging, shifting and differing analyses of contingent facts lead to differences and disputes. Thus it happens that many, who accept without reservation the social teaching of the Church, may differ in matters of application and policy.

Fundamental Rights. Recent encyclicals have enumerated nearly a score of basic rights, but those connected with socioeconomic problems are apposite here.[1] In this sphere, the right to live is most fundamental. This conforms with the deep-rooted instinct of self-preservation, which is so clearly a part of man's nature. Negatively, this right is expressed in the commandment "Thou shalt not kill." Positively, it involves the right to the necessary means for existence. This means not only a minimum of food, clothing, and shelter, but the obtaining of this minimum in a manner conforming with human dignity. It demands a socioeconomic order which affords men the opportunity to live as human beings. Mere animal survival is not living in a human sense.

---

[1] For a lengthy enumeration, with many quotations from the popes, see Robert Kothen, *L'Enseignement social de l'Église*, pp. 166–214. J. A. Messner, in his volume *Social Ethics* (St. Louis: Herder, 1949), pp. 222–226, lists fourteen basic rights. Other listings may be found in the *Code of Social Principles*.

Family rights are closely connected with the right to live. The physical, emotional, and spiritual needs of man are normally satisfied only in a family environment. The instinct to propagate the race is deep-rooted in our nature. Furthermore, we know from divine revelation, reason, and experience that monogamous family life is the only acceptable way for preserving the human race. Accordingly, a sound social order must minister to the needs of family life.

The right to possess property is also fundamental. Individual and family living in a human way would not ordinarily be possible otherwise. If all goods were in common, we would face an intolerable choice between two evils. On the one hand, there could be a disorderly struggle for immediate needs. Organized economic life would be impossible, and strife and contention the normal course of events. On the other hand, the community could control all wealth. But this would place in the hands of the collective group, and its ruler, absolute power over the individual and the family. Neither way of life meets the demands of human nature.

The right of association likewise springs from man's nature. We are social creatures, intimately dependent upon one another. The full powers of the individual are realized only in conjunction with others. In the economic sphere, organization is normally necessary for efficient and orderly production. So universal is this instinct for association that it can be called a basic human trait. Hence man has the natural right to form groups or teams for lawful ends.

Finally, the social order should be so organized that higher rights, not enumerated here, should be protected. Man has spiritual and cultural needs in addition to the physical. Rights in this sphere are generally of a higher order than those connected with bodily needs. The lower should minister to the higher; certainly it should not impede or conflict with nobler ends.

The Equality of Man. On the basis of man's nature and fundamental rights, we can say that "all men were created equal." Men are equal in origin, nature, and destiny. All are created alike by God. All possess the same basic human qualities of reason and free will. All have immortal souls destined to eternal life. All are called to the higher destiny revealed in the teachings of Christ.

While men have a moral equality, at the same time they have individual differences which may not be ignored. Not all have the same talents or dispositions. There are varying degrees of intelligence among individuals. Characters differ, as do tastes and aptitudes. In addition to inborn variations, circumstances and environment affect people deeply. Family care, the degree of education, and economic status are bound to make a difference.

As a result, it would be contrary to human nature to expect or to demand absolute equality among men. There is nothing inherently wrong in the distinction between leaders and followers, the well-to-do, and those less endowed with material goods, the educated and the uneducated. These distinctions could be wrong, however, if their source were vitiated or their unnecessary continuance were contrary to the common good. Leadership based on force and violence could be unjust. Unequal distribution of wealth could proceed to extremes which would be harmful to society.

An intriguing question concerns political equality. The Church has been traditionally reluctant to pronounce judgment upon forms of government. Its concern has rather been that governments be just, that they rule under law, and that this be in conformity with the law of God. Because of the inequalities of men, some Churchmen have even been hesitant in past centuries to espouse the idea of popular sovereignty. In this light, it is interesting to note the observation made by Pope Pius XII in his Christmas broadcast of 1944: "If then, we consider the extent and nature of the sacrifice demanded of all the citizens, especially in our day when the activity of the state is so vast and decisive, the democratic form of government appears to many as a postulate of nature imposed by reason itself."

On the same line of reasoning, there are current demands for greater industrial democracy. Granted the inequalities among men, it is still true that modern economic life is so pervasive in its influence and so exacting in its demands, that those partaking in it should have a greater voice in directing its course. In earlier societies, life was so organized that men could keep a basic independence, even though economically subject to another. There was more opportunity to shift from one job to another, to become an independent craftsman or to own a small enterprise. Today even the directors of huge factories are often subordinate officials, taking orders from a central office or from financial groups who control the company. It may well be questioned whether all inequalities existing today spring from unequal ability, or whether some come from a form of social organization which is encroaching upon the basic rights of the individual.

A problem of inequality which, while not strictly economic, has important social and economic overtones involves racial discrimination, particularly against Negroes. There is hardly any need to elaborate upon the un-Christian nature of such practices. A conception of life which would deny basic rights to a whole race merely because of the accident of color is essentially barbaric. By contrast, a true Christian social order calls for the harmonious integration of all groups into the social body. It does not reject the fact of diversity, but it achieves an organic union of various groups within the body politic and economic.

While the principles enunciated here are by their nature universal, it is useful to state explicitly that justice and right must be given to minority groups. Indeed, many of our social problems exist in heightened form among exploited peoples. Thus, Negroes, Mexicans, and Puerto Ricans suffer more than others from poverty, inadequate housing, insufficient facilities for medical care and education, and poor working conditions. Hence the obligations outlined in these pages apply especially where the abuses are greater. This is particularly true of the need for *organized* social action, as demanded by the virtue of social justice. Education, laws, and other forms of community influence and pressure should be used to counter these evils. Indeed, broad programs for social reform are not likely to be successful, if one group can be exploited with impunity. The competitive pressure from such underpaid workers would lower standards for all.

It is shameful that the most vocal proponents of racial justice have been the American communists. It speaks well for the basic good sense of minorities that communists have found so few recruits from their midst. Nevertheless, there is no assurance that Negroes and others will always remain unresponsive to the pleas of agitators. Moreover, in the present world struggle Americans would be indeed shortsighted were they to overlook the propaganda value for the Soviet Union derived from American discrimination. The great peoples of the Orient, especially, feel bitter about racial slurs. It would be tragic were our domestic prejudices to drive them into the Soviet orbit, while we were spending billions for an anticommunist foreign policy. These points will be developed in Chapter XV.

MAN IN SOCIETY

The discussion of rights thus far has centered primarily upon the individual and only incidentally upon society. In a sense, this emphasis is correct. Society exists for the individual, and not the reverse. But in another sense the approach just taken needs completion. Man is a social animal, as well as a person with rights and duties based upon his individual nature. Indeed, social living is essential to the full development of the human personality. Moreover, it is an aspect which needs stress in the

United States, since our traditions have been heavily individualistic. Only recently has our Catholic educational system begun to emphasize the requirements of social living. Again, we have the reputation of being a nation of many laws, but yet restive under law and occasionally defiant of law. Our frontier tradition of resourcefulness and individual initiative has persisted long after the frontier has been closed, and has been felt in fields where social co-operation is also needed.

The Social Nature of Man. Man's physical and psychological being shows that he is social. Physically, man is helpless without society. At birth, he is weak and puny. He needs the fostering care of the family to survive. He matures slowly, in contrast to the animal kingdom, where the young are rarely dependent for more than a few months or a year. In the struggle for survival, man does not have the physical resources to meet the challenge of savage nature. He has not the strength of the lion or tiger, the fleetness of the antelope, the cunning and sensitiveness of the fox, the natural defenses of the porcupine, the protective coloration of the rabbit, the agility of the squirrel, or other of the qualities, refined senses, or instincts which nature gives to animals for their self-protection. Without society, the child would freeze in the winter, starve for lack of food, or be the easy prey of any predatory animal.

Psychologically, man needs society. In contrast to the animal, we are born with few instincts. We do not sense dangers, nor do we realize what natural foods are good and what poisonous. We only learn from others in these vital matters. Moreover, our rational nature develops only in society. Men who live isolated lives rarely achieve fully balanced personalities, and often lose their sanity. Even the family is too small a unit for the full development of personality. Introverted, ingrown families are not adapted for living in this complex world. The overprotected and excessively sheltered child becomes a problem. Our minds, wills, and characters grow and become strong only in the give and take of social living.

Man has strong aspirations for social living. He seeks the company and values the esteem of his fellow man. The desire to love and to share in the love of others is among the deepest traits of our nature. Hence it is only to be expected that a rich social life characterizes human existence. Even our relationships to lower orders of being tend to be social. Thus, man the worker exercises dominion over the world. He performs, as it were, a task of creation in changing and ennobling lesser goods. But he has found that work must be performed as part of a harmonious pattern of social life, if it is to be fully effective.

Society is almost essential for economic life and the physical survival of
the race. It may be just possible for a single family in a suitable environment to meet its economic needs. By heavy and unceasing toil, it could
obtain the bare minimum of food, clothing, and shelter necessary to survive. Only a few families could be maintained under such conditions. Even
the primitive farming, hunting, grazing, and nomadic societies afforded a
living to but a relatively few. For the large population of modern times,
social organization is essential.

In economic life, organization permits needed forms of specializa-
tion, division of labor, and large-scale production, with consequent multi-
plication of skill and efficiency. When men specialize, they acquire great
skills in their particular fields. By division of labor, a large operation can
be broken down into many simple tasks, which each worker can perform
more efficiently. As individual tasks become simpler, they are subject to
mechanization, whereby human skills can be multiplied greatly. The machine takes over the skill of the individual worker, and power resources
concentrate in a small factory energies which could be supplied only by
thousands of workers. Thus, the essentials of living can be obtained for
large populations with relatively small effort, and time is made available
for luxuries, cultural living, social relationships, and other characteristically
human occupations.

Man's Social Rights and Obligations. Since social living is part of
man's nature, this fact is bound to modify our concept of rights and duties
based on the individual person. Not only are individual rights qualified by
the impact of equal or even superior rights of others, but specific rights
and duties arise from the fact of social living.

Among the more fundamental rights is the right of association mentioned earlier. What man's nature impels him to do is clearly a right
provided it is exercised within the bounds of reason. The associations of
interest here are those connected with the economic order. They include
business partnerships and corporations, labor unions, various forms of co-
operatives, industrial councils, and similar natural groupings. The functioning of these societies should, of course, be governed by the laws of
justice and the common good. Within these bounds, they have a right to
exist peaceably. Any effort by a more powerful society to destroy them is
morally wrong. Such would be the case in a totalitarian state, which permits only organs under its absolute control to survive. Again, if a corporation were to use its economic power to dissolve a labor union desired by
its workers, it would be acting unjustly.

Basic among the social duties of man is the obligation to contribute, according to his position, to the common good. Since society is natural to man, he must share the responsibilities as well as the privileges of social living. Of course, not all societies are equally necessary. Some, such as the state or the family, flow from nature itself. Others, such as choral groups or bridge clubs, are purely matters of taste and convenience. There is a third group which occupies an intermediate position which is difficult to classify today. This comprises associations which are virtually indispensable to achieve some necessary good. Thus, some argue that in modern society the labor union is a practical necessity in order to achieve some basic rights of man. This point will be discussed subsequently, but it illustrates the complex nature of the common good. However, the principle is clear: when a society is necessary to achieve some basic end springing from man's nature, we are not privileged to be neutral.

While society exists to serve man, it is also necessary for his welfare. By using society for the welfare of all, each individual secures his own well-being. This means that a proper balance must be struck between individual rights and social responsibility. The working out of this formula in detailed problems is not easy, but it is a task which may not be shirked. In facing this problem, the principles given earlier in regard to the priority of rights will enable us to secure results fully consonant with human nature.

THE PURPOSE OF ECONOMIC LIFE

The type of society most germane to the present study is the economic order, with all its ramifications among other social institutions. One of the major problems of modern times is the reorientation of economic life, so that it may conform to God's purpose in creating material things.

Goals Sought. Of first importance is the realization that economic life is subordinate to higher values. It deals with the material order, and this by its nature is inferior to matters cultural and spiritual. The lower should minister to the higher. Hence the basic purpose of economic life is to provide man with the necessities for survival, and the foundations for cultural and spiritual life. It will achieve this when every willing and able worker can earn at least a stable decent wage for himself and his family. This wage will provide necessities, a minimum opportunity for comfort and leisure, and some chance to realize nonmaterial aspirations according to the interests and talents of the individual.

Economic life should furnish, insofar as possible, opportunity for individuals to develop and utilize their personal talents. It should be the material foundation of an educational system which will bring out abilities and skills. For those whose aptitudes are mechanical, this would mean at least adequate vocational training. Where abilities tend toward the intellectual or the professional spheres, there should be sufficient opportunities for advanced study. In general, the trend should be toward an increase in leisure, so that man can be freed from excessive preoccupation with material things.

An important step toward this goal would be the wider distribution of wealth, particularly the actual ownership of property. In this way, individuals would have greater independence. They would be able to exercise personal choice as to the use of their resources for themselves and their families. There would also result a greater stability in economic life, to the extent that a smaller proportion of individuals would depend upon giant economic organizations. In principle, this method of securing cultural benefits is preferable to organized efforts by the state to provide for many of the needs of its citizens. Of course, we should not condemn social insurance, grants-in-aid for education, or civic recreational and cultural developments. In modern times these are necessary. But it is still desirable that individuals have the greatest possible freedom to direct their own lives in these fields. A more equitable distribution of resources would help bring this about.

Although widespread diffusion of ownership is the most desirable foundation for individual freedom and economic stability, it is nevertheless a fact that many will remain in the status of wage earners. Under these circumstances, a goal of social policy must be the preservation and enhancement of human dignity under conditions of economic dependence. The wage earner must at the minimum be accorded his basic rights and treated as befits a human being. Above this level of essential rights there are opportunities for giving the worker greater participation in the economic process. He could be given a more definite voice in matters which greatly affect his welfare. In this way, to use the language of Pope Pius XII, he would no longer be a mere object — a passive factor in the economic planning of others — but he would be a subject, a person exercising some control over his own destiny. Society would not be mechanical — a mass held together by external force — but it would be organic, based on the intelligent co-operation of free men and independent but collaborating social groups.

In attaining material wealth, technical progress can be a substantial help.

The popes have insisted that, in condemning certain abuses in the socio-economic sphere, they were not minimizing the value of modern technology. Wisely used, these processes can bring about the abolition of want. They can make food, clothing, and housing abundant for the needs of all. Moreover, they can provide leisure and comfort for many, and ultimately for all. Such goals are in themselves desirable from the viewpoint of Christian virtue. Excessive poverty brings a preoccupation with material things which injures the dignity of human nature and is contrary to the law of God. Of course, this wrongful solicitude about material things can come from an opposite extreme, when men seek wealth for its own sake and become preoccupied with amassing riches. Greed, vanity, and lust for power are also contrary to the law of God.

Most important today is the need for stability in economic life. Alternations between inflation and deflation are upsetting to higher values. Family life is strained. Men cannot make reasonable plans for the future. They are unhappy in good times for the fear of what is to come. Stability is mainly a problem of organization. It is obvious that we have the natural resources, technical skill, power, machines, labor supply, and managerial talent to abolish want and produce a high standard of living. It is equally obvious that we have not so organized these factors that we are able to utilize them fully. This is the problem and challenge of our age. Organization in turn is a social problem. It involves the harmonious working together of individuals and groups. The many organizations and institutions needed to effectuate policy will vary in different times and places. Economic science, prudential judgment based on experience, and social ethics will work together in bringing about the desired result. This would be the Christian social order, the restoring of all things in Christ.

Reform of Institutions. The first steps toward this goal will be the infusion of Christian principles of justice and charity into the various classes of society. Four great groups are important in this connection: capital, labor, the farming community, and government. By capital is meant, not merely finance, but the ownership of all productive property. This would include industry, business, and the service trades. The aim would be the spread of social justice and charity among each of the four groups so that each would seek the common welfare as well as individual goals. This would not be primarily a matter of forming a Christian conscience among individuals, important as this is. Rather it would involve a reform of the *institutions* of society. If the institutions of society tend toward wrong ends, the efforts inspired by personal good will are likely to be nullified. On the other hand, if the institutions of society are sound, they will contain and constrain men of ill will, preventing them from doing serious harm.

The work of reform is committed to all classes of society. In one sense, the state, as the supreme social group, should take the lead in seeking to reform social institutions. The common good is its very reason of being. But at the same time, the state itself may often be in need of reform. In modern times, it has reacted from a *laissez-faire* individualism, where it stood by impotently in the face of great injustice, to some approximation of statism, where it absorbed powers which should be committed to lesser groups. The state best seeks social justice by aiding subordinate groups to perfect institutions which bring about harmonious and prosperous economic life. Other groups in turn, inspired by Christian principles, should endeavor to correct evils in their spheres of action, and to direct their aims in the light of justice and charity. Thus we would achieve a basic reorientation of society.

Clearly this is an immense task. But it is made easier by the fact that other alternatives are being rejected. In much of the world, the old order has been cast aside. But some of the newer forms, such as communism, are worse than those which they supplanted. As extremes are shown to be unsound, men are bound to respect the moderation and sanity of the Christian social ethic. If we can formulate it in detail, and show its applicability to a complex society, it may well be received as were the first good tidings of the Gospel.

READINGS*

J. Messner, Social Ethics, pp. 1–122, 188, 207, 222–226, 908–911.
G. Clune, Christian Social Reorganization, Chap. 10.
R. Kothen, L'Enseignement social de l'Église, Chap. 3.
J. Villain, S.J., L'Enseignement social de l'Église, Vol. I, pp. 35–45.
H. Johnston, Business Ethics, Chaps. 3, 6.
Social Order: John R. Connery, S.J., "Catholicism," September, 1951; "On Reconstructing the Social Order," January, 1956; "The Christian Conscience and Economic Growth," April, 1957.

* For further readings, see List No. 3 in the Appendix.

Chapter IV

THE SOCIAL VIRTUES

JUSTICE

Commutative Justice

Pius XI, Quadragesimo Anno

47. That justice called commutative commands sacred respect for the division of possessions and forbids invasion of others' rights through the exceeding of the limits of one's own property; but the duty of owners to use their property only in a right way does not come under this type of justice, but under other virtues, obligations of which "cannot be enforced by legal action."

110. . . . the twofold character, that is individual and social, both of capital or ownership and of work or labor must be given due and rightful weight. Relations of one to the other must be made to conform to the laws of strictest justice — commutative justice, as it is called, with the support, however, of Christian charity.

Pius XII, Sertum Laetitiae, November 1, 1939

37. Now if the rich and prosperous are obliged out of ordinary motives of pity to act generously toward the poor, their obligation is all the greater to do them justice. The salaries of the workers, as is just, are to be such that they are sufficient to maintain them and their families.

Distributive Justice

Leo XIII, Rerum Novarum

49. Consequently, among the numerous and weighty duties of rulers who would serve their people well, this is first and foremost, namely, that they protect equitably each and every class of citizens, maintaining inviolate that justice especially which is called distributive.

Pius XI, Quadragesimo Anno

25. The function of the rulers of the state, moreover, is to watch over the community and its parts; but in protecting private individuals in their rights, chief consideration ought to be given to the weak and the poor.

Pius XII, Address to Catholic Employers, May 7, 1949

It would be just as untrue to assert that every particular business is of its nature a society, with its personal relationships determined by the norms of distributive justice to the point where all without distinction — owners or not of the means of production — would be entitled to their share in the property, or at the very least in the profits, of the enterprise. Such a conception stems from the assumption that every business belongs naturally within the sphere of public law. The assumption is inexact. Whether the business is organized in the form of a corporation or an association of all the workmen as part owners, or whether it is the private property of an individual who signs a wage contract with all his employees, in the one case as in the other it falls within the competence of the private-law discipline of economic life.

Social Justice

Leo XIII, Immortale Dei

22. Nevertheless, as We have laid down, to take no share in public matters would be equally as wrong (We speak in general) as not to have concern for, or not to bestow labor upon, the common good.

Leo XIII, Rerum Novarum

14. . . . however the earth may be apportioned among private owners, it does not cease to serve the common good of all. . . .

48. For the state is bound by the very law of its office to serve the common interest.

50. . . . all citizens, without exception, are obliged to contribute some-thing to the sum-total common good.

52. It is not right, as We have said, for either the citizen or the family to be absorbed by the state; it is proper that the individual and the family should be permitted to retain their freedom of action so far as this is possible without jeopardizing the common good and without injuring anyone.

Pius XI, Quadragesimo Anno

25. . . . Just freedom of action must, of course, be left both to individual citizens and their families, yet only on condition that the common good be preserved and wrong to any individual be abolished.

49. It follows from what We have termed the individual and at the same time social character of ownership, that men must consider in this mat-ter not only their own advantage but also the common good.

57. Therefore, the riches that economic-social developments constantly increase ought to be so distributed among individual persons and classes that the common advantage of all, which Leo XIII had praised, will be safeguarded; in other words that the common good of all

society will be kept inviolate. By this law of social justice, one class is forbidden to exclude the other from sharing in the benefits.

71. Every effort must therefore be made that fathers of families receive a wage large enough to meet ordinary family needs adequately. But if this cannot always be done under existing circumstances, social justice demands that changes be introduced as soon as possible whereby such a wage will be assured to every adult workingman.

74. Hence it is contrary to social justice when, for the sake of personal gain and without regard for the common good, wages and salaries are excessively lowered or raised; and this same social justice demands that wages and salaries be so managed, through agreement of plans and wills, insofar as can be done, as to offer to the greatest possible number the opportunity of getting work and obtaining suitable means of livelihood.

85. The most important among these interests is to promote the cooperation in the highest degree of each industry and profession for the sake of the common good of the country.

88. Loftier and nobler principles — social justice and social charity — must, therefore, be sought whereby this dictatorship may be governed firmly and fully. Hence, the institutions themselves of peoples and, particularly, those of all social life, ought to be penetrated with this justice, and it is most necessary that it be truly effective, that is, establish a juridical and social order which will, as it were, give form and shape to all economic life.

101. But it does violate right order when capital hires workers, that is the nonowning class, with a view to and under such terms that it directs business and even the whole economic system according to its own will and advantage, scorning the human dignity of the workers, the social character of economic activity and social justice itself, and the common good.

110. The public institutions themselves, of peoples, moreover, ought to make all human society conform to the needs of the common good; that is, to the norm of social justice.

Pius XI, On Atheistic Communism

51. In reality, besides commutative justice, there is also social justice with its own set obligations, from which neither employers nor workingmen can escape. Now it is of the very essence of social justice to demand from each individual all that is necessary for the common good. But just as in the living organism it is impossible to provide for the good of the whole unless each single part and each individual member is given what it needs for the exercise of its proper functions, so it is impossible to care for the social organism and the good of society as a unit unless each single part and each individual member — that is to say, each individual man in the dignity of his human personality — is supplied with all that is necessary for the exercise of his social functions. If social justice be satisfied, the result will be an intense activity in economic life as a whole, pursued in tranquillity and order.

53. It happens all too frequently, however, under the salary system, that

individual employers are helpless to insure justice unless, with a view to its practice, they organize institutions the object of which is to prevent competition incompatible with fair treatment for the workers. Where this is true, it is the duty of contractors and employers to support and promote such necessary organizations as normal instruments enabling them to fulfill their obligations of justice.

Pius XII, La Solennità della Pentecoste, June 1, 1941

1685. Hence, it follows that the care of such a common good does not imply a power so extensive over the members of the community that in virtue of it the public authority can interfere with the evolution of that individual activity which We have just described, decide directly on the beginning or — excepting the case of legitimate capital punishment — the ending of human life, determine at will the manner of his physical, spiritual, religious, and moral movements in opposition to the personal duties or rights of man, and to this end abolish or deprive of efficacy his natural rights to material goods. To deduce such extension of power from the care of the common good would be equivalent to overthrowing the very meaning of the word common good, and falling into the error that the proper scope of man on earth is society, that society is an end in itself, that man has no other life which awaits him beyond that which ends here below.

Pius XII, Message on Centenary of St. Thomas the Apostle, December 31, 1952

. . . the social teaching of the Church . . . is based on social justice, on the duty of each to the community, and of the community to each; its goal is peace in the social order, a composing of conflicting interests, so that the humblest in a nation may have at least what is sufficient; its strength is in its uncompromising reverence for the honor and natural rights of every human being.

Pius XII, To Spanish Social Week, May, 1956

A social sense teaches individuals precisely the contrary. It makes them conscious of their social duties, it urges them to take into account in all their activities their membership in a community, to be preoccupied with the welfare of their neighbors and with the common good of society. It works on the social conscience of men and, as a *habitus*, it disposes them to reach the purposes which God and society expect from them. This is, therefore, the sense of general or legal justice of which scholastic philosophers speak and which the pontifical documents often call social justice.

Code of Social Principles

175. Economic life is dependent on justice and charity.

Along with commutative justice, which governs contracts, and distributive justice, which regulates social burdens and benefits, due place must be given to social or legal justice, which relates to the common good, of which authority has the care and which each individual member of the social body is bound to serve and enrich. The individual, as the beneficiary of this common good, is in some measure its guardian, although it is the rulers who are primarily responsible for it.

Social justice should permeate the institutions and the entire life of the people. Its efficacy should be especially manifest in the creation of a juridical and social order which informs the whole economic life.

St. Thomas Aquinas, Summa Theologiae

The common good is the end of each individual member of a community, just as the good of the whole is the end of each part (II, II, 58, 9, ad 3).

The good of the individual is subordinate to the good of the many (II, II, 47, 11, ad 3).

The common good . . . and the particular good of the individual differ not only in respect of the many and the few, but also under a formal aspect (II, II, 58, 7, ad 2).

The common good takes precedence over the private good if it be of the same genus (II, II, 152, 4, ad 3; see also, I, II, 113, 9, ad 2).

Every law is directed toward the common good . . . any command toward a particular object does not have legal effect, except insofar as it is directed toward the common good (I, II, 90, 2).

The common good is to be preferred to private good (II, II, 32, 6).

Right reason . . . judges that the common good is better than the good of an individual (II, II, 47, 10).

He who seeks the common good of the many consequently seeks his own good as well . . . private good cannot exist without the common good of the family, or the city, or the state (ibid., ad 2).

Among human goods, the public good is pre-eminent over private good (II, II, 117, 6).

SOCIAL CHARITY

Pius XI, Quadragesimo Anno

4. Quite agreeable, of course, was this state of things to those who thought it in their abundant riches the result of inevitable economic laws and accordingly, as if it were for charity to veil the violation of justice which lawmakers not only tolerated but at times sanctioned, wanted the whole care of supporting the poor committed to charity alone.

88. Social charity, moreover, ought to be as the soul of this order, an order which public authority ought to be ever ready effectively to protect and defend.

137. But in effecting all this, the law of charity, "which is the bond of perfection," must always take a leading role. How completely deceived, therefore, are those rash reformers who concern themselves with the enforcement of justice alone — and this, commutative justice — and in their pride reject the assistance of Charity! Admittedly, no vicarious charity can substitute for justice which is due as

an obligation and is wrongfully denied. Yet even supposing that everyone should finally receive all that is due him, the widest field for charity will always remain open. For justice alone can, if faithfully observed, remove the causes of social conflict but can never bring about union of minds and hearts. Indeed all the institutions for the establishment of peace and the promotion of mutual help among men, however perfect these may seem, have the principal foundation of their stability in the mutual bond of minds and hearts whereby the members are united with one another. If this bond is lacking, the best of regulations come to naught, as we have learned by too frequent experience. And so, then only will true co-operation be possible for a single common good when the constituent parts of society deeply feel themselves members of one great family and children of the same Heavenly Father; nay, that they are one body in Christ, "but severally members one of another," so that "if one member suffers anything, all the members suffer with it." For then the rich and others in positions of power will change their former indifference toward their poorer brothers into a solicitous and active love, listen with kindliness to their just demands, and freely forgive their possible mistakes and faults. And the workers, sincerely putting aside every feeling of hatred or envy which the promoters of social conflict so cunningly exploit, will not only accept without rancor the place in human society assigned them by Divine Providence, but rather will hold it in esteem, knowing well that everyone according to his function and duty is toiling usefully and honorably for the common good and is following closely in the footsteps of Him, who, being in the form of God, willed to be a carpenter among men and be known as the son of a carpenter.

Pius XI, On Atheistic Communism

46. Still more important as a remedy for the evil we are considering, or certainly more directly calculated to cure it, is the precept of charity. We have in mind that Christian charity, "patient and kind," which avoids all semblance of demeaning paternalism, and all ostentation; that charity which from the very beginning of Christianity won to Christ the poorest of the poor, the slaves. And We are grateful to all those members of charitable associations, from the conferences of St. Vincent de Paul to the recent great relief organizations, which are perseveringly practicing the spiritual and corporal works of mercy. The more the workingman and the poor realize what the spirit of love animated by the virtue of Christ is doing for them, the more readily will they abandon the false persuasion that Christianity has lost its efficacy and that the Church stands on the side of the exploiters of their labor.

47. But when on the one hand We see thousands of the needy, victims of real misery for various reasons beyond their control, and on the other so many round about them who spend huge sums of money on useless things and frivolous amusement, We cannot fail to remark with sorrow not only that justice is poorly observed, but that the precept of charity also is not sufficiently appreciated, is not a vital thing in daily life.

48. . . . There is a divine regenerating force in this "new precept" (as Christ called it) of Christian charity.

Its faithful observance will pour into the heart an inner peace which the world knows not, and will firmly cure the ills which oppress humanity.

49. But charity will never be true charity unless it takes justice into constant account. A "charity" which deprives the workingman of the salary to which he has a strict title in justice, is not charity at all, but only its empty name and hollow semblance.

The wage earner is not to receive as alms what is his due in justice. And let no one attempt with trifling charitable donations to exempt himself from the great duties imposed by justice. Both justice and charity often dictate obligations touching on the same subject matter, but under different aspects; and the very dignity of the workingman makes him justly and acutely sensitive to the duties of others in his regard.

Pius XII, Summi Pontificatus, October 20, 1939

1437. . . . the re-education of mankind must be, above all things, spiritual and religious. Hence, it must proceed from Christ as from its indispensable foundation; must be actuated by justice and crowned by charity.

Pius XII, To the International Institute on the Middle Classes, October 25, 1956

Society's proper balance has its surest basis in a moral order which is inspired, not by cold, calculating logic concerned exclusively with equitable distribution of material goods, but rather by justice and generous charity, by the example of Christ, which is to say by that generous love which entails forgetfulness of self, renunciation, and sacrifice.

Pius XII, To Italian Workers, May 1, 1958

Let other workers' associations say "justice is enough for us!" as though the virtues of justice and charity were enemies of one another. The contrary is certainly true. There is in fact no genuine justice which is not preceded and prepared by the warmth of charity.

Pastoral Letter, 1919

The settlement of our industrial problems would offer less difficulty, if, while upholding its rights, each party were disposed to meet the other in a friendly spirit. The strict requirements of justice can be fulfilled without creating animosity; in fact, where this arises, it is apt to obscure the whole issue. On the contrary, a manifest desire to win over, rather than drive, the opponent to the acceptance of equitable terms, would facilitate the recognition of claims which are founded in justice. The evidence of such a disposition would break down the barriers of mistrust and set up in their stead the bond of good will. Not an armistice but a conciliation would result; and this would establish all parties in the exercise of their rights and the cheerful performance of their duties.

The Church and Social Order

63. Unfortunately there has been a tendency among too many to dissociate the virtue of justice from the virtue of charity, with the result that life has been made even more selfish and heartless. Charity is no substitute for justice, but it cannot be ignored or derided without failing utterly to comprehend its meaning and its potent influence in regulating and sublimating our social relations and responsibilities. We need justice without doubt or equivocation, but we also need charity if we are to put our lives in harmony with God's plan and promote that spirit of benevolence which will lift the burdens not only from the backs but also from the souls of men.

Code of Social Principles

176. But justice is far from exhausting the whole of one's duty towards others. Over and above its requirements, there is a limitless field for that brotherly love which men owe to each other as sons of the same Heavenly Father and descendants of the same first parents; a field of initiative, service and personal sacrifice for the common good. Charity thus finds a most important part to play in economic life. . . .

As to social charity, it ought to be the soul of that juridical and social order, which is the care of the public authorities and which ought to inform the entire economic life, as has been said above.

SUBSIDIARY VIRTUES

Pius XI, Quadragesimo Anno

47. . . . the duty of owners to use their property only in a right way does not come under this type of justice [commutative], but under other virtues, obligations of which "cannot be enforced by legal action."

50. The Sacred Scriptures and the Fathers of the Church constantly declare in the most explicit language that the rich are bound by a very grave precept to practice almsgiving, beneficence, and munificence.

IN ORDER to secure the proper organization of economic life, as briefly outlined in the preceding chapter, three requirements must be met. First, men must have a proper view of man and society, particularly economic society. This may be called an informed Christian conscience. Next, they must develop habits of acting in accord with these truths. These habits are the social virtues which are treated in the present chapter. They help us live up to the demands of both personal and social morality, explained in Chapter II. Finally, the personal virtue of men of good will must take institutional form in the laws, customs, and organizations of society. In this way right conduct will be given a pervasive and permanent influence. Selfish and evil actions will be prevented or counteracted.

Of the social virtues, justice is commonly considered the most important. It deals with rights and duties and hence fixes precisely the obligations of all persons participating in economic society. But justice is complemented by the bonds of charity and by certain subsidiary virtues related to charity.

JUSTICE

Kinds of Justice. Justice is defined as a constant habit or intention of giving each person his due. Persons in this definition include moral persons, such as corporations or government bodies. They too have rights and duties. When we speak of rights, we refer to the moral power to possess or obtain something. The idea of right involves a definite and clear obligation, not merely proprieties. Contracts, for example, involve rights and duties. By contrast, the laws of etiquette, generally speaking, express proprieties. They oblige in terms of considerateness and gentility, not justice.

We ordinarily speak of three kinds of justice. The first is general or legal justice, which calls for giving society its due. Under this virtue we are bound to consider the common good as well as our particular aims in all our actions. Some writers do not consider legal justice as a strict virtue, in the sense that it commands us to do certain acts which are proper to it alone. Rather, according to their point of view, it gives an overtone and direction to other virtues, directing their exercise in the light of the general welfare. Thus, almsgiving is commanded under the virtue of charity, but in helping the unfortunate legal justice binds us to consider the common good. Legal justice would incline us to one form of charity in preference to another. Other authors, however, do speak of specific actions commanded by legal justice in its own right. This is particularly true of the aspect of legal justice which is called social justice. Whichever view is held, legal justice involves the duties of the individual in regard to the community. He is obliged to seek the common good.

In contrast to general justice are the more particular forms of this virtue, called distributive and commutative justice. Distributive justice deals with the obligations of the community and its leaders toward the individual members. It calls for an equitable and proportional distribution of benefits and burdens to the members of society. Thus, legislators must be fair in giving out benefits (such as social insurance) or burdens (such as taxes). A father must be equitable in treating his children. Equity in such cases does not necessarily mean equality, since the needs of one may be greater than those of another. The socialist maxim: "From each according to his ability, to each according to his needs," is a fair approximation of distributive justice. If we could use mechanical terms to apply to virtues, we might say that the direction of flow is reversed when one compares legal and distributive justice. The one involves the individual's duty to society; the other, the rights of the person in connection with a given society. Hence some authors call social justice "contributive justice."

Finally, there is commutative justice, often called strict justice or exchange justice. Commutative justice differs from the other forms, in that the rights or duties concerned are specific, definite, and clearcut. Contributive and distributive justice create real obligations, but it is often difficult to pinpoint their precise implications. Men of good will could differ as to what is a fair tax rate or upon the citizen's obligation to vote in any given election. By contrast, the right to possess or obtain something, such as a specified piece of property, is quite definite. This right usually originates through exchange, such as the purchase of goods or services or a contract specifying wages to be paid for a certain amount of work.

Each of these three forms of justice is important for social life. This will be elaborated in the treatment to follow.

Commutative Justice. Commutative justice normally applies in two ways: the right to possess and the right to obtain. We have the right to possess property, including intangible wealth such as good will or reputation, that truly belongs to us. Our original title to the object in question may have derived from purchase, contract, or discovery. It may be conferred or made specific by law, as in the case of copyrights or patents. If we do not already have the object, we may have the right to obtain it. For example, a fire-insurance contract permits us to claim compensation for covered damages in case of fire. When we make a loan, we have the right to recover at a specified time.

The practice of strict justice is essential for our economy. Indeed it is questionable that organized economic society could exist, if most men were not honest. Yet dishonesty is one of the plagues of our society. It creates or intensifies many social problems. A few examples will make this clear.

When we buy some product in a store, we expect to get our money's worth. We look for the equality of exchange called for by commutative justice. If the object we purchase does not work well, breaks down frequently, or soon wears out, we normally feel that we have been cheated.

Here we meet a frequent source of injustice in our present economic system. Too often the consumer has no way of knowing the worth of his purchase. This is particularly true of complex products, such as household appliances, television sets, automobiles, and even clothing. There is no excuse for manufacturing or selling worthless goods. Equally blameworthy is any misrepresentation of quality so substantial that the buyer is deceived into purchasing a given item. Such actions are violations of strict justice. The buyer is given something essentially different from what he expected.

Justice also applies to the price of goods and services. Even when the quality is adequate, the price may involve exploitation of the consumer. When medieval moralists spoke of a just price, they meant a price that would return a reasonable profit to the seller. If a higher price is secured through exploitation of the need or ignorance of the buyer, this action is unjust. Unfortunately, the worst offenders in this regard are stores which cater to the poorer elements of the community. They often sell shoddy goods at high prices, using the lure of allegedly cheap credit. Most of the time this credit is also very high priced.

Related to these two abuses is the practice of fraudulent advertising. It is understood in our society that an advertiser will exaggerate the worth of his product. He may concentrate upon nonessential qualities that have a certain glamour appeal. Our courts have held that "puffing" and one-sided praise of a product do not constitute misrepresentation. Moralists may accept this judgment. But the files of any Better Business Bureau are usually filled with cases that go far beyond the bounds of conventional exaggeration. Once again, the very poor are often the victims of these exploiters. They are eager for bargains, yet often unable to distinguish the real quality of goods. Hence they fall prey to those who have no scruples in their advertising practices.

Injustice can also be committed by the worker who fails to give a reasonable amount of work in return for his pay. The proper pace of work is a rate that does not undermine the health of the worker over the span of his working life. It would be unfair to determine work norms on the basis of the maximum possible output of a young man. Obviously he cannot keep up this pace until he retires. Yet it is equally unfair to restrict output because of laziness. Normally it is not sound to slow down in a job, so as to stretch out work and cut down unemployment. Lower productivity weakens an economic system. More basic solutions than stretchouts or shorter work weeks must be found for the problem of unemployment.

These examples show the impact of strict justice in economic life. Yet it would be a mistake to ignore the social factors that may partially explain objectively unjust actions. A merchant, facing the policies of unscrupulous competitors, may feel compelled to adopt some of them in order to stay in business. He may even argue that, if he did not do so, the field would be monopolized by the least desirable business firms. Again, a worker is often under extreme social pressure to conform to the norms set by his fellows. It is no solution of these problems to say: "Let justice be done, though the heavens fall." The real solution is to prevent the economic pressures that force men to choose between dishonesty and bankruptcy. This can be done only by community action. For this reason, commutative justice needs to be supplemented by distributive and social justice.

Distributive Justice. In the traditional usage, the term "distributive justice" is applied to rulers of states. It obliges them to secure for each citizen his due and proportionate share of both the advantages and the burdens involved in the conduct of civil society. The older theologians talked of the fair distribution of public offices, on the one hand, and of taxes on the other. A more modern example is social legislation or public subsidies. Benefits thus distributed are not given on a basis of arithmetical equality, but rather in consideration of need and other special circumstances. Thus, a federal subsidy for education which would be based only on the tax contributions of the states would be self-defeating. The states which were able to pay the most taxes would be least in need of subsidies. In this regard, Pope Leo XIII stated that governments should look out especially for the needs of the poor, since the rich can often take care of themselves. Benefits distributed by the state can be very important in modern economic life. Examples of this are subsidies for low-cost housing; subsidies for farmers or high-cost producers of needed goods; justified tariffs; distribution of social-insurance benefits in view of needs as well as contributions; contributions for public hospitals in rural areas; and grants to special groups, such as reasonable pensions for soldiers. The same observation applies to the sharing of burdens. On the basis of distributive justice, it is fair that the wealthy should pay proportionately higher taxes than the poor. Taxes on luxuries are more equitable than taxes on necessities.

Older moralists often applied the principles of distributive justice to private industry. They argued, for example, that the needs of workers are often greater than those of stockholders. Hence, they concluded, a living wage must be paid, even though as a result no profits were available. The flaw in this reasoning stems from the fact that business property is not community property. It is not in the same category as civic or family possessions. For this reason, Pope Pius XII stated, using European legal terminology, that the business firm is in the private-law rather than the public-law category in respect to its property and profits.[1] It may be affected by distributive justice because it is subject to the state. But its relations with its employees are governed by commutative and social justice, not distributive.

Indeed, it is well to remember that, even in government itself, policies suggested by distributive justice are not absolutes. Should they conflict with the common good, with the demands of social justice, they must yield to the higher claims of the public welfare. For example, progressive taxation, based on ability to pay, is a sound policy. But if the rates are set so high for the wealthy that they discourage private enterprise and prevent investment for industrial expansion, the common good suffers. Under these circumstances, social justice requires a rate that permits new investment, with consequent increase in employment and living standards. Only when we understand fully the demands of social justice can we determine accurately the proper spheres of commutative and distributive justice.

Social Justice.   We noted above that moralists do not agree completely upon all phases of legal and social justice. In view of this fact, it is best not to begin with a definition of social justice. Instead we shall proceed inductively from the writings of Pope Pius XI and note how he viewed the nature and function of this virtue.

In the first place, the Pope often contrasts organized effort with individual effort, social morality with personal morality. Many times he notes the helplessness of the individual when confronted with a difficult social problem, such as ruthless competition. His remedy in each case is organized effort to cure the evil. What employers and workers cannot do as individuals, they can often accomplish as citizens or as members of economic groups. In each case, the Pope insists that social justice compels them to act in an organized fashion. This is their duty, inasmuch as they are bound to contribute to the common good.

This point is particularly important in evaluating programs of social reform that emphasize personal leadership and example. Such programs are good, so far as they go. But often they do not go far enough. Leadership

---

[1] The reference to private law reflects the European practice of legal enforcement of certain regulations drawn up by private associations. The closest parallel here would be enforcement of medical- or bar-association rules.

can be an important first step in a program of organized effort. But if it does not lead to group action, it is often of little value in rooting out entrenched social evils.

Another point to remember is that not all social ills spring from individual malice. An economic society comprised only of virtuous members could suffer from many ills because of faulty organization. It could, for example, be plagued with economic depressions because it lacked a sound monetary and fiscal system. Another illustration is the employer who says that he does not need unions because he treats his workers fairly. He may indeed be endeavoring to pay good wages and to offer the best of working conditions. Yet he may lack the talent needed to set up a sound personnel policy. As a result, there may be countless frictions and grievances that lead to bad morale among his workers. His good will is not implemented by proper organization of his plant.

A second point emphasized by the Pope is the need for imbedding moral principles in the very fabric of society. He calls for the customs, institutions, and laws of a society to reflect God's demand upon the economic order. A reform of institutions, no less than a reform of morals, is a prime necessity. It is not enough to organize for a better society. The results of social action must be permanent. This means that the rules governing stable social patterns must be sound. Competition, for example, should be controlled so that it promotes the common good. This may be done by law. Or it may be accomplished by enforceable codes of business and labor ethics.

A good example in point is the reform attempt of organized labor during the years 1957–1958. Certain standards of ethics were drawn up by the A.F.L.-C.I.O. An Ethical Practices Committee was formed to police these standards. Penalty for violation was expulsion from the federation. These steps can be classified as organized action for the common good. But to make these principles an institutional part of organized labor, further steps are needed. One would be to revise the constitutions of the member unions, when necessary, so that the code of ethical practices and rules designed to protect union democracy would be part of the basic law of each union. In addition, outside policing power — either in the federation or in government — should prevent usurpation of power or summary disregard of constitutional standards.

It is naïve to imagine that sound customs, laws, and institutions will prevent all economic evils. Civil law does not prevent all crime. But the deterrent effect of good social patterns is great. Even when they are flouted, it is easier to correct the evil than it would be in the absence of such standards. This is particularly the case with American society, if certain sociological analyses are correct. It is asserted that Americans are, in the language of Riesman, "other-directed," in contrast to peoples who are "inner-directed" or "tradition-directed." In effect, this means that the influence of community opinion is more decisive than it is in societies whose members are more influenced by inner convictions or by accepted traditions.

If it is true that the average American wants to conform to group standards, to be liked and accepted by his fellows, it is most important that such standards conform to moral laws and the demands of the common good. The informal ethics of a business community, the customs developed by a body of workers, the rules of a profession, all may be highly influential in determining the moral tone of a community.

The third point emphasized by the Sovereign Pontiff is that our efforts be directed toward securing the common good. This common good may be described as conditions of social life that favor the proper ends of a society and its individual members. In the economic sphere, it means arrangements that lead to abundant production and equitable distribution of goods and services needed for the individual and the family. Any society, public or private, works toward the common good when its actions enhance the welfare of its individual members and society as a whole. It may be compared to a general condition of health in a living body that in turns aids the healthy functioning of individual organs of the body.

It is necessary to remember that the common good of society is judged by the effects any given program may have upon its members. For this reason, it would be wrong to consider any society as an end in itself to the detriment of the rights of its constituents. Statism, for example, is evil because it seeks to enhance the power of the state as such, even to the point of denying essential rights of citizens. Socialism is wrong because it emphasizes the material element in society, to the exclusion of more important values. An overcentralized state arrogates to itself functions that can and will be performed properly by lower bodies. This violates the principle of subsidiarity, which holds that power and responsibility should be decentralized as far as the general welfare permits.

On the other hand, the common good is more than the sum of individual goods. If everyone were to act merely for his own interest, we would have anarchy, not society. Organized effort and proper codes of conduct are needed to avoid certain evils and to promote prosperity and social harmony. While society exists to serve the individual and the family, it has its own rights which must be acknowledged if it is to function. Thus we steer a middle course between the twin evils of statism and unregulated individualism.

These abstract statements will take on more point and effectiveness when they are applied to particular problems in later chapters. But, even at this stage, it is clear that American life does not meet the ideal outlined here. Many of our economic societies are mere pressure groups, aiming to gain the most for their own members, whether or not the common good is obtained. There are even cases — racketeers in a few labor unions are an example — when they do not even seek the interests of their members. Because of this basic disorganization of economic life, there is terrific pressure for the state to force justice and morality upon the social order. While the state is doing its duty in meeting this need, the situation is not ideal. Excessive state intervention curbs initiative and destroys freedom. Social justice envisions a hierarchy of societies, each sensitive to the needs of the common good, with the state directing, stimulating, guiding, and co-ordinating such activities to the extent that the public interest demands.

Social justice may now be defined as a virtue which inclines the individual to seek the common good, and particularly directs him to seek in an organized fashion to achieve an economic society whose laws, customs, and institutions are directed toward the promotion of the common good.

SOCIAL CHARITY

Social charity seeks many of the ends of social justice, but its motivation is different. The emphasis is upon love of neighbor, not upon rights and duties. Justice cannot bring about the complete union and harmony that will make society a smoothly functioning body. It cannot procure the generosity, patience, and tolerance needed in the slow years of transition between a disorganized society and one that is united in the interest of the common welfare. In fact, because of the frailty of human nature, it often happens that the vigorous quest for justice may actually drive men asunder. In theory, we can condemn injustice and yet not pass judgment on the motives of those who perpetrate injustice. In practice, we do not always separate the man from his deeds. Hence, were we content to limit ourselves to denouncing social injustice, we might actually divide society into warring classes. Thus, if organized labor were to attack some business practices, the effect might be to produce a united front of one group against the other. Even those who do not condone injustice might feel a sense of solidarity with their group which is being attacked. We might have a form of the class struggle occasioned by the pursuit of justice.

From this, of course, one should not conclude that the fight for justice should be slackened. Rather, it must be completed by the kindly bonds of charity. This is the more true since much social injustice is not necessarily a product of individual malice. Where the institutions of society are unsound, it is possible for well-meaning individuals to be caught in the snares of a bad system. Conventions, customs, and institutions lead them to practices which they may deplore, but feel helpless to remedy by themselves. Unless we take the pessimistic attitude that most men are evil, we should be willing to appeal to the better instincts even of those who are enmeshed in objective evil. Without such attitudes, it is difficult to see how we can achieve the co-operation and organization postulated by social justice.

Social charity fits in well with the demands deriving from the dignity of the human person. Many of these obligations, it is true, hold in terms of justice. But the recognition of a man's individual worth also calls for a certain good will toward him as a person. He does not then feel that he is submerged in a large group, whether this be civil society, a labor union, or a factory working force. Rather he senses the bonds of human relationship between himself and others, whether they be his fellow workers or his employer. Indeed, the prolific literature currently produced on human relations as a key to industrial labor relations is mainly an effort to implement the Christian virtue of charity. Personnel experts speak of the need for communication, participation, and teamwork in the factory. They stress individualized treatment of a worker's problems in the plant and elsewhere. Such techniques are said to be the key to the building of a happy and efficient working force. Yet we do not exaggerate in saying that these human-relations programs could well be implementations of the commandment second only to the law of love for God.

Just as human-relations programs are the employer's expression of charity, so also we might call union-management harmony efforts the union's way of living up to this virtue. When a union seeks to meet with the employer on terms of co-operation rather than enmity, it is acting in a Christian fashion. The idea of essential class struggle is Marxist, not Christian. There is no inherent conflict between a worker's loyalty to his union and his loyalty to his company. Even granting the historical fact that many unions were formed to remedy injustice and hence often grew up in an atmosphere of bitterness, it is not necessary to perpetuate such attitudes. With intelligence and good will on both sides, relations of genuine friendliness are possible. Indeed, they are more common in American industry than is generally realized. Furthermore, personal contacts between union officials and industrial leaders, particularly in solving common problems, can bring about a mutual respect which is the prelude for deep co-operation. Such a phenomenon was observed in various joint government committees during World War II, such as the War Labor Board or the War Production Board.

In the socioeconomic field, co-operation is often facilitated by referring to issues as problems, which they often are, rather than immediately denouncing them as injustices. A problem offers a challenge to the participants to reach a solution. Discussions may be had as to feasible methods of meeting the issue. After much give-and-take, it is often possible to reach a sound conclusion. By contrast, denunciations and the proposal of ready-made solutions often stir up resentments. A man who is condemned for practicing injustice often feels bound to defend his position and yields only reluctantly and with poor grace. But if the same man is asked to co-operate in meeting a problem, even though it is mainly of his own making, he often shows more good will. Furthermore, he can thus save face without difficulty.

Social charity is particularly useful in dealing with problems that involve explosive emotional overtones. An example is the race situation in the United States. Racial discrimination is unjust and we must never retreat on this point. But the actual working out of a program of racial betterment calls for immense amounts of good will on both sides. This was proved by the uneven pattern of results in the United States during the late 1950's. Carefully prepared and quiet programs of school integration succeeded. Ill-conceived and poorly prepared plans in the same area failed. It is easy to demand and denounce, while it is often most difficult to get a meeting of minds on complex evils rooted in long traditions. The former is the approach of justice alone, the latter involves justice tempered by charity. Lasting social reform usually needs the healing touch of social charity.

Subsidiary Virtues. Social charity is sometimes aided by certain subsidiary virtues often mentioned in connection with social problems. Among these are almsgiving, liberality, and munificence.

Almsgiving is compassionate giving to the needy, motivated by love of

God and neighbor. Social reforms may never remove all forms of poverty and need. Even if we do have social institutions to take care of most problems, there is still a place for personal giving and kindness. Moreover, there are many projects that may be useful for the community, yet unsuitable for government or other organized aid. Private donations in substantial amounts have done much good in this borderline field.

Liberality is the right use of external goods, a mean between prodigality and avarice. It involves a proper type of indifference to worldly wealth. Pope Pius XI indicates as a special function of this virtue the investing of superfluous wealth in productive enterprise. Thus community wealth is increased and new jobs are made available. Today a wealthy man might use his funds to aid promising new projects, instead of seeking the safe haven of tax-exempt bonds.

A special form of liberality is munificence, or the parting with great sums of money. This indicates a great freedom of spirit in regard to possession of external goods and a notable devotion to the common welfare. A common form of this virtue is the establishing of foundations with large fortunes as their bases. Many worthwhile community enterprises have been fostered in this manner. Substantial donations to hospitals, schools, and universities, works of charity, and religious enterprises belong in this category. An interesting example with socioeconomic implications is the setting aside of a fund to promote new enterprises involving unusual financial risk but holding great promise for the community. A wealthy American family is currently supporting such a project. Another illustration is a giant limited-dividend and relatively low-cost housing program sponsored by a large insurance company. Such use of wealth can promote social goals and mitigate the evils which might otherwise be expected from large concentrations of funds and of economic power.

The tendency toward equalization of incomes, and tax laws that make it difficult to accumulate large fortunes, will diminish opportunities to exercise the virtue of munificence. Indeed, the traditional sources of supply for university and other endowment funds have been drying up. Future donations for such causes may of necessity come from hitherto untapped sources, such as corporations, labor unions, or service clubs. New methods may be devised for securing help from the large number of persons who, although not wealthy, are in comfortable circumstances. In this way, many worthwhile activities may survive without the dangers involved in seeking government aid.

Finally, we may list among the virtues pertinent to the solution of the social problem the virtue of prudence. Prudence is often misunderstood as a virtue that inclines a person to move with restraint so as not "to upset the boat." Actually, prudence dictates the right choice of means in seeking an end. At times, when the end sought is urgent, prudence may well counsel vigorous and forthright action. Reasonable means to an end do not necessarily involve a timorous course of conduct.

In all matters concerned with the exercise of practical reason, prudence calls for careful study of problems and principles, the weighing of alternative courses of action, and the final selection of a course that seems most likely to produce the best results. Of itself, it leads neither to caution nor boldness. It may best be phrased: "Think before you act, and then act reasonably."

READINGS*

J. Messner, *Social Ethics*, pp. 122–235, 793–794.
St. Thomas Aquinas, *Summa Theologiae*, II, II, q. 31, 32, 58, 61, 78, 117, 134.
J. A. Ryan, *Distributive Justice*.
B. W. Dempsey, *The Functional Economy*, Chaps. 8, 11, 19.
W. J. McDonald, *The Social Value of Property According to St. Thomas Aquinas*, Chap. 2.
H. Johnston, *Business Ethics*, Chaps. 4–5.
Social Order: John E. Cantwell, S.J., "A Fourth Species of Justice," June, 1954; William Ferree, S.M., "Social Justice and Social Order," May, 1956; Francis J. Brown and Cornelius J. Eller, S.J., "The Process of Social Reform," September, 1956; Bernard W. Dempsey, S.J., "The Range of Social Justice," January, 1957; Charles N. R. McCoy, "Social Justice in *Quadragesimo Anno*," June, 1957.

---

* For further readings, consult List No. 3 in the Appendix.

Chapter V

CURRENT AND RECENT SOCIAL PHILOSOPHIES

INDIVIDUALISM

As a Philosophy

Pius XI, Quadragesimo Anno

10. He [Leo XIII] sought no help from either Liberalism or socialism, for the one had proved that it was utterly unable to solve the social problem aright, and the other, proposing a remedy far worse than the evil itself, would have plunged human society into greater dangers.

25. With regard to civil authority, Leo XIII, boldly breaking through the confines imposed by Liberalism, fearlessly taught that government must not be thought a mere guardian of law and of good order, but rather must put forth every effort so that "through the entire scheme of laws and institutions . . . both public and individual well-being may develop spontaneously out of the very structure and administration of the state."

78. Things have come to such a pass through the evil of what we have termed "individualism," that, following upon the overthrow and near extinction of that rich social life which was once highly developed through associations of various kinds, there remain virtually only individuals and the state.

133. Strict and watchful moral restraint enforced vigorously by governmental authority could have banished these enormous evils and even forestalled them; this restraint, however, has too often been sadly lacking. For since the seeds of a new form of economy were bursting forth just when the principles of rationalism had been implanted and rooted in many minds, there quickly developed a body of economic teaching far removed from the true moral law, and, as a result, completely free reign was given to human passions.

Pius XI, On Atheistic Communism

38. There would be today neither socialism nor communism if the rulers of the nations had not scorned the teachings and maternal warnings of the Church. On the bases of Liberalism and laicism they wished to build other social edifices which, powerful and imposing as they seemed at first, all too soon revealed the weakness of their foundations, and today are crumbling one after another before our eyes, as everything must crumble that is not grounded on the one cornerstone which is Christ Jesus.

Bishops' Statement, 1933

The social philosophy prevailing during recent centuries has carried human society far from its safe moorings.

That philosophy denied and denies, in reality, the oneness and the solidarity of mankind. In its light, wealth, business, and the power that material prosperity gives are in themselves supreme ends. Human rights must be sacrificed to those ends, and humanity itself must become the mere instrument in the production of wealth, not the master controlling it. Such a philosophy has always been and will ever be false and un-Christian in principle and application. It has literally taken God out of the world.

As an Economic System

Pius XI, Quadragesimo Anno

88. Just as the unity of human society cannot be founded on an opposition of classes, so also the right ordering of economic life cannot be left to a free competition of forces. For from this source, as from a poisoned spring, have originated and spread all the errors of individualistic economic teaching. Destroying through forgetfulness or ignorance the social and moral character of economic life, it held that economic life must be considered and treated as altogether free from and independent of public authority, because in the market, i.e., in the free struggle of competitors, it would have a principle of self-direction which governs it much more perfectly than would the intervention of any created intellect. But free competition, while justified and certainly useful provided it is kept within certain limits, clearly cannot direct economic life — a truth which the outcome of the application in practice of the tenets of this evil individualistic spirit has more than sufficiently demonstrated. Therefore, it is most necessary that economic life be again subjected to and governed by a true and effective directing principle. This function is one that the economic dictatorship which has recently displaced free competition can still less perform, since it is a headstrong power and violent energy that, to benefit people, needs to be strongly curbed and wisely ruled. But it cannot curb and rule itself.

107. This concentration of power and might, the characteristic mark, as it were, of contemporary economic life, is the fruit that the unlimited freedom of struggle among competitors has of its own nature produced, and which lets only the strongest survive; and this is often the same as saying, those who fight the most violently, those who give least heed to their conscience.

108. This accumulation of might and of power generates in turn three kinds of conflict. First, there is the struggle for economic supremacy itself; then there is the bitter fight to gain supremacy over the state in order to use in economic struggles its resources and authority; finally there is conflict between states themselves, not only because countries employ their power and shape their policies to promote every economic advantage of their citizens, but also because they seek to decide political controversies that arise among nations through the

use of their economic supremacy and strength.

109. The ultimate consequences of the individualist spirit in economic life are those which you yourselves, Venerable Brethren and Beloved Children, see and deplore: free competition has destroyed itself; economic dictatorship has supplanted the free market; unbridled ambition for power has likewise succeeded greed for gain; all economic life has become tragically hard, inexorable, and cruel. To these are to be added the grave evils that have resulted from an intermingling and shameful confusion of the functions and duties of public authority with those of the economic sphere — such as, one of the worst, the virtual degradation of the majesty of the state, which although it ought to sit on high like a queen and supreme arbitress, free from all partiality and intent upon the one common good and justice, is become a slave, surrendered and delivered to the passions and greed of men. And as to international relations, two different streams have issued from the one fountainhead: on the one hand, economic nationalism or even economic imperialism; on the other a no less deadly and accursed internationalism of finance or international imperialism whose country is where profit is.

Pius XII, To Delegates to International Foundry Congress, September 28, 1954

The demands of competition, which is a normal consequence of human liberty and ingenuity, cannot be the final norm for economics. There are inalienable values involved, the misunderstanding of which or contempt for which will be recompensed, after a more or less brief lapse of time, with dangerous social and political disturbances.

THE SYSTEM OF CAPITALISM

Leo XIII, Quod Apostolici Muneris

9. The Church, with much greater wisdom and good sense, recognizes the inequality among men, who are born with different powers of body and mind, inequality in actual possession also, and holds that the right of property and of ownership, which springs from nature itself, must not be touched and stands inviolate.

Leo XIII, Rerum Novarum

26. Therefore, let it be laid down in the first place that a condition of human existence must be borne with, namely, that in civil society the lowest cannot be made equal with the highest. Socialists, of course, agitate the contrary, but all struggling against nature is vain. There are truly very great and very many natural differences among men. Neither the talents, nor the skill, nor the health, nor the capacities of all are the same, and unequal fortune follows of itself upon necessary inequality in respect to these endowments. And clearly this condition of things is adapted to benefit both individuals and the community; for to carry on its affairs

community life requires varied aptitudes and diverse services, and to perform these diverse services men are impelled most by differences in individual property holdings.

Pius XI, Quadragesimo Anno

101. With all his energy Leo XIII sought to adjust this economic system according to the norms of right order; hence, it is evident that this system is not to be condemned in itself. And surely it is not of its own nature vicious. But it does violate right order when capital hires workers, that is, the nonowning working class, with a view to and under such terms that it directs business and even the whole economic system according to its own will and advantage, scorning the human dignity of the workers, the social character of economic activity, and social justice itself and the common good.

103. But, with the diffusion of modern industry throughout the whole world, the "capitalist" economic regime has spread everywhere to such a degree, particularly since the publication of Leo XIII's Encyclical, that it has invaded and pervaded the economic and social life of even those outside its orbit and is unquestioningly impressing on it its advantages, disadvantages, and vices, and, in a sense, is giving it its own shape and form.

Pius XII, On Women's Duties, October 21, 1945

On the other hand, can a woman, perhaps, hope for her real well-being from a regime dominated by capitalism? We do not need to describe to you now the economic and social results that issue from it. You know its characteristic signs, and you yourselves are bearing its burden: excessive concentration of population in cities, the constant all-absorbing increase of big industries, the difficult and precarious state of others, notably those of artisans and agricultural workers, and the disturbing increase of unemployment.

*   *   *

Pius XII, To the Italian Federation of Commerce, February 17, 1956

Freedom of economic activity cannot be justified and maintained except on condition that it serves a higher freedom, and has the ability, when need arises, to renounce a part of itself, in order not to fall short of the moral imperative. Otherwise, it will be difficult to restrain the ever-growing tendency towards a type of society whose economic and political organization constitutes the very negation of any sort of freedom.

Pastoral Letter, French Cardinals, September 8, 1949

By condemning the actions of communist parties, the Church does not support the capitalist regime. It is most necessary that it be realized that in the very essence of capitalism — that is to say, in the absolute value that it gives to property without reference to the common good or to the dignity of labor — there is a materialism rejected by Christian teaching.

Whatever their rank in society or their power in the economic life of the various nations, Catholics whose pride of class or attachment to worldly riches induces them to object to any change in the social structure are certainly not acting in the spirit of Jesus Christ. They are, without doubt, accomplices of the enemies of His Church and serve as the forerunners of communist revolution.

SOCIALISM

Leo XIII, Rerum Novarum

7. To cure this evil, the Socialists, exciting the envy of the poor toward the rich, contend that it is necessary to do away with private possession of goods and in its place to make the goods of individuals common to all, and that the men who preside over a municipality or who direct the entire state should act as administrators of these goods. They hold that, by such a transfer of private goods from private individuals to the community, they can cure the present evil through dividing wealth and benefits equally among the citizens.

8. But their program is so unsuited for terminating the conflict that it actually injures the workers themselves. Moreover, it is highly unjust, because it violates the rights of lawful owners, perverts the functions of the state, and throws governments into utter confusion.

Pius XI, Quadragesimo Anno

113. [Present-day] socialism, is surely more moderate. It not only professes the rejection of violence but modifies and tempers to some degree, if it does not reject entirely, the class struggle and the abolition of private ownership. One might say that, terrified by its own principles and by the conclusions drawn therefrom by communism, socialism inclines toward and in a certain measure approaches the truths which Christian tradition has always held sacred; for it cannot be denied that its demands at times come very near those that Christian reformers of society justly insist upon.

114. If the foregoing happens, it can come even to the point that imperceptibly these ideas of the more moderate socialism will no longer differ from the desires and demands of those who are striving to remold human society on the basis of Christian principles. . . .

116. Yet let no one think that all the socialist groups or factions that are not communist have, without exception, recovered their senses to this extent either in fact or in name. For the most part they do not reject the class struggle or the abolition of ownership, but only in some degree modify them. Now if these false principles are modified and to some extent erased from the program, the question arises, or rather is raised without warrant by some, whether the principles of Christian truth cannot perhaps be also modified to some degree and be tempered so as to meet socialism halfway and, as it were, by a middle course, come to agreement with it. . . .

117. But what if socialism has really been so tempered and modified as to the class struggle and private ownership that there is in it no longer anything to be censured on these

points? Has it thereby renounced its contradictory nature to the Christian religion? . . . Whether considered as a doctrine, or an historical fact, or a movement, socialism, if it remains truly socialism, even after it has yielded to truth and justice on the points which we have mentioned, cannot be reconciled with the teachings of the Catholic Church because its concept of society itself is utterly foreign to Christian truth.

119. Because of the fact that goods are produced more efficiently by a suitable division of labor than by the scattered efforts of individuals, Socialists infer that economic activity, only the material ends of which enter into their thinking, ought of necessity to be carried on socially. Because of this necessity, they hold that men are obliged, with respect to the producing of goods, to surrender and subject themselves entirely to society. Indeed, possession of the greatest possible supply of things that serve the advantages of this life is considered of such great importance that the higher goods of man, liberty not excepted, must take a secondary place and even be sacri-ficed to the demands of the most efficient production of goods. This damage to human dignity, undergone in the "socialized" process of production, will be easily offset, they say, by the abundance of socially produced goods which will pour out in profusion to individuals to be used freely at their pleasure for comforts and cultural development. Society, therefore, as socialism conceives it, can on the one hand neither exist nor be thought of without an obviously excessive use of force; on the other hand, it fosters a liberty no less false, since there is no place in it for true social authority, which rests not on temporal and material advantages but descends from God alone, the Creator and last end of all things.

120. If socialism, like all errors, contains some truth (which, moreover, the Supreme Pontiffs have never denied), it is based nevertheless on a theory of human society peculiar to itself and irreconcilable with true Christianity. Religious socialism, Christian socialism, are contradictory terms; no one can be at the same time a good Catholic and a true Socialist.

Pius XII, Christmas Message, 1955

They think they are establishing complete security on an ever-increasing productivity and on the uninterrupted flow of a continually greater production in the national economy. This, they say — on the basis of a full and increasingly perfected automatic system of production, and supported by better methods of organization and accountancy — will guarantee to all workers a continuous and progressive return for their labor. In a subsequent phase, this return will become so great that, by means of social measures, it will be able to take care of the security of those who are not yet able or are no longer able to work — the young, the old, the sick. To achieve security, they conclude, there will no longer be any necessity to have recourse to property, whether private or collective, whether in nature or in capital goods.

Now, this way of ordering the means of security is not one of those forms of adaptation of natural principles to new developments, but almost a frontal attack on the essence of man's natural relationships with his fellow men, with work, with society. In this excessively artificial system, man's security with regard to his life is dangerously divorced from the arrangements and the forces for the ordering of society inherent in human nature itself, which alone render possible the association of men in solidarity. In one way or other, although necessary adjustment must be made to the times, family and property have to remain among the fundamentals in a free systematization of persons. Somehow the lesser social units and the state must be able to come together as complementary agents of security.

NONCOMMUNIST STATISM

Pius XI, Non Abbiamo Bisogno

49. And here We find Ourselves confronted by a mass of authentic affirmations and no less authentic facts which reveal beyond the slightest possibility of doubt the resolve (already in great measure actually put into effect) to monopolize completely the young, from their tenderest years up to manhood and womanhood, for the exclusive advantage of a party and of a regime based on an ideology which clearly resolves itself into a true, a real pagan worship of the state — the "statolatry" which is no less in contrast with the natural rights of the family than it is in contradiction with the supernatural rights of the Church.

57. A conception of the state which makes the rising generations belong to it entirely, without any exception, from the tenderest years up to adult life, cannot be reconciled by a Catholic either with Catholic doctrine or with the natural rights of the family.

Pius XI, Quadragesimo Anno

(Summarized.) 91–96. The Pope describes the syndicalist and corporative organization of production in Italy, whereby all economic activity is directed by state-controlled syndicates. Workers and employers are represented in these groups, but the state has the final word. The advantages of this system are class collaboration and a unified economic life. Its disadvantages follow from the state's substituting itself for the free activity of the parties, political and involved administration, and the serving of particular political ends rather than the reconstruction and promotion of a better social order. These evils may be overcome if moral and religious principles are integrated with the system. There should also be a broader participation in the control of the system on the part of those who could contribute technical, occupational, and social knowledge and experience.

Pius XII, Summi Pontificatus, October 20, 1939

1420. To consider the state as something ultimate to which everything else should be subordinated and directed, cannot fail to harm the true and lasting prosperity of nations. This can happen either when unrestricted dominion comes to be conferred on the state as having a mandate from the nation, people, or even a social class, or when the state arrogates such dominion to itself as absolute master, despotically, without any mandate whatsoever. If, in fact, the state lays claim to and directs private enterprises, these, ruled as they are by delicate and complicated internal principles which guarantee and assure the realization of their special aims, may be damaged to the detriment of the public good, by being wrenched from their natural surroundings, that is, from responsible private action.

1429. The idea which credits the state with unlimited authority is not simply an error harmful to the internal life of nations, to their prosperity, and to the larger and well-ordered increase in their well-being, but likewise it injures the relations between peoples, for it breaks the unity of supranational society, robs the law of nations of its foundation and vigor, leads to violation of others' rights, and impedes agreement and peaceful intercourse.

Pius XII, Address to Sacred College of Cardinals, June 2, 1945

He [Pope Pius XI] proclaimed to the world on Passion Sunday, 1937, in his encyclical *Mit Brennender Sorge* what National Socialism really was: the arrogant apostasy from Jesus Christ, the denial of His doctrine and of His work of redemption, the cult of violence, the idolatry of race and blood, the overthrow of human liberty and dignity.

To the Holy Roman Rota, October 2, 1945

Equally unsatisfactory . . . is that conception of civil power which may be termed "authoritarian," for this shuts out citizens from any effective share or influence in the formation of the social will. Consequently it splits the nation into two categories, that of the rulers and that of the ruled, whose relations to each other are reduced to those of a purely mechanical kind, governed by force, or else based on purely biological foundations.

THE preceding chapters explained some fundamentals of a Christian social order and also alluded to evils poisoning economic life. It is now timely to examine in a systematic fashion the roots of these evils. The first topic treated, individualism, is the philosophy that contributed to the overthrow of the medieval social system and led in great part to the growth of our modern economic order. While it inspired many great commercial and industrial achievements, it also spawned appalling abuses. Capitalism is historically connected with this spirit of individualism, although in many areas it has changed in the direction of accepting social responsibility.

In reaction to individualism the social and political pendulum often swung to the other extreme of statism. Statism in modern times has taken two main forms. When the emphasis was primarily economic, it appeared in the guise of socialism. By contrast, where the problem was mainly political, the overcentralized state took the form of political dictatorship, fascism or national socialism. In these latter cases, patterns of ownership were not usually changed, but the owners were subjected to extreme political control.

Communism, of course, belongs among these systems. Ideologically, it is a branch of socialism. In its actual development since it took root in Russia in 1917, it has consistently exhibited a totalitarian pattern of government. It may be said to combine the bad features of socialist economic life and totalitarian political life. For this reason it is treated separately, rather than as a branch of socialism. Because of its obvious impact upon the modern world, it is the subject of a separate chapter.

INDIVIDUALISM

Individualism, called Liberalism by Pope Pius XI and most European writers, is considered the primary source of the social evils described in the encyclicals. As a system, it is roughly described in the phrase "every man for himself." It has developed in two forms, corresponding to different historical stages. In its earlier form, it exhibited these characteristics: morally and philosophically, it held that man was a law unto himself and that self-seeking is the prime rule of life; economically, it manifested itself in the form of unregulated free competition; and politically, it maintained that the state should hold aloof from economic life, except when it was protecting property rights.

The later form of individualism was conditioned by the economic changes resulting from its earlier form. Extreme competition was modified by the development of large firms; the absorption of competitors; trends toward monopoly; economic dictatorship made possible by centralized financial controls; and the effort of the business community to win control of the state, so that its power could be used to the advantage of this group. Consequently, individual selfishness yielded to group individualism; free competition was modified and sometimes replaced by monopoly; and the state became a partisan prize whose control was sought by competing groups, rather than the aloof policeman of laissez-faire days.

The historical roots of individualism were outlined briefly in Chapter I. It was a reaction to the religious and moral controls of the medieval period, and the political controls of eighteenth-century nationalism in France and England. Philosophers such as Jean Jacques Rousseau and Thomas Hobbes contributed its ideological basis, arguing that man was good (Rousseau) or hopelessly predatory (Hobbes). If man is good, then he does not need state control to do what is right. If he is completely bad, one cannot stop ruthless competition. These philosophical views were often reinforced by certain religious trends in Lutheranism and Calvinism, as well as by the Jansenist heresy within the Catholic Church.

At the same time, the classical economists, particularly Adam Smith, David Ricardo, and John Stuart Mill, contributed an economic justification of the trend. They argued that unlimited competition forces every man to work his hardest. It leads to the best possible goods at the cheapest prices. Thus maximum production and optimum distribution are obtained. The encyclicals refer to these writers as the Manchester School.

It is obvious from what has been said in preceding chapters that these arguments spring from a faulty view of human nature. Man is neither wholly good nor wholly bad by nature. He is wounded by original sin, but he is capable of natural virtue and of even greater achievements when he has the guidance, inspiration, and divine help obtained through acceptance of religious faith. He needs society, not because he is evil, but because God created man for social living. Even if unlimited selfishness were capable of creating the material benefits promised by the Manchester School, it would have to be rejected as contrary to man's nature and hence God's law. Actually, history records that a laissez-faire economic system produced great social evils and limited economic benefits.

From a strictly economic viewpoint, it is significant that many businessmen constantly strive to soften the impact of competition. Trends toward consolidation, monopoly, fair-trade laws, price fixing, and sharing of markets show that unlimited competition is not always accepted by the business community. Its consequences in the form of exploitation of labor, waste of natural resources, and the social waste caused by periodic depressions led to a constantly growing body of social legislation.

Hardly anyone in the United States today, except a few theoretical writers, seems willing to face in practice the rigors of unlimited competition. This does not mean that the theory has been abandoned in social polemics. On the contrary, business groups are often willing to apply it to farmers, farmers to organized labor, and labor to business. But each group wants to hold on to the benefits it has obtained from favorable legislation. Business would remove farm price supports, but fights for the protective tariff. Labor would punish business monopoly, but it rejects the application of antitrust laws to its own actions. Thus, as was noted before, atomistic individualism has been replaced by group individualism.

For these reasons, it is pointless to discuss in detail the ill effects of eighteenth-, nineteenth-, or early twentieth-century individualism. So far as we can see, there has been an irrevocable decision against either the atomistic competition of earlier days or the more recent economic dictatorship. What we have today is a society still partially infected by the philosophy of individualism, but subject to strong political and social controls. Powerful economic groups try to swing the state in directions they favor. However, as their power becomes excessive, countervailing forces arise and check them.[1] None of these clashing forces seems likely to achieve permanent domination over the others.

The current impact of individualism is twofold. First, as a philosophy that stresses selfishness and rejects the common good, it pushes society in a direction contrary to Christian social teaching. Obviously it cannot be reconciled with the principles outlined in Chapters III and IV. Second, the reaction to individualism has its own dangers. Present-day American economic life is obviously sounder than the earlier forms that provoked the demand for social controls. But the trend toward centralization is disturbing. Politically, it has led to enormous enhancement of the power of the federal government. In economic society, it has made more difficult the survival of smaller units in business, farming, and labor. The result is the phenomenon of increasingly centralized power, remote from the individual, the family, and small, easily controlled groups. This threatens a loss of liberty and a diminution of the status of individual members of the political and economic communities. These are the problems that Americans must solve if economic life is to be infused with Christian principles.

CAPITALISM

In many areas of the world, the spirit of individualism just described is considered as identical with capitalism. We in the United States, however, think that our form of capitalism is different. In general American usage, capitalism may be described as an economic system characterized by private ownership of the means of production, substantial freedom of enterprise to determine the main economic conditions of production, stress on the profit motive, and the use of funds invested in land, resources, buildings, and machines in a notable portion of enterprises. Succinctly, private ownership, free enterprise, the profit motive, and the use of invested funds are the main elements of our capitalistic system.

---

[1] See J. K. Galbraith, *American Capitalism: The Concept of Countervailing Power* (Boston: Houghton Mifflin, 1952).

Few Americans seriously dispute the value of private capitalism. We take our system for granted, almost as much as we do the air around us. Hence it comes as a shock to many to read European condemnations of capitalism, especially when these come from Catholic circles and even from the papacy itself. This would be less of a problem, were we to examine the ideas behind the term used. In Europe, capitalism is often used as synonymous with excessive concentration of wealth, exploitation of workers, and an antisocial mentality among employers. Many who condemn capitalism in Europe admire the American system. This applies even to doctrinaire socialists.

The specific elements which characterize our economic system are not at variance with Catholic social teaching. The Church favors private property and free enterprise, always with the proviso that there are social obligations as well as rights attached to these institutions. Nor is there anything immoral in seeking a profit or using saved funds to build new physical capital. It is true that American business has at times abused its power. But we speak of such abuses as deviations from moral norms in a system that is not intrinsically wrong.

The Wage Contract. Historically, one of the notable features of capitalism has been the wage system, whereby one or more workers contribute skill and energy, using the property of another, to produce goods or services. The products of such activity are sold by the owner of the property, who pays the workers for their contribution and retains a part as payment for his own share in the process, namely, the use of his property. Such a system, says Pope Pius XI, "is not to be condemned." "It is not of its own nature vicious." But it is a grave abuse when capital uses its power in such a way that it scorns "the human dignity of the workers, the social character of economic activity, and social justice itself and the common good." Accordingly, the hiring of workers by an employer is an acceptable mode of economic life, provided the social aspect of the process is not ignored.

In the modern world, it would be almost impossible to have any other system. World population has expanded to such a degree that the use of machines and mass-production methods seems essential if we are to maintain even a minimum standard of living. Increases in living standards almost invariably involve an increase in invested capital. Thus, in the United States, it can be shown that real wages per worker have gone up in direct proportion to increased capital investment. Today the typical American worker has at his disposal about fifteen thousand dollars' worth of tools, buildings, and resources. These multiply his skill and efficiency to such a degree that he can work only half as long as was customary fifty years ago, and yet receive three times as much real income. Such is the contribution of physical capital, which may be defined as the machines and resources bought with money capital. Even socialism and communism acknowledge the value of physical capital, although under these systems it is generally owned by the state. Socialist enterprises hire workers in much the same way as do their capitalist competitors.

An even more fundamental reason for the owner-worker distinction was noted by Pope Leo XIII, namely, human inequality. Men differ in skills, abilities, character, zeal, energy, and like qualities. Some are timid and retiring; others are forthright and resolute. There are men who are conservative and cautious, whereas their fellows may be daring and even reckless. With such major diversities in human nature, it is not surprising that men should be divided into the skilled and the unskilled and into leaders and followers. Nor is it remarkable that unequal talents are among the factors leading to inequality in wealth. In some cases individuals saved from their income, at times through several generations, to build up a great enterprise. In other instances, promoters used the money of others, obtained by borrowing or the sale of shares of ownership, to create some firm. Within an enterprise, men of exceptional ability are given the positions of responsibility. On lower levels, workers are classified according to their skills.

Of course, not all economic inequality is traceable to differences in ability. Elements of luck, ruthlessness, favoritism, and similar factors not connected with genuine ability have been important factors in many well-known success stories. But, at least there are enough variations in human qualities that inequality is not necessarily a result of exploitation. In general, this thesis need not be argued in America. Few in our midst accept the Marxian idea that capital is essentially predatory, stealing a surplus value which really belongs to the workers. Nor do we object to inequality of fortune or position, provided it is based on evident ability and not dishonest means. The average worker does not begrudge the manager of an enterprise his salary, nor the owner his profits provided they are "fair." But this element of fairness requires considerable definition and clarification, as will be further explained in Chapter VIII.

SOCIALISM

The Theory of Socialism. In contrast to individualism, socialism exalts the state in the economic sphere. Socialism has taken so many forms within the past century that it is difficult to specify its exact meaning today. Generally speaking, socialism calls for community ownership of the means of production. On the theory that private property in productive goods is the basis of economic exploitation, and the premise that free enterprise varies between wasteful competition and antisocial monopoly, it is held that drastic remedies are needed. Nothing less than community ownership of productive property will permit planned production without exploitation.

The degree of proposed socialization varies among the several schools of socialists. The system has moderated somewhat from an earlier position which would take over all forms of productive property. Some socialists would exempt small business firms and land held by small farmers. They would concentrate upon large, dominant enterprises. Likewise, there is variety in the type of control advocated. Some would have direct state ownership. Others would favor independent state corporations. Finally, there is a school which would have smaller groups, such as guilds of workers, taking over enterprises.

Most modern socialism holds for democratic methods of seizure, with fair compensation for the former owners. Likewise, it professes that control of the seized property should be democratic, at least through popular participation in a socialist government. In some cases the tendency toward class warfare has been mitigated. Socialists attack the inefficiency of present owners rather than their alleged exploitation of workers. These moderating trends were noted in *Quadragesimo Anno*.

A formal distinction must be made between socialism and nationalization. It is possible to achieve socialism through progressive nationalization of enterprises, but it is also feasible to have considerable state ownership without socialism. A similar distinction can be made between socialism and economic planning, although not all would admit this. In theory, it is possible to have private enterprise with a substantial degree of state control. Some writers would contend that such a situation would inevitably lead to socialism or worse. This, however, is a debatable point.

A Critique of Socialism. Pope Pius XI observed the great changes which have come about in socialism. He even stated that many of its concrete proposals do not differ greatly from the just demands of Christian social reformers. He noted with approval its recession from positions regarding the class war and revolutionary violence. Nevertheless, he stated that true socialism, based on its historical principles, is incompatible with Christian teaching.

One basic objection to socialism is its inherent materialism. It organizes social life exclusively in the interests of economic efficiency. With greater and greater production the main aim of society, it is evident that higher values are sacrificed for the sake of material goods. It may be objected that capitalism is likewise materialistic. But capitalism is not identical with civil society. Moreover, it is hardly a reform of capitalism to take over and intensify one of its less desirable features.

Socialism likewise endangers human liberties. If all economic power is concentrated in the hands of the state, such a state has absolute power. Even if it is organized along democratic lines, there are great pressures toward absolutism. Here is a concentration of power much more extensive than under the most dictatorial forms of capitalism. Such centralization is inherently dangerous, no matter what safeguards against abuse are established. Moreover, there are persuasive arguments that central control of economic life is possible only by totalitarian methods. When other incentives are removed, compulsion remains as a last resort. It is not unlikely that a socialist government must either put down resistance by workers or lapse into anarchy. But if it acts against the group that gives it political support, it must either yield power to the opposition or consolidate it by dictatorial methods. There is no easy escape from this dilemma.

There are also strong economic reasons against the practicability of socialism. The idea that a planned economy is more efficient than a well-functioning free economy is a fallacy. Central planning imposes the decisions of the few upon the many. Under a free economy each consumer through his purchases participates in planning. Businessmen through their investments likewise plan. Their activities are co-ordinated in the market through the price mechanism. In this way the quantity and quality of goods, the distribution of labor and capital, and the rewards to producers are calculated in terms of consumer needs and available resources. It is true that defects exist in the actual functioning of our market economy, as was noted earlier in this chapter. But the remedy is a free economy working for sound social ends, not a controlled economy which squanders the initiative and planning of the many only to replace it with the plans of the few. Quite apart from the elements of compulsion inherent in socialism and central planning, it is quite doubtful that centralism can use human and material resources as efficiently as a free economy. To repeat, the issue is not between planning and anarchy, but between the planning of the few and the decisions of the many.[2]

It is for these reasons that the Pontiff states that no Catholic may be a socialist. He calls the term "Christian Socialism" a contradiction. However, this stricture applies only to socialism in the literal sense of the term. Too often, in the United States, the term socialism is loosely applied to any proposed reform measure which would extend government authority in the economic field. Thus, health-insurance measures are sometimes mislabeled socialism or socialized medicine. Obviously, socialism in the technical sense has a very definite meaning. Even extensive nationalization is not of necessity socialism, although it may be undesirable for other reasons. Only if such measures are part of a pattern leading to complete state ownership of industry or control over services can we call them socialist.

NONCOMMUNIST STATISM

While socialism is the antithesis of individualism by virtue of state ownership of productive property, there are other forms of statism where control rather than ownership is the distinguishing feature. Thus, national socialism and fascism did not take over private industry, but they subjected economic life to strict state control. The system of ownership was undisturbed, but the owners were by no means their own masters in running their businesses. Prices were often regulated, production quotas set, and rigid patterns of working conditions imposed. The owners were allowed to receive profits, but they were often told how these must be invested in terms of economic expansion. Like every other phase of life in a totalitarian economy, business was forced to accept state dictatorship.

In discussing these varieties of statism, a sharp distinction must be made between state control of economic life and totalitarian control of all phases of life. This distinction is vital in appraising many modern government systems. Totalitarianism is essentially evil. By its very nature, it embodies a false concept of society. It denies basic rights to individuals. The total state intrudes in fields where government has no normal authority to enter. It probes deeply into family relationships, ignores parental

---

[2] For a succinct treatment of this problem, see J. Messner, *Social Ethics*, pp. 818–823, and L. von Mises, *Human Action* (New Haven: Yale University Press, 1949), Chap. 26.

authority in education, suppresses vital individual freedoms, and thus makes the citizen the slave of the state. It is unnecessary to elaborate in detail how all this perverts the notions of individual dignity, the function of society, and the true nature of the common good.

By contrast, the absence of popular democratic control is a relative rather than an absolute evil. Historically, monarchy, tribal rule, and forms of dictatorship have been, until recent centuries, the prevailing political forms among most of mankind. While it is well to emphasize the virtues of democracy, it is the part of realism to note also its preconditions. It is difficult to have true democratic rule without a minimum of popular general education, adequate means of communication, the existence of a middle class, and some economic security for the poorer classes of society.

For this reason, it is difficult to form valid generalizations about dictatorships in contemporary political society. In older states, such as Spain and Portugal, dictatorships entered when democratic government had broken down. In Spain, the reason was civil war. In Portugal, it was corruption and inefficiency, which bankrupted the government. In Latin America, the problem is often one of the absence of a middle class and the wide gulf between rich and poor. There is still another problem with nations, particularly in Asia and Africa, newly emerged from colonialism. Here we may find that the preceding colonial rule had not prepared an adequate civil service, so that the new nations find severe and often impossible handicaps to the practice of democracy.

For these reasons, we may accept the fact that some dictatorships are unavoidable. The indictment against this form of rule is based, not necessarily upon its beginnings in a nation, but upon its desire to perpetuate itself. When a ruler fails to use his power to prepare a nation for a viable democracy, he is betraying the best interests of his people.

CONCLUSION

In theory, as we shall note in Chapter XIII, it is not the form of government that matters, but the justice of its rule. But the power of the modern state is so absolute that the citizen rarely has recourse against injustice. For this reason it is safe to say that any condition that tends to overcentralize political power is dangerous. Individualism may produce such a result through reaction to the problems it creates. Socialism and statism directly enhance the power of the state. They must all be rejected as inadequate in terms of the needs of mankind.

The ultimate test of any society is its total impact on man and the family. If it promotes conditions consonant with man's dignity and rights, it is seeking the true common good. When its emphasis is distorted and man suffers, then it is lacking, no matter what material or political benefits it may obtain. Man lives in society, but society exists to help the individual and the family.

READINGS*

On Individualism and Socialism:
J. Messner, Social Ethics, pp. 543–565, 816–823, 927–930, 935–943.
C. Clune, Christian Social Reconstruction, Chap. 6.
O. von Nell-Breuning, Reorganization of Social Economy, Chaps. 14–15.
J. Villain, L'Enseignement social de l'Église, Vol. I, pp. 138–162, 165–187, 225–231.
On Statism:
J. Messner, Social Ethics, pp. 566–579.
R. Kothen, L'Enseignement social de l'Église, Chap. 7.
C. Dawson, Religion and the Modern State.
H. A. Rommen, The State in Catholic Thought.
H. Johnston, Business Ethics, Chap. 12.
Social Order: Philip S. Land, S.J., "Capitalism," November, 1951; Richard M. McKeon, S.J., "New Capitalism vs. Old," March, 1953; Bernard W. Dempsey, S.J., " . . . but don't call it CAPITALISM," May, 1954; Thomas P. Neill, "Liberalism," October, 1954; Ross J. S. Hoffman, "Conservatism," December, 1955; Francis G. Wilson, "Catholics and the New Conservatism," June, 1956; Paul F. Douglass, "New Concepts of Industrial Man," October, 1956; Arnold F. McKee, "Selling American Capitalism," November, 1956.

---

* For further readings, see List No. 4 in the Appendix.

Chapter VI

COMMUNISM

Pius XI, Quadragesimo Anno

112. Communism teaches and seeks two objectives: unrelenting class warfare and absolute extermination of private ownership. Not secretly or by hidden methods does it do this, but publicly, openly, and by employing every and all means, even the most violent. To achieve these objectives there is nothing which it does not dare, nothing for which it has respect or reverence; and when it has come to power, it is incredible and portentlike in its cruelty and inhumanity. The horrible slaughter and destruction through which it has laid waste vast regions of eastern Europe and Asia are the evidence; how much an enemy and how openly hostile it is to Holy Church and to God Himself is, alas, too well proved by facts and fully known to all. Although We, therefore, deem it superfluous to warn upright and faithful children of the Church regarding the impious and iniquitous character of communism, yet We cannot without deep sorrow contemplate the heedlessness of those who apparently make light of these impending dangers, and with sluggish inertia allow the widespread propagation of doctrine which seeks by violence and slaughter to destroy society altogether. All the more gravely to be condemned is the folly of those who neglect to remove or change the conditions that inflame the minds of peoples and pave the way for the overthrow and destruction of society.

Pius XI, On Atheistic Communism

8. The communism of today, more emphatically than similar movements in the past, conceals in itself a false messianic idea. A pseudo-ideal of justice, of equality and fraternity in labor impregnates all its doctrine and activity with a deceptive mysticism, which communicates a zealous and contagious enthusiasm to the multitudes entrapped by delusive promises. This is especially true in an age like ours, when unusual misery has resulted from the unequal distribution of the goods of this world. This pseudo-ideal is even boastfully advanced as if it were responsible for a certain economic progress. As a matter of fact, when such progress is at all real, its true causes are quite different, as for instance the intensification of industrialism in countries which were formerly almost without it, the exploitation of immense natural resources, and the use of the most brutal methods to insure the achievement of gigantic projects with a minimum of expense.

9. The doctrine of modern com-

munism, which is often concealed under the most seductive trappings, is in substance based on the principles of dialectical and historical materialism previously advocated by Marx, of which the theoreticians of Bolshevism claim to possess the only genuine interpretation. According to this doctrine there is in the world only one reality, matter, the blind forces of which evolve into plant, animal, and man. Even human society is nothing but a phenomenon and form of matter, evolving in the same way. By a law of inexorable necessity and through a perpetual conflict of forces, matter moves toward the final synthesis of a classless society. In such a doctrine, as is evident, there is no room for the idea of God; there is no difference between matter and spirit, between soul and body; there is neither survival of the soul after death nor any hope in a future life. Insisting on the dialectical aspect of their materialism, the Communists claim that the conflict which carries the world toward its final synthesis can be accelerated by man. Hence they endeavor to sharpen the antagonisms which arise between the various classes of society. Thus the class struggle with its consequent violent hate and destruction takes on the aspect of a crusade for the progress of humanity. On the other hand, all other forces whatever, as long as they resist such systematic violence, must be annihilated as hostile to the human race.

10. Communism, moreover, strips man of his liberty, robs human personality of all its dignity, and removes all the moral restraints that check the eruptions of blind impulse. There is no recognition of any right of the individual in his relations to the collectivity; no natural right is accorded to human personality, which is a mere cogwheel in the communist system. In man's relations with other individuals, besides, Communists hold the principle of absolute equality, rejecting all hierarchy and divinely constituted authority, including the authority of parents. What men call authority and subordination is derived from the community as its first and only font. Nor is the individual granted any property rights over material goods or the means of production for, inasmuch as these are the source of further wealth, their possession would give one man power over another. Precisely on this score, all forms of private property must be eradicated, for they are at the origin of all economic enslavement.

12. What would be the condition of a human society based on such materialistic tenets? It would be a collectivity with no other hierarchy than that of the economic system. It would have only one mission: the production of material things by means of collective labor, so that the goods of this world might be enjoyed in a paradise where each would "give according to his powers" and would "receive according to his needs." Communism recognizes in the collectivity the right, or rather, unlimited discretion, to draft individuals for the labor of the collectivity with no regard for their personal welfare; so that even violence could be legitimately exercised to dragoon the recalcitrant against their wills. In the communistic commonwealth morality and law would be nothing but a derivation of the existing economic order, purely earthly in origin and unstable in character. In a word, the Communists claim to inaugurate a new era and a new civilization which is the result of blind evolutionary forces culminating in a humanity without God.

14. Such, Venerable Brethren, is the new gospel which Bolshevistic and atheistic communism offers the world

as the glad tidings of deliverance and salvation! It is a system full of errors and sophisms. It is in opposition both to reason and to divine revelation. It subverts the social order, because it means the destruction of its foundations; because it ignores the true origin and purpose of the state; because it denies the rights, dignity, and liberty of human personality.

15. How is it possible that such a system, long since rejected scientifically and now proved erroneous by experience, how is it, We ask, that such a system could spread so rapidly in all parts of the world? The explanation lies in the fact that too few have been able to grasp the nature of communism. The majority instead succumb to its deception, skillfully concealed by the most extravagant promises. By pretending to desire only the betterment of the condition of the working classes, by urging the removal of the very real abuses chargeable to the liberalistic economic order, and by demanding a more equitable distribution of this world's goods (objects entirely and undoubtedly legitimate), the Communist takes advantage of the present world-wide economic crisis to draw into the sphere of his influence even those sections of the populace which on principle reject all forms of materialism and terrorism. And as every error contains its element of truth, the partial truths to which we have referred are astutely presented according to the needs of time and place, to conceal, when convenient, the repulsive crudity and inhumanity of communistic principles and tactics. Thus the communist ideal wins over many of the better-minded members of the community. These in turn become the apostles of the movement among the younger intelligentsia who are still too immature to recognize the intrinsic errors of the system. The preachers of communism are also proficient in exploiting racial antagonisms and political divisions and oppositions. They take advantage of the lack of orientation characteristic of modern agnostic science in order to burrow into the universities where they bolster up the principles of their doctrine with pseudoscientific arguments.

17. There is another explanation for the rapid diffusion of the communistic ideas now seeping into every nation, great and small, advanced and backward, so that no corner of the earth is free from them. This explanation is to be found in a propaganda so truly diabolical that the world has perhaps never witnessed its like before. It is directed from one common center. It is shrewdly adapted to the varying conditions of diverse peoples. It has at its disposal great financial resources, gigantic organizations, international congresses, and countless trained workers. It makes use of pamphlets and reviews, of cinema, theater, and radio, of schools and even universities. Little by little it penetrates into all classes of the people and even reaches the better-minded groups of the community with the result that few are aware of the poison which increasingly pervades their minds and hearts.

22. For the first time in history we are witnessing a struggle, cold blooded in purpose and mapped out to the least detail, between man and "all that is called God." Communism is by its nature antireligious. It considers religion as the "opiate of the people" because the principles of religion which speak of a life beyond the grave dissuade the proletariat from the dream of a Soviet paradise which is of this world.

23. But the law of nature and its Author cannot be flouted with impunity. Communism has not been able, and will not be able, to achieve

its objectives even in the merely economic sphere. It is true that in Russia it has been a contributing factor in rousing men and materials from the inertia of centuries, and in obtaining by all manner of means, often without scruple, some measure of material success. Nevertheless we know from reliable and even very recent testimony that not even there, in spite of slavery imposed on millions of men, has communism reached its promised goal. After all, even the sphere of economics needs some morality, some moral sense of responsibility, which can find no place in a system so thoroughly materialistic as communism. Terrorism is the only possible substitute, and it is terrorism that reigns today in Russia, where former comrades in revolution are exterminating each other. Terrorism, having failed despite all to stem the tide of moral corruption, cannot even prevent the dissolution of society itself.

57. In the beginning communism showed itself for what it was in all its perversity; but very soon it realized that it was thus alienating the people. It has therefore changed its tactics, and strives to entice the multitudes by trickery of various forms, hiding its real designs behind ideas that in themselves are good and attractive. Thus, aware of the universal desire for peace, the leaders of communism pretend to be the most zealous promoters and propagandists in the movement for world amity. Yet at the same time they stir up a class warfare which causes rivers of blood to flow, and, realizing that their system offers no internal guarantee of peace, they have recourse to unlimited armaments. Under various names which do not suggest communism, they establish organizations and periodicals with the sole purpose of carrying their ideas into quarters otherwise inaccessible. They try perfidiously to worm their way even into professedly Catholic and religious organizations. Again, without receding an inch from their subversive principles, they invite Catholics to collaborate with them in the realm of so-called humanitarianism and charity; and at times even make proposals that are in perfect harmony with the Christian spirit and the doctrine of the Church. Elsewhere they carry their hypocrisy so far as to encourage the belief that communism, in countries where faith and culture are more strongly entrenched, will assume another and much milder form. It will not interfere with the practice of religion. It will respect liberty of conscience. There are some even who refer to certain changes recently introduced into Soviet legislation as a proof that communism is about to abandon its program of war against God.

58. See to it, Venerable Brethren, that the Faithful do not allow themselves to be deceived! Communism is intrinsically wrong, and no one who would save Christian civilization may collaborate with it in any undertaking whatsoever. Those who permit themselves to be deceived into lending their aid toward the triumph of communism in their own country, will be the first to fall victims of their error. And the greater the antiquity and grandeur of the Christian civilization in the regions where communism successfully penetrates, so much more devastating will be the hatred displayed by the godless.

Congregation of the Holy Office, July 13, 1949

The Supreme Sacred Congregation of the Holy Office has been asked: (1) Whether it is lawful to enlist in or show favor to the communist party? (2) Whether it is lawful to publish, read, or disseminate books, newspapers, periodicals, or leaflets in support of communist doctrine and practice or write any articles in them? (3) Whether Catholics who knowingly and freely perform actions as specified in Nos. 1 and 2 above may be admitted to the sacraments? (4) Whether Catholics, who profess and particularly those who defend and spread, the materialistic and anti-Christian doctrine of the Communists, ipso facto, as apostates from the Catholic faith, incur excommunication reserved especially to the Holy See?

The most eminent and reverend fathers, charged with the defense of matters pertaining to faith and morals, after having previously heard the opinion of the consultors at a plenary session held on Tuesday, the 28th day of June, 1949, decreed that the above-mentioned questions be answered as follows:

To No. 1 — In the negative, for communism is materialistic and anti-Christian. Besides, communist leaders, although they sometimes verbally assert that they are not opposed to religion, show themselves nevertheless, both by doctrine and by action, to be in reality enemies of God, of the true religion, and of the Church of Christ.

To No. 2 — In the negative, inasmuch as this is prohibited by law itself (of Canon 1399, Corpus Juris Canonici).

To No. 3 — In the negative, in accordance with the common principles governing refusal of the sacraments to those not having proper dispositions.

To No. 4 — In the affirmative.

And on the following Thursday, the 30th of the same month and year, His Holiness Pope Pius XII, when informed of the decision in the usual audience granted to His Excellency, the Most Reverend Assessor, approved and ordered to be published the above answers in the Acta Apostolicae Sedis.

Pius XII, Christmas Message, 1955

We reject communism as a social system by virtue of Christ's doctrine, and We have a particular obligation to proclaim the fundamental principles of natural law. For the same reason, We likewise reject the opinion that the Christian ought today to see communism as a phenomenon or a stage in the course of history, almost a necessary point in its evolution, and consequently to accept it as if it were decreed by Divine Providence.

But at the same time, We again warn Christians of the industrial age, in the spirit of Our immediate predecessors in the supreme pastoral and teaching office, against being satisfied with an anticommunism founded on slogan and on the defense of a liberty devoid of content. Rather We urge them to build up a society in which man's security rests on that moral order the necessity and implications of which We have often set forth, looking as it does to true human nature.

French Hierarchy, The Church in the Modern World, June, 1954

The Church has always refused to be associated with a political anti-communism that denies the existence of social injustice, which is, nevertheless, the real cause of communism. She reminds us that "all error contains an element of truth." To seek to improve the lot of the working classes, to suppress the very real abuses caused by the liberal economy, and to bring about an equitable distribution of wealth are undoubtedly perfectly legitimate objectives.

Addressing warm-hearted Catholics who may allow themselves to be attracted by the immediate aims of communism, the Hierarchy asks them to look further ahead and to try to understand the true dimensions of the problem and what is really at stake. The Church has condemned Marxist communism first of all because it is wrong in itself by virtue of its atheistic materialism, which permeates not only its doctrine but also its socio-economic principles, its tactics, propaganda, and activities. She has condemned it also because of the religious persecution it instigates wherever it can and, lastly because of the consequences it involves, especially for the human person and the family.

THE analysis of communism made in 1931 and 1937 by Pope Pius XI is, to say the least, a remarkable example of historical insight. To the Catholic, it is a tangible indication of divine guidance of the Church. Little that is written there needs to be changed to apply to the powerful communist empire of the late 1950's. Yet, at the time it was written, the world's keenest statesmen and political analysts considered the Soviet Union as a backward power, repulsive in its cruelty, but in no sense a menace to world peace and freedom. In view of what subsequently happened, the insight and foresight of the Pope were truly unique.

Now we judge communism in the light of astounding scientific and military achievements, sharp political victories, amazing success in subversion and psychological warfare, and notable gains achieved through economic penetration of developing nations. There is no need today to argue its power or emphasize the danger it poses to Christian civilization. Our need, rather, is to understand the movement and to see its strength as well as its weakness. Such understanding can be a first step toward safeguarding human freedom, and ultimately restoring freedom to the hundreds of millions under communist control. To achieve this understanding, we must first know communist theory, tactics, and practice.

The Theory of Communism. Communism is a system of dialectical materialism. It is based on the premise that matter is the only reality, with God, the soul, and spiritual values but fictions. Material forces dominate the evolution of the world. Most important of these are economic forces, since they determine man's ability to survive. In any society, the organized methods of production are the absolute determinants of that culture. Civil government, the family, the Church, and other social groups are merely by-products of economic organization.

This materialism is dialectical in the sense worked out by the German philosopher, Hegel. History is seen as a dynamic process, whereby groups of forces dominate a given period of time. But every action leads to an equal and opposite reaction. Applying dialectical materialism to the nineteenth-century world, Marx considered capitalism to be the dominant economic system which determined contemporary history. The heart of capitalism is the institution of private property, which enables a few persons to secure control of economic life. Property, of course, is fundamental, since it furnishes the means of existence for man. When property is in private hands, its owners thereby control the lives of other men, who are nonowners. They can force others to work for them at whatever wages the owners may choose. That such wages would be the minimum needed for subsistence was argued by the capitalist economist, Ricardo. Hence private property is essentially a means of exploitation. Economic value is created only by work, but the owners return to the workers only a fraction of what they produce. The remainder, the surplus value, is retained for the immense profits of the capitalists.

To safeguard this system of exploitation, owners have developed two institutions for repressing the proletariat, the non-owning workers. The first is the state, which through its various powers protects the property owner. Most important of these powers is the police force which cows the workers. The courts, law, and such institutions are but elaborate developments of police and military power. Moreover schools, the bourgeois press, and other opinion-forming agencies are tools of the capitalists. Even the family, in its present form, embodies the capitalist mentality. Monogamy and parental control of children are but extensions of the ownership principle. Hence civil society is but a protective integument for monopolistic owners.

The second institution created to defend property is organized religion, the opiate of the people. Religion is an anodyne which deadens the frustrations of the workers by promising them justice in another world. In the crude language of the Industrial Workers of the World (I.W.W. — Wobblies), it offers "pie in the sky, instead of pie on earth." Religion sanctions property ownership in its command: Thou shalt not steal. It teaches to its votaries meekness and submission. The other-world mentality robs them of the ambition to remedy abuses here and now. It is an ideal tool for the capitalists.

Nevertheless, the dialectical forces of history may not be denied. The process of exploitation creates the weapons whereby it will ultimately be abolished. First, it arouses in the workers an ever increasing sense of anger and resentment. They become embittered at their lot, the more so when they contrast it with the wealth and luxury secured by others with the fruits of their labor. The next step naturally follows. The workers are "disciplined, united, organized, by the very mechanism of the process of capitalist production itself." These workers, given solidarity by their oppressors, unite in a revolutionary upsurge. "Centralization of the means of production and socialization of labor at last reach a point where they become incompatible with their capitalist integument. This integument is burst asunder. The knell of capitalist private property sounds. The expropriators are expropriated."[1]

The communist party exists to aid in the class struggle and thereby accelerate processes of history. It must educate the workers to realize their oppression and the means of deliverance. It must take advantage of poverty and exploitation, but especially it must capitalize on the recurring depressions and imperialist wars which are inevitable in the existing system. The unemployed offer a fertile field for recruits. In pursuing this aim, the communists must not be deviated by the prospects of short-term reforms. While they may agitate for reforms, so as to win the allegiance of the workers, their demands must be insatiable, so that issues will always remain. This point is vital. Proletarian reform groups which would be satisfied with anything less than total revolution are traitors to the working class. They are more dangerous enemies than the capitalists themselves. The class struggle must be intensified, not mitigated.[2]

Since the struggle is world wide, communist organization must be international. From the beginning, communism took the form of various international movements. The best known was the Third International, also called the Comintern, which closely ruled various communist parties throughout the world. This movement was dissolved, at least ostensibly,

---

[1] Karl Marx, quoted in H. Laski, *Communism* (New York: Holt, 1927), p. 108.

[2] This element of communist theory is of vital importance for understanding communist tactics. Communists want issues, not reforms. American labor leaders and liberal legislators can cite scores of instances where our native communists killed reforms by making impossible demands or through propaganda which alienated middle-of-the-road groups. Noncommunist leftist movements, such as Social Democracy, understand this tactic and are far more bitter enemies of communists than are liberals or even conservative capitalists.

during World War II. It has not yet been replaced by a comparable organization of world communists. Yet the unity of action of various communist parties indicates that other means have been found to achieve centralized control of world communism.

Communist Tactics. The main function of international communism is to win over the oppressed workers and peasants and to prepare for a series of proletarian revolutions. Communist dictatorships are to be set up in order to liquidate the enemies of the people. This is an interim process, according to Marx. Once true socialism is achieved, the state will wither away, since there will be no need for it. Instead, the workers' soviets will rule, with each person contributing according to his ability, and receiving according to his need.

While Marxism as a theory enjoyed some successes throughout the world, it did not become a potent force until Vladimir Lenin perfected the tactics for revolutionary seizure of power. It is difficult to overstate the diabolical brilliance of Lenin. The world-wide success of his tactics is proof of their remarkable flexibility and appeal.

The center of all activity is the communist party. This is organized upon secret and conspiratorial lines, partly to avoid government repression, but also in part voluntarily. Secrecy aids subversion. At the same time it helps the party to obtain complete control over its members, since they are not subject to outside pressures. Internal organization of the party is dictatorial. Under its "democratic centralism" discussion is permitted prior to decisions, but once the ruling forces issue a command, it is absolute. Deviationists are summarily dismissed. Even drastic and contradictory changes in the party line must be accepted without questioning.

Under such strict control, recruiting is naturally a slow and careful process. There is no one type which could be called characteristic material for communism. Most of its recruits, however, fall into one of three groups: the seriously disgruntled, misled idealists, or ambitious opportunists. The first type is obvious material for a revolutionary movement. It includes victims of economic, racial, national, and religious or cultural discrimination. Many workers who become communists do so because of crass exploitation or bitter class-struggle experiences in trying to better economic conditions. In the United States, recruitment for this reason alone has not been too successful. The American party has achieved better results among middle-class and even occasional well-to-do persons who are victims of racial, religious, or cultural discrimination. Certain foreign-language groups are considered good prospects. Of the average seven thousand

American communists, about 80 per cent belong in minority groups of one type or other.

The idealists who become communists are often intellectuals. Their interest may be either negative, revulsion against oppression; or positive, attraction for a planned society or some features of Soviet communism. Published material in Canadian and American espionage cases indicates that misguided idealists play an important part in communist plans. The initial appeal is made in terms of social justice, freedom of science, peace, or some other exalted consideration. The victim is gradually led to believe that his ideals can be realized only under communism. This explains, in part, why high-paid and respected scientists and other intellectuals joined the Soviet espionage apparatus in England, Canada, and the United States.

A third class of recruits includes ambitious persons who feel that the communist party is a source of advancement or protection. Obvious examples are the former nazis, fascists, and collaborators in Europe who quickly joined their respective communist parties to gain immunity and power. In Latin America and India, many intellectuals find little opportunity to use their talents. Some embrace communism as the best hope for their future. When communist infiltration into government and labor in the United States was at its peak, many found a party card a real opportunity for advancement. The same was true, at certain times, in the literary and entertainment fields.

When a subject is brought into the party, he is given a thorough indoctrination in the principles of Marx and Lenin. What is even more important, he is hermetically isolated from the capitalist world. He is led to distrust all bourgeois sources of information and to cut off friendly contacts with noncommunists. With such complete dependence upon the party, even for his thoughts, he soon becomes a fanatic. This explains in part the zeal which provokes admiration even from the enemies of communism. Another explanation of communist fanaticism is in terms of Darwinian selection: only zealots are attracted to such an extreme system and survive its rigorous demands upon its members.

Much of the secret of communist success lies in its strict organization and iron discipline. It is axiomatic that an organized, disciplined minority can usually outmaneuver a disorganized majority. In addition, communists use the weapon of massive deceit, the principle of the "big lie." By constantly calling their opponents warmongers and aggressors, and by appropriating to themselves the banners of peace and democracy, they have been able to confuse a large portion of the world.

The small communist party multiplies its influence by many tried and proved devices. It acts openly in the "united-front" approach, whereby it joins with other organizations for common action for a special objective. It is hoped that in such campaigns the party will be able to take over the movement and thus lead the larger groups. As a minimum result, it can gain good will, contacts, and respectability. Moreover, it is then in a position to press for ever higher demands, precluding real reform but embittering other participants in the process.

A second approach is the method called "boring-from-within." In these cases, secret communists secure places in influential organizations, such as government, labor unions, representatives of minorities, and organs for propaganda, such as press, radio, the screen, publishers, and book-review publications. Here the minimum aim is influencing policy along communist lines. The maximum objective is capture and control of such groups.

A third tactic is the formation of "front organizations," or groups apparently noncommunist but secretly organized and controlled by the party, which aim at ostensibly sound objectives. The method used here involves the determining of a high-sounding aim, such as peace, democracy, or some social reform. Then a core of names of prominent but naïve persons is secured as the organizing committee. On this basis, more names are obtained and fund-raising is started. With funds and names, it is possible to secure publicity, pressure upon government, and like objectives. The success of this tactic is amazing. While it has been exposed time and again, and individuals involved have realized their error in particular cases, it remains a reliable device for multiplying communist effectiveness. There seems to be an inexhaustible fund of prominent persons, who feel that they must be on record in favor of every worthy cause, but too busy to look into the real control of the group or to take any active part in the administration of the movement.

In addition to these broad programs, special approaches are developed for various interest groups, such as labor, Negroes, youth, women, consumers, tenants, the unemployed, pacifists, religious organizations, scientists, lawyers, doctors, teachers, social workers, librarians, book readers, and even businessmen. Thousands of such organizations have been listed by American investigative agencies. The amount of time, energy, and money which goes into such work is unbelievable in relation to the small size of the Communist Party, U.S.A.

Communist tactics have achieved results which are almost beyond belief. In scores of nations they have reached positions of real power. They can influence public opinion and government policy, even when they are a small minority. Often they achieve political success through balance-of-power tactics, siding with the group which offers them the most promises. Even more remarkable is their tenacious hold upon their spheres of influence, even after public opinion has been revolted by Soviet expansionist tactics. Their power of adaptation and deception is unique.

Soviet Communism. Communist theory was put into practice, for the first time on a large scale, in Russia. In 1917, the Russia of the Tsars gave way to a democratic government, which was then overthrown by the Union of Soviet Socialist Republics. At its very beginning, the communists put into effect their theories both of violent revolution and of contempt for moderate or even mildly radical reform. The actual communist revolt was not against the Tsars, but against the moderate Social Democratic government of Kerensky, which had earlier replaced the monarchy. The well-disciplined communist forces under Lenin instigated the second or "October" revolution.

Soviet conduct may be viewed under three aspects: economic organization, internal political life, and foreign policy. In each of these three spheres the general principles of Marx have been observed, but with strategic and tactical modifications by his successors. The path toward their ultimate goal has at times been brutally direct, but at other times devious and roundabout, with many diversions and even retreats.

In the economic sphere, after uncertain beginnings, certain definite policies began to emerge. Agriculture was forcibly collectivized, partly in the hope of more efficient production, but mainly to liquidate the last segments of private ownership. Industrial activity was controlled by a series of five-year plans, with primary emphasis upon heavy industry and scientific research. This concentration provided an excellent base for military power, but it left little for the Soviet consumer. Housing, clothing, and food have been consistently inadequate.

Production generally operates under centralized control, although some local autonomy has been promised. A centralized planning agency works out production quotas and prices. State banks finance individual factories in accord with the master plan. Thus far the factory managers have had little discretion in their operations, but they are rewarded for exceeding quotas and may be punished for falling behind. As a result, there is a tendency to exploit workers or to skimp on quality in order to obtain the quantity demanded. An exception to this rule is the production of military and scientific goods. Usually the best workers, engineers, and managers are assigned to this field. Results have been correspondingly good.

The Soviet worker has only limited freedom. For a long time, it was virtually impossible for him to quit a job without permission from the party. Even though this rule has been relaxed, housing difficulties tend to keep him in one place. Poor as his accommodations may be, he at least is certain of them so long as he remains with his current job. Wages vary according to the type of work and individual accomplishment. But even the better paid manual workers in the Soviet Union have the lowest living standards in all Europe. Because of this most wives also work. Yet the possession of money does not automatically insure food and clothing. Often stores are out of supplies. Long queues are the rule rather than the exception for many purchases. Nor can workers appeal to unions for redress of grievances, since their unions are party-controlled and aim to spur production rather than help their members. Strikes are virtually unheard of in the Soviet Union, although they have occurred in some of the satellite states.

In addition to technically free workers, there are slave workers. Their current number and status are uncertain. Under Stalin nearly twenty million workers lived in utmost misery in various slave-labor camps. Most of these were victims of political purges or scapegoats for failures in different projects. Since the death of Stalin, there are indications that purge and deportation tactics are less frequently used or even abandoned. By contrast, the Chinese People's Republic has millions in slave-labor camps. Conditions are fully as bad as those of the worst Soviet camps of the Stalinist era. In addition, the communes, with separate barracks for men, women, children, and the aged, plus communal kitchens, are a form of barbarism so terrible that even European communists are revolted by it. They are 1984 brought to life, almost as if Mao had read Orwell's novel and took it for a blueprint instead of a satire. Never has slavery been so total and inhuman as in China in 1959.

Farm policies have been subject to some experimentation since Stalin's death, but the basic pattern has not changed. New state farms were opened in hitherto untilled areas of Siberia, with mixed success. In older farming areas, the collective farm is still the mainstay for food production. However, current plans point in the direction of more and more state farms, with the peasant deprived of what few possessions he had under the collective farm.

The economic results of these policies have been uneven. The Soviet Union has been able to achieve excellent results in high-priority areas, such as military production. Production for civilian use has been inadequate in quantity and poor in quality. Nikita Khrushchev, however, has promised to equal or excel capitalist living standards by the early 1960's. It is difficult to see how this can be achieved in a short time, unless there is a massive diversion of economic effort from the military field to the civilian economy. There are no current indications that such a shift is being planned.

In the internal political sphere, conditions apparently are in a state of transition, with the direction uncertain. After Stalin died, the seemingly monolithic Soviet system exhibited severe internal strains. Apparently strong demands for some economic betterment and a minimum of civil rights were being made. The new managerial class, communist bureaucrats, leaders of the armed forces, intellectuals, and students indicated dissatisfaction with the police state. As a result, the power of the secret police became less evident. Leaders were purged from office, but their lives and freedom were not threatened. But the duration of this display of "Soviet legality" is unpredictable. In favor of its continuance are the demands for freedom made by important groups in the Soviet Union. Against it is the logic of dictatorship that brooks no opposition. Death is the only permanent way to silence potential rivals or enemies of the ruling faction.

Even relaxations from the iron rule of the Stalin era have not given Soviet citizens any appreciable advance toward democratic rights. There is practically no real freedom of speech or assembly. The state has a monopoly of press, radio, and education. Propaganda and indoctrination are still normal features of Soviet life. Persecution of religion in the U.S.S.R. is not so blatant as before, but the state-controlled Church exists only on sufferance. Other religious groups barely survive. The Catholic Church has been bitterly persecuted in the satellite nations, along with Lutherans and Jews.

There are good reasons to believe that tyranny, terror, and total subjection are essential elements of the communist system. This does not mean that no easing of the burdens is possible. But a communist dictator faces a terrible dilemma in this regard. If he yields to pressures from dissatisfied groups, he faces the possibility that concessions may lead to ever increasing demands, until the system is radically changed. Should he fail to yield, there is always the possibility of revolt by the armed forces, seizure of power by an opposing faction, or the breakdown of a complex economic system because of passive resistance. Communism had to educate its people to develop its military and economic power. It may find it difficult to control its restless intelligentsia. This dilemma may prove the fatal weakness of communism.

The Soviet Union and World Communism. Prior to World War II, the Soviet Union endeavored to spread communism almost exclusively by subversion and propaganda. While it was often successful in gaining prestige and influence by such methods, it did not bring into being any permanent communist governments. The war changed the picture tremendously. Poland and the Baltic states were annexed by direct conquest. The Balkans were taken over by subversion backed by the forces of the Red army. China, weakened by its long war with Japan and deprived of strong aid and guidance by the United States, could not resist the attacks of its communist armies. As a result of these events, the number of victims of communism increased to six times the prewar figure. One third of the human race, one billion persons, was in the shadow of the Red flag.

Even though the Soviet Union became the greatest colonial power in the world, it successfully exploited the resentments of former colonial nations. This third of the world's population generally proclaimed neutrality in the struggle between communism and its opponents. Often this neutrality was only apparent, as the new rulers listened to the siren song of Moscow. Agitation by internal communist parties, clever Soviet propaganda, judicious economic aid, and the appeal of the rapid industrialization of the Soviet Union all proved potent arguments in many capitals of Asia and Africa. Intervention in the Arab-Israeli struggle gave the U.S.S.R. a foothold in the strategic Near East and its prizes of oil and the Suez Canal. The cumulative effect of these successes left its impact in Latin America. It created strains in the various defensive alliances set up to counter the Soviet threat. While the West concentrated upon missiles and thermonuclear weapons, the communist world threatened to win most of mankind without firing a shot. Its political, economic, and subversive moves were paying increasing dividends.

Paradoxically, while communism was scoring external successes, it was meeting with increasing internal difficulties. In 1956, Hungary staged an ill-fated revolt that was soon crushed by the Red army. Poland tried a more subtle approach, accepting Soviet control of its foreign policy, but demanding internal freedom to seek "its own path to socialism." First steps in this path were concessions to farmers, workers, intellectuals, and to the Church. A considerable degree of freedom of speech, assembly, and religion was granted. Unfortunately, the severe economic exploitation of Poland by the Soviet Union made it impossible for the Polish government to raise the living standards of its people. Furthermore, there were both external and internal pressures upon the Polish government to revert toward more classical communist methods. The result has been considerable uncertainty as to the reality and permanence of Polish "independence."

By contrast, the Chinese People's Republic seems to be developing a different type of independence. It gives the public impression of following a strong "Stalinist" line at the time that liberalizing trends seemed to have the ascendancy in the Soviet Union. Apparently the immense numbers of Chinese, and the strategic position of Red China in relation to Asia, give the rulers of this land considerable power and status in the ruling communist hierarchy. The Chinese People's Republic must be considered a partner rather than a satellite in relation to the Soviet Union.

Soviet emphasis upon penetration of developing nations did not preclude it from seeking to influence citizens of nations allied against it. In addition to native communist parties, it has a number of international groups formed along familiar "front-organization" lines. There are the World Federation of Trade Unions and various groups and congresses for youth, women, intellectuals, the promotion of peace, agitation against nuclear tests (by Western nations), and encouragement of trade between East and West. Often these groups have had considerable success in making propaganda and confusing public opinion in free nations. For example, the 1957 World Youth Congress not only enlisted some American delegates, but it sent these delegates to Peiping in defiance of American passport policy. This fits in with the technique of agitation, or propaganda through action.

Some persons consider proposals for cultural and scientific exchanges between East and West in the category just described. This, however, is debatable. While much of the initiative for such moves came from Moscow, many intelligent opponents of communism hold that the West should welcome these opportunities. They agree that the Soviet seeks both propaganda advantages and scientific and economic information from such visits. Nevertheless, it is argued that the budding demands for freedom in the Soviet world would be fostered by contacts with the free world. In view of the fact that the Soviet seems to be able to get most of the information it seeks on American scientific and economic life, there seems to be little to lose from person-to-person exchanges. It is not consistent, on the one hand, to complain about the Iron Curtain erected about the Soviet Union and, on the other, to react adversely when the curtain is lifted, even partially. The more that the communist world sees the fruits of freedom, the more likely it is that internal pressures for change will increase.

Communism in the United States. The Communist Party, U.S.A., plays its appointed role in the international communist conspiracy. It is hardly expected to arrange for the revolutionary overthrow of the United States government. But it can help recruit espionage agents; endeavor to infiltrate government, labor, the entertainment and communication fields, and similar power centers; and devise methods for confusing and influencing American public opinion.

The current size of the communist party here is not accurately known, but the best estimates place its strength at about 7000 members. This is the lowest total in many years, although top membership never exceeded 100,000, even in the palmiest days. In addition to formal members, there are fellow travelers — persons who think and act like communists, but who are not actually subject to party discipline. Next there are the relatively large number of individuals who can often be duped by communist causes. Usually such persons are susceptible only in one or two areas, such as peace, labor policy, or racial issues. The number of fellow travelers and dupes cannot be estimated accurately. The director of the Federal Bureau of Investigation often states that there are ten fellow travelers for every party member. It is doubtful, however, that any constant ratio exists. Unfavorable events, such as the Korean War, the denunciation of Stalin, revelation of Soviet anti-Semitism, and the Hungarian revolt, tend to cut sharply the number of fellow travelers and dupes. The reverse is also true, as was noted during World War II, when Soviet popularity reached a peak in this country.

Recruitment of members and tactics for achieving communist goals follow the lines outlined earlier in this chapter. Peaks of Soviet achievement in the United States were the years 1935–1939, when the united-front program against Hitler was in effect; 1941–1947, the period of American alliance with Russia; and 1954–1956, when Stalin's successors seemed to be following a more reasonable policy. Low points were 1939–1941, because of the Hitler-Stalin alliance; 1947–1954, when the Soviets took over much of Eastern Europe and instigated the Korean War; and the period following the Hungarian revolt in 1956.

The results of a climate favorable to communism included: strong penetration of the entertainment, writing, and communication fields during most of the period 1935–1947; substantial power in the Congress of Industrial Organizations, especially during the years 1941–1947; successful infiltration into government, starting about 1935 and declining sharply after the congressional investigations of 1947-1950; and highly efficient espionage operations, particularly during World War II.

When the climate became unfavorable, communists did not slacken their activities. They merely changed emphasis. Their protection against domestic harassment was a stepped-up but undercover campaign in the civil-liberties field. They constantly attacked congressional investigators, with emphasis on the freewheeling methods of Senator Joseph McCarthy. Through legal actions they were successful in curtailing Justice Department prosecutions under the Smith Act. Execution of federal government loyalty programs became more difficult, as many persons concentrated upon the flaws and limitations of various procedures. Unfortunately, there were excesses in some investigative and loyalty procedures that gave a certain plausibility to attacks upon security measures. These attacks in turn coincided with increasing national awareness of civil-liberties problems, culminating in a series of Supreme Court decisions in 1957. Some of these decisions had the effect of hampering existing procedures in the investigative and security fields. No serious student of the situation credits the communists with creating this climate of opinion, but they certainly showed their shrewdness and sense of timing in capitalizing upon an issue that afforded them maximum protection in their activities.

Likewise, communists had considerable success in pushing issues such as the banning of nuclear tests, recognition of the Chinese People's Republic, expansion of trade between East and West, disarmament proposals favorable to the Soviets, and suggestions for direct negotiations between the United States and the U.S.S.R., to the exclusion of our allies. They have not yet succeeded in getting these proposals adopted, but they have helped in getting them discussed at the highest levels. Of course, many of these views are sincerely held by noncommunists and even anticommunists. The reason communist influence is attributed to these occurences is a sequence of events which happens too often to be merely coincidental. Thus, an issue (such as banning nuclear tests as a unilateral Western action) is first raised in the communist press. Next it is taken up by commentators and writers who have consistent fellow-traveling records. Then a committee is formed, normally directed by a fellow traveler or even a concealed communist. Finally public agitation becomes intense, causing strong pressures upon our government to adopt the policy in question.

It is a paradox that the communist party can have any status at all in the United States, considering the universal rejection of communism and fear of the Soviet Union among the American public. Communist achievements can be explained in two ways. First, there is the extraordinary talent of communists for propaganda and agitation. They have shown real genius in presenting issues cleverly and obtaining sympathizers who have no knowledge of the real source of these views. Second, communists have benefited from the habit of many Americans of going to extremes. Few among us seem to have the patience for calm and careful study of this problem. The result is that some opponents of communism make exaggerated and inaccurate statements. This creates sympathy in the liberal community and makes it susceptible to the civil-rights arguments raised by the communists. In the ensuing clash between the opposing camps, communists are often free to work with a minimum of hindrance.

In addition to these general considerations, there is an important observation that applies to the powerful, opinion-making intellectual community in the United States. This group has, for various historical reasons, been inclined toward liberal views. It has been more friendly toward socialism or even communism than it has been toward other forms of statism. Many important writers and commentators, whatever their views today, had sympathetic contacts with the left during the 1930's and 1940's. For this reason, they are less than happy with government investigations and related programs directed against erstwhile associates. They are quick to see the good points of Soviet policy and ever hopeful that methods of collaboration and accommodation can be found. As a result, the "far left" has a status of respectability that is astonishing when one soberly considers the fundamentally reactionary nature of communism.

The Free World Fights Communism. The impact of communism upon the world is so many-sided that no single method of countering it is likely to be successful. For example, it is relatively easy in the United States to answer Marxist theory. Our economic system is proof that a free, private economy can raise the living standards of workers. It can achieve sound democratic remedies for abuses. Such arguments are less effective in some parts of Europe, and in much of Asia, Africa, and Latin America. These areas see too much of the nineteenth-century brand of capitalism, with exploitation and sharp contrasts between the very poor and the enormously wealthy, to be impressed by arguments against the class struggle and the theory of surplus value. Vigorous social reform and real efforts to raise living standards are needed in these areas, if Marxism is to be countered.

Again, in the United States the argument that communism sacrifices essential spiritual values is fully appreciated. Even were the Soviet Union to exceed our own living standards, we would consider the cost too high, because freedom is more prized than luxury. But in nations in which the average man has few freedoms, except in theory, he may take a different view of communist propaganda. Even proof that communism is materialistic and godless does not always have the impact it might have. Many persons consider our own culture as sensual and materialistic. Hence they feel that there is little difference between communist and free powers in this regard. The free world needs more sensitive information services and more extensive programs for educating foreign students and exchanging visitors, if it is to win the war for the minds of uncommitted peoples.

But the struggle against communism is not merely a struggle against an ideology. We must never forget the immense military, diplomatic, economic, and subversive resources of the Soviet Union and related communist nations. The military threat is obvious, and the free world has reacted along two major lines. It has endeavored to keep equally strong or stronger armed forces, with nuclear weapons and missiles to deliver them. It has reinforced its defensive position by a world-wide series of alliances and pacts. At the same time, it has remained willing to seek disarmament and peaceful settlement of differences. Thus, the communist world is confronted with the choice between massive retaliation against aggression and the willingness of other nations to work out a durable and just peace.

The diplomatic, economic, and subversive offensive of communism is more difficult to meet. Communists can be ruthless in exploiting complex disputes, such as Arab-Israeli tensions or various colonial situations, whereas their opponents often find it difficult to unite on a policy regarding such problems. Communists can use trade and aid as weapons, while the West is often internally divided on economic measures. Moreover, Western measures of technical assistance to developing nations have been nonpolitical. By contrast, communists fully exploit any aid they give. The noncommunist world does not have its agents and native parties in the strategic areas which the communists are trying to win over. But the communists have highly organized and well-trained communist natives as their allies in seeking to subvert newly developing nations. Great resourcefulness, intelligence, and flexibility are needed to counter this infiltration. One promising method involves stepped-up programs of exchange of persons and student scholarships for Asia and Africa. The free world should train future leaders in developing nations and give them a full understanding of the values of democracy and freedom.

In countering communism, we would make a mistake were we to ignore the small but effective communist party in the United States. Loyalty and security programs, exposure of communist tactics and propaganda, and properly conducted congressional investigations still remain necessary. There are too many evidences of past and even present communist successes for us to remain complacent. But we must approach this task with sanity and moderation. There seems to be little justification, for example, for efforts to dig up past communist connections of persons who presently have broken with the movement. Such tactics create strong resentments and may well explain why many liberals are prejudiced against anticommunist programs. The test of any security program or investigation effort should be the present views of a person and the present security of the United States. Mistakes made in the past, particularly when the climate of opinion was vastly different, should not, without serious justification, be judged by present-day standards.

Likewise, it would be a mistake to ignore the possibilities for change within the communist empire. There are evidences of internal strains within the Soviet Union and its satellites. It is unlikely that any of these pressures will lead to successful revolt, unless the Soviet army were to rise up and take charge. But astute diplomacy, the wise use of exchange programs, and the acceptance of every opportunity to present the views of free nations to those within the communist world could do much to intensify pressures for greater freedom. If there is any chance that communism can be changed from within, the opportunity should be seized.

No easy task confronts the world as it faces a powerful and ruthless movement for world expansion of communism. It can be countered only by strength, leadership, intelligence, and sacrifice. The Christian world must meet its greatest challenge. Courage and dedication alone will meet this challenge and save the world from apocalyptic ruin.

READINGS*

J. Messner, Social Ethics, pp. 106–109, 930–934.
F. J. Sheed, Communism and Man.
R. N. Carew Hunt, The Theory and Practice of Communism.
J. Villain, L'Enseignement social de l'Église, Vol. I, pp. 188–224.
Social Order: Douglas Hyde, "Witness," October, 1952; Geza B. Grosschmid, "Communism vs. Religion," September, 1953; Cyril A. Zebot, "Communism Unmasked," October, 1957; Cyril A. Zebot and others, "Views on Communism and the Soviet Union," June, 1958.

* For further readings, see List No. 5 in the Appendix.

Chapter VII

THE IDEAL SOCIAL ORDER

CO-OPERATION, NOT CONFLICT

Leo XIII, Rerum Novarum

28. It is a capital evil with respect to the question We are discussing to take for granted that the one class of society is of itself hostile to the other, as if nature had set rich and poor against each other to fight fiercely in implacable war. This is so abhorrent to reason and truth that the exact opposite is true; for just as in the human body the different members harmonize with one another, whence arises that disposition of parts and proportion in the human figure rightly called symmetry, so likewise nature has commanded in the case of the state that the two classes mentioned should agree harmoniously and should properly form equally balanced counterparts to each other. Each needs the other completely: neither capital can do without labor, nor labor without capital. Concord begets beauty and order in things. Conversely, from perpetual strife there must arise disorder accompanied by bestial cruelty. But for putting an end to conflict and for cutting away its very roots, there is wondrous and multiple power in Christian institutions.

33. But the Church, with Jesus Christ as her teacher and leader, seeks greater things than this; namely, by commanding something more perfect, she aims at joining the two social classes to each other in closest neighborliness and friendship.

Pius XI, Quadragesimo Anno

39. Rather did our Predecessor draw from the Gospel and, therefore, from an ever living and life-giving fountain, teachings capable of greatly mitigating, if not immediately terminating, that deadly internal struggle which is rending the family of mankind.

Pius XII, Address to Catholic Employers, May 7, 1949

We have just made reference to the preoccupations of those who are engaged in industrial production. Mistaken and disastrous in its consequences is the prejudice, alas! too widely held, which sees in these problems an irreducible clash of rival interests. The opposition is only apparent. In the economic domain management and labor are linked in a community of action and interest. To disregard this mutual bond, to strive to break it, can only betray a pretension to blind and preposterous despotism. Employers and workers are not implacable adversaries. They are co-operators in a common task. They eat, so to speak, at the same table, seeing that they must live, in the last analysis, from the gross or net profits of the national economy. Each receives his income, and in this regard their mutual relations do not in any way imply that one is at the service of the other.

To receive one's wage is a prerogative of the personal dignity of anyone who makes his productive contribution in one form or another, as employer or laborer, toward the output of the nation's economy. In the accounting of private industry salary totals may be listed under costs to the employer. But in national economy there is only one type of costs, which consists in the national resources utilized with a view to national production, and which must, in consequence, be constantly replenished.

From this it follows that both parties are interested in seeing to it that the costs of national production are in proportion to its output. But since the interest is common, why should it not manifest itself in a common outward expression? Why should it not be allowable to assign to the workers a just share of responsibility in the establishment and development of the national economy? Especially today when the scarcity of capital and the difficulty of international exchange are paralyzing the free flow of expenditure on national production?

ORGANIZED ECONOMIC LIFE

Pius XI, Quadragesimo Anno

81. First and foremost, the state and every good citizen ought to look to and strive toward this end: that the conflict between the hostile classes be abolished and harmonious co-operation of the Industries and Professions be encouraged and promoted.

82. The social policy of the state, therefore, must devote itself to the re-establishment of the Industries and Professions. In actual fact, human society now, for the reason that it is founded on classes with divergent aims and hence opposed to one another and therefore inclined to enmity and strife, continues to be in a violent condition and is unstable and uncertain.

83. But complete cure will not come until this opposition has been abolished and well-ordered members of the social body — Industries and Professions — are constituted in which men may have their place, not according to the position each has in the labor market but according to the respective social functions which each performs. For under nature's guidance it comes to pass that just as those who are joined together by nearness of habitation establish towns, so those who follow the same Industry or Profession — whether in the economic or other field — form guilds or associations, so that many are wont to consider these self-governing organizations, if not essential, at least natural to civil society.

84. Because order, as St. Thomas well explains, is unity arising from the harmonious arrangement of many objects, a true, genuine social order demands that the various members of a society be united together by

some strong bond. This unifying force is present not only in the producing of goods or the rendering of services — in which the employers and employees of an identical Industry or Profession collaborate jointly — but also in that common good, to achieve which all Industries and Professions together ought, each to the best of its ability, to co-operate amicably. And this unity will be the stronger and more effective, the more faithfully individuals and the Industries and Professions themselves strive to do their work and excel in it.

85. It is easily deduced from what has been said that the interests common to the whole Industry or Profession should hold first place in these guilds. The most important among these interests is to promote the co-operation in the highest degree of each industry and profession for the sake of the common good of the country. Concerning matters, however, in which particular points, involving advantage or detriment to employers or workers, may require special care and protection, the two parties, when these cases arise, can deliberate separately or as the situation requires reach a decision separately.

97. What We have taught about the reconstruction and perfection of social order can surely in nowise be brought to realization without reform of morality, the very record of history clearly shows. For there was a social order once which, although indeed not perfect or in all respects ideal, nevertheless, met in a certain measure the requirements of right reason, considering the conditions and needs of the time. If that order has long since perished, that surely did not happen because the order could not have accommodated itself to changed conditions and needs by development and by a certain expansion, but rather because men, hardened by too much love of self, refused to open the order to the increasing masses as they should have done, or because, deceived by allurements of a false freedom and other errors, they became impatient of every authority and sought to reject every form of control.

Pius XI, On Atheistic Communism

32. The means of saving the world of today from the lamentable ruin into which amoral liberalism has plunged us, are neither the class struggle nor terror, nor yet the autocratic abuse of state power, but rather the infusion of social justice and the sentiment of Christian love into the social-economic order. We have indicated how a sound prosperity is to be restored according to the true principles of a sane corporative system which respects the proper hierarchic structure of society; and how all the occupational groups should be focused into a harmonious unity inspired by the principle of the common good. And the genuine and chief function of public and civil authority consists precisely in the efficacious furthering of this harmony and co-ordination of all social forces.

54. If, therefore, We consider the whole structure of economic life, as We have already pointed out in Our Encyclical Quadragesimo Anno, the reign of mutual collaboration between justice and charity in social-economic relations can only be achieved by a body of professional and interprofessional organizations, built on solidly Christian foundations, working together to effect, under forms adapted to different places and circumstances, what has been called the Corporation.

Pius XII, To Italian Workers, March 11, 1945

As for "the democratization of economy," it is equally endangered by monopolies — that is, by the economic tyranny of an anonymous conglomeration of private capital — and by the preponderant power of organized masses, ready to use their power to the detriment of justice and the rights of others.

The time has come to repudiate empty phrases, and to attempt to organize the forces of the people on a new basis; to raise them above the distinction between employers and would-be workers, and to realize that higher unity which is a bond between all those who co-operate in production, formed by their solidarity in the duty of working together for the common good and filling together the needs of the community. If this solidarity is extended to all branches of production, if it becomes the foundation for a better economic system, it will lead the working classes to obtain honestly their share of responsibility in the direction of the national economy. Thus, thanks to such harmonious co-ordination and co-operation; thanks to this closer unity of labor with the other elements of economic life, the worker will receive, as a result of his activity, a secure remuneration, sufficient to meet his needs and those of his family, with spiritual satisfaction and a powerful incentive toward self-improvement.

Pius XII, Letter to Semaines Sociales, July 18, 1947

Over and above the distinction between employer and employee, which threatens more seriously every day to become a pitiless separation, there is human labor itself: the work to be done, the job to which every man contributes something vital and personal, with a view to supplying society with goods and services adequate to its needs. It lies in the very nature of labor, understood in this sense, to draw men together in a genuine and intimate union, and to restore form and structure to a society which has become shapeless and unstable. This in turn would infuse new life into the relations between society and the state.

Pius XII, To Catholic Employers, May 7, 1949

Our Predecessor of imperishable memory, Pius XI, had suggested the practical and timely prescription for this community of interest in the nation's economic enterprise when he recommended in his Encyclical Quadragesimo Anno "occupational organization" for the various branches of production. Nothing, indeed, appeared to him more suited to bring economic Liberalism under control than the enactment, for the social economy, of a public-law statute based precisely on the common responsibility which is shared by all those who take part in production. This feature of the encyclical stirred up a host of objections. Some saw in it a concession to modern political trends, while for others it meant a return to the Middle Ages. It would have been incomparably more sensible to lay aside the flimsy prejudices of the past and to get down to work sincerely and courageously to make the proposal, with its many practical applications, a living reality.

Pastoral Letter, 1919

In his pronouncement on Labor [Rerum Novarum] Pope Leo XIII describes the advantages to be derived by both employer and employee from "associations and organizations which draw the two classes more closely together." Such associations are especially needed at the present time. While the labor union or trade union has been, and still is, necessary in the struggle of the workers for fair wages and fair conditions of employment, we have to recognize that its history, methods, and objects have made it essentially a militant organization. The time seems now to have arrived when it should be, not supplanted, but supplemented by associations or conferences, composed jointly of employers and employees, which will place emphasis upon the common interests rather than the divergent aims of the two parties, upon co-operation rather

than conflict. Through such arrangements, all classes would be greatly benefited. The worker would participate in those matters of industrial management which directly concern him and about which he possesses helpful knowledge; he would acquire an increased sense of personal dignity and personal responsibility, take greater interest and pride in his work, and become more efficient and more contented. The employer would have the benefit of willing co-operation from, and harmonious relations with, his employees. The consumer, in common with employer and employee, would share in the advantages of larger and steadier production. In a word, industry would be carried on as a co-operative enterprise for the common good, and not as a contest between two parties for a restricted product.

American Hierarchy, The Christian in Action, 1948

Catholic social philosophy has a constructive program for this organic development of economic life. Pope Pius XI, rounding out the social principles formulated by Leo XIII, laid down the broad outlines of this program seventeen years ago. In line with that constructive program we advocate freely organized co-operation between the accredited representatives of capital and labor in each industry and in the economy as a whole under the supervision but not the control of government. The agencies of this freely organized co-operation have been called by various names: Occupational Groups, Vocational Groups,

or more recently, Industry Councils. American Catholic students of the social encyclicals have expressed their preference for the name "Industry Councils" to designate the basic organs of a Christian and American type of economic democracy into which they would like to see our economic system progressively evolve. This evolution can come only as the fruit of painstaking study and effort to safeguard, in justice and charity, the rightful interests of property and the rightful interests of labor in the pursuit of the dominant interest of all, which is the common good.

A FLEXIBLE PROGRAM

Leo XIII, Rerum Novarum

76. Furthermore, if citizens have free right to associate, as in fact they do, they also must have the right freely to adopt the organization and the rules which they judge most appropriate to achieve their purpose. We do not feel that the precise character in all details, which the aforementioned direction and organization of associations ought to have, can be determined by fast and fixed rules, since this is a matter to be decided rather in the light of the temperament of each people, of experiment and practice, of the nature and character of the work, of the extent of trade and commerce, and of other circumstances of a material and temporal kind all of which must be carefully considered.

St. Pius X, Il Fermo Proposito

A certain freedom of organization should be allowed them, for it is not possible when many persons meet together, that all should be modeled on the same pattern or follow one single direction. Their organization should spring spontaneously from the works themselves; otherwise they will be like buildings of fine architecture, but without solid foundations, and therefore quite unstable.

It is also necessary to take into account the natural disposition of separate populations. Different usages and tendencies are found in different places. The important thing is to have a good foundation of solid principles, maintained with earnestness and constancy, and if this be the case, the method and form of the various works will be only accidental.

Pius XI, Quadragesimo Anno

86. The teaching of Leo XIII on the form of political government, namely, that men are free to choose whatever form they please, provided that proper regard is had for the requirements of justice and of the common good, is equally applicable in due proportion, it is hardly necessary to say, to the guilds of the various Industries and Professions.

87. Moreover, just as inhabitants of a town are wont to found associations with the widest diversity of purposes, which each is quite free to join or not, so those engaged in the same industry or profession will combine with one another into associations equally free for purposes connected in some manner with the pursuit of the calling itself. Since these free associations are clearly and lucidly explained by Our Predecessor of illustrious memory, We consider it enough to emphasize this one point: People are quite free not only to found such associations which are a matter of private order and private right, but also in respect to them "freely to adopt the organization and the rules which they judge most appropriate to achieve their purpose." The same freedom must be asserted for founding associations that go beyond the boundaries of individual callings. And may these free organizations now flourishing and rejoicing in

their salutary fruits, set before themselves the task of preparing the way, in conformity with the mind of Christian social teaching, for those larger and more important guilds,

Industries and Professions, which We mentioned before, and make every possible effort to bring them to realization.

Code of Social Principles

82. If authority is necessary in the profession to regulate the activity of its members, it is still more necessary that there be a supreme authority over all the professions, with power to regulate their mutual relations and to direct their activity towards the common good. The social order, therefore, requires interprofessional organization on regional, national, and even international lines.

83. Experience shows that vocational groups are exposed to a grave danger: induced by a certain group selfishness, they tend to forget and to neglect their chief duty, which is to work together as effectively as possible for the general welfare of the country. Hence a just relationship of dependence should be established and maintained between the state, guardian of this welfare, and the vocational groups. Vocational organization should relieve the state of many tasks which at present weigh heavily upon it, without, however, absorbing or weakening it, but rather perfecting and strengthening it.

84. Once the vocational bodies have been established, three tasks will remain to be accomplished: (i) To unite kindred associations into federations; (ii) To gather together the vocational groups and federations under one supreme vocational authority; (iii) To bestow on this supreme authority the powers required for its purpose and thus to reach the culminating point towards which the vocational organization tends and in which it ought to find its full realization.

85. Yet, in order to be effective, they will have to adapt themselves to national temperament, to traditions, to the particular needs of each country and, at their beginning, to what occupational elements already exist. In the same manner, within each vocational group, account must be taken of the particular needs of that occupation.

86. Vocational organization does not exclude the freedom of trade unions and employers' associations.

THE PRINCIPLE OF SUBSIDIARITY

Leo XIII, Rerum Novarum

20. Wherefore, assuming, of course, that those limits be observed which are fixed by its immediate purpose, the family assuredly possesses rights, at least equal with those of civil society, in respect to choosing and employing the things necessary for its protection and its just liberty. We

say "at least equal" because, inasmuch as domestic living together is prior both in thought and in fact to uniting into a polity, it follows that its rights and duties are also prior and more in conformity with nature.

Pius XI, Quadragesimo Anno

79. Just as it is gravely wrong to take from individuals what they can accomplish by their own initiative and industry and give it to the community, so also it is an injustice and at the same time a grave evil and disturbance of right order to assign to a greater and higher association what lesser and subordinate organizations can do. For every social activity ought of its very nature to furnish help to the members of the body social, and never destroy and absorb them.

80. The supreme authority of the state ought, therefore, to let subordinate groups handle matters and concerns of lesser importance, which would otherwise dissipate its efforts greatly. Thereby the state will more freely, powerfully, and effectively do all those things that belong to it alone because it alone can do them: directing, watching, urging, restraining, as occasion requires and necessity demands. Therefore, those in power should be sure that the more perfectly a graduated order is kept among the various associations, in observance of the principle of "subsidiary function," the stronger social authority and effectiveness will be and the happier and more prosperous the condition of the state.

Pius XII, Letter to Semaines Sociales, July 18, 1947

On the other hand, it is clearly our bounden duty today, when the former propensity for the "hands-off" system of *laissez faire* shows serious signs of weakening, to beware of plunging to the opposite extreme. In organizing production, we must guarantee full weight and directive influence to the principle, advanced time and again in the social teaching of the Church, according to which the activity and services of society must play a merely "subsidiary" role, aiding or supplementing the activity of the individual, the family, and the profession.

SOCIAL ORDER AND THE UNITED STATES

G. Gundlach, S.J., The Social Question, Essen, Fall, 1951

The Church believes — as follows from *Quadragesimo Anno* — that with the idea of the "vocational order" it shows to the anticapitalistic tendencies of our age a positive road which avoids the negative and pseudo-solutions of socialism or communism. The necessity to walk this road can be denied only by those who believe that the free market economy could be saved by providing for judicial authority against the positions of power in the market. Such a course may seem still possible in a country like the United States, where the spaciousness of the territory and the abundance of natural resources still allow it to circumvent all frictions of a more serious character, or easily to overcome the harm done by them. But over there the anticapitalistic tendencies are not yet powerful either; an almost naïve trust in unlimited progress still holds its sway there; as a consequence, there exist neither the real nor the moral prerequisites for a true understanding of the idea of the "vocational order," and still less for its realization.

*   *   *

The social doctrine of the Church provides, as Pope Pius XII pronounced only last year, that employers and employees shall participate on a footing of equality in the suprafirm functions of the regional and vocational groups.

*   *   *

. . . For the vocational order — as a framework for a free market economy — assumes firms which, at least in principle, are anchored in the right of private property and with which society interferes only in a co-ordinating way. But under the conditions that now exist, suprafirm organs will mean a dual function of the union and, at best, provide new jobs for new people.

THE social teaching of the Church is clear and definite in regard to the nature of man and society, the purpose of economic life, and the virtues which should govern man the producer. It rejects both individualism and statism as totally inadequate to organize economic life according to God's plan for mankind. Instead, Pope Pius XI outlines a completely different approach to economic society.

The papal plan, in essence, calls for an organization of economic life, and indeed all social life, in terms of the common interests and goals of all producers and families. Workers and employers in each industry and profession would band together to co-operate for their own mutual interests and for the common good of the country. When this is accomplished, the economic system would reach its maximum efficiency. Production of wealth would attain the highest levels possible in terms of available skills and resources.

This type of organization would incorporate into economic society the principles of sound social morality. It would be formed on the basis of co-operation, not conflict. It would aim at seeking the common good, not merely the selfish interests of individuals and classes. In effect, it would afford an institutional framework for policies based on the virtue of social justice.

Pope Pius XI considered this proposal the heart of his program for social reform. He proposed it first in 1931 and reiterated it strongly in 1937. His successor, Pope Pius XII, likewise referred repeatedly to this form of economic life as the only hope for a thorough renewal of industrial society. In spite of this repeated emphasis, there are considerable elements of obscurity about the precise import of the papal program. Numerous efforts have been made to interpret and apply the principles laid down in *Quadragesimo Anno*. Yet no clear and universally accepted explanation has been produced as a result of these studies. Perhaps some light can be obtained by a study of the background of the papal proposal.[1]

Background Considerations. It is clear from the papal documents involved that a number of factors prompted the analysis summarized above. Some of these considerations involve negative and destructive elements in existing economic life against which the Pope was reacting. Others concern both historical and theoretical reasons for the proposed organization of industrial society.

One negative element is the class struggle. All the modern popes have insisted upon the folly and destructiveness of the internecine war between capital and labor. It is obvious that management and workers must co-operate in the actual production of goods and services. No one questions the fact that the prosperity of any given company is greatly affected by the degree of harmony and understanding in the factory. Yet there is rarely any organized effort to intensify and extend this process. Generally what co-operation exists is the product of understandings reached at the collective-bargaining table. But these understandings come from groups organized for entirely different purposes. Labor unions and their management counterparts seek primarily to protect the rights and interests of their partisans, not necessarily the common good of the industrial community.

Another negative element is unregulated competition, to the extent that it obtains in a given nation. Competition is an important part of economic life. It stimulates incentive, weeds out the slovenly and inefficient, and tends to vitalize and energize the economy. But it can also atomize producers and prevent the formation of organizations dedicated to their common interests. Too often its rigors lead businessmen to the other extreme, to the formation of monopolies or the seeking of arrangements to stifle competition completely. The ideal social order would avoid these extremes. Businessmen would compete, but within a framework of organization that protects both their mutual interests and the common good. Some mutual interests, for example, would be research, advertising, standards of quality, and the social obligations of the industry.

Finally, among the negative elements, is the relation of the modern state to society. This has varied from the extremes of *laissez-faire* indif-

---

[1] The Pope's program is generally called by American Catholics the Industry Council Plan. Industry councils are the equivalent of the *ordines* and *collegia ordinum* of *Quadragesimo Anno*, translated in the text used here as "industries" and "professions." Other terms used are "occupational groups," "vocational groups," "modern guilds," and "corporative society."

ference to totalitarian statism. We have neither in the United States, but we do have some other evils mentioned by the popes. One is the burdening of the state with an infinity of duties that could be handled, within a properly organized social order, by organized economic groups. If these groups were truly seeking the common good, and had sufficient powers, they could take over many of the regulatory and social functions now restricted to government bodies. To cite one example from a thousand possible instances, the meat industry could be organized to set up and administer proper standards for grading and branding meats.

Among the more positive considerations mentioned in papal documents is the success of medieval economic society during its golden period. Before decay set in, it had achieved methods of regulating economic life in accord with the principles of morality. Pope Pius XI did not state that this social order was perfect or ideal, but it did meet "in a certain measure the requirements of right reason, considering the conditions and needs of the time." It failed, not because of inherent weaknesses, but because of selfishness and rebellion against authority.

Undoubtedly another factor inspiring the Pope was the writings of Heinrich Pesch, the originator of the system called solidarism. He and his disciples and fellow Jesuits, Oswald von Nell-Breuning and Gustav Gundlach, saw clearly the dangerous trends in modern economic society. They called for a new approach more in accord with the demands of human nature, with both production and the organization of economic society based on the true needs of man and the family. There is sufficient similarity between papal proposals and the writings of these scholars to warrant the use of these sources in interpreting *Quadragesimo Anno*.[2]

Some writers have asserted that the papal proposals were based on the corporate state of Mussolini. Actually, nothing could be farther from the truth. The purpose of the reform of social order is to lessen, not increase, state control of economic life. The corporate state features excessive controls. Corporative society would restore controls to properly organized economic groups.

We mention these background factors to give a definite idea of the evils in society that industry councils would cure, and also to indicate possible parallels that might help clarify the encyclical presentation. The Pope wishes to substitute order for disorder, harmony for the class struggle,

---

[2] See O. von Nell-Breuning, S.J., *Reorganization of Social Economy* (Milwaukee: Bruce, 1936), and R. E. Mulcahy, S.J., *The Economics of Heinrich Pesch* (New York: Holt, 1952).

and decentralized power in place of concentration of political or economic might. He desires social institutions that will of themselves facilitate the practice of justice. This is the basic distinction between social order and a society that lacks such order, even though individuals in the latter may endeavor to practice virtue in their economic relationships.

Elements of Social Order. Certain points seem clear in regard to the proposed industry councils. First, they comprise industries and professions. They should not be considered in terms of labor-management collaboration at the factory level. This collaboration, of course, is desirable but it is not the type of co-operation discussed here. What is envisioned is the organization of an entire industry or occupation, such as steel, automobile production, or farming. All the members of the occupation will be represented in the organization. Workers and employers, for example, will both be on the council in any given industry.

The type of organization should be determined by those concerned, "provided that proper regard is had for the requirements of justice and of the common good." Hence it would be quite improper for any commentator to draw up a detailed blueprint of economic society and present this as the papal program. At best, any blueprint would be the author's considered application of basic principles to the needs of a particular time and place. For example, there has been some controversy over the position of labor unions in respect to an industrial council. Would they furnish the representatives of labor, or would some other method of selection be used? Such questions cannot be answered in advance. Prudential judgment, considering "the requirements of justice and the common good" under the circumstances, should give the answer in each instance.

The Pope makes a distinction between industry councils and "free associations" which are a "matter of private order and private right." The implication is clear that industry councils would not be considered free associations (such as labor unions, trade associations, or research councils), but rather semipublic bodies. This means that every member of the industry or occupation would be expected to belong to the councils and would be bound by their regulations.

Here we introduce a concept somewhat strange to American legal customs. We do not have many groups that have such regulatory powers over their members. The closest parallels would be the medical and the bar associations. Private organizations, of course, can impose rules upon their members. But normally no one is compelled to join them or to retain membership. We would need drastic revisions of our antitrust laws to accept such concepts of regulatory powers.

Industry councils would not supplant free associations. Present organizations should prepare the way for a social order based on co-operation for the common good. But they would continue to remain in being in order to handle matters that are the special concerns of management or labor, in contrast to those which reflect the mutual interests and the common problems of the industry or occupation.

The purpose of industry councils is the co-operation of all involved individuals in seeking the welfare of each industry or occupation, and their working together for the common good of all. Presumably this calls for some type of higher co-ordinating council, although Pope Pius XI was not explicit in this regard. He simply spoke of "that common good, to achieve which all Industries and Professions together ought, each to the best of its ability, to co-operate amicably." He also mentioned "professional and interprofessional organizations." Here again it would seem inadvisable to draw up blueprints prematurely. Decisions can be made at the proper time in accord with the demands of the common good.

The Pope did not specify how the councils should function in seeking the welfare of their industries or occupations and the common good. Their task would be to infuse justice into economic life. The means used would be determined by their prudent judgment, motivated by Christian principles, in the light of the laws, customs, and economic realities of the time.

There was a tendency among some earlier commentators to envision the councils as a giant economic planning body, with controls over investment, prices, profit, markets, and wages. It is difficult to see how such a type of organization would actually promote the common good. It would increase centralization of power if the government had to make the final decisions, as it undoubtedly would. Furthermore, such a system would be rejected by most people as merely another brand of socialism.

Prices, profit, investment, and markets seem to belong in the area of management economic decisions that Pope Pius XII characterized as within the competence of the owners of property. Wages would be determined mutually, but by the free associations representing management and labor. Of course, all these decisions have social aspects and should be made in the light of the common good as well as individual interests. But their social aspects do not make them mutual concerns of labor and management, to be decided on the industry level by industry councils. Rather the parties directly concerned have the prime responsibility to decide, subject to considerations of the common good, directed first by their own consciences and ultimately, when necessary, by the state as the supreme custodian of the common good.

Nevertheless, there are many industry-wide economic problems that would seem to fall within the competence of industry councils. These would include studies and policies designed to increase productivity, standards of justice that aim to keep competition within proper bounds, regional economic problems, and national problems such as the quest for economic stability and orderly economic growth. When problems transcend the boundaries of an individual industry or occupation, there would seem to be a need for a higher level of industry councils and undoubtedly some degree of government participation.

The examples just given, of course, represent interpretation and application of the encyclical program. The popes deliberately couched their counsels in general terms, leaving the utmost latitude for individual economies to apply them according to their special needs and customs. The essential point in any effort at interpretation and application is a conscientious effort on the part of any commentator first to keep faithful to the spirit of the entire body of papal teaching, and then never to confuse doctrinal teaching of the Church with his own economic analysis. This latter point is especially important when debatable schools of economic thought are being followed. Economic debate, when it does not involve moral principles, should be labeled properly, and not blanketed into interpretations of Catholic social teaching.

It may be objected that the type of co-operation sought by the Pope is impractical, given man's selfishness. This objection was foreseen, as Pope Pius XI explicitly stated that the reconstruction and perfection of social order "can surely in nowise be brought to realization without reform of morality." But reform of morality does not mean the rooting out of selfishness and greed from the hearts of all men. It means that there should be enough men of good will seeking to bring about a right social order, and having the power to draw up binding rules and regulations that would implement the demands of justice and charity. As was noted earlier, sound laws, customs, and institutions can bring about a good society, even though evil men may be members of that society.

Industry Councils in American Life. The industry-council program has been widely publicized in American Catholic circles, but its impact upon economic thinking in the United States is uncertain. Some American economists have reached similar conclusions by independent means. Others have examined the proposals and offered their criticisms. Still others have been understandably confused by the lack of unanimity in Catholic interpretation and application of papal proposals.[3]

American thinkers who are most concerned about group individualism and its disruptive impact upon the economy are predisposed to think along lines parallel to papal proposals. They are worried about concentrations of power in both labor and business, and the too frequent insistence upon group interests to the neglect of the common good. They feel that a new approach is needed, if our system is to live up to its full potentialities. Only by this method, they assert, can we avoid instability caused by recurrent inflation and deflation. They would in addition seek to remedy newer forms of income maldistribution, whereby favored groups can siphon off special shares of the national income, to the detriment of those who lack the economic or political organization to protect their interests.

On the other hand, there are also thinkers who feel that certain economies, such as those of the United States and West Germany, have achieved already a substantial measure of social justice. They argue that it would be dangerous to tinker with a working system that is producing excellent results. According to this thinking, we would conclude that the American system has secured the purposes sought in the encyclicals, even though we have not always used the precise means prescribed there.

After weighing these viewpoints, it seems that the better arguments lie with those who would improve the American economy along the principles of the encyclicals. As was noted in Chapter I, our system does not produce justice for many groups of our citizens. It is afflicted with serious instabilities. Its unity is often precarious, subject to conflicting pressures from powerful groups, such as industry, labor, and the farm community.

The case for sober consideration of papal principles is strengthened when we examine their major implications for American life. Certainly no one would question the desirability of higher levels of labor-management co-operation. Hostility and the class struggle are not forces of strength in our economy. We are strong despite, not because of, these clashes.

---

[3] An explicit critique, from a Protestant viewpoint, is found in H. R. Bowen, *Social Responsibilities of the Businessman* (New York: Harper, 1953). Such authors as Roepke, Schumpeter, Polyani, and J. M. Clarke often parallel encyclical ideas.

Likewise, the existence of common interests in our economy is not debatable. We grant the many merits of competition, but we have in practice modified the struggle among competitors. Industry-wide advertising and research are common today. Few industries lack trade associations to promote mutual concerns. Indeed, we can rightly assert that we have already adopted many policies that harmonize with encyclical counsels. But we can go further and seek the general common good, as well as the needs of industry, in our various organizations in industry and the professions.

Nor is there much disagreement in principle over the desirability of lessening government burdens and transferring controls and regulations to the groups directly concerned with the problems. While we have political debates over specific government functions, even those who seem to favor extended federal action do not support centralization as such. They merely argue that in certain cases the government must act because other groups have defaulted upon their social obligations.

At least, we can note certain trends and beginnings that conform to encyclical standards of social justice. Nor is it unrealistic to expect that these trends may be strengthened. Social control in the United States, generally speaking, has been imposed upon unwilling groups of business and labor. As recently as thirty years ago the dominant philosophy of the nation was individualistic, even though some measure of social reform had been instituted at the end of the nineteenth century. It will take time for various groups to accept fully the primary demands of the common good. Once this hurdle has been surmounted, it is quite possible that they will choose co-operation and self-regulation, at least as an alternative to continuing government controls.

Steps Toward Social Justice. Granted the soundness of encyclical principles on social order, the important question is how they are to be promoted in the United States. It would be a mistake, in the light of American temperament and general patterns of historical change, to try to draw up an elaborate, detailed pattern which would be labeled the Industry Council Plan. Social change normally is evolutionary, not revolutionary. It involves modification of existing institutions, not the establishment of entirely new patterns. Pope Pius XI spoke of "preparing the way" for these councils and making "every possible effort to bring them to realization." Education and experimentation will bring us closer to our goal.

One field of action that should be increasingly emphasized is that of labor-management co-operation. This has been the subject of much research in recent decades, but almost exclusively at the level of the single plant or company. Management has studied new psychological techniques. Efforts have been made to instill in the worker pride in his job and pride in his company. The worker is consulted. Proposed changes are explained to him and he is given the opportunity to state his views on the subject. This stress on teamwork exists in unionized and nonunion plants alike.

Co-operation on the industry level is less common. The United Mine Workers have co-operated with management in seeking to expand markets for coal. Several unions in the clothing field have done commendable work in helping promote the products of their industry. But generally organized labor is not so co-operative. The tradition of many unions has been to seek gains for their members and to leave to the employer the problem of absorbing these costs and selling his product. Yet, in fairness to organized labor, it must be noted that the employer often influences union attitudes in regard to co-operation. If he is aloof and unfriendly, the union will remain at a distance.

The element of divergence is even greater so far as national economic policies are concerned. Employers charge that unions often restrict production, force price increases as a result of excessive wage demands, and fail to realize the profit needs of an expanding economy. Unions in turn justify wage increases as necessary to offset inflation or to increase purchasing power. They claim that profits are excessive. They further assert that mass markets are needed to stimulate investment. The value of these arguments will be considered in later chapters. But the wide divergence of opinion is a challenge to both sides to seek competent and independent analysis of their claims.

So long as these fundamental cleavages exist, it is not likely that they will be solved by any council made up of the conflicting parties. Discussion, as such, can only clear up misunderstandings. It rarely can lead to the removal of basic conflicts of interest. If we were to organize a national economic council in the United States today, for example, one would hardly expect business, labor, and farm groups to agree completely upon what constitutes the economic common good of the nation. Government would have to make the final decisions, as it does today.

One historic effort to seek broad co-operation between labor and management was the President's Economic Conference of 1951. While the Conference broke up in failure, more agreement was reached than is generally realized. It failed primarily because highly controversial topics were put at the top of the agenda. Perhaps a more skillfully prepared high-level meeting would prove to be more successful. Certainly it is distressing that few efforts are made to narrow the gap between labor and management.

Realism compels us to face these difficulties. But they are not insurmountable. One method for seeking greater unity is to seize every possible opportunity to bring together conflicting groups to discuss matters upon which they do not diverge. These could include questions of public policy — local, state, national, and international. One good example is the problem of race relations and discrimination in employment. Membership in public-service organizations is another suitable meeting ground. Contacts made in "neutral" activities can bring about personal understandings, which often carry over to the fields where conflict prevails.

Another method is to promote public debate of issues. When members of interest groups are challenged by expert and impartial critics, they are less likely to rely upon weak arguments or unfounded opinions. They are not able to argue that their opponents are clouding issues in order to promote their own interests. In this regard, the radio and television industries can render a public service by airing the economic conflicts that divide our nation. Once public opinion is informed and aroused on any point, even the strongest pressure groups are likely to give way.

We should not overlook the value of labor-management co-operation on the factory or company level. If real understanding and trust are reached at these levels, they are bound to influence broader policies. The plant manager today may be the corporation president tomorrow. A local union leader may advance to a position of national influence. Assuming that the majority of such executives are men of good will, they are bound to re-examine basic clashes with those whom they have grown to admire and trust.

In addition to promoting labor-management co-operation on a broad front, it is desirable to restudy our pattern of social controls. The purpose of this would be to substitute, where possible, self-regulation in place of government regulation. The question might be raised, for example, whether or not our organized security exchanges could take over some of the functions of the Securities and Exchange Commission. It may be that the financial community has progressed sufficiently in twenty-five years to warrant such trust. Such transfers of power need not be total, at least in the beginning. Government regulatory commissions could remain as watchdogs over the performance of private groups, with power to intervene when serious abuses arose.

The important point is that we develop an awareness regarding centers of power. The more that control is removed from individuals and smaller groups, the more difficult it is for the average citizen to influence those who exercise power. We should be consciously striving to keep real life in local government, local unions, and local units of large corporations. This does not mean that we blindly oppose any activities of the federal government or national groups. Rather it means that we consistently use the principle of subsidiarity — keeping power decentralized so far as this is consistent with the common good.

One method of moving toward an ideal social order is to utilize every available opportunity to insist upon the importance of the common good. The principle that business and labor should serve the general welfare is widely accepted, so far as public statements go. It is rare today that any economic conflict is carried out merely as a power struggle. To an ever increasing degree, the belligerent parties try to win the support of public opinion. They argue that their claims are right and that their position would benefit the nation. This recognition of the power of an aroused citizenry can be a valuable asset in the fight for social justice.

Those who are seeking a better social order can deal with various economic groups and their programs in terms of the impact upon the entire economy. They can argue for policies that benefit the nation, not merely a particular group. This is an understandable and acceptable approach in terms of American psychology. It is much more likely to produce results, in contrast to efforts to introduce an industry-council plan in one step.

In brief, we can be constantly aware of the main objectives of a just social order, and the main obstacles to it. The objectives, as listed in papal writings, are organized effort to seek the common good, and co-operation as a pattern in economic life. The obstacles most often cited are the class struggle, unsocial forms of competition, and various evils connected with the relation of the state to economic society — excessive concentration of power, efforts of economic groups to control the state, and misuse of civil power with resulting prejudice to the common good.

Policies that promote the objectives sought, or remove obstacles to their attainment, should be the main concern of Catholic social action. This will be the Church's answer to the social problem outlined in

Chapter I. Thus we seek a social order in accord with God's purpose for man and in line with the social virtues. We offer a means to remedy past abuses and an alternative to unacceptable social and political systems.

The detailed analysis of capital, labor, property, and the state, in the section to follow, gives the rights and duties connected with each of these great institutions. As each conforms more and more to the demands of social justice, it is better prepared to take its proper place in a well-organized social order. Detailed problems connected with each topic must be judged in the light of our transcendent goal — the complete reform of economic society. The vision and insight of Pope Pius XI have given us a pattern for justice integrated in our economy. As we are guided by this vision, our contribution to social policy will gain in wisdom and enduring value.

READINGS*

J. Messner, *Social Ethics*, pp. 138–143, 196–200, 332–346, 705–710, 749–752, 818–823, 867–923, 935–947.
B. W. Dempsey, *The Functional Economy*, Chaps. 14–17.
G. Clune, *Christian Social Reorganization*, Chap. 21.
O. von Nell-Breuning, *Reorganization of Social Economy*, Chaps. 10–12.
———— "Vocational Groups and Monopoly," *Review of Social Economy*, September, 1951.
J. Villain, *L'Enseignement social de l'Église*, Vol. III, pp. 111–243.
C. Bruehl, *The Pope's Plan for Reconstruction*, Chaps. 19–29.
H. Johnston, *Business Ethics*, Chap. 9.
Social Order: "International Bibliography on Vocational Order," September, 1953; Peter de Bruin, S.J., "Toward Economic Order," February, 1951; Philip S. Land, S.J., "Guides for Social Reform," March, 1951; "Heinrich Pesch," April, 1951; Philip S. Land, "International Bibliography on Vocational Order," April, 1953; Goetz A. Briefs, "Economics of Heinrich Pesch," December, 1953; Philip S. Land, S.J., "Protestants on Industry Councils," January, 1954; Henry J. Schmandt, "State Intervention — When?" December, 1954; Cornelius A. Eller, S.J., "Roots for Reform," November, 1954; Bernard W. Dempsey, S.J., "Economic Community, Industrial Municipalities Need Home Rule," April, 1955; *Quadragesimo Anno: An American Symposium*," January, 1956.

* For further readings, consult List No. 3 in the Appendix.

Part II

SOCIAL PRINCIPLES AND MAJOR
SOCIOECONOMIC INSTITUTIONS

Chapter VIII

RIGHTS AND DUTIES OF CAPITAL

THE RIGHT TO PROFITS

Pius XI, Quadragesimo Anno

53. And in the application of natural resources to human use the law of nature, or rather God's will promulgated by it, demands that right order be observed. This order consists in this: that each thing have its proper owner. Hence it follows that unless a man is expending labor on his own property, the labor of one person and the property of another must be associated, for neither can produce anything without the other. Leo XIII certainly had this in mind when he wrote: "Neither capital can do without labor, nor labor without capital." Wherefore it is wholly false to ascribe to property alone or to labor alone whatever has been obtained through the combined effort of both, and it is wholly unjust for either, denying the efficacy of the other, to arrogate to itself whatever has been produced.

54. Property, that is, "capital," has undoubtedly long been able to appropriate too much to itself. Whatever was produced, whatever returns accrued, capital claimed for itself, hardly leaving to the worker enough to restore and renew his strength. For the doctrine was preached that all accumulation of capital falls by an absolutely insuperable economic law to the rich, and that by the same law the workers are given over and bound to perpetual want, to the scantiest of

livelihoods. It is true, indeed, that things have not always and everywhere corresponded with this sort of teaching of the so-called Manchesterian Liberals; yet it cannot be denied that economic-social institutions have moved steadily in that direction. That these false ideas, these erroneous suppositions, have been vigorously assailed, and not by those alone who through them were being deprived of their innate right to obtain better conditions, will surprise no one.

55. And therefore, to the harassed workers there have come "intellectuals," as they are called, setting up in opposition to a fictitious law the equally fictitious moral principle that all products and profits, save only enough to repair and renew capital, belong by very right to the workers.

57. Therefore, the riches that economic-social developments constantly increase ought to be so distributed among individual persons and classes that the common advantage of all, which Leo XIII had praised, will be safeguarded; in other words, that the common good of all society will be kept inviolate. By this law of social justice, one class is forbidden to exclude the other from sharing in the benefits. Hence the class of the wealthy violates this law no less, when, as if free from care on account

143

of its wealth, it thinks it the right order of things for it to get everything and the worker nothing, than does the nonowning working class when, angered deeply at outraged justice and too ready to assert wrongly the one right it is conscious of, it demands for itself everything as if produced by its own hands, and attacks and seeks to abolish, therefore, all property and returns or incomes, of whatever kind they are or whatever the function they perform in human society, that have not been obtained by labor, and for no other reason save that they are of such a nature.

58. To each, therefore, must be given his own share of goods, and the distribution of created goods, which, as every discerning person knows, is laboring today under the gravest evils due to the huge disparity between the few exceedingly rich and the unnumbered propertyless, must be effectively called back to and brought into conformity with the norms of the common good, that is, social justice.

136. Those who are engaged in producing goods, therefore, are not forbidden to increase their fortune in a just and lawful manner; for it is only fair that he who renders service to the community and makes it richer should also, through the increased wealth of the community, be made richer himself according to his position, provided that all these things be sought with due respect for the laws of God and without impairing the rights of others and that they be employed in accordance with faith and right reason.

Pius XII, To the Italian Federation of Commerce, February 17, 1956

Every exchange of products, in fact, quite apart from satisfying definite needs and desires, makes it possible to put new means into operation, arouses latent and sometimes unexpected energies, and stimulates the spirit of enterprise and invention. This instinct, which is innate in mankind, of creating, improving, and making progress explains commercial activities as much as and more than the mere desire for gain.

DUTIES OF OWNERS

Leo XIII, Graves de Communi

15. Certainly, the path of popular improvement is better assured and more quickly traversed, the more we have the co-operation of the well-to-do, with their wide opportunities of effectual aid. We would have them reflect upon the fact that they are not free to choose whether they will take up the cause of the poor or not; it is a matter of simple duty. Men live in a civic society not only for their own good, but also for the good of all. Some are too poor to contribute their share to the common stock; those, therefore, who can should contribute more generously. The extent of this obligation is in proportion to the amount of riches received. The larger it is, the stricter must be the account we shall have to render to God, who gave it to us. We learn the same lesson from the plague that spreads its calamity and unless a remedy be applied in time, will break out to the ruin and destruction of all classes. He who neglects to take up the cause of the poor acts without regard to his personal interest as well as that of his country.

Leo XIII, Rerum Novarum

31. The following duties, on the other hand, concern rich men and employers: workers are not to be treated as slaves; justice demands that the dignity of human personality be respected in them, ennobled as it has been through what we call the Christian character. If we hearken to natural reason and to Christian philosophy, gainful occupations are not a mark of shame to man, but rather of respect, as they provide him with an honorable means of supporting life. It is shameful and inhuman, however, to use men as things of gain and to put no more value on them than what they are worth in muscle and energy. Likewise it is enjoined that the religious interests and the spiritual well-being of the workers receive proper consideration. Wherefore, it is the duty of employers to see that the worker is free for adequate periods to attend to his religious obligations; not to expose anyone to corrupting influences or the enticements of sin, and in no way to alienate him from care for his family and the practice of thrift. Likewise, more work is not to be imposed than strength can endure, nor that kind of work which is unsuited to a worker's age or sex.

32. Among the most important duties of employers the principal one is to give every worker what is justly due him. Assuredly, to establish a rule of pay in accord with justice, many factors must be taken into account. But, in general, the rich and employers should remember that no laws, either human or divine, permit them for their own profit to oppress the needy and the wretched or to seek gain from another's want. To defraud anyone of the wage due him is a great crime that calls down avenging wrath from Heaven. "Behold, the wages of the laborers . . . which have been kept back by you unjustly, cry out: and their cry has entered into the ears of the Lord of Hosts." Finally, the rich must religiously avoid harming in any way the savings of the workers either by coercion, or by fraud, or by the arts of usury; and the more for this reason, that the workers are not sufficiently protected against injustices and violence, and their property, being so meager, ought to be regarded as all the more sacred. Could not the observance alone of the foregoing laws remove the bitterness and the causes of conflict?

Pius XI, On Atheistic Communism

50. Therefore, We turn again in a special way to you, Christian employers and industrialists, whose problem is often so difficult for the reason that you are saddled with the heavy heritage of an unjust economic regime whose ruinous influence has been felt through many generations. We bid you be mindful of your responsibility. It is unfortunately true that the manner of action in certain Catholic circles has done much to shake the faith of the working classes in the religion of Jesus Christ. These groups have refused to understand that Christian charity demands the recognition of certain rights due to the workingman, which the Church has explicitly acknowledged. What is to be thought of the action of those Catholic employers who in one place succeeded in preventing the reading of Our Encyclical, Quadragesimo Anno, in their local churches? Or of those Catholic industrialists who even to this day have shown themselves

hostile to a labor movement that We Ourselves recommended? Is it not deplorable that the right of private property defended by the Church should so often have been used as a weapon to defraud the workingman of his just salary and his social rights?

Pius XII, Christmas Message, 1952

This solidarity of men with each other demands, not only in the name of brotherly love, but even of mutual advantage, that everything possible be done to maintain and increase employment. Therefore, let those who are able to invest capital consider in the light of the common good — and with due regard to their economic condition, to risks involved and opportunity offered — whether they can reconcile with their conscience their neglect and failure to make investments because of unreasonable caution.

Pius XII, Address to Delegates of World Petroleum Congress, June 10, 1955

. . . the concern of management is more and more with the men themselves who serve as its collaborators. It is important that these men put forth all their initiative on behalf of the employer. But they will be led to do this only if industry first takes care to fulfil their basic human needs, which are not completely satisfied either by a just salary or even by the appreciation that is due their professional competency.

Pius XII, To the International Conference on Human Relations in Industry, February 4, 1956

We are happy to ascertain, nevertheless, that pure technique has vividly brought out the importance, so long ignored, of human relations in labor.

CODETERMINATION

Pius XI, Quadragesimo Anno

64. First of all, those who declare that a contract of hiring and being hired is unjust of its own nature, and hence a partnership contract must take its place, are certainly in error and gravely misrepresent Our Predecessor whose Encyclical not only accepts working for wages or salaries but deals at some length with its regulation in accordance with the rules of justice.

65. We consider it more advisable, however, in the present condition of human society that, so far as is possible, the work contract be somewhat modified by a partnership contract, as is already being done in various ways and with no small advantage to workers and owners. Workers and other employees thus become sharers in ownership or management or participate in some fashion in the profits received.

Pius XII, To Catholic Employers, May 7, 1949

The owner of the means of production, whoever he be — individual owner, workers' association, or corporation — must always — within the limits of public economic law — retain control of his economic decisions. It goes without saying that his income is higher than that of his collaborators. But it follows that the material prosperity of the entire population, which is the objective of social economy, lays upon him, more than upon the others, the obligation of contributing by savings to the increase of the nation's fund of capital. As we must not forget, on the other hand, that it is supremely advantageous to a healthy social economy when this accumulation of capital derives from the greatest possible number of sources, it is very desirable, in consequence, that the workmen also should be enabled, by the fruit of their savings, to share in the creation of the capital resources of their country.

Pius XII, To Catholic International Congresses for Social Study and Social Action, June 3, 1950

The wisdom of Our Predecessor Pius XI has made that quite clear in the Encyclical Quadragesimo Anno, where he denies, in consequence, that there is any need in the nature of things to pattern the wage-contract on the contract of partnership. That is not to disavow the usefulness of what has thus far been achieved in this direction, "in various ways, to the no small gain of both wage-earners and employers." But in the light of principles and facts the right of economic joint-management lies beyond the field of these possible achievements.

Pius XII, To Austrian Catholics, September 14, 1952

. . . the pontiffs of the social encyclicals, and also We Ourselves, have declined to deduce, directly or indirectly, from the labor contract the right of the employee to participate in the ownership of the operating capital, and its corollary, the right of the worker to participate in decisions concerning operations of the plant (Mitbestimmung). This had to be denied because behind this question there stands that greater problem — the right of the individual and of the family to own property, which stems immediately from the human person. It is a right of personal dignity; a right, to be sure, accompanied by social obligations; a right, however, not merely a social function.

IN THE first part of this work, our intellectual camera used a broad focus. The "social question" was presented in sweeping outlines. The right and the duty of the Church to pronounce upon moral aspects of social and economic problems were explained. In furthering this concept, two chapters were devoted to the pertinent moral principles and virtues.

Next, general social systems were examined, including papal directives for a sound approach to social order.

In the present section, our focus is narrowed. Important social institutions, such as capital, labor, the family, property, and the state, are scrutinized in terms of the demands of justice and charity. In each case, the emphasis is upon major current problems and rights and duties pertinent to current situations. Of necessity, the treatment is selective rather than comprehensive. Stress is laid upon actual present-day issues, rather than historical or abstract considerations. Thus, for example, in dealing with capital and business management, the main rights emphasized are those connected with salaries and profits. The duties treated are those toward labor and the public. A similar selectivity is practiced in the other chapters of Part II. It was deemed more important to concentrate upon vital issues of the day than to force each treatment into a preconceived uniform pattern.

Capital was chosen as the first topic primarily because of the tremendous impact that physical capital — billions invested in factories and machines — has made upon our standard of living. The term itself, as used in the encyclicals, has many meanings. Sometimes it refers to the capitalist class, in the sense of promoters, managers, or owners of productive property. At other times it means physical capital, or capital goods. Here allusion is made to the machinery, buildings, and natural resources used as agents of production. Still again, it can mean invested funds and the "profits" secured from such investment. For the sake of clarity, it is best to consider separately these different contributions to the productive process and the returns each deserves.

We must decide not only what are the proper returns for capital, but also to whom they should be allocated and in what proportion. In making this decision, both commutative justice and social justice should be consulted. To the extent that what is clearly due in strict justice can be defined, we should do so. In addition we should try to determine what the common good demands of capital.

OUR PROFIT SYSTEM

Management and Promotion.   Since the questions of profits and interest are highly complex, it is easier to consider first the reward to the capitalist as promoter or manager of a firm. It is possible that the promoter may contribute nothing from his own funds to a given enterprise. Yet he may have vision, daring, or experience which insures great success with the use of borrowed or invested money. A person of this nature makes a definite contribution to economic life and is entitled in justice to a reward for this function. Organization, correct calculation of risks, and awareness of opportunities are real values and add to the wealth of the community. One could even say that the speculator, often despised as a parasite, is not necessarily nonproductive of economic value. Stock exchanges and commodity markets, when properly regulated, smooth out the functioning of the price system and actually lessen risk to producers. The actual return imputed to the efforts of promoters is difficult to assess accurately. In a free economic system, however, the law of supply and demand tends to bring about a rough approximation of what the business community attributes to these agents. If labor is able to demand a proper wage, money capital receives its fair share, and management is suitably rewarded, the surplus remaining in a competitive enterprise is usually credited to the promoter.

Management of an enterprise is likewise a distinct function, not necessarily connected with the initial promotion of a firm or the furnishing of funds for its needs of physical capital. This distinction is clearly seen in the corporation, where day-by-day direction of the company may be in the hands of a president who is not even a stockholder. Broad policies may be laid down by a board of directors, representative of the stockholders, but the actual running of the firm is left to skilled management. In many of the largest corporations, management controls the appointment of directors through the use of the proxy machinery. In small companies, the owners are usually their own managers. In such cases, their salary for management is lumped in with other "profits," but in fact the directing of a firm is distinct from both its promotion and its ownership.

The contribution of management is best seen when a succession of managers run the same company. It frequently happens that a firm may approach bankruptcy under poor management and make large profits under a new president, with economic conditions, market for the product, and wages remaining the same. In other cases, several competitive firms may be equally close to raw materials and market, have the same power and transportation facilities, pay the same wage rate, and yet one company may be highly successful and others barely survive. Obviously, such results reflect different management policies.

In view of the economic contribution made by management, it follows that salaries based on this contribution are not necessarily unjust. Some moralists are appalled at the differential between wages paid to workers and the salaries and bonuses given to corporation executives. Yet published salaries, and actual income after taxes, are often quite different. Under present tax laws, it is quite difficult to get rich on salaries, no matter how high they may seem. If the net salary incomes of most top corporation executives were apportioned equally among their workers, it would be unusual were this to add as much as ten dollars a year to the wages of each worker.

When we apply the rules of strict justice to corporation salaries, we conclude that they are not of themselves unjust. Good executives can earn millions of dollars annually for many firms. When they are paid a small portion of what they contribute, certainly we cannot say that their income is excessive. From the viewpoint of social justice and the common good, we note that good management helps provide jobs, worthwhile products, and vital economic incentives. All these contributions lead to a healthy economy and national prosperity.

These comments, of course, are generalizations about American business. Undoubtedly there are exceptions to the rules just stated. Some executives may obtain their positions through favoritism and may be overpaid in terms of their contributions. There are those whose policies are antisocial. While they may add to the financial soundness of their firms, they do not enhance the common good of the nation.

Given this defense of executive salaries, it is nonetheless socially desirable to emphasize incentives other than economic. Many public servants perform duties fully as complex as those of corporation executives, but receive only a minor fraction of the latters' salaries. This shows that service to the community, a sense of creative achievement, and similar nonmonetary incentives can also be attractive. If such attitudes could be created, there would be less need for disproportionate salaries, which may give rise to social tensions.

Profits. The term "profits" has many meanings in current usage and in the papal encyclicals. Many persons, particularly small businessmen, use the term to denote the net annual return from a firm. They do not calculate separately their salaries for managing the company. Economists, on the other hand, do not consider return on capital as profits. To them profits constitute a residue after wages, salaries, and other expenses have been paid; depreciation allowed on investment; and payment made for money invested or borrowed.

In these pages, profits are used to denote a return on money invested in a firm. They exclude salaries paid or imputed for management and also interest paid on borrowed money. This usage is closest to that of the encyclicals and hence makes interpretation and comment on these documents more accurate. Particular emphasis is laid upon corporate profits, since these are often subjects of controversy.

The right to profits must be judged both in terms of commutative and of social justice. In strict justice, capital makes a contribution to economic life by furnishing a necessary factor of production. Machines and raw materials contribute to the productive process by enhancing and multiplying the effectiveness of human labor. Capital goods are purchased as a result of the savings of investors and lenders, who reserve a part of their current income, thus diverting some economic effort from the making of goods for consumption to the making of goods for production. This contribution is made in prospect of at least two types of rewards. At the minimum, the sum contributed should be returned. The corporation does this for lenders by setting aside reserves for the retirement of its bonds. For investors, it keeps their property in good repair and may make depreciation allowances to cover the cost of capital equipment.

The second return to lenders and investors is a charge for the use of their money. The moral justification of this charge is treated subsequently in connection with interest. Interest to bondholders is called such, whereas with stockholders it is a part of their dividends, together with a payment for the added risk they assume and, at times, a share of profits in the strict, scientific sense. Stockholders should receive more than the going rate of interest in view of two types of risk. They run the chance of nonpayment in poor years (corporations today tend to use depression reserves more to keep the firm alive than to pay out dividends) and they may lose their principal if business changes lead to bankruptcy of their company.

While strict justice looks upon profits in terms of payment for service rendered, social justice weighs them in the light of the common good. Here the overruling consideration is the health of the economy taken as a whole. This point has occasioned much recent controversy in the United States both in terms of principles and of facts. On the level of principle, it is sometimes argued that when profits are too high they lead to excessive investment. It is alleged that industries expand capacity beyond the absorptive power of the market, with consequent overproduction and unemployment. The suggested remedy, according to this school, is higher wages (to create mass markets) and lower profits.

A completely different viewpoint is held by those who favor a high investment level and continuing economic expansion. They argue that new or better products create consumer demand and hence stimulate the economy. At the same time, these new products offer more employment to a constantly increasing labor force. If the new investment involves modernization of existing plants or replacement of obsolete facilities, then productivity increases and prices decline. This also leads to higher living standards.

The history of the American economy, in contrast to that of some European nations, generally favors the second analysis. A high level of investment has led to increases in productivity and fairly constant economic expansion. Employment has kept pace with this growth, and real incomes of workers have consistently mounted. An even more dramatic example, under exceptional circumstances, was the recovery of the German Republic after World War II. Starting with its currency reform in 1949, and particularly after military controls were lifted, Germany bounded ahead to unparalleled prosperity. One feature of this recovery was an unusually high investment rate, needed to replace war-damaged or destroyed property.

The conclusions given here refer largely to American experience since the conclusion of World War II. There were earlier periods in our history, when the income distribution pattern was different, that warranted the charge of excessive profits. Moreover, these general comments apply to the economy as a whole. Undoubtedly, individual firms have made excessive profits. Individual companies or even industries may have expanded unwisely. But the over-all pattern has been healthy in terms of production, jobs, and general living standards.

At this stage, it is fair to conclude that reasonable profits are justified in strict justice. The principal loaned or invested should be safeguarded through sufficient charges for depreciation. After this is done, reasonable profits should be sufficient to pay a fair rate of interest to bondholders and stockholders, and to make adequate allowance for risks assumed. Moreover, social justice upholds the profit incentive as a means for promoting economic expansion and higher living standards. It calls, however, for the consideration of profits in the light of the total national economic picture, so that the economic system will function for the common good of all.

Calculation of Fair Profit.   While it is easy to lay down general principles about fair profits, it is most difficult to apply these principles to concrete situations. Otherwise, we would not be having the almost interminable controversies over business prices and profits. Labor unions, columnists, and congressional committees rather regularly attack the level of dividends and profits. Business in turn is equally strident in defending its case. Indeed, it often claims that profit levels are too low for a healthy economy.

In order to think clearly about these matters, we must know the answers to three questions bearing on profits. They are: What should we consider profits in the context of these public controversies? What are fair profits in strict justice? What does social justice say about profits?

To answer the first question, we must begin by determining the proper method for computing profits. Management apologists, for example, often talk in terms of profit per unit of sale. Some argue that the public considers 6 per cent a fair return, and that few concerns make more than this amount per dollar of sales. Actually, this form of polemics is quite misleading. A supermarket, with a high turnover rate, might make good profits annually if it nets one cent on the sales dollar. By contrast, a furniture store, with low turnover rates, might need to net twenty cents on its sales dollar to secure a fair annual return on its investment. Obviously this method of calculating profits, while useful for cost-control purposes, has no relevance to controversies over fair profits. The really important test is the profit level as a percentage of the *current net worth* of a firm. This will determine whether or not it is receiving an adequate return on its capital investment.

Next, we should speak of profits after taxes, not gross profits. Since the federal government generally taxes over half of corporation profits, there is no basis for assuming that the stockholder benefits from the gross amount. Gross profits are useful in calculating shares of national income and for collective bargaining, but they are not pertinent to discussions on fair returns to investors.

When dealing with individual firms, it is normally unfair to concentrate upon profits for any given year. Only the average over a suitable number of years will determine the general profit level of a firm. By "suitable" we mean a period long enough to balance boom and recession periods and to allow for unusual situations, such as especially good or bad years, or uniquely favorable or unfavorable contracts. Thus, if American Motors should become a prosperous firm, we should certainly allow for its long period of deficits. We must also calculate the effect of any long-term inflationary trend upon profits. This forces many firms to set aside extra reserves for replacement of equipment, since tax laws permit deductions based only upon actual cost. Such additional reserves should not be considered profits.

If we consider profits for the entire business community, it is not fair to stress gains over earlier periods, unless we also note how other components of the economy have fared. For example, while business profits increased in the ten years 1948–1957, returns to labor increased much more rapidly.[1] In this context also we should consider the psychology of investors. If investors made only a modest profit on successful corporations, their total return would be quite low, since some of the firms they support may turn out badly. Hence, to preserve investment incentives, we must expect that some firms will receive quite high profits. Otherwise, we dry up the risk funds that contribute to our economic expansion.

These qualifications may seem to make the entire problem rather difficult and complex. But they are necessary, precisely because of the multiple aspects of the profit situation. Only by using such distinctions can we answer our remaining questions as to fair profits in terms of strict and social justice.

What are fair profits in terms of strict justice? A rough answer is that average profits after taxes, expressed as a percentage of return on current net worth, can be twice the interest rate a firm would currently pay for its bonds. The bond rate presumably gives the cost of money to that firm. The extra amount compensates for risks taken by stockholders and provides an incentive for persons of means to continue investing. If a company earns above this amount consistently, the burden of proof should be upon the firm to show that these returns represent exceptional efficiency or unusual situations, and not exploitation of workers or consumers.

The figures just cited constitute an amount that business executives can, in strict justice, seek to obtain. In terms of recent bond yields, this would mean a range of about 8 to 12 per cent upon the net worth of a company. When we bring in considerations of social justice, we ask if still higher profits are ever justified in terms of the common good. This

---

[1] See Table 1, p. 272, for statistics in this regard. The percentage of national income going to profits declined during the period, although profits rose in absolute figures. Profits of manufacturing corporations, as percentages of net worth, were 12 per cent in 1956 and 10.7 per cent in 1957, close to the maximum considered allowable in the analysis to follow.

question can be answered only in terms of the impact of a firm's profits upon the economy at any given time.

We might consider, for example, the situation of General Motors during the years when its costs were considerably below those of its main competitors. If it cut its prices, it might have bankrupted its competitors and become a monopoly. This would have been contrary to American public policy. Nor could it have paid substantially higher wages than its competitors, given the realities of union politics. Presumably the common good was best served by permitting General Motors its high profits.

Another example would be a firm or an industry that pioneers in new processes that may greatly benefit the economy. An illustration would be the desalting of sea water or the use of boron as a solid fuel. High profits in such situations may even be warranted by strict justice, because of exceptional risks. But certainly the common good is promoted by farsighted pioneers who often do what others consider impossible. Were we to cut off economic incentives from such a class, the general economic good would suffer.

Our conclusions thus far seem to be weighted in favor of the business side of the profit controversy. This emphasis has been deliberate, since moralists often fail to understand the complexity of the problem. Nevertheless, to redress the scales and seek even justice, we must note that many firms achieve high profits through monopolistic situations, without any corresponding benefit to the economy. Price-fixing, the abuse of patents and mergers, covert allocation of markets, and similar devices can lead to exploitively high prices and profits. The critical test in most of these situations is the presence or absence of substantial competition. It is possible to have a high degree of competition even when prices are almost identical (as in the automotive industry), but the burden of proof in such cases lies upon the allegedly competing firms in the industry.

Nor should we leave the impression that labor unions fail to comprehend the need for business profits. The following quotation from a labor economist shows a keen understanding of the problem.

> The chance to make a profit is a mainspring to efficiency and good management in a free enterprise system. To compete against other business, to pay the steady wage increases demanded by labor and still make a profit, a business firm must invent new processes and install new techniques. Labor feels that competition and the profit incentive are necessary to assure good management and productivity. Our high living standards exist because we produce more per manhour than any other nation.

Profits provide business with capital needed to carry on operations, improve machinery and expand plant. Better machines produce greater value per manhour of work, the basis for higher wages; expanded plant capacity creates more jobs. Profits also furnish the tax money that pays a major part of government expenses.[2]

But there are other labor spokesmen who show less insight into the profit needs of American business.

Our conclusion, then, is that polemics about profits often cause misunderstandings. Only a careful consideration of all the circumstances surrounding the profit situation of any firm or industry, including the impact upon the common economic good, can lead to fair and objective appraisal of business profits.

The Right to Interest. The question of interest formerly loomed large in moral treatises. Pure interest was forbidden by medieval theologians because money was considered a consumption good which was used up in the process of spending. It was analogous to food. When a housewife borrows ten pounds of sugar, she is expected to repay that amount and no more. The sugar, in contrast to land, animals, or other productive property, does not produce an income that can be considered a title justifying an extra charge.

Medieval writers allowed extrinsic claims, such as a loss incurred, a gain forgone, or a premium to cover risk, as justification for interest. But a charge for the use of money as such was considered exploitive. The Church ban on interest charges was gradually relaxed as the complex world of business provided more and more extrinsic titles for a return on money. The presumption now is that any lender either passes up a possible gain, or at least incurs the sacrifice of losing the liquidity of his funds. Moreover, the common good of the community is served by the availability of loan capital. Indeed, our modern economic system could not function without it.

It is more difficult to determine what is a just rate of interest. Basic loan rates today are determined by supply and demand factors. The amount of money available for loans depends partly upon savings decisions by income receivers and partly upon funds released by central-banking systems (e.g., the Federal Reserve System). The demand for money is influenced by business conditions and by consumer needs for financing.

Since the general bank rate is influenced by central-banking decisions, the presumption is that it is a just rate, determined by considerations of

---

[2] *Labor's Monthly Survey*, September, 1948, p. 6.

the common economic good. In the United States, the governing board of our central-banking system is appointed by the President with the consent of Congress. Hence it is an agency of the state, committed to seek the common good.

Higher rates based on greater risks or higher collection costs are also morally justified. Even the relatively high rates of finance companies (3 per cent a month, or 36 per cent a year) may not be excessive, since these firms have high investigation, bookkeeping, and collection costs. Injustice is more likely to occur in some installment-sale practices. First, the buyer is often deceived as to the real charges he is incurring. Second, many contracts are so framed as to keep a borrower in constant debt. Most larger stores and sales agencies avoid such practices, but they are common among firms that cater to poor credit risks or less educated buyers. Such firms lend freely at exorbitant rates and let the courts become their collection agencies. Even worse are the "loan sharks" who prey upon improvident borrowers. It is not uncommon for such persons to lend "until payday" (for example, lending five dollars and collecting six), thus getting 20 per cent interest for a loan of a few days. This, of course, makes an annual rate in excess of 1000 per cent.

Usurious exploitation, while cruel and unjust, is not a major economic problem. It can be remedied by better laws (such as the New York State law calling for full disclosure of installment charges), promotion of credit unions, and by adequate economic education in our schools. Even then there will always remain a residue of truly improvident persons who cannot manage money or who gamble or drink away their incomes. These persons need moral guidance and possibly psychiatric treatment. Laws and social institutions rarely help such cases. But society should be concerned with those who, through unavoidable necessity or even ignorance, are victimized by exploitive moneylenders.

DUTIES OF OWNERS AND MANAGERS OF CAPITAL

Duties Toward Labor

The basic social obligation of "capital," in relation to workers, is to respect their human dignity. From this fundamental outlook, many detailed duties may be deduced. Thus, the claim of workers for a fair wage springs from their human dignity. Their right to form unions may be derived from this source. These and other considerations will be treated more at length in the chapters immediately following.

One suggestion given in *Quadragesimo Anno*, however, may be discussed at this point. This is the suggestion that the work contract be modified by a partnership contract, with the workers sharing in the profits, management, and ownership of an industry. The Pope does not advocate this move as a strict right, but he does feel that one or more of these degrees of partnership might be more consonant with the human dignity of workers. Steps in this direction would mean a cautious approach toward greater industrial democracy and the unity of economic society. At the same time, however, we must be aware of the obstacles and pitfalls surrounding these methods, at least in the light of American experience.

Profit-Sharing. Profit-sharing normally involves the dividing of a portion of net profits among the workers in accord with a previously developed formula. Thus, in a given company, some figure may be taken as the fair compensation of stockholders, after suitable reserves had been set aside for bad years. It may then be agreed that of the net profits remaining, 60 per cent (to use an arbitrary figure) may be divided among workers, with the remainder going to salaried employees, executives, and, possibly, stockholders. This would be in addition to a fair wage determined by normal collective bargaining. Such a procedure emphasizes the common interests of workers and employers, gives labor an incentive to cooperate with management, and tends to increase workers' loyalty to the company employing them.

Some firms frankly emphasize the incentive element in profit-sharing. After a basic wage is fixed, supplementary returns depend upon increased production at lower cost. In this way, output is increased and hence workers can be paid at a higher annual rate. The Lincoln Electric Company, in Cleveland, is a strong proponent of this method. On the other hand, the incentive method of profit-sharing often causes much suspicion and even hostility on the part of organized labor. Many workers fear that this is a device to speed up production by developing a pace of operations which cannot be sustained indefinitely. To them, it is reminiscent of piece-rate methods in which unit rates were cut after employees earned a good salary by increasing output. They argue that labor shares the losses during depression times by virtue of unemployment; hence its basic wage should be independent of the ups and downs of the business cycle.

Since these objections are rather widespread and since many profit-sharing plans have failed, it is clear that caution should be used in approaching the problem. As far as any conclusion may be reached from the many plans tried in the United States, it is this: profit-sharing is not normally a good initial means to establish employee good will toward the employer; but if understanding and co-operation have been built up by other means, then profit-sharing is a sound auxiliary device for strengthening bonds already established. Where mutual trust already exists, the sharing of profits is a legitimate incentive to higher productivity, stability in employment, and greater employee loyalty.

A sound profit-incentive plan is based on the theory that there are untapped reserves in the working force which can be utilized through co-operation. Workers often have suggestions for new methods of production, devices to increase quality and cut down waste, safety programs, and the lessening of absenteeism and labor turnover. It may even happen that they could work faster without undue fatigue if the proper stimulus were applied. But the evolving of such patterns of co-operation is a complex psychological problem which will never be met by an unaided profit-sharing plan. Profit-sharing can be successful only if previously complete trust in management's integrity and competence has been developed.

One of the most successful forms of profit-sharing is the so-called Scanlon plan. The heart of this plan is the attempt to make the entire plant work as a team in increasing efficiency and lowering costs. Group rather than individual incentive is the keystone. Management and its workers jointly set a productive norm. They work together in cutting costs. Their teams are constantly screening suggestions and seeking better methods of performance. Results of this method have been remarkable, provided that a pattern of trust and co-operation pre-existed its adoption.

Sharing Management. While the idea of profit-sharing has met with indifference on the part of business and some hostility from labor, suggestions for sharing management usually provoke violent reactions from business and indifference from a large part of labor. Business is acutely sensitive to the "prerogatives of management." It insists that responsibility must be centralized, meaning that it should rest in the hands of owners or their representatives. On the other hand, many labor unions are not interested in sharing any of management's burdens. On some specific points, such as the rate of production, they may demand a voice in what was formerly considered the exclusive field of management, but there is little general interest in any broad participation. This is even more true, as a rule, of the average worker in a factory. He has a limited conception of the broad problems of management and even less interest in assuming a share of them. Thus, at first glance, it might appear that proposals for management-sharing are unrealistic; convincing perhaps to intellectuals, but unappealing to those directly concerned.

Yet, in another sense, sharing of management not only is sound, it is one of the most important developments in recent years. Most of the adverse reaction springs from one limited interpretation of the proposal. Thus, it has been presented as involving employee representation on a board of corporate directors with (presumably) minority status. Business balks at such a notion and labor is not very interested in it. On the other hand, thousands of businessmen are becoming deeply interested in the "human-relations" literature and experience of the past twenty-five years. Learned studies have been made and experiments attempted to prove that "teamwork, communication, and participation" are necessary for a smoothly functioning industrial unit. Educational programs have been developed to make workers feel an identity with company interests and a sense of common responsibility in meeting problems.

In the literature mentioned above, there is great emphasis upon treating a worker as an individual, with full recognition of his personal traits. When a worker is hired, his aptitudes and desires are ascertained and he is fitted to a suitable job. He is trained, not only for his special work, but also in the broad problems of his company. He is made to feel that the firm's problems are his own. Communication is a two-way process. His point of view is solicited; and ultimate decisions are explained to him, not merely handed down as peremptory orders. The ultimate aim is teamwork between workers on all levels and management. Such practices at the factory level are harmonized with the union contract, and with the workers' representatives as definite parts of the pattern of consultation and teamwork.

It is also noteworthy that there is much postwar discussion of management-sharing, on the part of European Catholic groups. Europeans frequently make the distinction, in discussing this problem, between social and economic questions, with the workers having a clear right to participate in the former area, but less right to enter into economic decisions. Under the heading of social questions would come various personnel matters and the problems of social welfare. These considerations are often included in collective bargaining and social legislation in the United States. Economic matters include prices, output, profits, investment, and similar management decisions. American labor has not gone deeply into this field, except to the extent implied by collective bargaining over wages and other costs.

The results of European experiments, particularly those in Germany since codetermination was introduced by law in 1951, are not impressive. At any rate, the historical and cultural patterns behind such moves are quite different from those prevailing in the United States. Our temperament inclines toward partnership situations built on mutual trust, not those imposed by law.[3]

Sharing Ownership. Sharing of ownership usually involves employee stockholding in corporations. Plans of this nature were tried extensively during the 1920's to promote worker interest in a firm. But the stock-market crash of 1929 caused most of these plans to founder. Some companies today retain the practice, particularly in connection with pension or profit-sharing plans. Sears, Roebuck, & Company is an outstanding example.

Most firms, however, have been reluctant to inaugurate stock-ownership plans. Their executives feel that stock prices are too unstable and that workers might become disillusioned when the value of their shares dropped. Moreover, ownership of stock does not give any substantial degree of participation in the control of a modern corporation. Stockholders are too scattered, as a rule, to exercise any personal supervision over the companies in which they have invested. In addition, most American workers are concerned with tangible wage returns, rather than the prospect of dividends.

It would be a mistake so to emphasize means and devices that the ultimate end is overlooked or slighted. The sharing of profits, management, or ownership belong in the category of means toward the end of further emphasizing the human dignity of the worker. Moreover, the form they may take is in large part a matter of experience and prudential judgment. It would seem that the trend of American experience is in the direction of emphasizing worker participation in management at the level where it has concrete and daily impact on his life. If workers are day-by-day partners in the productive process, and their unions are included in the area of broad co-operation, participation, and consultation, then we shall have a greater degree of partnership than has ever previously existed in the American economy.

---

[3] For recent literature on codetermination and human relations see the conclusion of List No. 6 in the Appendix.

Duties Toward the Public

Management must seek the public good, as well as proper relationships with its workers. One aspect of this has already been mentioned, the element of fair prices and reasonable profits. It is a matter of simple justice to give the consumer value for his money. Monopoly or practices in restraint of trade are exploitive. The selling of inferior products or any element of substantial deception of the consumer is unjust.

Beyond this, one of the great needs in the business world is a genuine feeling for the public economic good. Business, like labor and farmers, often becomes a captive of class psychology. As a result, it tends to equate the common good with its own immediate interests. "What is good for business is good for the nation." This attitude, for example, makes some business spokesmen seek tax cuts at a time when national defense precludes such relief. It leads others to oppose removal of trade barriers and to denounce foreign economic aid as a waste of taxpayers' money. It often produces a captious and negative attitude toward government.

Any of these positions may be supported by arguments that appear sound. The holding of any of them is not necessarily a sign of anti-social tendencies. Here the real test is why they are held. Is the businessman reading only arguments that favor his preconceptions? Is he seeking reasons to bolster the short-term interests of his company, and neglecting the national welfare? It is not easy to give general answers to such questions, but there are reasons to believe that it is readily possible for a businessman to drift into a narrow and self-centered position.

In the first place, his own psychology poses problems. By the nature of his calling, he is a man of self-reliance and independence. He is used to giving orders and making firm decisions. He has successfully relied on personal energy and resourcefulness to see him through difficulties. As a result, he is often temperamentally unprepared for the tortuous ways of politics and diplomacy. He wants direct action in fields where it often cannot be had. Then he feels frustrated and hostile and vents his feelings in denunciations of Washington or the United Nations.

Again, many businessmen are so tied down with their own problems that they do not have the time for general reading. They get their information in capsule form from business letters and special sources, such as their trade associations or national business groups. Many of these sources, unfortunately, cater to views designed to please their clients. The result is a reinforcement of originally narrow opinions by the ability to quote "experts" and "authorities."

In this connection, it is a paradoxical fact that often big business, so frequently damned as antisocial, is more advanced than the small businessman. Managers of large corporations of necessity acquire a national and even international point of view. They consult with economists and professional analysts of public policy. They even have some independence in regard to their stockholders and can often take a larger and more long-range viewpoint than is likely with small businessmen. At the same time, their prestige with smaller businessmen is so great that, as our allies in presenting a social philosophy, they are powerful forces for good. Hence the use of publications such as the *Harvard Business Review* or *Fortune*, and of statements by organizations such as the Committee on Economic Development or the American Management Association, are more effective than quoting material compiled by a government or labor group. In citing business leaders, it is often more compelling to use a mild but progressive assertion by acknowledged leaders than a stronger position urged by some highly publicized businessman who lacks real influence in his own community. Thus, a quotation from the Chamber of Commerce of the United States, noting that central fiscal and monetary policies are important in preventing depressions, is more useful than a powerful plea for economic planning by some businessman who is considered a maverick by his colleagues.

While we find in many businessmen a tendency toward parochialism, it is only fair to note that they are not the only offenders. The pressure of modern life tends to make persons in many occupations narrow and overspecialized. Labor leaders can be as guilty or as unfortunate as business leaders in this regard. It is important, in terms of Catholic social action, to have some degree of understanding for these human limitations. We can more readily convince people toward whom we have sympathy.

It is particularly regrettable when Catholics fall into the Marxist attitude of class hostility and blanket denunciation. Some among us have been slow to forget the business abuses of the 1920's, even in the changed climate of the 1950's. Others are equally severe in condemning wrongs in the labor movement, with no credit for the idealism and good will that prevail in so much of this field. Neither extreme shows the healing spirit of social charity, which is the distinct contribution of Christian social teaching. Patient persuasion and sympathetic teaching may win people to seek the common good, whereas group condemnation only confirms them in past positions.

To correct these abuses, it is the work of all who would reform society to preach the value of co-operation for the good of the nation and of all mankind. "What is good for the country, is good for business, labor, and farmers." A truly healthy economy benefits all members of that economy. Short-term selfish advantages usually boomerang in the long run. If recognition of these truths could replace group individualism, everyone would benefit.

READINGS*

J. Messner, Social Ethics, pp. 262–264, 670–674, 697–861 (especially 751–753, 798–800, 811–817, 837–843), 927–930.
B. W. Dempsey, The Functional Economy, Chaps. 18, 20–21.
J. A. Ryan, Distributive Justice.
———— A Better Economic Order, Chap. 7.
O. von Nell-Breuning, Reorganization of Social Economy, Chap. 7.
J. Villain, L'Enseignement social de l'Église, Vol. I, pp. 85–134; Vol. II, pp. 15–109.
G. Clune, Christian Social Reconstruction, Chap. 20.
H. Johnston, Business Ethics, Chaps. 8–9.
Social Order: "The Enterprise," May, 1952; Paul F. Douglas, "New Concepts of Industrial Man," October, 1956; Francis J. Corrigan, "Justice in Stock Exchanges," February, 1953; Francis J. Corrigan, "Accelerated Amortization," April, 1954; Leo C. Brown, S.J., "Profit Sharing Pays," February, 1951; James A. O'Brien, "Profit Sharing and Organized Labor," March, 1954; A. A. Ahner, "Human Labor Relations," March, 1951; Leo C. Brown, S.J., "Labor-Management Cooperation," May, 1951; William J. Nicholson, S.J., "Human Factors in Management," November, 1952; Bernard W. Dempsey, S.J., "The Human in Economic Activity," November, 1956; Quentin Lauer, S.J., "Co-Management in Germany," January, 1951; Alfred R. Desautels, S.J., and Joseph M. Fallon, S.J., "Social Achievements in Belgian Industry," October, 1951; John F. Cronin, S.S., "Social Exchange Today," December, 1951; Henry K. Junckerstorff, "Co-Management: a Trojan Horse," January, 1953; Robert J. McNamara, S.J., "Co-determination and Socialism: a Note," March, 1953; E. A. Kurth, "Codetermination in Germany — Peace at Last?" January, 1954.

---

* For further readings, consult List No. 6 in the Appendix.

Chapter IX

CAPITAL-LABOR RELATIONSHIPS

THE DIGNITY OF LABOR

Leo XIII, Rerum Novarum

31. Workers are not to be treated as slaves; justice demands that the dignity of the human personality be respected in them, ennobled as it has been through what we call the Christian character. If we hearken to natural reason and to Christian philosophy, gainful occupations are not a mark of shame to man, but rather of respect, as they provide him with an honorable means of supporting life.

62. To work is to expend one's energy for the purpose of securing the things necessary for the various needs of life and especially for its preservation. "In the sweat of thy face shalt thou eat bread" (Gen. 3:19). . . . In fact, to preserve one's life is a duty common to all individuals, and to neglect this duty is a crime. Hence arises necessarily the right of securing things to sustain life, and only a wage earned by his labor gives a poor man the means to acquire these things.

Pius XII, La Solennità della Pentecoste, June 1, 1941

1688. To the personal duty to labor imposed by nature corresponds and follows the natural right of each individual to make of labor the means to provide for his own life and that of his children; so profoundly is the empire of nature ordained for the preservation of man.

1689. But note that such a duty and the corresponding right to work is imposed on and conceded to the individual in the first instance by nature, and not by society, as if man were nothing more than a mere slave or official of the community.

Pius XII, Christmas Broadcast, 1942

1850. He who would have the star of peace shine out and stand over society should give to work the place assigned to it by God in the beginning. As an indispensable means toward gaining over the world that mastery which God wishes for His glory, all work has an inherent dignity and at the same time a close association with the perfection of the person; this is the noble dignity and privilege of work which is not in any way cheapened by the fatigue and the burden, which have to be borne as the effect of original sin, in obedience and submission to the will of God.

Pius XII, Christmas Message, 1955

Man can consider his work as a true instrument of his sanctification because by working he makes perfect in himself the image of God, fulfills his duty and the right to gain for himself and his dependents the necessary sustenance, and makes himself a useful contributor to society. Bringing this order into existence will obtain for him security, and, at the same time the "peace on earth" proclaimed by the angels.

Pius XII, To Directors of Chemical Products Organizations, January 10, 1958

Respectful of persons and their inalienable rights, conscious of the profound solidarity that makes him one with the most humble of his fellows, the man with a heart — the Christian above all — does not allow the judgment of economic facts and social situations in the light of the determinism of blind laws or of an inexorable historical evolutionism. He suffers deeply to see the worker of our day too often a stranger to his work, chained to a task which chokes him in an iron collar instead of giving him the opportunity to develop, no matter how modest that opportunity may be.

Competent people realize that the worker, when faced with a job which distorts or degrades his personality to the vanishing point, slows down his productive effort and thus reduces considerably the advantages gained twenty-five years ago by mechanization.

Psychologists have tried to classify the numerous influences which determine the behavior of the worker at his task.

It seems that the most outstanding of these is an active interest in his task, which engages the attention of the man and gives him the feeling of putting his personal resources into his work and developing them.

The worker then feels that he is using not only his muscular power but also his very soul, and that his labor is recompensed, first of all, by pride in the work accomplished, which grows within him.

Instead of seeing in his work only a means for making a living, he finds in it a sense of life and the measure of his personal and social being.

If from the point of view of productivity alone this factor merits the serious attention of industrial chiefs, it is even more impressive when one considers it from the more lofty point of view of the human conscience and its absolute responsibilities.

These responsibilities were succinctly expressed by Christ when He as Supreme Judge declared that, all that is done for the least of His, is as though it were done for Him (cf. Matt. 25, 40).

THE RIGHT TO ORGANIZE

Leo XIII, Rerum Novarum

72. For man is permitted by a right of nature to form private societies; the state, on the other hand, has been instituted to protect and not to destroy natural right, and if it should forbid its citizens to enter into associations, it would clearly do something contradictory to itself, because both

the state itself and private associations are begotten of one and the same principle, namely, that men are by nature inclined to associate.

76. Furthermore, if citizens have free right to associate, as in fact they do, they also must have the right freely to adopt the organization and the rules which they judge most appropriate to achieve their purpose. We do not feel that the precise character in all details which the aforementioned direction and organization of associations ought to have can be determined by fast and fixed rules, since this is a matter to be decided rather in the light of the temperament of each people, of experiment and practice, of the nature and character of the work, of the extent of trade and commerce, and of other circumstances of a material and temporal kind, all of which must be carefully considered. In summary, let this be laid down as a general and constant law: workers' associations ought to be so constituted and so governed as to furnish the most suitable and most fitting means to attain the object proposed, which consists in this, that the individual members of the association secure, so far as possible, an increase in the goods of body, of soul, and of property.

Pius XI, Quadragesimo Anno

30. They were with criminal injustice denying the natural right to form associations to those who needed it most to defend themselves from illtreatment at the hands of the powerful. There were even some Catholics who looked askance at the efforts of workers to form associations of this type as if they smacked of a socialistic or revolutionary spirit.

35. Under these conditions, Catholics seem almost forced to join secular unions. These unions, however, should always profess justice and equity and give Catholic members full freedom to care for their own conscience and obey the laws of the Church. It is clearly the office of bishops, when they know that these associations are on account of circumstances necessary and are not dangerous to religion, to approve of Catholic workers joining them, keeping before their eyes, however, the principles and precautions laid down by Our Predecessor, Pius X, of holy memory. Among these precautions the first and chief is this: side by side with these unions there should always be associations zealously engaged in imbuing and forming their members in the teaching of religion and morality, so that they in turn may be able to permeate the unions with that good spirit which should direct them in all their activity. As a result, the religious associations will bear good fruit even beyond the circle of their own membership.

Pius XII, Sertum Laetitiae, November 1, 1939

1468. Because social relations is one of man's natural requirements and since it is legitimate to promote by common effort decent livelihood, it is not possible without injustice to deny or to limit either to the producers or to the laboring and farming classes the free faculty of uniting in associations by means of which they may defend their proper rights and secure the betterment of the goods of soul and of body, as well as the honest comforts of life. But to unions of this kind, which in past centuries have procured immortal glory for Christianity and for the professions an untarnishable splendor, one cannot everywhere impose an identical discipline and structure which therefore can be varied to meet the different temperament of the people and the diverse circumstances of time.

But let the unions in question draw their vital force from principles of wholesome liberty; let them take their form from the lofty rules of justice and of honesty, and, conforming themselves to those norms, let them act in such a manner that in their care for the interests of their class they violate no one's rights; let them continue to strive for harmony and respect the common weal of civil society.

Pius XII, To German Catholics, September 4, 1949

May the day be not distant that those organizations of self-defense, which the defects of the hitherto existing economic system and, above all, the lack of Christian mentality have made necessary, could cease to function.

Pius XII, To Belgian Workers, September 11, 1949

Unions have arisen as a spontaneous and necessary consequence of capitalism embodied in an economic system. As such, the Church gives her approval to them, always with the condition that, depending on the laws of Christ as their unshakable foundation, they endeavor to promote a Christian order in the world of workers.

Pius XII, To Railroad Workers of Rome, June 26, 1955

No true Christian can find fault if you unite in strong organizations to defend your rights — while remaining aware of your duties — and to arrive at an improvement in your conditions of life. On the contrary, precisely because the harmonious action of all groups in the state is a Christian duty, no individual citizen ought to become a victim of the arbitrary act or tyranny of others. You are therefore acting in full conformity with the Church's social teaching when, by all means morally permissible, you vindicate your just rights.

We said by all means morally permissible. It is unnecessary to remind you that acts of violence which damage the liberty and the goods of others are not even contemplated by true Christians. When, therefore, they use the power of their organizations to win recognition for their rights, it is essential that, in the first place, they use the means suitable for the negotiation of a peaceful settlement. Then, in particular, there must be taken into consideration whether the results being aimed at are in reasonable proportion to the damage which could result from force.

The Church and Social Order

26. Labor can have no effective voice as long as it is unorganized. To protect its rights it must be free to bargain collectively through its own chosen representatives. If labor when unorganized is dissatisfied, the only alternative is to cease work and thus undergo the great hardships which follow unemployment.

Hierarchy of Quebec, Pastoral Letter, February, 1950

100. Present circumstances render more pressing and more imperious the *obligation* for workers . . . to exercise this right [to join unions].

101. Every man has an obligation to seek to protect the security of his professional [economic] interests. He has the duty to seek to obtain for himself and his family all that is necessary in order to live a truly human life and to safeguard them against future hazards. He has the duty to contribute to the welfare of his fellows, especially those united to him in common interests. He has the duty to collaborate in restoring a social order which would be more balanced in favoring respect for justice in all the activities of labor, industry, and commerce. The isolated worker cannot do this. But union with his fellow workers will permit him to fulfill this imperious social duty. In the present state of things, accordingly, there exists a moral obligation to participate actively in one's economic organization.

RIGHT TO WORK AND UNION SECURITY

Pius XII, Christmas Message, 1952

. . . access to employment or places of labor is made to depend on registration in certain parties, or in organizations which deal with the distribution of employment. Such discrimination is indicative of an inexact concept of the proper function of labor unions and their proper purpose, which is the protection of the interests of the salaried worker within modern society, which is becoming more and more anonymous and collectivist.

In fact, is not the essential purpose of unions the practical affirmation that man is the subject, and not the object of social relations? Is it not to protect the individual against collective irresponsibility of anonymous proprietors? Is it not to represent the person of the worker against those who are inclined to consider him merely a productive agent with a certain price value?

How, therefore, can it be considered normal that the protection of the personal rights of the worker be placed more and more in the hands of an anonymous group, working through the agency of immense organizations which are of their very nature monopolies? The worker, thus wronged in the exercise of his personal rights, will surely find especially painful the oppression of his liberty and of his conscience, caught as he is in the wheels of a gigantic social machine.

Statement of Ohio Bishops, March 20, 1958

Man has a right and duty to work for his livelihood. This right cannot be circumscribed to the extent that a man loses his liberty of choice of a vocation; nor to the extent that he is deprived of an opportunity to support himself and his family. It does not follow that a man has the unconditional right to work in any and every industry or business at will.

For reasons of social justice it may be desirable and often advantageous to the common good that man's right be restricted by certain specified conditions. One of these imposed conditions may require that he belong to a labor union or at least be obliged to join the union subsequently, so as to share responsibility with his fellow workmen in support of the union.

Just as a citizen of the United States is free to live in Ohio, Kentucky, or Pennsylvania, yet is obliged to observe the laws of the particular state as a condition of citizenship, so also in respect to his right to work; he is free to work in any industry of his choice, but only on condition that he abides by the rules adopted by that particular industry as a condition of employment.

In other words, the right to work is a general right and cannot be denied to men in the aggregate; but the right to work in a specific industrial plant or business can be subject to special conditions.

If state statutes were to make such a condition of union maintenance mandatory, we would oppose them as unwise, if not unjust. If state statutes however were to forbid the enforcement of such a condition, when mutually accepted by management and labor through collective bargaining, then we would be equally opposed.

We believe it is unwise to encourage state intervention in this matter, whether it be in favor of "right-to-work" laws or against them.

There are certain abuses which sometimes creep into the labor movement, but we are convinced that "right-to-work" laws are not the proper means to correct them. Corruption of certain labor leaders has been one of these current abuses. The denial of the democratic processes and the denial thereby of responsibility to the rank and file of union membership, whether in election to office or in the determination of union policy, are prolific causes of these abuses.

COLLECTIVE BARGAINING

Strikes

Leo XIII, Rerum Novarum

56. Labor which is too long and too hard and the belief that pay is inadequate not infrequently give workers cause to strike and become voluntarily idle. This evil, which is frequent and serious, ought to be remedied by public authority, because such interruption of work inflicts damage not only upon employers and upon the workers themselves, but also injures trade and commerce and the general interests of the State; and, since it is usually not far removed from violence and rioting, it very frequently jeopardizes public peace. In this matter it is more effective and salutary that

the authority of the law anticipate and completely prevent the evil from which it would seem that conflict between employers and workers is bound to arise.

Pius XII, To Christian Associations of Italian Workers, June 7, 1957

. . . only one word of advice is possible for the organized parties to the labor contract: it is better to bargain than to fight one another. This is the only conclusion they can adopt before their own consciences and the people at large.

Australian Hierarchy, Peace in Industry

Under modern conditions, the right to organize in trade unions and the right to strike, under certain defined conditions, are inseparable.

It would be futile to urge the formation of trade unions if the Church did not realize that this involves recognition of the right to strike, as a last resort, and when other measures of achieving social justice have failed.

Four conditions of a just strike have been laid down commonly by theologians: (1) The cause of a threatened strike must itself be just and rightful. (2) There must be sufficient hope of success. It is morally wrong to plunge workers into a strike in which they have no hope of success and from which they will emerge in a worse condition than before. Nevertheless it does not always follow that because a strike is lost it is in vain. (3) The benefit to be gained must not be out of proportion to the harm inflicted. In the case of strikes which seriously affect the entire community, the onus thus placed on those who decide to strike is therefore very great. (4) Before a strike is declared, every effort must first be made to settle the dispute peacefully through conciliation, arbitration, and other more peaceful methods.

Hierarchy of Quebec, Pastoral Letter, February, 1950

179. There are certain categories of workers who would seriously imperil the common good, were they to strike. In this not too frequent situation, the law may suppress or suspend the right to strike, but not without at the same time giving such workers some compensating methods which are adequate to obtain justice. The law should, for example, provide for compulsory arbitration, adequately safeguarded in regard to impartiality, effectiveness, and promptness of decision.

180. Since strikes always involve serious consequences and are justifiable only after normal means for securing a just agreement have been exhausted, the law may limit the exercise of the right to strike, for all workers, by imposing on the parties the obligation to submit to certain procedures such as negotiation, conciliation, and arbitration, before recourse to a work stoppage.

181. (Summarized.) Since laws which suspend or delay the right to strike have the effect of maintaining the status quo, such laws should be carefully drawn to prevent any appearance of partiality. When workers feel that delay is both unnecessary and prejudicial to their interests, they become extremely restless under the law. The state should improve existing laws so as to avoid such dangers.

Code of Social Principles

131. The public interest is the first criterion for estimating the lawfulness or unlawfulness of any concerted cessation of work. To this criterion must be added regard for justice and charity.

132. This public interest is more immediately at stake when it is a question of services directly established for the good of the country and of undertakings, even private ones, that supply the most essential common needs. Certain services are even so indispensable to the community that it is difficult to put forward any supposition that would justify a strike.

133. The danger of such strikes justifies the legislative measures that, in many countries, forbid the use of this dangerous arm by those employed in the public services. But it is also the duty of the legislator to seek by study, and supply by law, such guarantees as will in a less costly fashion assure, especially to those who are forbidden to strike, the gain or the advantages which might be the outcome of a strike that is justifiable both in its aim and methods.

DUTIES OF WORKERS

Leo XIII, Rerum Novarum

30. Among these duties the following concern the poor and the workers: To perform entirely and conscientiously whatever work has been voluntarily and equitably agreed upon; not in any way to injure the property or to harm the person of employers; in protecting their own interests, to refrain from violence and never to engage in rioting; not to associate with vicious men who craftily hold out exaggerated hopes and make huge promises, a course usually ending in vain regrets and in the destruction of wealth.

Pius XI, Quadragesimo Anno

140. No less praise must be accorded to the leaders of workers' organizations who, disregarding their own personal advantage and concerned solely about the good of their fellow members, are striving prudently to harmonize the just demands of their members with the prosperity of their whole occupation and also to promote these demands, and who do not let themselves be deterred from so noble a service by any obstacle or suspicion.

Pius XII, To Members of Italian Electrical Industry, January 25, 1946

To obtain the desired concord between labor and capital, recourse is had to the professional organization and the labor union, understood not as weapons destined exclusively for a defensive or offensive war which would provoke reactions and reprisals, not as a flowing river which submerges and separates, but rather as a bridge to unite these groups.

Pius XII, To Christian Association of Italian Workers, June 29, 1948

But if you are not to grow faint along the road, if you are to keep alive the flame that burns in your hearts, if especially you are to win over the young to your cause, you must keep always before your eyes the noble objective toward which your movement is on the march. Your ultimate purpose is the formation of authentic Christian workingmen, equally distinguished for skill in the practice of their profession and for fidelity in the practice of their religion; men who are capable of reconciling harmoniously the stubborn defense of their economic interests with the strictest sense of justice, and with the sincere disposition to collaborate with the other classes of society toward Christian reconstruction in every walk of social life.

Do not let yourselves deviate from this goal, which is more important than any purely transitory form of union organization. The future of the unions themselves depends on the faithfulness with which you pursue this goal. In fact, if ever they should aim at exclusive domination in the state and society, if they should seek to exercise absolute power over the worker, if they should reject the strict sense of justice and sincere good will to collaborate with the other social classes, they would betray the expectations and the hopes which every honest and conscientious worker places in them. What must be thought when a worker is kept from his labor because he is not *persona grata* to the union, when workers are forced to abstain from labor for political purposes, when they are led astray down not a few other mistaken paths that lead very far away indeed from the true good and often invoked unity of the working class?

Pius XII, To Belgian Workers, September 11, 1949

The temptation to abuse the force of organization [is] a temptation as strong and as dangerous as that of abusing the power of private capital.

. . . The force of organization, however powerful one may wish to suppose it, is not of itself and considered in itself an element of order.

Pius XII, To Administrative Council of the International Labor Organization, November 19, 1954

The labor movement cannot rest content with material success, with a more perfect system of guarantees and assurances or with a greater measure of influence on the economic system. It cannot visualize its future in terms of opposition to other social classes or of the excessive ascendancy of the state over the individual. The goal it pursues must be sought on the very plane on which the Organization places it, that is to say, on the plane of universality — as is proposed in the Encyclical *Quadragesimo Anno* — in a social order where material prosperity is the result of the sincere collaboration of all for the welfare of all and serves as a support for the higher values of culture and, above all, for the indissoluble union of minds and hearts.

The Australian Hierarchy, Morality in Public Life, September, 1950

The basic Christian virtues of justice and charity are the concern of the trade union no less than of political parties, of governments, employers' organizations and of other organized bodies which have obtained such vast power in this century.

This responsibility to base union policy on justice and charity has become all the more pressing in recent years, during which economic life has become so complex that a strike in one small section of an industry can often bring about general industrial paralysis and cause untold sufferings to large numbers of innocent people.

THE discussion of management's duties toward labor, presented in the preceding chapter, was professedly limited in scope. It dealt primarily with the suggestion of Pope Pius XI that the wage contract be supplemented by some form of partnership. It is appropriate now to extend this treatment by considering broader aspects and moral implications of the contacts between workers and management. We do this in two stages, treating first the worker as an individual dealing with his employer and then discussing their collective relationships in union-management affairs.

THE WORKER AND HIS INDIVIDUAL RIGHTS

Much has been said in earlier pages of this book about the rights of man and the dignity of the individual. These points were treated positively and directly in Chapter III, and indirectly in connection with the virtues of justice and charity and in our rejection of individualism and statism. Natural law teaches that man enjoys certain inherent rights, regardless of differences in individual ability and achievement. Our immediate concern is how this truth is applied in work situations that affect nearly seventy million Americans.

Work: A Right and a Duty.   First of all, we note that work is a duty and a right for mankind. It is a duty, since most persons can only thus procure their means of livelihood. Even those who may not have the economic need to work must find an equivalent form of activity, or otherwise face physical, mental, and spiritual decline. Idleness is harmful to human character, whereas the discipline of work can develop many virtues, such as fortitude, patience, and brotherly co-operation.

Work participates in the miracle of creation, since man thereby brings into being new forms and materials not found in nature. Hence there is no need for the worker to feel ashamed of his lot, no matter how humble it may seem. Some of the most difficult types of work are most necessary for the general welfare. Few persons may like such tasks as street cleaning or garbage removal, yet the community would suffer intensely if such tasks were neglected. Again, domestic and personal service is often in disrepute today. To the extent that such attitudes are the result of low wages and poor working conditions in the past, they are quite natural. But it would be wrong to feel that direct personal service is inherently undignified and unworthy. Some of the most respected professions, such as medicine and teaching, embody personal service. A mother's devotion to children is one of the highest forms of this work.

If man has the duty to work as a means of earning his livelihood, he must also have the right to secure work. The God-implanted instinct of self-preservation warrants reasonable access to the wealth of the earth. In most cases, the appropriate form of access is through the creation of new wealth by work. Therefore we can say that man's right and duty to live in effect mean a right to work. This right is directed toward the economic system and owners of property in general. It is not a right to any specific job, but merely a moral claim against economic society. Society meets this claim when it makes every effort so to organize its laws, customs, and institutions that a maximum degree of employment consistent with the common good be created. Its aim should be a job opportunity for every willing and qualified worker.

Although the right to work is not a claim to any specific job, the question arises as to the possibilities of a strict right — in commutative justice — to a definite job, rather than a broad claim in social justice to a fair opportunity to earn a livelihood. Such a strict right, either to obtain or retain a job, can arise from a contract. But most persons, not being motion-picture or baseball stars, do not have contractual rights to a job. Are there, then, any strict rights that may be asserted either in getting or keeping a specific job?

Job Discrimination. In the matter of obtaining a job, the moral problem is that of the responsibility of an employer who practices discrimination against work applicants. No individual applicant has a right to a particular job, but this does not mean that an employer may arbitrarily hire whom he pleases. Obviously he may not, if his discrimination is based on an unworthy motive. Employers are not necessarily bound to hire the most qualified applicants — a certain exercise of whim or irrationality in choice need not be reprehensible. But serious moral fault can be present when the grounds of rejection are immoral.

When a qualified applicant is refused an available job merely because of race, religion, national origin, union affiliation, or similar reasons, the refusing employer can be guilty of grave sin. He is at least violating the virtue of charity. He can also be co-operating in a collective act of injustice. Such can be the case, for example, if all employers in a community refuse skilled work to a qualified Negro, thus forcing him to accept unskilled work at lower pay. If individual employers feel that they are hopelessly coerced by unjust community pressures, they are bound in social justice to try to correct the situation that caused such pressures.[1]

A special problem of some concern today involves the hiring of persons over forty years of age. It is becoming increasingly difficult for workers in this age group to find new jobs, should they lose their former positions. Employers' objections to hiring them stem from pension plans, fear of sickness and injuries, and preference for more energetic and younger workers. Yet older workers bring skill and experience that often more than compensate for any difficulties involved in hiring them. They are usually stable and reliable. It is hoped that field studies being made regarding this problem will convince employers that they are seriously mistaken in regard to the disabilities of older workers. Just as industry learned to appreciate the assets of the handicapped worker, so likewise it can understand the real merits of older applicants for jobs.

Once a worker is hired and performs satisfactorily, he does not, barring some contractual arrangement, acquire a right in strict justice to retain his job. An employer who replaces him with a favored nephew may be acting contrary to charity and equity, but he is not breaching a strict right. To preclude actions of this nature, unions generally and rightly insist, as part of their contracts, upon seniority features and provisions for impartial review of discharges. Some moralists, however, would not accept the analysis just given. They hold that implied in the contract of hiring is the assumption that a worker may retain his job, so long as conditions do not change and his work remains satisfactory. If this condition is really a part of the work contract in modern times, then arbitrary and unwarranted discharge would be a violation of strict justice.

It would be unfortunate if the somewhat negative features of this treatment of the right to a job were to leave an impression that this right is meaningless. Serious rights and duties can exist apart from the claims of commutative justice. The fact that most of the duties connected with

---

[1] The problem of discrimination, and techniques to be used in fighting it, will be treated later in Chapter XV.

employment involve social justice, equity, and charity does not make them less binding. It merely indicates that different means may be needed to enforce them. Social justice, for example, may call for group action rather than unilateral efforts to remedy a situation.

Human Relations. Nor does reserve about the right to retain a job mean that any worker may be mistreated with impunity in this work. On the contrary, the dignity of man demands that the worker be considered as a moral equal who happens to be in a subordinate position. There is nothing inherently wrong in the idea of one person's being in authority over another. On the contrary, authority and subordination are necessary for orderly society. Parents should be able to give commands to their children. Policemen must have the power to direct traffic and keep public peace. But authority rightly used respects the rights of the person in an inferior position. It is used for his welfare, either directly or through his participation in the common good. This principle should be used as a test of industrial relations.

Recognition of the dignity of the worker in industrial life calls for many complex adjustments. At the very beginning of the employee relationship, the element of respect should enter. When a worker is hired, he should be treated as an individual, not merely as another name on the payroll. This means an effort to secure the right person for a job, careful explanation of his duties, opportunity to discover and correct his mistakes, transfer possibilities when needed, and a consistent program aimed at making a worker feel that he is a welcome partner in production. In-service training and advancement programs also help worker morale and minister to his human dignity. Finally, more enlightened firms have methods for taking care of the maladjusted and personality problems, ranging from workers who are merely "difficult" or odd to full-fledged alcoholics or the chronically antisocial.

It is important in this connection to note attitudes rather than techniques. The essential point is consideration of the basic dignity of employees; the means used may vary from plant to plant and from industry to industry. A sensitive employer will try to root out any element of unfairness in hiring workers, autocracy in the issuance of orders, a pace of operations too rapid for older workers, or any policies that prove to be irritants in labor-management relations. An employer should be benevolent, without being paternalistic. While kindness is important, consistent justice and equity are essential. Workers prefer fairness and a predictable set of principles, even though this means strict treatment, to changeable outbursts of good will and generosity. Likewise, if a choice were necessary, most would take equitable rules, minus the latest psychological techniques, in preference to techniques not backed up by principle. Of course, no dichotomy need exist here; it is possible to have both good principles and good techniques.

Even when the employer is fair in treating his workers, considered as individuals, he has not exhausted the possibilities inherent in their relationships. Workers rarely react to their work situation in a purely individualistic fashion. As a rule they form various types of social groupings, formal or informal, ranging from labor organizations to bowling teams or credit unions. Often strong loyalties to the groups concerned are developed. These loyalties need not conflict with loyalty to the company, unless management itself insists upon opposing a particular grouping. In most cases, the problem area is that involving the labor union. Because of the special importance of union-management relationships, the remainder of this chapter will be devoted to the complex issues they engender.

THE WORKER AND HIS UNION

Why Workers Organize.   Workers organize into labor unions for one primary reason: to deal more effectively with their employer. Even when the employer is fair in his personnel policies, his employees may still need a union to protect their interests. The sheer complexity of many modern plants often makes it impossible to have good labor relations without the aid of independent representatives of the workers. There are too many layers of authority between top management and the man at the machine, too many opportunities for misunderstanding or misinterpretation of instructions, and too many occasions for damaging rumors to arise. For the employer's own protection, he often needs experienced union leaders to handle grievances and negotiations.

The case for the union is even stronger when an employer is not prepared to give his workers equitable treatment. In such cases, he has an enormous advantage over his employees, if they come to him as individuals. The average worker lacks the ability, experience, and knowledge necessary to present his case to an employer. He cannot usually marshal economic statistics to buttress a wage plea or quote legal authorities to support his rights. Even were he to make a good case, he has no economic power to back up his argument against an unyielding management. He needs the job more than the job needs him. By contrast, a union can give such workers economic information and legal aid. It also enables them to mount against the employer the serious economic threat of a concerted work stoppage. Under such circumstances the job does need the workers. Most employers are quite reluctant to provoke strikes, especially if they are not sure of the justice of their own position.

The right of workers to organize into unions of their own choosing is widely accepted both as a legal and a moral principle. Legally the right of organization is protected in the United States by federal law and often by state law as well. Morally, a labor union enjoys the general protection given by man's natural right of association, and the specific sanction given to a means necessary to secure certain basic human rights. Today it is rare for any responsible person in the United States to attack labor's right to organize. Even the most determined foes of unions deny that they oppose unionism as such.

We come to a more controversial point when we examine the question of a duty to join a union. Such a duty could arise because a labor union is necessary to secure essential ends for the worker, his family, or economic society. For example, it might be that only a union could obtain wage rates adequate for the health and welfare of the worker and the needs of his family. Or it might be argued that good unions are a first step in the direction of organized social order, as treated in Chapter VII. To prove these points, and thereby establish a duty to join a union, it is necessary to show that the union is uniquely able to secure a necessary end. This is often difficult to do without arguments so complex and involved that an opponent is rarely convinced. For instance, if the worker is satisfied with wages and working conditions in a nonunion plant, is one compelled to argue that he should develop "divine discontent" and seek changes? It is also possible that a worker may be dissatisfied, but unconvinced that unions would be effective or that they would not bring as many disadvantages as advantages. Finally, the argument that all must join unions in order to bring about a just social order begs the question in regard to the position of unions in relation to industry councils.

A more fruitful approach is to stress instead the virtue of social justice and the obligations it imposes upon all members of economic society. Undoubtedly the common good, under some circumstances, may be achieved only by the existence of a union in a particular plant and by universal participation in such a union. Even when a worker may be personally unconcerned with the goals sought by his fellow workers in organizing a union, he may not thereby remain indifferent. For example, he as a single worker may be content with his wage. But he must share the concern of married workers who contend that it is inadequate for their needs. Such obligations, in social justice and charity, are clear and beyond debate. It is better to emphasize definite duties of this nature rather than to hazard the more difficult task of establishing a universal duty to join unions. The end result may be the same in most cases, but the task of persuasion and conviction may be easier if we try the less ambitious approach. In view of the widely publicized charges that both communism and corruption have infected segments of the American labor movement in the past twenty years, an unqualified assertion that every worker has a duty to join a union may be a source of scandal to many of the faithful.

Duty to Recognize Unions. If workers have the right to form unions, employers have correlative duties to recognize such unions and to deal with them in collective bargaining. Such obligations are usually part of federal and state laws protecting union organization. But the moral principle goes further than most laws. For example, government bodies and nonprofit organizations are sometimes exempt from laws protecting unions. But there is no reason why employees of the government or of religious or charitable organizations should be considered second-class citizens in regard to union organization. Even where the right to strike may be surrendered (as with hospitals), it does not follow that collective bargaining is useless.

In general, employers should accept unions chosen freely by their workers. They have a moral and legal right to counsel their workers on the choice of a union, but they may not coerce them or interfere with them. If the union chosen turns out to be corrupt or communist-dominated, employers may be morally justified in fighting it or refusing to recognize it. Corrupt or communist influences may so divert a union from its legitimate ends that it ceases, in fact, to be primarily a labor union. But employers must be sure of their facts in regard to charges of this nature. Too often allegations of radicalism or corruption are made without sufficient evidence. Even when employers have moral certainty in regard to charges made against a union, they are still bound by law to deal with such a union, provided that it has fulfilled all the conditions required for National Labor Relations Board protection.

When churchmen act as employers, they have the same obligations toward workers as have other employers. Indeed, in the light of papal teaching, their conduct should be exemplary in regard to union recognition and collective bargaining. They would be expected to negotiate freely and willingly, invoke conciliation where differences have not been resolved, and even use arbitration in matters where its value is generally recognized. At the same time, it must be remembered that the Church as an employer has the same moral rights as other employers. Its negotiators may argue inability to pay, the need for safeguarding a going business, the case for considering ability above seniority in regard to promotions, and similar pleas. These representatives may fight union claims, even to the point of provoking a strike, when they are considered unjust. It is legitimate to refuse recognition to a communist-dominated or racketeering union. Good example does not involve automatic concession of every union claim. It simply means that Church employers practice the principles of social justice with fidelity and generosity.

Right-to-Work Laws. A particularly difficult problem connected with union organization involves right-to-work laws. These are laws which outlaw compulsory unionism. The nineteen or more states having such laws acknowledge labor's right to organize, but they forbid the union shop or any other device which forces a worker either to join a union or to retain membership after he has joined. It is argued, in favor of such laws, that it is un-American to force workers into unions. Furthermore, it is alleged that compulsory union membership favors racketeers and communists in unions. Workers are unable to leave such unions and thereby deprive vicious leaders of their support.

The traditional argument in favor of the union shop is that workers who receive the benefits of union protection should also pay the costs incurred by the union. It is also asserted that a union shop is the only real guarantee of workers' rights to organize, when the employer is hostile and there is a considerable degree of labor turnover. Otherwise, a union must spend all its time and energy organizing, merely to replace workers who have left the plant or the union. Finally, proponents of the union shop maintain that it is a precondition for labor-management peace. This is true because a union that lacks security must be constantly fighting management to justify its existence. A secure union, on the other hand, is free to work in a friendly and unaggressive fashion with employers.

The ethical arguments against compulsory union membership are not conclusive. The right to work is not an unconditional or unqualified right. It is usually surrounded by many social obligations, ranging from security checks to medical examinations, or from compulsory pension plans to requirements that workers buy company products. Nor are these limitations necessarily wrong. The right to work, like many other rights, must be exercised in the context of the common good.

It is true that the union shop probably makes it easier for racketeers and communists to maintain their power in a union. This point should not be exaggerated, however, since corrupt and Red-led unions seem to do as well in right-to-work states as do their more reputable fellows. At any rate, it is better to seek more direct methods for curing abuses within the union movement, and not to forbid a practice which long has fulfilled a legitimate need in American labor-management relations.

An unusual argument against the union shop is one directed exclusively to Catholics. It holds that the popes favor Catholic unions and merely tolerate neutral unions, at the same time demanding proper safeguards for the faith of the workers. Hence it is difficult enough to justify the joining of secular unions by Catholics, and impossible, they say, to excuse devices that force the faithful into such unions.

Catholic unions were originally formed to counter the virulently Marxist and antireligious unions of certain European nations. As such, they performed a needed function both of preserving the faith of workers and of indicating the Church's interest in the working class. No such unions were formed in Ireland, since there was little if any Marxist tradition in the Irish labor movement. By contrast there are Catholic unions in Quebec, but it is possible that they may merge with the secular A.F.L.-C.I.O. There has been no movement in the Catholic hierarchy of the United States in favor of Catholic unions. In view of such wide diversity of action throughout the world, known to the Holy See and at least tolerated by it, it seems a bit farfetched to bring up this point in connection with the right-to-work controversy.

The arguments cited in favor of the union shop are not absolute. They are presented in connection with American conditions at a given time. As such, they may not be valid in a nation where employers generally accept unions without question. They may even cease to be valid here, were conditions to change drastically. The best that one can do, in matters such as these, is to exercise the most careful prudential judgment as to what the common good demands in the circumstances. Others, holding the same Catholic principles, may see the facts differently and thus come to different conclusions. Principles are based on faith and authority, as well as upon sound reason. As such, they do not change. Policy, to the contrary, being based upon prudential judgment in concrete matters, allows for diversity and even disagreement.[2]

There is no doubt but that the Holy See has been concerned with monopolistic tendencies in labor unions. The June, 1948, address *To the Italian Workers*, two addresses in September, 1949 (*To Belgian Workers* and *To the German Catholics*), and the Christmas, 1952, message clearly indicate these concerns. The Pope is most unhappy about conjoining "access to employment" with abusive political or social demands by unions. Certainly those who defend the union shop as best suited for labor peace in the United States should be equally vocal, as were the Ohio bishops, in insisting that proper measures be taken to see that the unions they defend are indeed worthy of such help.

A possible way out of the impasse connected with the union shop is what may be termed a "service-charge" agreement. Under this clause, all workers in the collective-bargaining unit pay a service charge to the union that bargains for them and handles their grievances. Membership in the union, however, is optional. Those who pay the slightly higher charge for union membership have the right to vote for officers, to vote on strike calls, and to share strike benefits and other privileges dispensed by the union.

American law has consistently favored the principle that a chosen bargaining agent should have exclusive rights to bargain for all members of the unit. The alternative here would be chaos in industrial relations. Since a chosen union is committed by law to serve all workers, whether members or not, it is reasonable to ask all workers to pay a fair charge for these services. Workers who object to union membership may remain outside, without being called "free loaders." They should have legal protection against excessive charges, in addition to their existing right to request decertification of an unsatisfactory union. Such an arrangement should give adequate security to unions and yet avoid the odium of compulsory union membership.

COLLECTIVE BARGAINING

The most common purpose of union organization is collective bargaining over wages, hours, and working conditions. Unions represent their

---

[2] In the United States, the overwhelming majority of bishops and Catholic social scientists who have stated public views on right-to-work laws opposed such enactments. Several priests, however, have been articulate in favor of these laws.

members in seeking agreement upon a contract which governs their employment. This fact implies many rights and duties both in regard to unions and employers.

Aims of Collective Bargaining. Union-management negotiations in collective bargaining should seek to give both workers and employers their rights and their equitable claims in matters of wages, hours, and working conditions. Workers have a right to a just wage and hours and working conditions consonant with their human dignity. The employer has a right to a fair profit and responsible performance of work by his employees. Moreover, the public has a right to expect conscientious dealings on both sides, so that unnecessary strikes or lockouts will not cause serious inconvenience or even hardship. In addition to rights there are equitable claims. The worker is seeking higher standards of living than the minimum of strict justice. The employer desires wholehearted co-operation from his workers. And the public wishes to share in the gains achieved through increased productivity.

The real problems in collective bargaining usually fall within the domain of claims for better conditions, rather than the area of rights. The demand for a living wage, for hours which do not endanger health or interfere with family life, and for working conditions consonant with human dignity is not likely to cause serious theoretical objections from the employer. At most he might object that he is unable to meet all the demands, but he is not likely to contest their justice. Thus, the right to grievance machinery, assuring the worker of a system of appeals against conditions which he finds oppressive, is a matter of justice. It is a recognition of human dignity. Social justice likewise favors provisions regulating job security. Protection against arbitrary discharge is equitable. More controversial are seniority provisions regulating layoffs and promotions. In view of the fact that older workers are generally family men, it is consonant with human dignity to afford them job protection. The employer is benefited through the retention of a stable and contented working force. Likewise, it is equitable to invoke seniority in promotion where abilities are equal. The principle of absolute seniority in promotion, disregarding ability, is less acceptable. It might be legitimate where the nature of work is such that skills do not vary appreciably. But it would not be suitable in regard to promotion to executive positions where abilities are usually the controlling factor.

Other items in union contracts, such as paid vacations and holidays, are more in the nature of claims than rights. They raise the worker's standard of living and may legitimately be sought when the condition of business permits. But an employer who might give two week's vacation with pay would be within his rights in turning down a request for a third. The same reasoning would apply to claims such as pensions, a guarantee of work or wages, and medical insurance. If the employer is not paying a living wage, the workers may in justice demand either a living wage or its equivalent through pensions and medical plans. But where these are claims above the minimum standard, it is equally legitimate for workers to ask them and for employers to deny them. These are problems of equity rather than justice.

The fact that demands in collective bargaining often go beyond the realm of rights into the more shadowy ground of claims and interests does much to explain the difficult problems connected with strikes or lockouts. If every work stoppage were based upon clear problems of justice, it would be relatively simple to judge who was right and to provide machinery for enforcing the rights involved. In fact, however, it is extraordinarily difficult to judge the merits of a strike or a lockout.

Justice in Strikes. Strikes are to collective bargaining what quarrels are to married life. They are temporary breakdowns of unity, leading to widely varying results. They can clear the air and bring a new and better understanding. Or they may create lasting bitterness, smoldering beneath a surface truce. Finally, they can cause a complete break in relationships between the affected parties. Furthermore, like quarrels between spouses, they are often the source of serious suffering to innocent third parties. Because of the problems occasioned by industrial disputes, sound social principles circumscribe the right to strike with many qualifications.

That workers in general have the right to strike is usually conceded. Some authors are so concerned with possible evils that they consider the strike a weapon of extreme desperation, to be used only when its necessity is clear and overwhelming. Others are not so rigorous in demanding justification for work stoppages. The American public justifies strikes on the grounds that workers cannot be compelled to remain at the job. Moralists are more likely to emphasize the justice of workers' claims as the excusing circumstance. They permit a strike for a just cause when other means of securing fair treatment fail. Many writers compare a strike to war and pose similar conditions for its justification. The strike must be (1) for a just cause; (2) necessary because other means have failed; (3) such that the gains sought will outweigh the evils occasioned, with a reasonable hope for success in the strike; and (4) carried on by lawful and morally sanctioned means. These conditions imply many complex decisions.

A just cause involves at least some claim which is fair and equitable. As noted before, we do not limit collective bargaining (and consequently strikes) to matters of strict justice. Otherwise, workers would have little chance to improve their conditions. Indeed, the economy itself might suffer, since the constant goad of worker demands forces employers to use more efficient methods and thus benefit the entire nation. Between demands that are beyond doubt matters of justice and exactions that are clearly unjust lies a no man's land of claims and interests. Such claims may be pressed even to the point of a strike, but the employer who rejects them and permits the strike is not of necessity acting unjustly.

For this reason, and others, the concrete determination of the justice or equity of a strike issue is not easy. The critic must understand the realities of industrial relations to be able to appraise correctly the issues involved. Thus, a strike for noneconomic reasons, such as for union recognition, may be vitally important for the workers. Only when the union is recognized may they be sure that their rights can be enforced. Again, workers may strike over an unjustified discharge of a fellow worker. Here they feel that precedent is essential, in that if the principle of unjustified discharge is allowed, no worker may be safe. On the other hand, there have been strikes motivated by considerations of union or civic politics. It is unjust for a union leader to provoke a strike merely for the sake of his own personal pique or ambition. Political strikes, especially general strikes, are usually wrong, since there are better alternative methods in a democracy for securing political ends. They may not always be wrong, since sometimes they are a dramatic form of the right of petition, calling public attention to the inadequacy or injustice of administrative decisions. As an illustration, it sometimes happens that a legal means exists for settling a dispute without recourse to a strike, but that the use of this means involves intolerable delays, often for years. Direct efforts to secure a settlement seem justified here.

Even more difficult are problems connected with secondary, sympathy, and jurisdictional disputes. In these cases, the employer is often an innocent victim caught in the crossfire between warring parties. There is little difficulty when the employer of primary and secondary strikers is the same person. Thus, if Corporation A had a strike in its New York plant called for a just cause, workers in its Detroit plant could strike to enforce the just claim of their fellow employees. Again, if one employer in an industry had a strike, and workers for other employers in the same industry had reason to feel that conditions obtained through the strike would become general, they might reasonably go out for their own protection. Otherwise, they would be victims of the divide-and-conquer strategy. Father Clune goes further and justifies, on the principle of indirect voluntary, a strike against the main supplier of a mill which is trying to break a just strike through the use of strikebreakers.[3] But he would not concede the justice of a sympathy strike merely because what hurts labor in one place hurts all workers. In other words, where workers have a real and tangible, even though indirect and secondary, interest in a just strike, this may be an excusing reason for them to go on strike. But if the interest is remote and fanciful, they would not be justified in striking.

Jurisdictional disputes are strikes over the allocation of work. They may be sanctioned where the employer has clearly violated a contract or the unwritten customs of the trade. But where he is merely an innocent party, a victim to the conflict of claims between two unions, such a strike does not seem just. In such cases social justice would call for resort to other methods, such as an impartial board to arbitrate the claims. If the affected parties cannot agree to disinterested judgment, then the state has the right and duty to enforce such an agreement.

A common cause of jurisdictional disputes is the action of specialty employers, often employing only one craft, in spreading out to fields traditionally handled by other crafts. Contractors may be as often the cause as the victim of such disputes. The complexity of these issues shows the wisdom of the Taft-Hartley clause which encouraged union-management machinery to solve them. On the whole these committees have done a good job. They have proved the value of subsidiarity.

Likewise, there are industries and occupations where the public interest is so paramount that strikes may not be tolerated or, at best, permitted as a last resort. Here the clear demands of the common good transcend the interests of the parties. In such cases alternate methods for solving the dispute must be set up, even though they involve techniques (such as compulsory arbitration) that would otherwise be unacceptable. One might here distinguish between an absolute and a relative public interest. In the first case, even one day's strike would be intolerable. This would be

---

[3] Cf. G. Clune, *Christian Social Reorganization* (Dublin: Browne and Nolan, 1940), pp. 416–417. The moral principle of the indirect voluntary permits a person to perform an action which is in itself morally good or indifferent, but from which an evil result may follow. This is permitted provided that the agent acts from correct motives, that the good result does not follow as a result of the evil, and that the reason for acting is sufficiently serious to outweigh the unintended but foreseen evil. Thus, a woman might, to save her life, permit radium treatments for cancer of the cervix, even though this might result in sterility.

true of police, the army, firemen, emergency nurses in a hospital, electric power workers (if no service at all were maintained), or a total paralysis of all means of public transportation on a broad scale. In the second case, grave public inconvenience would be caused, but no disaster provided the strike were not prolonged unduly. This would be true of telephones, a major form of transportation, garbage collection, atomic energy production in time of international tension, war strikes in major industries, coal min-ing, oil transportation or production, milk and food delivery, or a limited strike in electric power production.

In the first instance, strikes should be prohibited by law, with com-pulsory settlement of disputes. In the second category, strikes should be delayed by law, with public hearings and other pressures for an equitable settlement and an emergency power to stop the strike when disaster threatened. It does not follow from this that all strikes by public workers are unjustified. Many public servants are not performing emergency duties. Often a strike is the only means for publicizing the conditions of under-paid or mistreated government workers. Federal or state laws to prohibit such strikes by public workers are unjust if they do not provide effective alternative means for meeting rights and equitable claims.

To summarize, in normal disputes between employers and their workers, a just cause for a strike may be found either in a right which has been denied or an equitable claim which is being pressed. This principle may be applied with limitations to secondary and sympathy strikes where the workers are striving for valid claims which otherwise might be lost. Even greater limitations should be imposed on jurisdictional strikes since satis-factory alternate methods for handling such disputes can be set up. Finally, in industries or occupations vitally affecting the public interest, the public good demands other means than a strike for deciding the justice of the case.

Other Conditions for a Strike. A strike for a just cause is not legiti-mate if other means of settlement are not exhausted. The normal means of settlement are negotiation, conciliation, and arbitration. Thus, it is unjust to call a "quickie" strike to settle a dispute, if no efforts have been made to negotiate the point. Damage is thus caused to the employer and the public, without reasonable attempts to forestall this evil. There may be cases where solid grounds exist to believe that negotiations would be useless and that the employer would use the time to prepare strikebreaking methods. In such a situation, a sudden strike might be justified. Normally, however, both parties should attempt to bargain in good faith until it is clear that no settlement can be reached. Genuine collective bargaining involves efforts by both sides to present reasonable offers and to discuss the merits of the issues in question. A take-it-or-leave-it attitude is permissible only after a complete breakdown of fair discussions. A certain amount of "padding" of claims or the use of poker-playing methods is not unfair, since such tactics are usually expected and discounted in advance.

When negotiations break down, federal or state conciliation machinery is usually available. At times, private parties may serve as mediators. Here again both groups are bound in justice to use such services, unless there are solid reasons to believe that conciliation is invoked merely to waste time and weaken the economic power of one party. Since there are profound psychological elements involved in the negotiation of contracts, it is often helpful to gain the aid of friendly or disinterested third persons.

If conciliation fails, it is possible to submit the dispute to judicial arbitration. Many industries have permanent arbitrators who handle contract disputes as well as grievances. In other cases, ad hoc arbitration is invoked when a situation reaches an impasse. On the other hand, most industries and labor unions are violently opposed to arbitration of issues, claims, and even rights in the negotiation of contracts. Employers claim that this means the abdication of basic managerial rights to an outsider who rarely can be as familiar with the industry as the parties directly concerned. Unions likewise are reluctant to entrust their rights or even claims to a third party. If disputes were only over rights, there would be less difficulty. But interests and claims are not easily subject to judicial decision. Even where economic rights are involved, such as a fair wage, an employer may be understandably reluctant to entrust to another a decision which may mean the life or death of the company.

Compulsory arbitration, enforced by law, amounts to complete government control over industry and labor, since the economics of collective bargaining are far-reaching in their implications. Moreover, the existence of an outside court often tends to break down normal collective bargaining. One party or the other merely goes through the motions, hoping to gain more from the outside agency than it could get directly. All these results are seriously contrary to the common good and hence involve a violation of social justice. Compulsory arbitration might more easily be justified in the administration of a contract previously reached by collective bargaining. The contract settles clearly defined and limited rights and claims, so that its carrying out is a matter of justice. Actually, most modern agreements do have such an arbitration clause.

Compulsory arbitration, with all its limitations, is likewise acceptable for jurisdictional disputes and absolute public interest disputes. In these cases, the evils caused by a strike outweigh the disadvantages attendant upon compulsory settlement of claims. Decisions in jurisdictional disputes are more akin to the interpretation of contracts and customs than they are to the awarding of claims. There is usually a body of precedent or analogy to similar situations which permits equitable decisions in such matters. In regard to absolute public-interest disputes, these industries or occupations are usually under a fair degree of government control already. Thus, compulsory arbitration would not here be extending appreciably the area of state penetration into private life.

The third major condition, that a strike should promise more good than the evil it occasions and that it have some chance of success, likewise must be judged in the light of industrial realities. Often workers remain on strike for a single cent an hour more than has been offered by the employer. It may take them years to gain what they seem to have lost in wages. Yet, there are intangibles involved in such situations which preclude an oversimplified treatment. Unions may feel that concessions made one year would be a precedent for further pressures later. There may be a principle of discrimination involved, with one union getting less than another. This could lead to the playing off of one against the other until both were rendered impotent. Or the surface cause of a dispute may be but a last straw in a long history of irritations, just as quarrels between individuals may erupt violently for apparently slight reasons. Thus, it is almost impossible to generalize as to which causes of strikes outweigh the attendant evils. This has to be done in each individual case by persons experienced in the ways of industrial life.

Finally, the last condition of a just strike is that it should be waged by morally acceptable means. It is not legitimate to engage in sabotage or other destruction of the employer's property. Nor is violence permissible, save in self-defense against clearly threatened violence from groups supporting the employer. If the employer uses strikebreakers against a just strike, the strikers would be permitted to boycott and attempt to persuade others to boycott goods so produced. This is merely inducing people not to co-operate in an unjust action by buying products made under unethical conditions. Picketing is lawful for the same reasons. Of course, there are forms of mass picketing which are conducive to violence. But mass picketing is not in itself wrong, since it has a legitimate purpose which may be intended. It is a more effective manner of advertising the strike. Striker morale and solidarity are aided when strikers see their fellows on the picket line. Not all strike violence is induced by strikers. In the past, and in some industrially backward parts of the country today, it was a standard employer tactic to provoke violence so as to discredit strikers.

If all the four conditions laid down are fulfilled, a strike may be just. Of course, it is impossible to make any generalization as to run-of-the-mill American strikes and to say whether or not they have often been just. Two points do have validity: with some exceptions, union leaders do not sanction strikes without serious reason, since the risk they run is too great; second, many newspapers do not give fair reports of the strikers' case, either through bias or through the necessary brevity found in tabloids or provincial papers largely interested in local news. Hence it is necessary to find the facts before judging.

If a strike (or lockout) appears to be justified by the criteria just outlined, we should blame any inconvenience caused by the strike or lockout upon the party who is responsible in the dispute. This, of course, need not be the party who ordered the stoppage. Moreover, we should not co-operate with the party at fault by any activity on our part. This could mean refusing to cross picket lines or buy "hot goods." Such an obligation would be particularly strong for a person in a position of influence, since his actions may well determine the success or failure of the work stoppage.

In conclusion, it might be said that the prevalence and importance of strikes is frequently overstressed. Strikes are dramatic, whereas industrial peace seems prosaic. Lincoln Steffens observed that any newspaper can "break" a police chief simply by reporting and headlining routine crime news. Similarly, a bad public opinion can be created in regard to unions by overemphasis upon exceptional strikes, to the neglect of continuing examples of labor-management co-operation. The percentage of total working time lost by strikes during the period of dramatic headlines (1947–1949) was 0.46. By 1958, the average had dropped to 0.27 per cent. These figures are somewhat low, since they measure only direct stoppages, not indirect effects. Nor do they allow for the unusual impact of highly critical strikes. But they do serve as a useful antidote to exaggeration.

THE DUTIES OF LABOR

Labor has duties as well as rights. It must deal fairly with employers. Unions should be honestly and effectively run. And, in all cases, the rights of the public must be observed.

Duties Toward Employers. A worker is bound in justice to work diligently and fairly in return for a decent wage. "An honest day's work for an honest day's pay" is the old maxim. Conscientious work means more than avoidance of loafing. It also involves care of property, concern with the quality of work, and a proper interest in the welfare of the employer.

Difficult practical problems arise in regard to such practices as stretching out work, "feather-bedding," or "made-work." Usually these practices are motivated by the effort to preserve and extend employment in a declining industry. Unfortunately, this approach is self-defeating, since it increases costs and hence accentuates the fall-off in demand for products or services. Labor must learn that production of wealth is the only basis for its income. Increases gained through abuse of a monopoly position, without any gain of productivity, are morally wrong and economically suicidal.

Organized labor should recognize the evils of restrictive practices, whatever their subjective justification. More than any other practice, they give unions a bad name in the public mind. The public expects fair value when it pays a worker. It is understandably resentful when necessities are high priced because of work limitation. This is particularly the case in times of full employment. Here soldiering and feather-bedding may well be contrary to strict justice. At any time, the unions concerned would be wise to prepare a constructive, long-range program for remedying the conditions which have occasioned these practices.

In this light a special duty of workers, in social justice, is their willingness to co-operate with management to secure more efficient production. Labor-management co-operation is one of the main techniques for raising living standards. Moreover, it is desirable for its own sake since class hostility is contrary to the nature of industrial life. As was observed before, the uniting force of production is as important as the divisive force of distribution. This duty of co-operation implies a corresponding willingness of employers to do their share in meeting the legitimate demands of labor. Workers must be assured that generous efforts on their part will not mean that they will work themselves out of their jobs. The resulting increase must be distributed fairly among the workers, as well as among stockholders and consumers.

With all the faults of some unions, employers must bear a large share of the blame for an aggressive situation. They often get the type of union that their own conduct calls for. When they are "hard boiled" and try to break the union, it will become a fighting organization. If they are coldly impersonal, the union normally takes a strictly business attitude. Here one has an armed peace rather than either co-operation or conflict. Occasionally one finds collusion rather than real co-operation, the difference being that both sides unite in policies contrary to the public interest. More frequently there is a situation which might be called accommodation, where common interests are recognized but only in a limited fashion. Conflict and hostility are avoided, but positive friendliness and complete mutuality are absent. The test of full co-operation is progression beyond normal collective bargaining to the level of joint efforts to increase productivity and to lower costs. It is this final stage which is the aim of Catholic social teaching.

Duties in Regard to Unions. Workers have many duties as union members. Among these one of the most important is that they make the effort to see that their union follows sound principles. This involves attendance at meetings, conscientious voting in union elections, and even running for union office. Where unions have gone bad, either through communism or racketeering, there is nearly always a history of poorly attended union meetings. Workers are often content to let small cliques or factions run their unions, provided they get results. At times, this produces an entrenched bureaucracy which consolidates its power either through a political machine or by changing the union constitution. In this light, the obligation to take interest in union matters might well be compared to one's civic obligations, the more so since unions today are quasi-public institutions. Union members should not emulate corporation stockholders in the doubtful practice of evading responsibility behind the anonymity of a large organization.

At the same time, workers should avoid the opposite extreme of undue pressure on union officers. Holding union office is a task beset with many trials and rewarded with ingratitude and abuse. It is almost a vocation rather than an attractive profession. While some union leaders may live well, a majority works long hours, particularly at night, under extreme tension. For one overpaid union racketeer, there are hundreds of underpaid and overworked servants of workers. So true is this that there exists at times a problem of social justice in relation to union employees. Unions, like church and similar groups, occasionally expect their workers to toil long hours at inadequate pay for the sake of the cause.

Union officers in turn have duties toward their members. They owe them faithful and honest service, representing them with integrity and courage. They should consider themselves as servants of the workers. Any trend in the direction of autocracy and dictatorship violates the human dignity of the members. This does not mean that some discipline and leadership are not useful in unions. On the contrary, they are essential if the union is to function smoothly. Since public interest demands that labor organizations act as responsible and trustworthy groups, their leaders must have some power to enforce continuity of policy. It would be intolerable if any agreement were subject to repudiation by a small but vocal minority of members.

Union officials should insist that orderly methods be followed in handling grievances, with no wildcat and unauthorized strikes. They should have the courage to stand for sound policy. When their experience tells them that membership wishes are unwise, they should use all their ability to persuade the members to follow a wiser course.

These same officials should serve the interest of their members in relation to the employer. While they should explore all forms of labor-management co-operation, such activities must be open and upright. Collusive, underhand dealing with employers to the detriment of the workers is thoroughly dishonest. A union official who accepts secret payments from company officials to "go light" in his demands upon them is like a grafting public official. He betrays trust and is guilty of dishonesty. If the betrayal is serious, one might say that he has no right in justice to the salary which he takes from the union. He is receiving it only through fraud and deception. Of course, there is no objection to personal friendliness between union officials and corporation executives. A private chat at the dinner table might solve problems in an hour which would take weeks in a grievance committee. The motivation behind such meetings should be the controlling factor in judging their propriety.

Finally, officers of unions should be honest in handling the funds of the membership. It is desirable to have preliminary financial reports of a local on a quarterly basis, at least, with an annual detailed audit of funds both of the local and of the parent union. Members likewise should have fair opportunity to vote for their leaders in an honest election. In view of past abuses, there is a case for government regulation of such matters, in the attempt to preserve genuine democracy in unions. Labor groups today are no longer private associations; they are quasi-public bodies and hence have public responsibility.

All these observations are particularly pertinent in connection with Senate hearings on labor corruption, held during the years 1956–1958.

Revelations of widespread abuse of power shocked the American public
and led to demands for reform legislation. Such legislation would be
directed at the goals of safeguarding union funds and preserving the
democratic process in unions. It is questionable, however, in the light of
previous experience that Congress will be able to legislate adequately in
its attempt to remedy this situation. It is extremely difficult to anticipate
all problems and to draw up comprehensive rules, without affecting the
legitimate and normal functioning of unions. Serious thought should be
given to an alternative method, patterned upon the Public Review Board
of the United Automobile Workers. Such independent boards would
have full power to investigate and remedy abuses in the democratic
process, misuse of funds, and similar breaches of trust.

Unions should be given a choice between setting up a genuinely independent board on their own initiative, or permitting their members to
appeal to a federal board or court established to guarantee the democratic
rights of union members. Such courts, for example, could supervise
nominations and elections, examine financial statements, and hear appeals
from disciplinary actions. They would have the discretion to hear complaints at the lowest level, or to act as an appeals system from the
procedures set up by the union constitution. In exercising this discretion,
they could follow the rules set up by civil courts of equity — granting
summary relief when irreparable damage is threatened, but otherwise
using standard appeal procedures.

Duties Toward the Public. One of the aspects of labor's duties toward
the public was examined earlier, in connection with the morality of
strikes. Strikes called for trivial or unworthy reasons cause hardships to
employers and to the public, without any compensating justification. In
addition, unions should carefully examine their position in regard to
charges of wage inflation. This point will be treated in the following
chapter.

The internal conduct of labor unions, also studied previously, is a
matter of public interest today. But good conduct is not merely a matter
of avoiding corruption or autocracy. It also involves positive acceptance
of community responsibilities and a certain maturity commensurate with
labor's power. Most labor leaders are eager to assume such duties. They
take their part in community-chest programs, Red Cross drives, and
public-school activities. But the labor movement could acquire more
finesse in public relations. It could drop the class-hostility approach in

its press and speeches, particularly in areas where employers are reasonable in dealing with unions. There is no reason why the labor press should often read like a page from a nineteenth-century socialist publication. Business as a whole has shown more awareness of the need for good public relations than has the labor movement. Fine words may not always be backed up by deeds in the business community. But labor too often has concealed fine deeds behind the smokescreen of careless public utterances.

Finally, labor would do its public duty by considering broader areas of co-operation with management and other economic interests, as outlined in Chapter VII. More is needed than protestations of public interest. There must be a detailed working out of common programs on all levels. From the single small factory, through giant industries, to the great national federations of business and labor, there should be a realization of common concerns and general responsibilities. Collective bargaining should move in the direction of co-operation for the welfare of all. It should never degenerate into collusion to exploit the consumer. Co-operation in turn should be carried into ever higher levels through frequent conferences of the various local and national organizations. It would be desirable that friendly relations and informal meetings be a normal thing between top labor and business leaders. Even more valuable would be close relations between the expert advisers, such as lawyers and economists, and the leaders in these fields. While economics is not an exact science comparable to mathematics or physics, there are nevertheless broad areas of agreement among experts. Certainly there is little justification today for juggling statistics or distorting trends in the attempt to prove a position taken merely for partisan reasons. Thus, all trained economists realize that living standards will rise only through increased productivity. This in turn can be achieved through capital investment and through labor-management co-operation. Gains obtainable through redistribution of present income are, on the whole, negligible, especially when considered in terms of their effect upon capital formation. Except where prices and profits are badly out of line, there need be little difference in the economic attitudes of capital and labor.

If business and labor both can develop a sense of broader interests and responsibilities, we can move toward replacing group individualism with a genuine sense of concern for the common good. Thus we approach, step by step, that happy unity of society which can bring industrial peace **and economic prosperity.**

READINGS*

J. Messner, *Social Ethics*, pp. 800–811.
B. W. Dempsey, *The Functional Economy*, Chap. 13.
J. Villain, *L'Enseignement social de l'Église*, Vol. II, pp. 57–101, 177–311.
M. E. Walsh and P. H. Furfey, *Social Problems and Social Action*, Chap. 10.
G. Clune, *Christian Social Reconstruction*, Chaps. 17–20.
H. Johnston, *Business Ethics*, Chaps. 9, 11.
Catholic labor periodicals: *Work*, the *Wage Earner*, the *Labor Leader*, and the *Labor Observer*.
Social Order: William A. Durbin, "The Right Not to Join a Union," September, 1952; William J. Smith, S.J., "The Duty to Join a Union," November, 1952; Gladys W. Gruenberg, "Unionism at the Crossroads," January, 1955; Leo C. Brown, S.J., " 'Right-to-Work' Legislation, Does Not Solve Problem," March, 1955; Leo C. Brown, S.J., "Unionization in Small Plants," April, 1956; Leo C. Brown, S.J., "Problems in Unionized Small Plants," May, 1956; Roy Lechtreck, "Bargaining with the State," September, 1956; Mortimer H. Gavin, S.J., "Trends in Christian Trade Unionism," December, 1956; Leo C. Brown, S.J., "Labor Arbitration," February, 1957; Leo C. Brown, S.J., "Union Public Review Boards," May, 1957; Leo C. Brown, S.J., "The Quandary Labor Faces Today," October, 1957; Gladys W. Gruenberg, "Union Monopoly?" March, 1958; Leo C. Brown, S.J., "Trade Unionism Appraised," October, 1958; Georges Jarlot, S.J., "Christian Trade Unions," February and March, 1959; August Vanistendael, "The Neutrality of American Trade Unions," March, 1959.

---

* For further readings, consult List No. 7 in the Appendix.

Chapter X

THE LIVING WAGE AND FULL EMPLOYMENT

THE LIVING WAGE

Leo XIII, Rerum Novarum

51. Nay, in this respect, their energy and effectiveness are so important that it is incontestable that the wealth of nations arises from no other source than from the labor of workers. Equity therefore commands that public authority show proper concern for the worker so that from what he contributes to the common good he may receive what will enable him, housed, clothed, and secure, to live his life without hardship. Whence it follows that all those measures ought to be favored which seem in any way capable of benefiting the condition of workers. Such solicitude is so far from injuring anyone, that it is destined rather to benefit all, because it is of absolute interest to the state that those citizens should not be miserable in every respect from whom such necessary goods proceed.

61. We shall now touch upon a matter of very great importance, and one which must be correctly understood in order to avoid falling into error on one side or the other. We are told that free consent fixes the amount of a wage; that therefore the employer, after paying the wage agreed to, would seem to have discharged his obligation and not to owe anything more; that only then would injustice be done if either the employer should refuse to pay the whole amount of the wage, or the worker should refuse to perform all the work to which he had committed himself; and that in these cases, but in no others, is it proper for the public authority to intervene to safeguard the rights of each party.

62. An impartial judge would not assent readily or without reservation to this reasoning, because it is not complete in all respects; one factor to be considered, and one of the greatest importance, is missing. To work is to expend one's energy for the purpose of securing the things necessary for the various needs of life and especially for its preservation. "In the sweat of thy face shalt thou eat bread." Accordingly, in man labor has two marks, as it were, implanted by nature, so that it is truly personal, because work energy inheres in the person and belongs completely to him by whom it is expended and for whose use it is destined by nature; and, secondly, that it is necessary, because man has need of the fruit of his labors to preserve his life, and nature itself, which must be most strictly obeyed, commands him to preserve it. If labor should be considered only under the aspect that it is personal, there is no doubt that it would be entirely in the worker's power to set

the amount of the agreed wage at too low a figure. For inasmuch as he performs work by his own free will, he can also by his own free will be satisfied with either a paltry wage for his work or even with none at all. But this matter must be judged far differently, if with the factor of personality we combine the factor of necessity, from which indeed the former is separable in thought but not in reality. In fact, to preserve one's life is a duty common to all individuals, and to neglect this duty is a crime. Hence arises necessarily the right of securing things to sustain life, and only a wage earned by his labor gives a poor man the means to acquire these things.

63. Let it be granted then that workers and employers may enter freely into agreements and, in particular, concerning the amount of the wage; yet there is always underlying such agreements an element of natural justice, and one greater and more ancient than the free consent of contracting parties, namely, that the wage shall not be less than enough to support a worker who is thrifty and upright. If, compelled by necessity or moved by fear of a worse evil, a worker accepts a harder condition, which although against his will he must accept because the employer or contractor imposes it, he certainly submits to force, against which justice cries out in protest.

Pius XI, Quadragesimo Anno

69. It is obvious that, as in the case of ownership, so in the case of work, especially work hired out to others, there is a social aspect also to be considered in addition to the personal or individual aspect. For man's productive effort cannot yield its fruit unless a truly social and organic body exists, unless a social and juridical order watches over the exercise of work, unless the various occupations, being interdependent, co-operate with and mutually complete one another, and, what is still more important, unless mind, material things, and work combine and form as it were a single whole. Therefore, where the social and individual nature of work is neglected, it will be impossible to evaluate work justly and pay it according to justice.

71. . . . . Every effort must therefore be made that fathers of families receive a wage large enough to meet ordinary family needs adequately. But if this cannot always be done under existing circumstances, social justice demands that changes be introduced as soon as possible whereby such a wage will be assured to every adult workingman. It will not be out of place here to render merited praise to all who, with a wise and useful purpose, have tried and tested various ways of adjusting the pay for work to family burdens in such a way that, as these increase, the former may be raised and indeed, if the contingency arises, there may be enough to meet extraordinary needs.

72. In determining the amount of the wage, the condition of a business and of the one carrying it on must also be taken into account; for it would be unjust to demand excessive wages which a business cannot stand without its ruin and consequent calamity to the workers. If, however, a business makes too little money, because of lack of energy or lack of initiative or because of indifference to technical and economic progress, that must not be regarded a just reason for reducing the compensation of the workers. But if the business in ques-

tion is not making enough money to pay the workers an equitable wage because it is being crushed by unjust burdens or forced to sell its product at less than a just price, those who are thus the cause of the injury are guilty of grave wrong, for they deprive workers of their just wage and force them under the pinch of necessity to accept a wage less than fair.

73. Let, then, both workers and employers strive with united strength and counsel to overcome the difficulties and obstacles and let a wise provision on the part of public authority aid them in so salutary a work. If, however, matters come to an extreme crisis, it must be finally considered whether the business can continue or the workers are to be cared for in some other way. In such a situation, certainly most serious, a feeling of close relationship and a Christian concord of minds ought to prevail and function effectively among employers and workers.

74. Lastly, the amount of the pay must be adjusted to the public economic good. We have shown above how much it helps the common good for workers and other employees, by setting aside some part of their income which remains after necessary expenditures, to attain gradually to the possession of a moderate amount of wealth.

Pius XI, On Atheistic Communism

32. We explained clearly [in Quadragesimo Anno] the right and dignity of labor, the relations of mutual aid and collaboration which should exist between those who possess capital and those who work, the salary due in strict justice to the worker for himself and for his family.

49. The wage earner is not to receive as alms what is his due in justice. And let no one attempt with trifling charitable donations to exempt himself from the great duties imposed by justice.

52. But social justice cannot be said to have been satisfied as long as working men are denied a salary that will enable them to secure proper sustenance for themselves and for their families; as long as they are denied the opportunity of acquiring a modest fortune and forestalling the plague of universal pauperism; as long as they cannot make suitable provision through public or private insurance for old age, for periods of illness and unemployment.

53. It happens all too frequently, however, under the salary system, that individual employers are helpless to ensure justice unless, with a view to its practice, they organize institutions the object of which is to prevent competition incompatible with fair treatment for the workers. Where this is true, it is the duty of contractors and employers to support and promote such necessary organizations as normal instruments enabling them to fulfill their obligations of justice. But the laborers, too, must be mindful of their duty to love and deal fairly with their employers, and persuade themselves that there is no better means of safeguarding their own interests.

Pius XI, Casti Connubii

123. And so, in the first place, every effort should be made to bring about that which Our Predecessor Leo XIII, of happy memory, has already insisted upon, namely, that in the state such economic and social meth-

ods should be adopted as will enable every head of a family to earn as much as, according to his station in life, is necessary for himself, his wife, and for the rearing of his children, for "the laborer deserves his wages" (Luke x, 7). To deny this, or to make light of what is equitable, is a grave injustice and is placed among the greatest sins by Holy Writ (Deut. xxiv, 14, 15); nor is it lawful to fix such a scanty wage as will be insufficient for the upkeep of the family in the circumstances in which it is placed.

126. If, however, for this purpose, private resources do not suffice, it is the duty of the public authority to supply for the insufficient forces of individual effort, particularly in a matter which is of such importance to the commonweal, touching as it does the maintenance of the family and married people.

Pius XII, To Spanish Employers and Workers, March 11, 1951

You know very well, beloved children, that a just salary and a better distribution of natural wealth constitute two of the most impelling demands in the social program of the Church.

Pius XII, Letter to Semaines Sociales, 1947

Touching this third section, We should like for Our part to emphasize a point on which sensible people today are generally agreed, namely, that the highly important question of dividing up the so-called "social product" has by this time received sufficient treatment. A more urgent problem requires our immediate attention. We must make sure that goods are made available for the use of men, and in increasing quantities. In a word, production is the problem of the hour.

Pius XII, To Sacred College of Cardinals, June 2, 1948

The relations between agriculture and industry within the single national economies, and of those latter with the economy of other nations, the manner and extent that each nation is to share in the world market — all these difficult problems present themselves today afresh and under aspects different from those of previous times. Upon their rational solution depends the productivity of the several nations, and consequently the welfare of individuals as well; for it is clear that there can never be sufficient distribution where there is not sufficient production.

Pius XII, To International Union of Family Organizations, September 20, 1949

The popes, in their social messages, have strongly favored the family or social wage, which gives the family the power to rear children in proportion to their increasing number. . . . Naturally, it is fitting to note that more attention is needed for large families: reduction of taxes, [granting] subsidies [and] allowances, considered not as pure gifts, but as a modest grant for the most valuable service rendered by the family, and especially the large family.

Pius XII, Social Function of Banking, April 25, 1950

A man's work ought to give to him and his family a sufficiency of daily bread. That sufficiency is not something which is added in a sort of extrinsic fashion; it is intrinsically connected with professional work according to the designs of God. Is it possible to imagine a more powerful stimulus to a just organization of our daily lives than this Christian conception of work?

Pius XII, To Spanish Workers, November 12, 1954

It is the Church's wish that those who labor be able to live a life which is really human, so they can live a Christian life, without too many earthly worries to keep them from thinking of heaven. The Church advocates a more just distribution of natural goods, based principally on a just salary, which will guarantee your own present life and that of your families, while allowing a certain amount of savings as a guarantee for the future.

American Hierarchy, The Christian Family, 1949

The family, to exercise its good influence in full effectiveness, needs a just measure of economic security. When, in a wealthy and prospering nation, diligent and willing parents are forced to live in grinding poverty; when parents have no opportunity of owning their own home; when the aid of government is extended to those who raise crops or build machines but not to those who rear children, there exists a condition of inequity and even of injustice. Social legislation and social action must concur to improve man's economic opportunity, to enable him to marry early, to free him from the peril of unnaturally limiting his family, and to afford him some certainty of sufficiently gainful employment and some assurance that death or accident will not reduce his dependents to the status of public charges.

Hierarchy of Quebec, Pastoral Letter, February, 1950

131. In the present state of labor relations, a collective bargaining agreement negotiated with a labor union may be considered as the normal means for determining a just wage. It ceases to be such a norm, however, if imposed by undue pressure from any source.

Australian Hierarchy, Standard of Living, September, 1954

In social justice, as distinct from strict justice, the state must come to the relief of the family man. Nor should it be urged that the state is asked to give a gratuitous subsidy to the family. For apart from the duty of Christian charity, the man who marries and rears a family renders an important and vital service to the stability, progress and defense of the state, and the state should willingly discharge its debt. Indeed, in Australia the state acknowledges this obligation when it provides child endowments and other social benefits.

The worker with a family responsibility, therefore, in addition to the wage which he, like the single man, is entitled to get from his employer, will receive from public funds a social benefit allowance for his wife and for each child dependent on him.

To apply these general principles in practice, we suggest the following arrangement:

1. There should be a Standard Wage, which would be that of a single man. This would cover his essential needs of food, clothing and shelter. It would provide a modest amount for recreation, and enable him to make partial provision for marriage. It would enable him to begin to make suitable provision, through public and private insurance, for old age, for periods of illness and unemployment. It would provide some opportunity whereby the prudent man, by the practice of thrift, could acquire a moderate amount of property for himself. The same amount would be fixed for either sex.

2. On his marriage, the worker would be entitled to an increase in income to provide now for his wife in addition to himself, and to provide also for savings in anticipation of the birth of a child. He would also be entitled to a bonus to enable him to purchase in part his house and furniture.

3. On the birth of each child, he would be entitled to an added weekly payment to cover the cost of his dependent children. Endowments for dependents should remain so long as dependency exists.

AUTOMATION

Pius XII, To Christian Union of Executives and Businessmen, March 7, 1957

It is also foreseen that the age of automation will constantly reassert the pre-eminence of intellectual values among the productive class: knowledge, ingenuity, organization, foresight.

There is no doubt that the period of transition may result in an increase of unemployment among older workers, who are less adapted to new training; but younger laborers as well are faced with the same danger whenever a nation is forced to hasten its steps toward automation because of competition with other countries.

This is why it is necessary to make suitable plans, starting now, so that the dynamism of technology may not result in a public calamity. In every case, producers must accept the principle that technology is at the service of the economy, and not vice versa.

Pius XII, To Christian Associations of Italian Workers, June 7, 1957

Automation involves, above all, the danger of confusing technical productivity with economic productivity.

. . . automation achieves a fantastic increase in . . . productive capacities. But will it, on the other hand, involve a true growth of productivity in the national economy? By this we mean a lasting and sure attainment of conditions which will make possible the material and human well-being of every member of the population, and in which all those who contribute immediately — with their labor, their property, their capital — to the national economy will receive a return corresponding to their investment. Further, such a state of economic production ought to be capable of giving an easy solution to social tensions.

*   *   *

Another important point regarding social life which must be carefully weighed is the technological unemployment which might well arise, according to circumstances, with the introduction of automation.

*   *   *

But even if these problems could be satisfactorily solved in the long run, the fact remains that increase in technological unemployment even for a brief period would represent in some countries a loss that could not be lightly incurred. In this area it is not at all legitimate to adopt the false principle which in the past impelled certain statesmen to sacrifice an entire generation in view of the great advantages that would accrue to succeeding ones.

*   *   *

New criteria, therefore, will have to be adopted to estimate the value of the paid worker, and new types of workers will have to be considered. These will present domestic problems for the labor unions and may even affect their present form, especially if it is borne in mind that, in certain sectors of the national economy, the working class will not in the future be notably affected by automation.

*   *   *

He will also be saved from the false notion that a man works in order to enjoy leisure. In reality, a man has leisure — apart from the natural and honorable rest from toil, which is needed to enable him to perfect his faculties and to fulfill better his religious, social, and domestic duties — in order to make him physically and mentally more competent in his work. Touching this matter, an unconsidered use of automation might give rise to no slight dangers, both with regard to personal morality and to the sound structure of production and consumption in the national economy.

Pius XII, Aspects of Automation, October 23, 1957

Now, if it is true that in the early stages the machine often enslaved man, who was supposed to control it, today machine tools have been perfected to a point where one can hope that an ever-increasing number of workers will be freed who have until now been subjected to the performance of purely material and monotonous tasks.

FULL EMPLOYMENT

Pius XI, Quadragesimo Anno

74. But another point, scarcely less important, and especially vital in our times, must not be overlooked: namely, that the opportunity to work be provided for those who are able and willing to work. This opportunity depends largely on the wage and salary rate, which can help as long as it is kept within proper limits, but which on the other hand can be an obstacle if it exceeds these limits. For everyone knows that an excessive lowering of wages, or their increase beyond due measure, causes unemployment. This evil, indeed, especially as we see it prolonged and injuring so

many during the years of Our Pontificate, has plunged workers into misery and temptations, ruined the prosperity of nations, and put in jeopardy the public order, peace, and tranquillity of the whole world. Hence it is contrary to social justice when, for the sake of personal gain and without regard for the common good, wages and salaries are excessively lowered or raised; and this same social justice demands that wages and salaries be so managed, through agreement of plans and wills, insofar as can be done, as to offer to the greatest possible number the opportunity of getting work and obtaining suitable means of livelihood.

75. A right proportion among wages and salaries also contributes directly to the same result; and with this is closely connected a right proportion in the prices at which the goods are sold that are produced by the various occupations, such as agriculture, manufacturing, and others. If all these relations are properly maintained, the various occupations will combine and coalesce into, as it were, a single body and like members of the body mutually aid and complete one another. For then only will the social economy be rightly established and attain its purposes when all and each are supplied with all the goods that the wealth and resources of nature, technical achievement, and the social organization of economic life can furnish. And these goods ought indeed to be enough both to meet the demands of necessity and decent comfort and to advance people to that happier and fuller condition of life which, when it is wisely cared for, is not only no hindrance to virtue but helps it greatly.

Pius XII, Christmas Message, 1952

In fact, the intention of guaranteeing full employment with a constantly rising standard of living may well evoke the anxious query, to what degree expansion is possible without provoking a catastrophe and, above all, without bringing in its wake mass unemployment. It seems, therefore, that efforts must be made to attain the highest possible level of employment, but at the same time means must be sought to insure its stability.

*   *   *

. . . where private initiative is inactive or inadequate, the public authorities are obliged to provide employment, so far as possible, by undertaking works of general utility, and to facilitate by counselling and other means the finding of employment by those who seek it.

Pius XII, To the International Association of Economists, September 9, 1956

. . . it is dangerous, for example, to increase industrial production without assuring the sale of the goods produced, to modify the volume of monetary circulation without taking into account the corresponding volume of commercial transactions, or to seek for full employment while neglecting to prevent the risk of inflation.

The Church and Social Order

37. . . . there must be a balance between various groups, both organized and unorganized. Unless this be true, the economic system cannot

function smoothly and there will inevitably be unemployment, because the one class of workingmen cannot buy the high-priced products of the other class of workingmen with their limited income. If skilled laborers, who, through rigid organization, have a monopoly control of their craft, raise their rate of hourly wages too high, they do not gain their advantage exclusively from the wealthy, but from the poor also, in terms of excessive prices. Higher wages as a rule should come out of excessive profits and not out of increased prices.

38. Heartening, indeed, are the beginnings toward the greater security of the people that have already been made through legislative enactment and public policy. The immediate benefits of these laws to working people may be small and some modifications perhaps desirable, but it is highly gratifying that the principle upon which they rest has become a part of our national policy.

Code of Social Principles

95. As for the "right to have work," it is the supposed right of an out-of-work man to demand from the state a paid occupation and a wage. Public authorities have the duty of forestalling unemployment and its consequences by all the means in their power. But it does not follow that every individual without work has the strict right to employment. But social organization should be such that men out-of-work should be able to subsist in times of involuntary unemployment, thanks to a system of social insurance or industrial provident funds, established for instance on a vocational basis, or by means of resources that come from a small-holding system.

HITHERTO we have discussed primarily the procedural aspects of labor-management relationships, although one major substantive matter — working conditions — was considered in some detail. The present chapter treats of two additional major substantive issues: wages and stability of employment. All these, of course, are closely connected with the concept of human dignity. Only if the rate of pay is adequate to support really human existence, and the stability of employment is such that man can have reasonable assurance about the future, can we say that a job meets the essential demands springing from a worker's rights. A living wage for the worker and a condition of full employment that bolsters job security are both needed if economic life is to meet human needs.

THE LIVING WAGE

Moral Concept of a Living Wage. The introduction of the concept of a living wage was a great moral achievement for the Church in the nineteenth century. Prior to that time, other and harsher doctrines were accepted both in theory and in practice. Both classical economic theory and the realities of the day left the wages of labor to the price-fixing mechanism of a free market. Labor was treated as a commodity, with its wage governed exclusively by conditions of supply and demand. Furthermore, it was widely held that the wage fund available for the payment of workers was a relatively stable amount, so that the pressure of increased population would only lead to misery and starvation. The Iron Law of Wages was a shackle binding labor to unending wretchedness.

At the time, some moralists justified this condition, at least in terms of the virtue of strict justice, in that the labor contract was freely entered upon. A worker agreed to accept a given rate of pay by the fact that he willingly accepted the job. Perhaps in charity, or even in distributive justice, there might be a claim for more. But contractual justice was satisfied when the wage agreed upon was paid. Moreover, the equality of justice was met when the worker received the market value of his services as determined by supply and demand. Hence the going rate for labor was considered the just rate.

Karl Marx and the socialists reacted strongly to this trend, swinging to the other extreme. They held that all value arose through labor, so that the worker was entitled to the full amount of the value of the product. Socialism denied to capital any right to a return from gains achieved through the labor of workers. The appropriation of such surplus value was considered theft.

Popes Leo XIII and Pius XI opposed both extreme views. While Pope Leo stated that through the labor of workers states grow rich, his successor clarified his thought by noting that labor's contribution is wonderfully enhanced by machinery and other physical capital. Both upheld the right of management and investors to their just share from the joint product. But, at the same time, they denied the theory that labor was a commodity whose value was to be determined exclusively by the market. In ringing words, Pope Leo stated that over and above the wage contract there is natural justice, the imperious demand that the wage be sufficient to support the worker who is thrifty and upright. Here again, his illustrious successor added clarity, by specifying that this wage be sufficient to support not only the worker, but his family as well.

The argument given to justify the claim in justice for a living wage derives basically from the dignity of man. In the labor market, a worker is selling more than an economic service. He is offering his work as the only normal means he has for human existence. The wage he receives affords him the wherewithal to live as befits a man. This means, not only food, clothing, and shelter for himself, but also the requirements for family living, since family life is normal for most men. He must receive enough to live in decency at any given time and to make provisions for sickness, old age, and like contingencies of existence.

Hence in human labor there is an intrinsic value, reflecting human dignity and needs, which is quite distinct from the market value determined by supply and demand schedules. The monetary expression of this intrinsic value is termed a living wage, a wage adequate for family needs paid to the head of a household. This sum should establish a minimum wage for persons who are the support of families. Above this minimum, there may be differentials based on skill, zeal, initiative, resourcefulness, and similar qualities. The evaluation of such additional contributions may be left to collective bargaining, the market for these added inputs, and other traditional methods for setting wages.

The standard of a decent living wage varies according to time and place. It is relevant to the resources and economic organization of a given country. Of course, there is an absolute basic minimum of food, clothing, and shelter necessary to sustain life itself. But the higher standard of decent comfort is relative to the economic conditions of a nation. An American housewife and her teen-age daughters would feel a sense of real deprivation today if they did not have nylon stockings. Such might not be the case with a Central European peasant woman. Hence, there is no absolute, world-wide living wage.

It may be objected that, in American social life, there is excessive emphasis upon conventional standards of living which are far more costly than such absolute needs as adequate food, clothing, housing, medical care, and education. Thus, it is held that as incomes rise needs also rise. What is a luxury today may be a conventional necessity tomorrow. We are like squirrels in a cage, very active but going nowhere. There is some merit in this objection, but it can be carried too far. In the United States today some families lack the minimum in the field of absolute needs. Here the productive ability and the earnings of the main wage earners must be enhanced so that they can provide adequate food, clothing, housing, and medical care for their dependents. The first need in social justice is a proper structure of economic society, so that all able and willing heads of households can earn a living wage for the care of their families. When such a stage is reached, we can then face the problem of conventional necessities, adjusting our standards to the productive capacities of our economy.

An Obligation in Justice. Papal statements on a living wage ended some controversies among theologians, but they also created new ones. Older writers sometimes asserted that an employer was obliged in justice to pay the contractual wage, and in charity a living wage. Now it seems clear that the payment of a living wage is a matter of justice. But is it commutative justice, with the obligation of restitution and strict bilateral claims against employers, or is it social justice, involving personal and group accountability, but not the obligation of restitution?

Earlier versions of this text took the viewpoint that papal authority seemed to be strongly in favor of an obligation in commutative justice. It was noted, however, that in practice "moral impossibility" often excused the individual employer from paying such a wage and from the obligation of restitution. Hence as a practical matter the duty to pay a living wage ended up as a problem of social justice, even though it began as a claim in strict justice. In view of these practical difficulties, and some uncertainties in regard to papal teaching, it is now held that the obligation to pay a living wage is primarily a matter of social justice. If the economy were so organized, through proper reforms, that the economic value of a worker's contribution at least equaled his claim upon an employer for a living wage, then the worker would also have a claim in strict justice for such a wage. The *aequalitas justitiae* would then exist, since the value of his services amounted to a living wage.[1]

At present, two classes of workers do not generally earn the economic equivalent of a living wage. One is the substandard worker — beginners, the aged, handicapped, and so forth. The other is the worker whose output is normal, but who is employed in an industry that is "disorganized" in the encyclical sense of the term. In such an industry, the economic value produced by the worker's efforts is not sufficient for a family wage. Hence an employer is incapable of paying such a wage. Either his competitors would pay lower wages or else the setting of an uneconomic wage would only increase his other economic difficulties. This was recognized by one of the best-known and most qualified commentators on *Quadragesimo Anno*, Father Oswald von Nell-Breuning:

> If, however, the economic structure is disturbed, or if it proves to be impossible to give labor its proper place in the system, then the value of

---

[1] See *Catholic Social Principles*, pp. 356–361, for papal quotations and problems connected with the strict-justice approach to the problem of a living wage.

work done will more or less fall short of family requirements. Then the employer cannot be required, either on the basis of commutative justice or for some other reason, to pay family wages. On the contrary, in this instance he is unable to pay them. The attempt to pay them in spite of it would merely result in further dislocation of the economic structure, and would endanger the employer himself.[2]

On this reasoning, the employer is bound in strict justice only to pay a going wage, but in social justice he must co-operate with other economic agents to make a living wage possible.

Problems of Implementation. Even in prosperous firms and industries, there may be serious problems involved in paying every worker, regardless of present family obligations, a living wage. This means in practice that, in order to have a suitable wage for heads of families, other wage earners must receive a substantial sum in excess of their personal needs. The economic implications of this demand have caused many writers to ask what type of wage we should seek as a result of reforms brought about through the practice of social justice. Should this be some absolute figure, designed to meet the needs of an average family in each country? Or should it be a flexible amount, tailored to the family needs of each worker through a family-allowance system or some equivalent device? Earlier editions of this work favored the flat sum, as more consonant with the strict-justice approach. It also is consistent with actual practice in such industrial nations as the United States and Germany.

This position was sharply and brilliantly challenged by Professor Michael P. Fogarty in the September, 1957, *Review of Social Economy* and by other authorities in private conversations. Objections to the flat-sum approach include the following: (1) It is difficult to decide fairly upon a so-called average or typical family. (2) Whatever level is chosen, unmarried workers or married workers with smaller families than average will receive a bonus in living standards. (3) Such bonuses tend to raise expectations and thus constantly keep a living wage unattainable. (4) Finally, this approach makes impossible demands upon our economic system, by requiring that all workers receive wages adequate for family needs, even though a given percentage of them will not be supporting a family at any one time.

The flexible system, based on a family-allowance plan, does not suffer

---

[2] *Reorganization of Social Economy,* p. 177. In reference to handicapped workers, see St. Thomas Aquinas, *Summa Theologiae,* II, II, 77, 1.

from these disabilities. If, for example, during a given year, there are fifty-three million children under the age of sixteen in the United States, the aim would be to provide 70 million working adults with wages adequate for the personal needs of each worker, and also to enable them to contribute to a fund that will give supplementary wages to parents so that they can support properly the children below working age. Presumably there would also be a contribution for the support of wives, and especially mothers, who are not working outside the home. This latter point was not treated by Professor Fogarty. The Professor then concludes:

> Re-interpreted on these lines, the Family Living Wage is free from the defects which attach to it when taken in Cronin's sense. It comes down from cloud-cuckoo-land into the realm of practical possibility. It can now take care, without setting up demands for a $6,000 or $7,000 minimum wage in an economy where this minimum alone would exhaust the entire national product, of all the families that are "normal" in the sense of including a substantial share of the community's children; of the families with four, five, or seven children as well as of those with one or two. It is consistent with — if this be taken as another possible criterion of wage justice — equal pay for equal work. It no longer involves chasing a standard of living which, like an electric hare, is guaranteed to keep always a little ahead; for, with the help of allowances, the standard of life of the large family can be raised to the conventional level without automatically making it possible for smaller families to push that level higher still. The conventional level will of course rise as productivity increases, and so on Catholic social theory it should; for the Living Wage is a dynamic concept, focussed as has been said on fair shares rather than on any absolute or ideal standard of life. But it will rise thanks to the advancing incomes and expanding consumption patterns of all families alike, not to permanent leadership of those families which happen to have few dependents. . . .[3]

The theoretical value of the flexible approach is indeed great. It does set an economically more practicable goal for a living wage. At the same time, it does away with the paradox of reaching the conclusion that, in the richest nation in the world, a majority of wage earners do not and cannot earn a living wage, even by the modest standard of the two-child family. On the other hand, there seems to be little sentiment in the United States for a family-allowance system of any type, whether the contributions be made from general taxes, employer wage payments, or worker wage receipts. It is doubtful that American employers and unions can soon be convinced about the desirability of family allowances. Unions generally favor a flat rate of pay "adequate for family needs." Many

---
[3] *Review of Social Economy* (September, 1957), p. 101.

Americans, in addition, feel that the size of the family should be tailored to income rather than the reverse.

It may be possible, however, to work toward the family-allowance system in an oblique manner. For example, stress can be laid upon maternity payments as a medical fringe benefit. If these were adequate enough to take care of prenatal, hospital, and postnatal (for a year) expenses, a substantial contribution toward meeting family burdens would be had. If other medical benefits were also on a family basis, we would be moving still closer to the goal sought. American unions are much more willing to make allowances for family needs in seeking fringe benefits than they are in the matter of basic wages. Since fringe payments are so substantial in many industries, this can be very important for the purpose of seeking family welfare.[4]

In addition, we should do much more to inculcate in our younger people realistic attitudes toward spending, saving, and living standards. If unmarried younger workers spend all their income in "having a good time," two serious evils result. First, they have no savings to fall back upon when they are married. Second, they develop impossible cravings in terms of living standards. Many young couples think it quite normal to buy an automobile, a house, and furniture during the first two or three years of marriage. They plunge so deeply into debt that any unforeseen contingency, such as unemployment, sickness, or even pregnancy may push them into insolvency.

In years past, families made a regular practice of saving so that they could meet the financial contingencies of family life and old age. Today more and more of these burdens are being met by the insurance principle: old-age insurance, medical insurance, unemployment compensation, and now proposals that the United States adopt a family-allowance system. There is nothing wrong with saving by means of insurance; indeed much can be said in its favor. But those who favor extension of such methods should give considerable thought to the method of payment. Specifically, it may be wise for workers to contribute directly to various funds, instead of having them financed exclusively by employer contributions or from general taxes. This may seem to be merely a bookkeeping matter at times — a choice between the employer paying directly into a fund or giving the worker higher wages (subject to his personal income tax). But, when the worker pays directly, he is more likely to realize that he is meeting his

---

[4] Other aspects of family allowances will be treated in Chapter XI.

family obligations, and not passing them on to the employer or the state. For this reason, in discussing the implementation of the living-wage theory, there is still much to be said for the older view (dominant still in the United States) that favored a wage suitable for the so-called "average family" (a concept attacked by Professor Fogarty), with reliance upon savings and resourcefulness to meet unusual needs. If, however, it is felt necessary that family needs be met through insurance, the principle of subsidiarity would favor Professor Fogarty's decentralized approach (employer-worker compacts) in preference to the state-controlled system advocated by the Australian bishops. All these points, however, must be considered as freely debatable proposals for implementing a moral principle that is beyond debate. The popes have made clear the moral claim of a worker for a family living wage. They have not discussed, except by way of illustration, the detailed means for securing such a wage.

Problems connected with a living wage and the dignity of labor should be a special concern of priests and religious who are in the position of employers. In the past, our record in this regard has not always been good. Church institutions have at times been notorious both for low wages and arbitrary practices, such as the discharge of workers who have given most of their lives to an institution, only to be let out either because of old age or a change of administration. Cynics have remarked that some in our midst apply vows of poverty to workers, even though Canon Law makes no provision for vicarious acceptance of religious vows. Undoubtedly, such situations occur with the best of motives. Church institutions rarely have adequate funds, so that their administrators understandably try to economize in the attempt to have the most money for the primary purpose of the venture. This would be especially true for schools, institutions of charity, and even some parishes. Yet charity should not be served at the expense of justice. We should give good example in regard to the social teaching of the Church as well as in matters of piety.

Many bishops now require that wages and working conditions be considered in letting construction contracts. It would be most desirable that when bids are let, the award go, not to the lowest bidder absolutely, but to the lowest bid from a reputable firm which pays decent wages and treats its workers fairly. Likewise, the Church as employer cannot afford to lag behind in other phases of industrial relations, such as proper hours, working conditions, grievance machinery, seniority provisions, protection from arbitrary discharge, security for old age, and such normal features of reasonable employment. These are usually matters of justice, not works of supererogation. We should be more reluctant than lay employers to seek excuse from such obligations on the grounds that we cannot afford to meet them.

Economics of a Living Wage.   Thus far we have discussed the ethical obligation in regard to a living wage and the method by which it should be paid. The conclusions reached were that the obligation was primarily in terms of social justice and that some form of family-allowance method was most likely to bring about the results sought.

Since the primary obligation is in the area of social justice, it logically follows that we should ask: What changes are necessary to make possible the payment of a living wage? Some might reply that the most important and immediate change would be a family-allowance system, so that distribution of current production would be directed in favor of families, rather than in favor of the unmarried and the childless married couples. This may be true, but it is rather unlikely that such a basic change will come about in the United States in the near future. We should seek special family help as a long-range project, and yet ask ourselves what can be done immediately to help workers who are paid under our present system of wage rates geared to the job rather than family status.

If we examine our economic system as a whole, we find it quite impressive in terms of resources, machinery, management and technical skills, and the quality and quantity of labor. For nearly twenty years, we have been able to divert an important share of our resources to nonproductive uses, such as the building of our military strength, and also give some of our wealth in foreign-aid programs, and yet maintain a high and ever increasing standard of living.

Moreover, developments in such areas as atomic energy, the discovery of new materials, and advances in electronics and automation all promise more rather than less wealth in the future. We seem on the verge of scientific breakthroughs that will put virtually unlimited energy resources at our disposal and will provide either natural or synthetic materials for nearly all our needs. In addition, the efficiency of labor, already multiplied many times by machines and managerial skills, will skyrocket as automation becomes more common. The electronic and chemical processes that make automation possible add a new dimension to the machine. In the past, machines made available immense and tireless sources of energy applied under the guidance of a skilled worker. But automation transfers to the machine a power of direction, correction, and even "judgment," that seems to duplicate human intelligence to a limited degree, but with a speed, accuracy, and tirelessness that man is not capable of achieving.

The ultimate implications of automation are difficult to assess. If these processes are extended widely throughout our economic life, undoubtedly we can have both substantially higher living standards and new vistas of leisure. Physical productive capacity alone will not solve our economic problems, as is evident from difficulties connected with farm surpluses. But unless we are able to produce, we cannot advance far even with the best distribution methods in the world. On this basis, the physical and technical capabilities of our economic system are most relevant to living standards and a living wage.[5]

World economic problems would be very simple if every increase in productive capacity would automatically mean more wealth, higher wages, and increasing living standards. Unfortunately economics is not that simple. Goods have to be sold at a price that will meet the cost of a producer. Here we run into one of the paradoxes that constantly frustrate those who dream of a simple economy of abundance. This paradox is the fact that, economically speaking, scarcity also has value. A person who can control the supply of wanted goods and services often makes out better, in the short run, by producing less rather than more. A manufacturer with a monopoly, or a union with strict control of the supply of workers in a given craft, can often "charge what the traffic will bear." They are paid, not primarily because of what they produce, but because of the artificial scarcity they have created. Of course these advantages are strictly short-run and self-defeating, like standing to get a better view of a football game. No society gets rich by restricting production. But individuals have become wealthy this way.

Over a long range, living standards can rise only by one method — increased output per worker. By education, good management, or by automation, the worker can turn out more in a given time with an unchanged or lower expenditure of energy. Thus labor costs per unit of product or service decline. This increase in productivity can be passed on directly to the worker in the form of higher wages. Or it can go to consumers as lower prices, to stockholders as higher profits, or to any combination of these factors. Other consequences also follow. It may happen that increased efficiency will mean that fewer workers will be

[5] See J. P. Dewhurst, ed., *America's Needs and Resources* (New York: Twentieth Century Fund, 1955).

needed or that less efficient plants can be retired. Such dislocations can cause hardships, but their ultimate effect is to keep all producers at top peaks of efficiency.

Policy Problems. The preceding treatment of the basic economics of a living wage is a highly simplified prelude to some important policy discussions. Two problems, in particular, are deserving of serious consideration: how union wage rates affect the distribution of productivity gains; and what is to be done about industries or occupations that do not easily adapt themselves to new processes and hence do not have productivity gains.

When we discuss union wages achieved through collective bargaining, we refer to the total package, including fringe benefits. These latter have mounted to such a degree that they often comprise one fifth of the total wage. Indeed, fringe benefits are sometimes a form of socialized saving, making less necessary personal saving for old age, sickness, unemployment, vacations, and the like. Yet workers often forget that they are getting these benefits, since they rarely affect take-home pay and current spending power.

The format of payment is in itself unimportant, provided we do not lose sight of total costs. Thus, when the guaranteed annual wage was asked of the automotive industry in 1955, few questioned the principles involved. Workers and their families eat by the year, not by the hour. It is highly desirable to have wage guarantees so that workers can plan their economic futures, including such major expenditures as the buying of a house. The practical problem was how to offer such guarantees without bankrupting an industry. The idea of limited, regular contributions to a fund to supplement unemployment compensation solved this difficulty. A limited guaranteed annual wage became a reality.

Where real problems arise is in industries where a tradition has arisen of substantial periodic wage gains, apparently in excess of any productivity increases within the industry. The leaders in this process are certain large industrial unions, such as those in the automotive, steel, and coal-mining fields. Similar patterns are followed by teamsters and many building-trade unions. The result of their demands is usually a round of price increases, leading to long-term inflationary trends in the nation. To some degree such wage demands are self-defeating, since higher prices may cancel some of the gains. Often, however, these unions are protected by cost-of-living clauses, so that the burden of inflation must be borne elsewhere.

Wages and Inflation. There seems to be neither moral nor economic justification for wage increases that are essentially inflationary. Inflation is a highly disruptive force in the economy. Any action that provokes it normally is contrary to the common good. It will be argued, of course, that the "bloated profits" of the large corporations can absorb these wage increases without the necessity of price rises. But the burden of proof here rests upon the union, since the corporate-profit sector of our economy has declined, in comparison with wages, in recent years.

Indeed, it is questionable that organized labor should even seek to capture the entirety of productivity gains for its members. Quite apart from the moral claims of capital (if new machines explain the productivity rise), there is the problem of workers in industries or occupations that do not lend themselves readily to automation or other devices to increase productivity. Are they to remain stagnant economically, while other workers make more and more gains? The answer is that, when the gap gets too great, teachers, policemen, barbers, and the like will demand wage increases. Since higher costs in these areas cannot be absorbed, they must be passed on and hence inflation is given another push upward.

This type of inflation could be avoided if productivity gains in industry were shared partly by the workers involved (as higher wages) and partly by consumers (as lower prices). Lower prices give some benefits to workers on fixed incomes or those in industries not having productivity increases. Lower prices in technologically advanced sectors also make a constant price level more feasible, since they permit price increases elsewhere in the economy when such are needed to help less favored groups.

All workers should share equitably in the benefits brought about by automation and similar methods for increasing production. The process just described will help bring this about. Of course, some industries resist pressures toward greater efficiency. Productivity in the building trades, for example, is notoriously low. High hourly wages, often coupled with restrictive labor practices; hand-production methods; multiple handling charges for materials; and obsolete building codes all contribute to low productivity in this field. Such practices cannot be justified in terms of social justice. They may even pose problems of conscience in terms of simple honesty.

While wage increases should be framed in terms of productivity gains, either in the industry or in the economy as a whole, this does not mean that workers must withhold their demands until the accountants have calculated the last penny of increased efficiency. A certain consistent pressure for higher standards forces employers to develop more efficient methods and thus make such standards feasible. But this pressure must be within reasonable bounds. No one, for example, expects the economy to bound ahead with an annual efficiency gain of 10 per cent, or even half that amount. Union wage demands that do not consider these facts are at best unrealistic and possibly are highly damaging to the economy.

In this regard, we must carefully evaluate the slogan often used in wage demands: "Wage increases mean more purchasing power needed to stimulate consumer buying." Such statements can be pure nonsense. If an industry cannot absorb wage increases without passing them on in the form of higher prices, then purchasing power has not increased at all. Only when wage increases can be absorbed without raising prices is there any net gain in purchasing power. It would be much truer to say that higher efficiency, leading to either lower prices or higher wages or both, is the only real source of increased purchasing power. Anything else is illusory.

We may conclude that sound wage increases either reflect or provoke productivity gains. Workers in high-wage industries should not seek increases in excess of efficiency gains. Generally they should take less, so that lower prices can be had. Workers in low-wage occupations may seek higher wages, either through union demands or minimum-wage laws, even in excess of productivity gains. Thus they share efficiency increases of other segments of the economy. They also force their own industries or occupations to seek lower costs and better use of the factors of production.

FULL EMPLOYMENT

Even more critical than the question of a living wage is the problem of employment security. Most men, if compelled to make a choice, would prefer a secure job with lower pay to a well-paying job whose future is uncertain. This is especially true of those who suffered during the great depression of the 1930's. Many, although able and willing to work, lost their life savings, their homes, and their other property. Their families suffered from anxiety, malnutrition, and even despair. It was a bleak tragedy to millions and they are not anxious to repeat it.

Recession and Depression. In discussing unemployment, our main interest is the economy-wide type of unemployment that characterizes business recessions and depressions. It is not that we are unconcerned with seasonal unemployment, loss of jobs from technical changes and automation, or depression confined to single industries. Each of these is a real problem and deserves serious consideration. The guaranteed annual wage, in the form of supplemental unemployment compensation, often is helpful in mitigating the rigors of seasonal job fluctuations. Employers can mitigate unemployment resulting from automation by keeping all workers, but not replacing those who leave for various reasons. Finally, declining industries can sometimes be revived by research and imaginative management. In other cases, communities must seek new industries to replace those that no longer furnish sufficient jobs.

By contrast, a recession or a depression, bringing nationwide unemployment coupled with a general decline in business activity, is not so easily handled. To clarify the terms used, economists generally speak of a decline or adjustment when there is a minor or short-lived dip in business activity. If the decline is deeper and longer-lived (over 7 per cent of the working force unemployed, and the decline lasting for a year or eighteen months) it is called a recession. A depression is still more serious and prolonged.

A variety of factors influence economic fluctuations. Such elements as the ability to postpone purchases, the influence of credit and money supply, government fiscal policies, price policies and inflation, and investment and income-distribution patterns — all these, either singly or in combination, can stimulate or retard business.[6]

Economic activity is basically unstable for many reasons. One factor is the fact that the purchases of durable goods can often be postponed. Automobiles, television sets, and machines can be repaired instead of replaced. Consumer and business spending for heavy goods is usually at a high level in boom times. Should uncertainties arise, it is easy to postpone such purchases.

Many of these items are purchased on credit, either consumer credit or business loans. When business is good, debt tends to increase. But in a decline, it is harder to get credit. Moreover, many persons tend to curtail purchases after a spending spree while they are paying off their debts. Thus declines tend to snowball. Tax policies can also affect the supply of money, making it more or less scarce. When governments spend more than they take in, business usually is stimulated. A government surplus has the opposite effect, as a rule.

Price policies can affect business activity. A little inflation, for example,

---

[6] For a simple treatment of the economics of the problem, see J. F. Cronin, *Problems and Opportunities in a Democracy* (Chicago: Mentzer-Bush, 1955), pp. 299–308.

is stimulating since businessmen and consumers buy to escape higher prices. But continued inflation disrupts price and wage relationships, makes business planning difficult, promotes speculative booms in the securities markets, and eventually can lead to serious reactions and possibly a depression.

Income-distribution patterns also influence economic stability. As a rule, the higher the level of an individual's income, the higher the proportion that is set aside in the form of savings. A high national level of savings, if invested, usually means many new plants and industries, with a consequent boom for construction and machine-tool industries, and also new employment opportunities. If savings remain idle, business activity declines. Hence it is important to have an income-distribution pattern that encourages needed investment, but does not discourage mass consumption. Tax policies also affect investment, both in terms of influencing the supply of savings and in terms of incentives (or lack thereof) to risk capital in new developments.

Antidepression Measures.   Since any of these, or other factors, can influence employment and prosperity, it is obvious that control of the economy is not an easy matter. The decisions of millions of persons may affect economic conditions. Co-ordinating such decisions is most difficult. At the present time, the most important control techniques are lodged with the federal government, particularly the authorities who control monetary and fiscal policies. For example, the Federal Reserve System has tools at its disposal to influence the amount of credit that banks may make available. Thus it can encourage banks to lend or discourage them from lending, as conditions warrant. Likewise, the total of taxes collected by the federal government has an important bearing upon business conditions. When the government accumulates a surplus, spending less than it takes, there is a dampening effect upon business. A deficit usually is stimulating, except that prolonged deficits sometimes have adverse effects upon business psychology.

As a result of the depression that began in 1929, both the government and private groups sought and obtained certain cushions against future depressions. Unemployment compensation and supplementary payments, federal old-age retirement funds and private pensions, farm benefits, military spending, federal insurance of bank deposits — all tend to soften the impact of a business slump and to make adjustments easier to achieve. Should these fail to do the job, there is little doubt but that the government today would take drastic steps, such as sharp tax reductions or major public-works programs, to restore economic activity.

While business declines and unemployment are regrettable, they can have incidental good effects. Sharp competition corrects certain careless practices that both business and labor tend to acquire in boom times. Business firms are forced to consider costs and thus step up their efficiency. Poor labor practices are remedied, as "work breaks" are substituted for "coffee breaks." Thus the dynamism of the economy is preserved by corrective processes set in motion by earlier abuses.

In view of the complexity of causes of business slumps, a question may arise as to the proper steps to be taken when the economy is depressed. First and most important for leaders in social-action movements is the need for making a fair, competent, and objective study of the causes. Many in our ranks have been too influenced by the allegedly Keynesian position that massive injections of purchasing power will always cure slumps. Presumably this position implies that shortage of disposable income is the prime cause of all declines. Such an analysis may not be borne out by income statistics. During phases of the 1957–1958 decline, for example, disposable income was rising for the economy as a whole. This particular recession seemed primarily to have been caused by declines in federal spending, business capital investment, and consumer spending for durable goods. Underlying some of these declines were reactions to steady inflationary trends. If inflation, caused by runaway costs, is the main factor, then injection of new "purchasing power" would tend only to increase the problem.

The effort to discover and cure the causes of a slump should not distract us from the primary need for taking care of the human tragedies caused by unemployment. Certainly we should work to make unemployment compensation, plus supplemental unemployment benefits, adequate to meet family needs when the main wage earner is out of work.

More specific cures will vary, depending upon whether the causes are economy wide (macroeconomic) or confined to specific sectors (microeconomic). Economy-wide fluctuations can be prevented or cured by adjustments in federal spending, taxation, and central-bank loan policies. Federal spending can be a stimulant or brake, as the need demands, and credit policy should go hand in hand with fiscal policy.

When the causes of trouble are more specific, such as a farm slump, decline in building, postponement of durable goods purchases by business or consumers, or uncontrolled costs leading to inflation and productivity declines, then the remedies in turn should be tailor-made. Farm aid, stimulants to private building (or public-works programs), tax incentives to spur business investment — each of these can be used as needed. There may even be a time when the harsh curative measures engendered by the slump itself may be permitted to act. When an economy is going "soft," with manufacturers careless about quality, cost, and efficiency; salesmen waiting for customers to seek them out; and workers taking more time for "coffee breaks" than "work breaks," much can be said for permitting the educational forces of declining sales and profits to bring back the dynamism and incentive of the economy.

Since economics has not reached the status of an exact science, there will be debates over causes and remedies of each business decline. But enough is known of the major causes, and the most effective remedies, that sound and workable policies can be achieved. Nevertheless, considerable study and work is necessary in each case; panaceas only intensify the malady.

The subject of recessions is technically distinct from that of unemployment caused by faulty pricing decisions of industry. For example, there was much discussion in 1959 about high administered prices in the steel and automobile industries adding to the severity of the 1958 recession and holding back the recovery. Unquestionably a faulty price structure, based on the idea of high unit profits even though this decreases total demand and employment, tends to make it difficult to cut down recession-caused unemployment. But, in itself, price-related joblessness is more akin to technological unemployment than to idleness caused by business slumps. It could happen in any given industry even in times of prosperity and almost full employment.

Two other points are important in regard to administered-price situations. First, high administered prices do not of necessity lead to exorbitant business profits. Indeed, if an industry guesses wrong on public reaction to prices, it may end up with lower profits than would be the case if it gambled on high volume and low unit profit. The second point is that much of the discussion on administered prices is tied up with problems of wage increases beyond productivity gains. In many instances, it was the increase in costs caused by such wage increases that caused the initial rise in prices. Of course, it is quite possible that certain industries reacted excessively and raised prices beyond the level needed to recoup added costs. Certainly temperate action by both industry and labor in such situations would add to employment and the economic health of the nation.

The problems discussed in this chapter are of the highest importance in terms of the common welfare. It is most desirable that workers should have secure jobs and that their income levels should increase regularly. This benefits business as well as labor. It is an objective which should be divorced from partisan politics. Yet in practice, some workers make substantial gains whereas others actually lose as a result of inflation. Organized labor and organized business, far from finding these problems matters of mutual interest, often disagree violently on steps to be taken. Likewise, many political leaders tend to favor one side or another. Thus a problem, which should be a perfect example of the common concerns discussed in Chapter VII, instead is considered in a context of group individualism. All have suffered as a result.

READINGS*

J. Messner, Social Ethics, pp. 599–600, 759–769, 800–811, 901–908.
B. W. Dempsey, The Functional Economy, Chaps. 11–12, 22.
J. A. Ryan, A Living Wage.
——— Distributive Justice, Section 4.
O. von Nell-Breuning, Reorganization of Social Economy, Chap. 9.
J. Villain, L'Enseignement social de l'Église, Vol. II, pp. 104–170.
H. Johnston, Business Ethics, Chap. 10.
Social Order: Edward Duff, S.J., "Family Wage," September, 1955; Michael P. Fogarty, "Family Living Wage: A Comment," December, 1955; Edward Duff, S.J., "The Living Wage," February, 1957; Francis J. Corrigan, "The Virus of Inflation," November, 1957; J. R. Kirwan, "Novelties in Wage Theory," December, 1957; James J. Lamb, "Automation: Its Effects," November, 1958; James J. Fairman, "The Future of Nuclear Power," February, 1959.

***

* For further readings, see List No. 7 in the Appendix.

Chapter XI

THE ECONOMIC PROBLEMS OF THE FAMILY

LIVING STANDARDS

Pius XI, Casti Connubii

126. If families, particularly those in which there are many children, have not suitable dwellings; if the husband cannot find employment and means of livelihood; if the necessities of life cannot be purchased except at exorbitant prices; if even the mother of the family, to the great harm of the home, is compelled to go forth and seek a living by her own labors; if she, too, in the ordinary or even extraordinary labors of childbirth, is deprived of proper food, medicine, and the assistance of a skilled physician, it is patent to all to what an extent married people may lose heart, and how home life and the observance of God's commands are rendered difficult for them. Indeed it is obvious how great a peril can arise to the public security and to the welfare and very life of civil society itself when such men are reduced to such a condition of desperation that, having nothing which they fear to lose, they are emboldened to hope for chance advantage from the upheaval of the state and of established order.

127. Wherefore, those who have the care of the state and of the public good cannot neglect the needs of married people and their families, without bringing great harm upon the state and on the common welfare. Hence, in making the laws and in disposing of public funds they must do their utmost to relieve the needs of the poor, considering such a task as one of the most important of their administrative duties.

Pius XII, To Italian Workers, June 13, 1943

Our Predecessors and We Ourselves have not lost any opportunity of making all men understand by Our repeated instructions your personal and family needs, proclaiming as fundamental prerequisites of social concord those claims which you have so much at heart: a salary which will cover the living expenses of a family and such as to make it possible for the parents to fulfill their natural duty to rear healthily nourished and clothed children; a dwelling worthy of human persons; the possibility of securing for children sufficient instruction and a becoming education, of foreseeing and forestalling times of stress, sickness, and old age.

Pius XII, Christmas Message, 1952

We are thinking of the consequences of poverty, still more of the consequences of utter destitution. For some families there is a dying daily, a dying hourly; a dying multiplied, especially for parents, by the number of dear ones they behold suffering and wasting away. Meanwhile, sickness becomes more serious, because not properly treated; it strikes little ones in particular, because preventive measures are lacking.

Then there is the weakening and consequent physical deterioration of whole generations. Whole masses of population are brought up as enemies of law and order, so many poor girls gone astray, pushed down into the bottom of the abyss, because they believed that that was the only way out of their shameful poverty. Moreover, not rare is the case where it is wretched misery that leads to crime. Those who in their works of charity visit our prisons affirm constantly that not a few men, fundamentally decent, have gone to prison because extreme poverty has led them to commit some unpremeditated act.

Pius XII, To Italian Catholic Workers' Association, May 14, 1953

. . . the more exclusively and incessantly one increases the tendency to consumption, all the more does the economy cease to have as its object the normal man in his reality, the man who orders and adjusts the demands of this earthly life to his last end and to the law of God.

If — as a hopeful painting has pictured it — the machine were destined to lessen ever more and, so to speak, diminish to the ultimate the time of labor and of physical effort, the free time would also necessarily have to lose its natural meaning of relaxation and rest between the two moments of activity. This would become the prime element of life and the occasion of new and often costly needs, as also, on the other hand, a source of gain for those who satisfy these needs. Thus the genuine relationship existing with a real and normal need, would be reversed through demands artificially created. The income therefrom would necessarily increase, but very soon it would become no longer enough. The lack of security would remain, because the social economy would take its rise from and would suppose a mankind deviated from the right and just measure of its being.

WOMEN WORKERS

Leo XIII, Rerum Novarum

60. Finally, it is not right to demand of a woman or a child what a strong adult man is capable of doing or would be willing to do. Nay, as regards children, special care ought to be taken that the factory does not get hold of them before age has sufficiently matured their physical, intellectual, and moral powers. For budding strength in childhood, like greening verdure in spring, is crushed by premature harsh treatment; and under such circumstances all education of the child must needs be foregone. Certain occupations likewise are less fitted for women, who are intended by

nature for work of the home — work indeed which especially protects modesty in women and accords by nature with the education of children and the well-being of the family.

Pius XI, Quadragesimo Anno

71. In the first place, the worker must be paid a wage sufficient to support him and his family. That the rest of the family should also contribute to the common support, according to the capacity of each, is certainly right, as can be observed especially in the families of farmers, but also in the families of many craftsmen and small shopkeepers. But to abuse the years of childhood and the limited strength of women is grossly wrong. Mothers, concentrating on household duties, should work primarily in the home or in its immediate vicinity. It is an intolerable abuse, and to be abolished at all cost, for mothers on account of the father's low wage to be forced to engage in gainful occupations outside the home to the neglect of their proper cares and duties, especially the training of children.

Pius XII, On Women's Duties, October 21, 1945

Indeed, We have on a former occasion pointed out that for the same work output a woman is entitled to the same wages as a man.

We see a woman who, in order to augment her husband's earnings, betakes herself also to a factory, leaving her house abandoned during her absence. The house, untidy and small perhaps before, becomes even more miserable for lack of care. Members of the family work separately in four quarters of the city and with different working hours. Scarcely ever do they find themselves together for dinner or rest after work — still less for prayer in common. What is left of family life? And what attractions can it offer to children?

As to the working classes, forced to earn daily bread, a woman might, if she reflected, realize that not rarely the supplementary wage which she earns by working outside the house is easily swallowed up by other expenses or even by waste which is ruinous to the family budget. The daughter who also goes out to work in a factory or office, deafened by the excited restless world in which she lives, dazzled by the tinsel of specious luxury, developing a thirst for shallow pleasures that distract but do not give satiety or repose in those revues or dance halls which are sprouting up everywhere, often for party propaganda purposes, and which corrupt youth, becomes a fashionable lady, despises the old nineteenth-century ways of life.

Pius XII, To the Federation of Italian Women, October 14, 1956

Because of this temporal goal, there is no field of human activity which must remain closed to woman; her horizons reach out to the regions of politics, labor, the arts, sports; but always in subordination to the primary functions which have been fixed by nature itself.

HOURS OF WORK

Leo XIII, Rerum Novarum

59. Now as concerns the protection of corporeal and physical goods, the oppressed workers, above all, ought to be liberated from the savagery of greedy men, who inordinately use human beings as things for gain. Assuredly, neither justice nor humanity can countenance the exaction of so much work that the spirit is dulled from excessive toil and that along with it the body sinks crushed from exhaustion. The working energy of a man, like his entire nature, is circumscribed by definite limits beyond which it cannot go. It is developed indeed by exercise and use, but only on condition that a man cease from work at regular intervals and rest. With respect to daily work, therefore, care ought to be taken not to extend it beyond the hours that human strength warrants. The length of rest intervals ought to be decided on the basis of the varying nature of the work, of the circumstances of time and place, and of the physical condition of the workers themselves. Since the labor of those who quarry stone from the earth, or who mine iron, copper, and other underground materials, is much more severe and harmful to health, the working periods of such men ought to be correspondingly shortened. The seasons of the year also must be taken into account; for often a given kind of work is easy to endure in one season but cannot be endured at all in another, or not without the greatest difficulty.

60. Let it be the rule everywhere that workers be given as much leisure as will compensate for the energy consumed by toil, for rest from work is necessary to restore strength consumed by use. In every obligation which is mutually contracted between employers and workers, this condition, either written or tacit, is always present, that both kinds of rest be provided for; nor would it be equitable to make an agreement otherwise, because no one has the right to demand of, or to make an agreement with, anyone to neglect those duties which bind a man to God or to himself.

HOUSING

Pius XII, To Women of Italian Catholic Action, July 24, 1949

First of all, We say that everything that can contribute to a sound social policy for the good of the family and Christian youth can always count on the efficacious support of the Church.

We repeat now to you what We said to the men of Catholic Action some two years ago. The Catholic Church strongly supports the requirements of social justice. These requirements include provision for the people of the necessary houses, and above all for those who desire to found a family or are already doing so. Can there be conceived a social need of greater urgency? How sad it is to see young people, at the age when nature is more inclined to marriage, forced to wait years and years, merely because of the lack of a place to live, and always with the danger that in this nerve-wracking waiting their morals may deteriorate. Encourage, then, as much as you can, with your propaganda and your labors, the provision of houses so that the dignity of marriage and the Christian education of children may not suffer from this need.

Pius XII, To Catholic International Congresses for Social Study and Social Action, June 3, 1950

The time has come to face squarely, in its full dimensions, the duty of providing for countless families, in their natural, moral, juridical, and economic unity, a just living space which meets, however modestly but at the very least in sufficient measure, the demands of human dignity.

Pius XII, To Autonomous Institute for Popular Housing, November 21, 1953

Public authorities ought, in regard to housing, as in other matters, seek to favor, and in no case oppose, private enterprise. In the case of popular housing especially, they should favor the enterprise of co-operatives.

Pius XII, To "Stations de Plein Air" Movement, May 3, 1957

Is it necessary to bring up the sad example of the exploitation of slum areas? Dilapidated, ramshackle houses without the most necessary hygienic installations sometimes yield a sizeable income to their owners without costing them a penny. Inevitably, they neglect to make necessary repairs in them for years on end.

Enough can never be said about the harm that these dwellings do to the families condemned to live in them. Deprived of air and of light, living in filth and in unspeakable commingling, adults and, above all, children quickly become the prey of contagious diseases which find a favorable soil in their weakened bodies. But the moral injuries are still more serious: immorality, juvenile delinquency, the loss of the taste for living and for working, interior rebellion against a society that tolerates such abuses, ignores human beings, and allows them to stagnate in this way, transformed gradually into wrecks.

Society itself must bear the consequences of this lack of foresight.

Because it did not wish to prevent the evil and to provide a remedy in time, it will spend enormous sums to keep up an appearance of curbing delinquency and to pay expenses for prolonged confinement in sanatoriums and clinics. How many millions authorized for the cure of evils that it would be easier and less expensive to prevent!

*   *   *

Persons of good faith who have only an inadequate knowledge of the matter readily believe that the majority of those who live in the slums or who must be satisfied with an income below the essential minimum are there through their own fault or negligence, and that welfare organizations are capable of helping anyone in need of it. The fact is, existing institutions which address themselves chiefly, as We have already said, to those who can help themselves, ought to be adapted and their activity extended to those who, for any reason whatsoever, are incapable of benefiting by measures already in force.

John XXIII, To Members of UN Housing Committee, November 14, 1958

Reflect then, on the basis of this premise, how the heart of every Christian should consider the duty it has to provide a house for him who has none as one of the bases of charity in general and of every complete apostolate.

Code of Social Principles

33. The family has the right to ownership and, in the first place, to own a home where a materially and morally wholesome family life can be lived to the full. Besides this, it is highly desirable that each family should possess a plot of its native soil. . . . It behooves that public authorities should favor, in an efficacious way, the system of family ownership. If, for special reasons, families cannot acquire dwellings of their own, it is preferable that independent organizations, which offer their members some attributes of ownership, should supervise housing, rather than private landlords or public authorities.

44. The housing shortage, affecting a very large number of families among the middle and working classes, the burden of domestic expenses and public taxation, the lack of domestic help make the bearing and upbringing of a large family particularly onerous and meritorious. A sound policy on population will be above all a family policy. It will include a complete program of cheap houses and public transport, of the organization of family help, of mutual assistance and tax-relief in favor of large families.

The building of garden cities, composed of dwellings set aside for separate families and situated in open country near work centers, adds an important contribution to the well-being of the family and to public hygiene. The family allowance system ensures a better balance between family resources and expenses.

152. (i) The system known as "family allowances" has, in recent years, shown satisfactory developments. It is fitting that the payment of these allowances should form part of all agreements, whether individual or collective, between employers and workers, and even that it should be made obligatory by law in favor of all families; further, distributive justice demands that the total of these allowances should be in proportion to family burdens, so as to ensure an equal standard of living to families of the same social class.

(ii) There is also a tendency for social insurance to become legalized. It must necessarily be made general, and it seems desirable that, admitting the principle of the plurality of assurance societies, it allows subjects the opportunity of joining the societies of their choice (vocational or not). In any case, if the State judges it necessary to insist on all the members joining one single society, it must see that this membership does not prevent them from choosing the social or health services which they prefer.

SOCIAL SECURITY

Pius XII, Christmas Message, 1950

For this reason We have repeatedly and with ever greater insistence proclaimed the fight against unemployment and the striving after a sound social security as an indispensable condition if all members of a nation, both high and low, are to be united in a single corporate body.

Pius XII, To the Italian Federation of Commerce, February 17, 1956

Undoubtedly, nowadays more than in the past, there is a growing desire to assure to all classes of society guarantees that will preserve them from the mishaps and chances inherent in the fluctuations of the economy; guarantees that will protect employment and its rewards; guarantees that will provide for sickness and incapacitating accidents that may reduce a man to idleness and deprive him of the means of livelihood. This solicitude is quite justified; but in many cases the present system of social security has not yet succeeded in putting an end to difficult situations or in healing wounds that are always open.

It is important, however, that the anxious desire for security should not prevail over the businessman's readiness to risk his resources to such an extent as to dry up every creative impulse; nor impose on enterprise operating conditions that are too burdensome; nor discourage those who devote their time and energy to commercial transactions.

IN THE preceding chapter, the moral claim for a living wage was urged. In addition, there was also the comment that a family-allowance system is a more practical means for implementing this ideal than the alternative of a fixed wage based upon the needs of the so-called average or normal family. Yet it is only the part of realism to note the difficulties facing the family-allowance system, so far as acceptance here is concerned. Because of this difficulty, the present chapter offers comments upon the economic problems confronting the family under existing social conditions.

Living Standards. In judging the welfare of the family, it is necessary to make clear the standards used. The pages to follow give some of the indications of poverty as well as the bases for commonly accepted standards of family living. There follows a discussion of housing and medical costs, since these are two of the more important components of the family budget. Then we face the methods used by many families to augment their incomes: additional work by the main wage earner, work by wives and mothers, and work by children. After these situations have been evaluated, a brief exposition of social-insurance and the family-allowance plan is offered.

While there may be some elements of the subjective in such terms as poverty, frugal comfort, and luxury, there are nonetheless sufficient objective standards to warrant some conclusions about proper standards of living. Thus propriety would call for a minimum of three bedrooms for most families with children, one each for parents, boys, and girls. We expect separate kitchen and bathroom facilities for each family. The cost of renting or buying such facilities can be priced in different cities. Likewise, we can make up and price a typical breadbasket for a family of various sizes. The same applies to clothing, medical care, transportation, and sundries. In this way a budget can be drawn up that estimates the monetary cost of a given level of living. The best known of such budgets was issued by the Bureau of Labor Statistics, U. S. Department of Labor, in 1947. Another well-known series of budgets is that of the Heller Committee of the University of California. The BLS budget was based on studies in thirty-four cities, while the Heller budgets deal with the San Francisco area.

The family used in the BLS budget consisted of four persons. The father was thirty-eight years old, the mother thirty-six and not gainfully employed, and the children included a thirteen-year-old boy in high school and an eight-year-old girl in grade school. It estimated costs in terms of a moderate budget, above the subsistence level and below the luxury level. The figure given would of necessity be adjusted for families of different sizes. The Bureau considers that a two-person family would need 65 per cent of the budget; a three-person family, 84 per cent; and a five-person family, 114 per cent. The budget includes actual costs of food, clothing, housing, medical care, taxes and contributions, and moderate comforts, such as cigarettes and motion pictures.

The family lives in a five-room dwelling where the wife does all the cooking, cleaning, and laundry without paid assistance. They have a mechanical refrigerator and a washing machine. Meat is served several times a week, with cheaper cuts on weekdays and a more expensive meat dinner for Sunday. Turkey is served on Thanksgiving. Little is allowed for luxury goods purchases: the children get an ice-cream cone and a bottle of soft drink per week, and the father one bottle of beer a week. He buys one heavy suit every two years and a light suit every three years. His wife gets a new heavy wool coat every four years and four dresses a year. In largest cities, transportation is public, but in smaller places, the family owns a cheap, used car. They have a small radio and attend a movie about once every three weeks. They do not have a telephone, but make three paid calls a week. A small amount of life insurance is carried. Modest contributions are made to religious and charitable groups.

For such a family, costs averaged $4,656 nationally in 1958. The Community Council of New York reached a total of $4,545 for a similar family in October, 1957. The Heller Budget, for the San Francisco area, is so much higher (totaling $5,831.70) that it must be considered as being based upon standards different from those of the other budgets.

It may be objected that the statistics quoted are deficient, in that they fail to include nonmonetary income in the family. Thus, a wife who is adept at sewing and cooking can contribute importantly to family income. She can sew clothes, draperies, and the like. She can also bake bread, make jams, and can various fruits and vegetables when they can be bought cheaply. The husband can learn to do elementary carpentry, plumbing, and electrical work around the house. If land is available, a vegetable garden can be cultivated. Growing children can share in these tasks as their strength and skills permit. Undoubtedly such methods have been used by many families to supplement an inadequate income. They are also useful in training children to habits of work and responsibility. But there are two difficulties to be faced, before we may feel that large families can become more self-supporting. The first is a problem of education. Our society tends more and more toward a tradition of seeking leisure time in ever greater quantities. The family which followed the pattern outlined above would be, to some degree, fighting a growing trend in the opposite direction. Second, many of these activities require more space than is available in city apartments. They presuppose home ownership. But the figures given above show how difficult it would be for the average couple to take the risk of purchasing a home.

Some families can meet budgets such as those outlined above without economic difficulty. Others meet and even excel these living standards, but pay the price by having more than one wage earner in the family. Still others fall below the standards given and suffer some deprivations and possibly even poverty. It is quite important that we give serious thought to the implications of these situations.

Alleviating Poverty.   Poverty connotes the idea of doing without at least some things that are generally considered essential. In a poor family, to cite one example, housing conditions may involve overcrowding, to the detriment of health and morale. It may be difficult, if not impossible, for children to have quiet and privacy for study. Their sleeping quarters may be overcrowded. They may be forced to use the streets as playgrounds, endangering their lives and often impairing their moral standards.

A poor family may lack essential foods. It may be forced to skimp on fruits, milk, meat, and fresh vegetables. As a result, diet may not be adequate for health. Yet this family cannot afford private medical care and must depend upon free clinics. Thus, it may or may not get medicines and treatment it needs. Poverty may also be felt in other ways, such as the quality and even quantity of clothing. It often is a barrier to educational advancement.

Many persons have noted the paradox of poverty in a nation considered to be the wealthiest in the world. There are evidences of poverty on all sides. Many family incomes are far below the level needed to meet even the most modest budget. We have both urban and rural slums. Beggars and drifters are found walking our streets. But we cannot conclude from these facts that all problems of poverty are economic and hence subject to improvement by the use of economic means alone.

A very important factor in poverty is a complex of social conditions that prevent many persons from earning adequate incomes. At times, this may be a matter of personal moral habits, as with the wage earner who gambles or drinks away a substantial portion of his income. Certain estimates place the number of problem drinkers as high as five million, including at least one million classed as alcoholics. Some persons have physical or mental deficiencies that make them virtually unemployable. Illiteracy or lack of skill may keep a worker at the lowest income level. A moron could hardly be allowed to handle complex and expensive machinery. Handicapped persons, such as the blind, deaf, or crippled, vary in earning ability. Some are excellent workers in the right jobs. Others, such as those totally disabled with arthritis, must depend upon outside support.

Racial or cultural discrimination may also be factors in inadequate earnings or housing. As will be noted more in detail in Chapter XV, Negroes and some Spanish-speaking people often find difficulties in getting the better types of jobs, no matter what may be their training and qualifications. All these types of poverty may properly be classed as noneconomic, in that the causes and remedies are primarily social.

In addition, there are cases of poverty attributable to economic causes, but these causes are so special and exceptional that general remedies, such as minimum wages or union organization, are of no avail. Such unusual conditions may persist even when the nation as a whole is enjoying high employment and broad prosperity. Two examples illustrate this point. The first is the marginal farmer who lacks land, capital, and often skills necessary to produce a profit from his work. Such farmers may receive cash incomes of less than $1,000 even when the bulk of farmers producing similar crops are prospering. A second example involves regions that are chronically depressed. Jobs may be scarce because of lack of demand for the product, as happened to anthracite coal. Or there may be an outmigration of industry to more favorable areas. Such was the case with many textile and shoe mills, particularly in New England. For both of these types of poverty, remedies must be specifically tailored to the situation. Poor farmers, for example, may be helped by the Rural Development Administration, described in Chapter XVI. Depressed areas need new industry and proper federal, state, and local programs to attract such firms.

Finally, there are persons with low incomes that may not be suffering real hardship as a result. Older families living partly upon capital and young student families living upon savings or borrowed funds may be living perfectly normal lives. Yet they show up in income statistics as being at the poverty level.

In the light of these distinctions, we should be careful in the matter of attributing blame for the pockets of poverty that persist in our nation. If the causes are primarily social, then the remedies are not usually economic. When the reasons for distress involve exceptional situations, we do not tinker with our general economic processes, especially when they seem to be functioning quite well. Many problems belong more to the social worker or the psychiatrist rather than to the economist or the politician. Nor should we overlook the possibilities in such simple remedies as credit unions and teaching persons home economics and the wise management of their funds.

Families with low incomes can often stretch their earnings by means of shrewd management. Many times this involves a willingness, and ability, to trade time and effort for little savings that can mount up. For example, in the budgets cited, food costs are important. But an ingenious cook can prepare less expensive items and still have good meals. The economy-minded will bypass convenient but expensive mixes and prepared foods and use their own time instead to prepare cakes, vegetables, and soups. But here we must be realistic and note that the busy mother of several young children may not have much energy for time-consuming, albeit economical, preparation of food. Nor may she be able to shop around for the best bargains.

Family needs emphasize the desirability of lower food costs, since they are so important in family budgets. Yet we must frankly admit that current trends are in the other direction. Every effort is being made, and rightly so, to increase farm income. Processing costs increase as consumers buy more and more of frozen and precooked foods. It is not easy to see where important savings can be made in this area, although isolated cases of excessive middleman charges may be turned up.

Whether or not a low-income family may better its lot by more shrewd spending, it at least should have the opportunity to try. Consumer education as part of high school social-science study, sewing lessons in adult-education courses, and similar aids may give families the option of using their time in the effort to secure savings in the purchase of food and clothing.

Housing Costs. One of the most critical factors in family living costs is the high price of housing. No other area of our economy has suffered so much from inflated costs. It is estimated that a typical house that cost $8,000 in 1941 sold for $20,000 in 1958. Rental housing has likewise increased in cost. The result is that many families are paying heavy charges for housing, to the detriment of other demands upon the family salary. Others are forced to live in housing below the standards they can reasonably expect. Still others are crowded into slums where an entire family may have but one room.

There are many reasons for this debacle, but the most important stem from a combination of inefficiency and greed. The construction industry has often resisted change in regard to materials, working practices, and methods of production. Land costs are often high, and likewise money costs. City building codes may force obsolete and antiquated methods of production. Prefabrication is the exception and individual building the rule, at least for single dwellings. Hourly wages for labor are among the highest in the land, and productivity is often quite low, hampered by feather-bedding practices and work-stretching traditions. The result is that housing often has priced itself out of the market.

An important reversal of this trend was promised in 1958, when the building-trade unions and the construction industry announced long-range plans to use more efficient production methods. While the initial announcement concerned only heavy construction, it is expected that the policy will gradually be carried over into residential housing. It certainly is an unwelcome paradox that, in the richest and most progressive industrial nation of the world, antiquated methods should be used for the provision of one of the major necessities for family life.

Even if the cost of construction is cut drastically, it does not follow that the cost of housing will always be within the reach of the family purse. This is particularly the case when urban rental housing is involved, especially in areas of high land costs. In many cases it is impossible for private builders to construct rental housing at prices suitable even for "middle-income" tenants, to say nothing of rehousing slum occupants. When land is extremely high-priced, the only alternative to costly rents is a high density of occupancy — the very slum conditions that most cities seek to eliminate. For this reason, it is generally necessary that the federal or local governments assume part of the costs, thereby making low-rent facilities available. It is customary, in the case of low-income families, for local authorities (with federal help) to build public housing. This, in effect, is subsidized housing, since the rents charged do not pay the costs of land, construction, and operation. Where middle-income families are involved, some cities or states offer special tax arrangements for limited-dividend housing projects. For instance, they may be taxed at a rate based upon previous unimproved use, instead of the current value of the project.

Where downtown city areas are involved, it is important that new housing fit in with an adequate pattern of planning and urban renewal. Otherwise, the core areas of large cities tend to decline when population migrates to the suburbs. Huge investments in stores, churches, schools, and like properties become impaired in value or even worthless, as population shifts leave them stranded. Obviously it is sound economy to utilize valuable central-city properties instead of building duplicates in the suburbs, unless population growth (rather than movement) makes these necessary.

In discussing housing problems, and related subjects of urban renewal and rehabilitation, much of the treatment has been in the abstract, with no reference to concrete governmental programs for lending money to home buyers (FHA, VA), purchasing bank mortgage loans (FNMA), slum clearance, urban renewal, and public housing. These programs are extremely important for any understanding of current government aids to the housing market. Yet since they are subject to frequent changes in detail and emphasis, it was considered more desirable in these pages to

leal with the principles concerned and to leave the details for study in
available reference manuals.

Medical Care. The problem of medical care is currently surrounded
by considerable controversy, much of it unnecessary in that it involves
avoidable misunderstandings. In this discussion, three points will be
treated: the physical availability of medical care, the costs of medical
care, and general health insurance.

In the United States, at this writing, there are important shortages of
medical facilities, particularly for rural regions and low-income states. In
these cases, there are not enough doctors, nurses, clinics, technicians, and
hospitals. It is unlikely that these needs can be met by private initiative,
particularly in the low-income states. An argument can be made for
federal subsidy both for the construction and equipping of buildings
and for the training of necessary personnel. A further problem exists in
cities where adequate facilities and trained personnel are available, but
where their cost is excessive for low- and middle-income families. The
most successful method for meeting this problem is the formation of
clinics, whereby a number of specialists work in the same building under
some type of common direction. This avoids unnecessary duplication of
expensive equipment and makes thorough medical care available at the
same price as is currently paid for less adequate treatment. At the same
time, it does not lower doctors' incomes or interfere with their full freedom of practice. The promotion of such clinics would be a form of social
justice especially suitable for Catholic doctors.

A valuable technique for handling medical costs for some moderate-
income families is the institution of industrial or union group health
plans. Since it has been estimated that the cost of sickness, in terms of
lost industrial production, is about eight billion dollars a year, or a productivity decline of 5 to 7 per cent, management often calculates that
such assistance saves money in the long run. Some firms feel that a direct
money profit is made by such programs, while others consider the gain
indirect, through better morale and industrial relations. One careful study
made by the Industrial Hygiene Foundation showed that a chemical
industry spent $21,335 in medical care and estimated its return at $87,032,
or $4.08 for each dollar spent. There was less sickness, fewer accidents,
and lower insurance costs. Labor turnover also declined. In addition to
industry, some labor unions have secured medical care for their members.
Thus, the Union Health Center of the International Ladies' Garment
Workers Union occupies seven floors of a New York skyscraper. It has

a staff of 143 doctors (11 of whom are full time), 40 nurses, 5 registered pharmacists, 4 junior pharmacists, and 30 technicians. This center served 42,352 persons in 1957 and 757,015 visits were made by these patients. No charge is made to Union members, and family dependents pay $1.25 a visit. Employer contributions pay most of the costs of the Union Health Center. The United Mine Workers Union also has elaborate health facilities, including a number of hospitals. Other unions use community services, such as Blue Cross or Blue Shield.

In regard to the costs of medical care, a distinction must be made between ordinary medical care and extraordinary problems. The cost of ordinary medical care is not unreasonable. The total amount spent for medical care in the United States is low, when compared with national expenditure for luxuries. Moreover, the rapid growth of prepayment plans indicates that the economic problems connected with certain types of illness are being met. Nevertheless, there is room for further improvement along these lines. Present-day coverage is more adequate for hospital care than for payment of doctors' bills and the cost of expensive medicines. Hence there is need both for extension of coverage in regard to existing plans and for rapid growth of plans which deal with fees and high-cost medicines. But sound social policy would dictate progress along lines which have proved their worth rather than radical experimentation with new devices.

Extraordinary medical care includes chronic illnesses, such as arthritis and certain forms of heart disease; crippling sickness, like poliomyelitis or mental illness; operations which are unusually costly; and disease which requires the constant use of high-cost drugs. Sickness of this type usually wrecks the finances of a family. If it strikes the main wage earner, income is cut off at the same time that needs are greatest. Moreover, such illness is not ordinarily met by present-day prepayment plans. Indeed, the prepayment method is not intrinsically suitable for these cases, since their incidence is scattered and unpredictable. The insurance method is the only logical device for such a situation, just as it is the only sound way for meeting the costs incidental to a fire. There are now available private insurance plans analogous to automobile collision insurance. An insurance company fixes a total annual amount to be paid by the patient either directly or through prepayment plans, and covers all costs above this amount. Plans of this type deserve every encouragement.

There is one possible hazard to the prepayment and insurance systems that poses a moral question. At times patients demand unneeded care even hospitalization, merely because they are covered. Again, certain doctors increase their fees when they know that a patient has medical coverage. The practice of causing unwarranted and unnecessary increases in the costs of medical plans threatens to endanger the stability of the entire program. Both patients and doctors alike are woefully shortsighted when they indulge in such improper activities.

The analysis just given does much to answer the question as to the advisability of national health insurance. If the approach advocated here is sound, there is no need for a detailed study of the arguments for or against such a plan. Clearly it is contrary to the principle of subsidiarity for the government to intervene in matters already being handled by private initiative. Even granting the present inadequacy of private approaches through prepayment plans and similar devices, it is better to aid methods which are basically sound rather than to replace them with a new and cumbersome approach. At the same time, the medical profession would be doing itself a great disservice were it to remain contented with a merely negative approach to the problem of the economics of medical care. It is not enough to fight proposals which it fears might lead to socialized medicine. The real problems which occasioned these proposals must be met adequately and within reasonable time. The state does have the moral right and duty to intervene in matters concerning the common good, when individual initiative fails to meet serious needs. It is primarily the duty of the medical profession to see that sound organization and adequate private payment plans answer the needs of the American public, so that in the future extensive government intervention will not even be seriously considered.

The economic problems of medicine afford an excellent opportunity for social action by thousands of Catholic doctors. They are well aware of our teaching in regard to family life and also know the medical costs of bringing children into this world and rearing them to maturity. Such doctors are within their rights in opposing programs for medical care which they consider unsound and dangerous. But they should at the same time be in the forefront in proposing practical plans for making medical care available, through prepayment, to all families and individuals. They, better than laymen, can suggest methods for lowering the costs of such care without decreasing quality or denying to doctors their proper incomes. Finally, they can endorse the insurance method, whether private or public, for the field where it is really needed, namely, for extraordinary and almost catastrophic expenses from chronic or crippling illness. Such a positive approach would meet the needs of our time, without risking the real values of private initiative and local autonomy.

Making Ends Meet. A worker may confront the problem of high living costs in two ways. First, he might try, individually or through social action, to cut costs in key areas. This approach has been discussed in the pages immediately preceding. Second, he or his family, or both, may try to earn additional income. This may involve seeking added sources of income in return for additional work by the main bread-winner, who usually is the father of the family. Or it may involve work by married women whose husbands also work. Finally, it can raise the problem of child labor. By 1958, almost half of American families had more than one pay check.

During World War II, the Korean War, and some phases of the post-Korean boom, it was possible for workers to earn considerable sums in the form of overtime pay. Most industrial workers are covered by the Fair Labor Standards Act (Wage and Hour Act) and thus usually receive time and one half for all time worked in excess of forty hours a week. If such overtime pay is available over a sustained period, many workers can accumulate substantial additional income. This permits such expenditures as down payments on a home, the purchase of a car, or payment for furniture. Moreover, as automation progresses in American industry, there will be increasing demands for a shorter work week without any pay decrease. This presents serious difficulties, but it is not economically impossible, provided that productivity per worker has risen enough to absorb the increased costs involved. If changes of this nature are made, it is likely that overtime pay will increase in importance as a source of additional family income.

In this regard, attention should be paid to the increasing practice of holding a second, part-time job. In factory argot, this is called "moon-lighting." It is estimated that four million workers today do additional work for a few hours at night, or on Saturdays and Sundays, in order to supplement family income.

Besides work done for pay, we should consider as income any productive work done at home. The do-it-yourself technique is often a real source of savings, as amateurs do painting, papering, plastering, tile-laying, and related activities that formerly were confined to skilled workers. A home owner who knows how to use the "cold-tube" method safely in repairing a malfunctioning television set can often effect really substantial economies. Just as with the housewife's shopping and cooking, time and effort used in making repairs and improvements can mean money saved.

From a social viewpoint, such extra income-producing activities are not to be condemned, provided they are important for the family and do not lead to impairment of health or neglect of parental duties. If a worker is able during his years of greatest energy to pay for a house and accumulate furniture and like possessions, he is less likely to be under severe economic pressure as he advances in age and suffers a decline in energy and health.

The same principle applies to the problem of women workers, to be treated presently. It is good, rather than bad, when young, unmarried women work. Even if they expect to make marriage their career, it is good for them to learn the discipline of work. They can also save money for their marriage. Older unmarried women and widows may need to work in order to earn their living. Married women who are not mothers may work outside the home, provided they are willing and prepared to accept their normal responsibility of motherhood. In addition, they should be sure that these extra duties do not impose a strain upon their marriage. It is always wise, when possible, to consider any such income as a supplement, not to be included in deciding family living levels. Thus, this income could be used to pay for a home, furniture, or other capital expenses in contrast to day-by-day living costs.

Women Workers. The position of women in industry has varied considerably during modern times. With the advent of the industrial revolution, women were employed in factories and mines. Gradually, their place in the factory was yielded to men, except that in both world wars the trend was reversed. In 1958, there were over 22 million women in the labor force in the United States, or more than one third of the women over fourteen years of age. Among the occupations heavily staffed by women are: secretarial, sales, teaching, clerical work, work in restaurants, nursing, and various kinds of personal service. A sizable group of women (over 4,000,000) work in manufacturing, such as textiles and clothing, paper and printing, shoe manufacturing, glassmaking, electrical manufacturing, and metal, rubber, and chemical industries. Women do light assembly-line work. In some industries, such as tobacco manufacturing or women's clothing, women comprise about 70 per cent of the working force. A high percentage also obtains in knit goods, woolen and worsted goods, radio manufacturing, gas and electric fixtures, boots and shoes, and men's clothing. But even in the masculine stronghold of heavy industry, about 12 per cent of the workers are women. Half the women in the labor force are thirty-eight years old or older. A majority of working women are married and about 40 per cent of these have children under eighteen.

The position of women in the business world has many social implications. These include the question of proper wages and working conditions, the effect on the home, and the impact on the economy in general.

Women are frequently paid lower wages than men, even for the same occupations. Thus, women schoolteachers often receive lower salaries than men doing the same task. The argument used is that men are more efficient, that they need the higher wages to support families, and that women do not remain in an industry or occupation long enough to be considered other than learners or apprentices. On the other hand, there is no question but that women are used to supplant male workers and thus depress the wage rate. Women often accept lower wages because they enter the working force either under some pressure or with the idea that the job is temporary. Married women workers frequently seek only a supplementary income, while single girls, often living at home, will accept lower wages since their expenses are lower. When these groups take jobs which are competitive with those of men, undoubtedly they depress standards. Moreover, the elements of pressure or temporary employment make them less amenable to unionization or other steps to raise wages. The net result is competitive lowering of living standards.

Women need special consideration in the matter of working conditions. They need periodic rest intervals, a more liberal sickleave policy, and also maternity leaves. As a rule, nightwork is considered unsuitable for women. They are less able than men to work long hours. Because of this, most states have laws regulating the employment of women. These laws may specify the maximum number of hours per day and week, rest periods, and similar considerations. Over half the states also have minimum-wage laws for women. Standards for minimum wages usually assume a self-supporting single woman, thus taking a middle ground between the single woman living at home and the married woman supporting a family. Most laws are flexible, considering both the cost of living and the economic status of an industry.

Those whose duty it is to advise young girls and married women in the matter of employment might well ponder the address on Women's Duties given by Pope Pius XII on October 21, 1945. With moving eloquence and insight, the Holy Father noted that a woman cannot be happy in a social order which does violence to her nature. Her whole being tends toward motherhood and family life. Even when by vocation, either freely chosen or in submission to Divine Providence, she may never have a family of her own, she can still choose a form of spiritual motherhood in her choice of occupation. Through such professions as teaching, nursing, or social work, she can dedicate her life to the care of others. If she is forced, on the contrary, to do work more suitable for the masculine temperament, she does violence to her nature and becomes frustrated and unhappy.

Child Labor. Another possible source of supplementary family income is work by children of the family. Until recent years, most of the emphasis in regard to child labor concerned its abuses and consequent undesirability. With the serious problems of juvenile delinquency that have beset the United States in the 1950's, it is likely that there will be more stress upon the formative effects of hard work as a source of discipline and character building. It is still useful to note abuses that may exist in regard to immature workers. But we note these evils only to seek sound forms of work, not to discourage any constructive activity by the young or to promote the purposeless forms of idleness that often lead to delinquency. When discussing dangers in child labor, we observe physical, moral, and cultural problems that may arise as a result of wrong types of work for youth.

Work by children is physically dangerous when it taxes their strength and exposes them to sickness or, at least, to a stunting of their normal development. Such is the case with work too difficult for their years, risky in terms of possible accidents or in unsuitable surroundings in the matter of either place or time. Factory work is generally unhealthy for boys under eighteen. Labor in the fields in itself is better, but often the long hours and exhausting tasks are too much for the growing boy. Even light work which carries on into the night can mean loss of sleep and hence be debilitating. Moreover, if a child works so incessantly in his free time that he has no time for recreation, he will suffer physically. Hence, it is wrong to expect full-time hard work from children still in early adolescence. Part-time work likewise should be such as not to impose too great a strain at a time when energy reserves may be low.

Child labor is morally dangerous when performed in surroundings which present unusual temptations to crime or vice. From the moral viewpoint, indiscriminate mingling of young boys with older workers in factories would be generally unwise. The tone of conversation in the average factory is hardly that of a Holy Name meeting. While adults with decent standards develop a certain protective indifference to such language, the situation is otherwise with young boys, even in this sophisticated age. A similar problem obtains with street trades, such as those of newsboys and bootblacks, especially when boys work until late in the night to catch the after-theater crowd. Night surroundings in large cities can often be corrupting.

Another drawback to certain forms of child labor is the neglect of education which they involve. This ranges from outright withdrawal from school to carelessness in regard to studies. It is generally felt in the United States that a high school education or its equivalent should be available to all children. While there may be some who lack the minimum talent or interest necessary for such training, it is still desirable that they secure a better preparation for life, perhaps in a trade school. Certainly it is unjust when a student who is willing and able to receive a standard of education considered normal in this country is deprived of this opportunity because of family poverty.

There are two moral aspects to child labor. The first is that no child should be permitted to work under conditions which are detrimental to his health, morals, or basic education. Such work injures him and hence is contrary to his human dignity. Second, it is unjust when economic conditions force a child to work because total family income is insufficient to maintain decent standards. The father of a family should normally receive wages sufficient to support his family in frugal comfort. This does not mean that children should be forbidden work suitable to their age and strength. The discipline of moderate work is good training for children. They may learn habits of industry and responsibility. The income received may permit the family or the children small luxuries otherwise unobtainable. In some circumstances, it may be possible for a boy, through afterschool and summer work, to save enough to go to college. Again, in the absence of a family-allowance system, older children in large families may work to supplement a wage adequate for an average family but unsuitable in their case. Even in this situation, the family-allowance method might be better in principle.

Child labor in the United States is regulated by the Fair Labor Standards Act, which forbids the employment of minors under the age of sixteen in mining and manufacturing or at any work during school hours. Minors between the ages sixteen and eighteen may not be employed in hazardous occupations. Employment certificates may be secured by children between fourteen and sixteen, when the work will not interfere with their education or physical development. This law, however, applies only to occupations involved in interstate commerce. Children employed by their parents in occupations other than manufacturing and mining are exempt from the act. By 1958, nearly 700,000 minors of fourteen and fifteen were at work, and 1,100,000 of the ages sixteen and seventeen. About 10 per cent of this group was employed in violation of law, mostly in agriculture. The definition of "at work" included those employed fifteen or more hours a week, and about half this group was working full time. Most significant is the fact that the number of minors working in 1958 represented a sharp increase over the 1940 figures.

Even more meaningful than the figures quoted is the fact that both federal and state governments do not have adequate appropriations to enforce the laws upon the statute books. As a result, many abuses flourish even when regulatory laws have been passed to prevent them. In addition, many laws have loopholes to favor certain groups, such as farmers, so that coverage is often incomplete.

Social Insurance. Not all income supplements create social problems. This is particularly the case with the so-called "fringe benefits" attached to the pay check, and also to social security and related programs. Fringe benefits, such as pensions, health plans, and paid vacations, constitute a real income gain to the worker, even though he may not always realize this fact. In effect, these benefits, plus social security, remove to a considerable degree the necessity for saving for sickness, old age, and unemployment. Hence a worker can devote a larger percentage of his pay to current needs.

In theory, it can be argued that workers should be paid enough that they can save for their own health and retirement needs. Actually, the whole trend of modern life is in the other direction. High-pressure advertising induces the worker to spend what he has and often to mortgage his future by installment purchases. We could not easily reverse this trend. In some cases, it may not even be desirable to try. For instance, we can probably have better medical care through industrial health plans or through group insurance than any worker could secure with the same funds spent piecemeal.

Likewise, it can be argued that the insurance principle is sound when dealing with the problem of unemployment. When a hazard is unpredictable in precise incidence as regards the individual, although predictable for a group, it is much easier to provide for this hazard through insurance rather than by individual saving. Workers are morally justified in seeking a level of unemployment benefits that permits a family to maintain its basic living standards. The reason that this is sought today through collective bargaining rather than through increases in state legislative benefits is partly economic and partly political. Economically some industries are in a good position to give supplementary unemployment benefits. From the viewpoint of politics, it is often easier to get gains through collective bargaining than to seek similar benefits through legislation. State legislators often view unemployment compensation with a jaundiced eye, as if it were a premium paid for idleness. Employers, on the other hand, are often more realistic in understanding that joblessness is unavoidable. Moreover, they are usually anxious to keep their work force intact when forced to lay off workers temporarily. Hence many of them, at least, are quite willing that their workers receive good benefits while unavoidably idle.

The Federal Advisory Council on Employment Security recommended at the close of 1958 that major changes be made in our unemployment compensation system. They favored a flat 30-week period of benefits, with benefits to average either half the worker's wage or two-thirds of the state's average weekly wage, whichever is lower. This would necessitate a major increase in practically every state in the Union. In addition, there was a call for simplifying and standardizing eligibility requirements. These proposals recognized the real importance of unemployment compensation to our economic system. It is more than a humanitarian measure; it is also a factor of stability in business fluctuations.

Finally, the combination of the industrial pension and federal old-age-and-survivors' benefits can often make the difference between destitution and security in old age. What was considered fantastic when proposed as the Townsend Plan some decades ago is almost a reality today — the availability of really suitable pensions for older persons without any means test or similar limitation. The time may come when the complex payment systems of today, both federal and private, will be replaced by pooled contributions based on the simple idea that the working force should take care of retired workers at any given time. We could thus avoid the tremendous bookkeeping problems, posed by present methods, as well as the economic implications of investing tens of billions for funded pension systems. Individuals and their employers could pay into this system according to their incomes. Payments to retired persons would be in terms of average previous income, regardless of how it was earned or for whom the pensioner worked. In this way there would be no need for huge investments and no problem of a pension tying a worker to a particular company for a lifetime.

In the meantime, certain adjustments are needed in the existing system of Old Age and Survivors' Insurance. For example the menace of inflation should be faced by some form of escalator clause tied to benefits. The extent of coverage should be still further broadened to include all persons in federal employment and the small groups of employed and self-employed still excluded from benefits. Finally, the age at which widows may receive payments should be further reduced. It is unrealistic, in most instances, to expect a widow to be self-supporting to the age of sixty-two.

Family Allowances. In connection with the economic problems posed by a living wage, it was noted that there are strong arguments for a system of family allowances. Thus the wage received (including allowances) would be geared to family needs. We would not then burden our economic system with the heavy, if not impossible, task of paying all workers a wage that will enable family heads among them to support their children. In order to understand how such a system might help with family economic problems, it is useful to note here a few facts about different systems and to consider the controversies over the best method for instituting such allowances.

Practically every industrial nation in the world has some form of aid for families. Over a score, including our neighbor, Canada, have direct allowances for children. Others have tax benefits, medical assistance, and other grants designed to help parents meet their burdens. These methods of help are based on several well-known facts. First, there is the fact that in our modern urban civilization children are an economic liability, not an asset. In earlier times, when farm and small-town life was predominant, large families were less of a burden, because children could work at home or near the home. Now it is often difficult for children to find suitable work, especially if they are young.

Second, total incomes for families with a large number of children tend to be low. One reason for this is that such families often have only one breadwinner, since the mother cannot be employed outside the home. Another factor is that the father is often relatively young and has not reached the peak of his earning capacity. Hence we find that families with the greatest needs are often low down on the family-income scale.

Apart from the element of need, some countries justify family help on the grounds that an expanding population is a national asset. Often it is a military necessity. It may be an economic advantage. Given the

248 SOCIAL PRINCIPLES — MAJOR SOCIOECONOMIC INSTITUTIONS

fact that so many families are childless, it is usually necessary to have a sizable number of large families (over four children) in order to maintain even a constant population level. On this ground, it can be argued that large families contribute to the general welfare and should in turn be rewarded for their contribution. Even totalitarian nations, such as the Soviet Union, have family allowances. Since it is notorious that such nations have little concern for human life or misery, one assumes that they support families as a source of national strength.

The form of allowance varies from country to country. Some give aid for all children, others for the third and following children, and so forth. Some systems decrease benefits per child as family size increases, others do not. Canada completely ignores the element of need, aiding even the children of the wealthy. The cost of aid may be met by general taxes or by special levies upon payrolls.

The types of argument used in the preceding chapter would favor an aid program closely tied up with the employer-employee relationship. Two reasons favor this, as contrasted with a state program based largely upon general taxation. One reason for payroll financing is the moral obligation of a living wage. This obligation is tied up with a work situation, not with the civic status of the worker. Hence employers, and workers also, should contribute to a fund designed to equalize family burdens. A second argument for the payroll-financed type of allowance plan is that it fits in more with the principle of subsidiarity. A state program would be another step in the direction of the welfare state. But here we must face up to the difficulty posed by low-wage industries. Obviously, an employer-financed plan would need supplementing from some general fund, if such industries were to pay an adequate wage to married workers with families.[1]

If a family-allowance system were to be inaugurated in the United States, there are good grounds for starting any system of payment with the third child. So much of our economic thinking has been in terms of the two-child family as normal, as indicated in the budgets analyzed earlier, that we can take for granted that most wages are supposed to meet this type of family obligation. A system of this nature would be less costly and less revolutionary in terms of established customs. Hence it would have a far better chance of being adopted than the theoretically better system of assistance for all family needs.

---

[1] For a temperate and factual analysis of the family-allowance program, see James C. Vadakin, *Family Allowances* (Miami, Fla.: University of Miami, 1959).

When the cost of family allowances is being considered, it is well to remember that contributions to the family may permit of savings in community social-service programs. Many existing welfare and relief programs could be curtailed if not abolished. In addition, there would be an enormous gain in terms of morale, as families got these services as matters of right, not because of their indigence. It may well be that, strictly on the basis of cost, aid to families may turn out to be a long-run saving to the community.

READINGS*

J. Messner, *Social Ethics*, pp. 283–317.

G. Clune, *Christian Social Reorganization*, Chaps. 11, 18.

J. Villain, *L'Enseignement social de l'Église*, Vol. II, pp. 170–175.

A. H. Clemens, *Marriage and the Family*, Chap. 17.

C. S. Mihanovich and others, *Marriage and the Family*, Chap. 5.

M. E. Walsh and P. H. Furfey, *Social Problems and Social Action*, Chaps. 10–11.

Social Order: A. H. Clemens, "Values in Family Living," March, 1953; Francis J. Corrigan, "The Consumer: Real and Ideal . . . and how to be a better one," February, 1955; Mary Clinch, "The Phenomenon of the Working Wife," October, 1956; A. H. Scheller, S.J., "How Co-op Health Plans Work," October, 1953; Edward Duff, "Medicine, a Public Utility?" March, 1954; Leo C. Brown, S.J., "The Economic Future of Medical Practice," June, 1958; Ralph A. Lassance, S.J., "Canada Provides for Her Children," February, 1952; Francis J. Corley, S.J., "Family Allowances; U. S. Plan," April, 1953; Francis J. Corley, S.J., "Why FEDERAL Family Allowances?" June, 1954; Francis J. Corley, S.J., "Are Family Allowances Doles?" February, 1956.

---

* For further readings, see List No. 8 in the Appendix.

Chapter XII

PROPERTY

THE RIGHT OF OWNERSHIP

Leo XIII, Rerum Novarum

10–17. (Summarized.) Man differs from beast in that he has the right of ownership. His ability to foresee the future and meet its needs is an added reason for this right. This is a natural right, anterior to the formation of the state and independent of it. But the broad right of ownership does not preclude the institution of private property. "However the earth may be apportioned among private owners, it does not cease to serve the common interest of all, inasmuch as no living being is sustained except by what the fields bring forth. Those who lack resources supply labor, so that it can truly be affirmed that the entire scheme of securing a livelihood consists in the labor which a person expends either on his own land or in some working occupation, the compensation for which is drawn ultimately from no other source than the varied products of the earth and is exchanged for them" (No. 14). Private possessions are clearly in accord with nature, since only by man's labor can nature be truly productive. Theories which permit use of land, but deny ownership [single tax], overlook the improvement of land through cultivation. "Rightly, therefore, the human race as a whole, moved in nowise by the dissenting opinions of a few, and observing nature carefully, has found in the law of nature itself the basis of the distribution of goods, and, by the practice of all ages, has consecrated private possessions as something best adapted to man's nature and to peaceful and tranquil living together" (No. 17). Civil and divine law [against theft] sanction such an institution.

18–23. (Summarized.) Property also fits in aptly with family obligations. A father protects his children through saving and the right of inheritance. The family is certainly prior to the state, even though subject to just laws. Moreover, the equality envisioned by socialism would in reality lead to turmoil and dissension. "Let it be regarded, therefore, as established that in seeking help for the masses this principle before all is to be considered basic, namely, that private ownership must be preserved inviolate" (No. 23).

55. But it will be well to touch here expressly on certain matters of special importance. The capital point is this, that private property ought to be safeguarded by the sovereign power of the state and through the bulwark of its laws.

Pius XII, Radio Address, September 1, 1944

Private property is in a special manner the natural fruit of labor, the product of an intense activity on the part of the man who acquires it through his energetic will to ensure and improve, by his own forces, his own living conditions and those of his family, to create for himself and those dear to him a field in which they may rightly enjoy, not only economic freedom, but political, cultural, and religious freedom as well.

Pius XII, To International Institute for the Unification of Private Rights, May 20, 1948

The recognition of this right [of property] harmonizes with the dignity of the human personality, the recognition of inviolable rights and duties inseparably inherent in the free personality received from God.

Only those who deny to men the dignity of free persons can admit the possibility of substituting for the right of private property (and consequently the very institution of private property) some system of insurance or legal protection by public law.

Pius XII, To Christian Associations of Italian Workers, June 7, 1957

. . . the independence of the family and the freedom of the citizen are naturally bound up with a sound functioning of private property as a stabilizing social institution.

The Church and Social Order

20. The Church has always defended the right to own private property and also to bequeath and to inherit it. We have vindicated this right even to the point of being falsely accused of favoring the rich against the poor. The Church teaches that the right to own property is based on the natural law of which God Himself is the author. By the law of nature man must provide for himself and his family and he can fully discharge this obligation only if there exists an established system of private ownership.

PROPERTY RIGHTS: SOCIAL AND INDIVIDUAL

Pius XI, Quadragesimo Anno

45. First, then, let it be considered as certain and established that neither Leo nor those theologians who have taught under the guidance and authority of the Church have ever denied or questioned the twofold character of ownership, usually called individual and social according as it regards either separate persons or the common good. For they have always unanimously maintained that nature, rather the Creator Himself, has given man the right of private ownership, not only that individuals may be able to provide for themselves and their families, but also that the goods

which the Creator destined for the entire family of mankind may through this institution truly serve this purpose. All this can be achieved in nowise except through the maintenance of a certain and definite order.

46. Accordingly, twin rocks of shipwreck must be carefully avoided. For, as one is wrecked upon, or comes close to, what is known as "individualism" by denying or minimizing the social and public character of the right of property, so by rejecting or minimizing the private and individual character of this same right, one inevitably runs into "collectivism" or at least closely approaches its tenets.

49. It follows from what We have termed the individual and at the same time social character of ownership, that men must consider in this matter not only their own advantage but also the common good. To define these duties in detail when necessity requires and the natural law has not done so, is the function of those in charge of the state. Therefore, public authority, under the guiding light always of the natural and divine law, can determine more accurately upon consideration of the true requirements of the common good, what is permitted and what is not permitted to owners in the use of their property. Moreover, Leo XIII wisely taught "that God has left the limits of private possessions to be fixed by the industry of men and institutions of peoples."

TAXATION

Leo XIII, Rerum Novarum

67. But these advantages can be attained only if private wealth is not drained away by crushing taxes of every kind. For since the right of possessing goods privately has been conferred not by man's law, but by nature, public authority cannot abolish it, but can only control its exercise and bring it into conformity with the common weal. Public authority, therefore, would act unjustly and inhumanly, if in the name of taxes it should appropriate from the property of private individuals more than is equitable.

Pius XI, Quadragesimo Anno

49. Yet when the state brings private ownership into harmony with the needs of the common good, it does not commit a hostile act against private owners but rather does them a friendly service; for it thereby effectively prevents the private possession of goods, which the Author of nature in His most wise providence ordained for the support of human life, from causing intolerable evils and thus rushing to its own destruction; it does not destroy private possessions, but safeguards them; and it does not weaken private property rights, but strengthens them.

Pius XI, On Atheistic Communism

75. The state must take every measure necessary to supply employment particularly for the heads of families and for the young. To achieve this end demanded by the pressing needs of the common welfare, the wealthy

classes must be induced to assume those burdens without which human society cannot be saved nor they themselves remain secure. However, measures taken by the state with this end in view ought to be of such a nature that they will really affect those who possess more than their share of capital resources, and who continue to accumulate them to the grievous detriment of others.

Pius XII, On Public Finance, October 2, 1948

The Church . . . addressing herself to those who have some share of responsibility in the treatment of public finance questions . . . beseeches them: In the name of human conscience, do not destroy morals from the top. Forego those measures which, despite their technical virtuosity, shock and wound the people's sense of the just and unjust, or which relegate to the background their vital urge, their legitimate ambition to harvest the fruits of their own labor, and their anxiety over family security, all considerations which merit first place in the mind of the legislator and not the last.

The financial system of the state should aim at reorganizing the economic situation in a manner that would assure the people the material conditions of life indispensable for following the supreme end assigned by the Creator: the development of intellectual, spiritual, and religious life.

Pius XII, To International Association for Financial and Fiscal Law, October 2, 1956

There can be no doubt concerning the duty of each citizen to bear a part of the public expense. It is the obligation of the state, however — insofar as it is charged with protecting and promoting the common good of citizens — to assess upon its citizens only necessary levies which are, furthermore, proportionate to their means. Taxation can never become, then, a convenient way for public authority to make up a deficit brought on by an improvident administration, or a means of favoring one industry or branch of business at the expense of another of equal utility. The state must forbid itself any waste of public funds; it must forestall abuse and injustice on the part of its employees, as well as evasion by those who are legitimately taxed.

Modern states tend today to multiply their interventions and to make themselves answerable for an increasing number of services; they exercise a tighter control over the economy; they intervene to a greater extent in the social protection of many classes of workers. Thus their need for money mounts in proportion to the degree to which they enlarge their administrations. Excessively heavy impositions often oppress private initiative, check the development of industry and commerce, and work to the detriment of good will.

*   *   *

May taxes continue to be adjusted, with increasingly sensitive and adequate criteria, to the true capabilities of the individual. Taxation will no longer, then, be regarded as a constantly excessive and more or less arbitrary burden. It will come to represent — in a state better organized and equipped for achieving the harmonious performance of society's various activities — a humble, perhaps, and very material, but nonetheless indispensable, aspect of civic unity and individual support of the common welfare.

Code of Social Principles

158. Taxation laws which are just, and justly applied, are binding in conscience. Catholic sociologists should endeavor to correct wrong opinions on this matter, and in the name of social justice to lead good people to participate loyally in the expenses of the state.

161. In theory, the ideal would be a single progressive tax on income. But in practice a part of the public revenue must be obtained through indirect taxes, which are more willingly accepted and do not so easily become oppressive.

162. Direct taxation has, however, the advantage of asking from the citizens a conscious sacrifice which gives them an interest in public affairs.

164. Justified in exceptional circumstances, such as a very defective division of material resources, excessive taxes and dues undermine the principle of ownership, scarcely differ from confiscation, and hinder the building up of national reserves.

DUTIES OF PROPERTY OWNERS

Leo XIII, Rerum Novarum

36. To own goods privately, as We saw above, is a right natural to man, and to exercise this right, especially in life in society, is not only lawful, but clearly necessary. "It is lawful for man to own his own things. It is even necessary for human life." But if the question be asked: How ought man use his possessions, the Church replies without hesitation: "As to this point, man ought not regard external goods as his own, but as common so that, in fact, a person should readily share them when he sees others in need. Wherefore the Apostle says: 'Charge the rich of this world . . . to give readily, to share with others'" (Summa, II, II, 66, 2). No one, certainly, is obliged to assist others out of what is required for his own necessary use or for that of his family, or even to give to others what he himself needs to maintain his station in life becomingly and decently: "No one is obliged to live unbecomingly." But when the demands of necessity and propriety have been sufficiently met, it is a duty to give to the poor out of that which remains. "Give that which remains as alms." These are duties not of justice, except in cases of extreme need, but of Christian charity, which obviously cannot be enforced by legal action. But the laws and judgments of men yield precedence to the law and judgment of Christ the Lord, who in many ways urges the practice of almsgiving: "It is more blessed to give than to receive," and who will judge a kindness done or denied to the poor as done or denied to Himself. "As long as you did it for one of these, the least of My brethren, you did it for Me." The substance of all this is the following: whoever has received from the bounty of God a greater share of goods, whether corporal and external,

or of the soul, has received them for this purpose, namely, that he employ them for his own perfection and, like-wise, as a servant of Divine Providence, for the benefit of others.

Pius XI, Quadragesimo Anno

47. In order to place definite limits on the controversies that have arisen over ownership and its inherent duties there must be first laid down as a foundation a principle established by Leo XIII: the right of property is distinct from its use. That justice called commutative commands sacred respect for the division of possessions and forbids invasion of others' rights through the exceeding of the limits of one's own property; but the duty of owners to use their property only in a right way does not come under this type of justice, but under other virtues, obligations of which "cannot be enforced by legal action." Therefore, they are in error who assert that ownership and its right use are limited by the same boundaries; and it is much farther still from the truth to hold that a right to property is destroyed or lost by reason of abuse or nonuse.

48. Those, therefore, are doing a work that is truly salutary and worthy of all praise who, while preserving harmony among themselves and the integrity of the traditional teaching of the Church, seek to define the inner nature of these duties and their limits whereby either the right of property itself or its use, that is, the exercise of ownership, is circumscribed by the necessities of social living. On the other hand, those who seek to restrict the individual character of ownership to such a degree that in fact they destroy it are mistaken and in error.

50. Furthermore, a person's superfluous income, that is, income which he does not need to sustain life fittingly and with dignity, is not left wholly to his own free determination. Rather the Sacred Scriptures and the Fathers of the Church constantly declare in the most explicit language that the rich are bound by a very grave precept to practice almsgiving, beneficence, and munificence.

51. Expending larger incomes so that opportunity for gainful work may be abundant, provided, however, that this work is applied to producing really useful goods, ought to be considered, as We deduce from the principles of the Angelic Doctor, an outstanding exemplification of the virtue of munificence and one particularly suited to the needs of the times.

A JUST DISTRIBUTION OF PROPERTY

Leo XIII, Rerum Novarum

65. We have seen, in fact, that the whole question under consideration cannot be settled effectually unless it is assumed and established as a principle, that the right of private property must be regarded as sacred. Wherefore, the law ought to favor this right and, so far as it can, see that the largest possible number among the masses of the population prefer to own property.

Pius XI, Quadragesimo Anno

57. Therefore, the riches that the economic-social developments constantly increase ought to be so distributed among individual persons and classes that the common advantage of all, which Leo XIII had praised, will be safeguarded; in other words, that the common good of all society will be kept inviolate.

58. To each, therefore, must be given his own share of goods, and the distribution of goods which, as every discerning person knows, is laboring today under the gravest evils due to the huge disparity between the few exceedingly rich and the unnumbered propertyless, must be effectively called back to and brought into conformity with the norms of the common good, that is, social justice.

60. The immense multitude of the nonowning workers on the one hand, and the enormous riches of certain very wealthy men on the other, establish an unanswerable argument that the riches which are so abundantly produced in our age of "industrialism," as it is called, are not rightly distributed and equitably made available to the various classes of people.

61. Therefore, with all our strength and effort we must strive that at least in the future the abundant fruits of production will accrue equitably to those who are rich and will be distributed in ample sufficiency among the workers . . . that they may increase their property by thrift, that they may bear, by wise management of this increase in property, the burdens of family life with greater ease and security, and that, emerging from that insecure lot in life in whose uncertainties nonowning workers are cast, they may be able not only to endure the vicissitudes of earthly existence, but also have assurance that when their lives are ended they will provide in some measure for those they leave after them.

63. . . . It will be impossible to put these principles into practice unless the nonowning workers through industry and thrift advance to the state of possessing some little property.

Pius XI, On Atheistic Communism

50. Is it not deplorable that the right of private property defended by the Church should so often have been used as a weapon to defraud the workingman of his just salary and his social rights?

Pius XII, Christmas Broadcast, 1942

1840. The dignity of the human person, then, requires normally, as a natural foundation of life, the right to the use of the goods of the earth. To this right corresponds the fundamental obligation to grant private ownership of property, if possible, to all. Positive legislation regulating private ownership may change and more or less restrict its use. But if legisla- tion is to play its part in the pacification of the community, it must prevent the worker, who is or will be a father of a family, from being condemned to an economic dependence and slavery which is irreconcilable with his rights as a person. Whether this slavery rises from the exploitation of private capital or from the power of the state which dominates all and controls the whole field of public and private life, even going into the realm of ideas and beliefs and of conscience, this lack of liberty can have more serious consequences, as experience shows and proves. . . .

1851. These exigencies include, besides a just wage which covers the needs of the worker and his family, the conservation and perfection of a social order which will make possible an assured, even if modest, private property for all classes of society. . . .

Pius XII, Radio Address, September 1, 1944

But the Church aims rather at securing that the institution of private property be such as it should be according to the designs of God's wisdom and the dispositions of nature: an element of social order, a necessary presupposition to human initiative, an incentive to work to the advantage of life's purpose here and hereafter, and hence of the liberty and the dignity of man, created in the likeness of God, who, from the beginning, assigned him for his benefit domination over material things.

The social and economic policy of the future, the controlling power of the state, of local bodies, of professional institutions cannot permanently secure their end, which is the genuine productivity of social life and the normal returns on national economy, except by respecting and safeguarding the vital function of private property in its personal and social values.

*   *   *

For the same purpose small and medium holdings in agriculture, in the arts and trades, in commerce and industry should be guaranteed and promoted; co-operative unions should ensure for them the advantages of big business; where big business even today shows itself more productive, there should be given the possibility of tempering the labor contract with a contract of co-ownership.

Pius XII, To Spanish Employers and Workers, March 11, 1951

The Church defends the right of private property, a right she considers fundamentally inalienable. But she insists also on the need for a more just distribution of property and deplores the unnatural social situation in which an enormous mass of impoverished people live beside a small group of very rich and privileged. There always will be economic inequalities. But all those who in any way are able to influence the progress of society must aim to obtain a situation which permits people who do the best they can not only to live, but to save. There are many factors which must contribute to a greater diffusion of property. But the principal one always will be a just salary. You know very well, beloved children, that a just salary and a better distribution of natural wealth constitute two of the most impelling demands in the social program of the Church.

Pius XII, To the International Institute of the Middle Classes, October 25, 1956

It is not that the middle classes constitute a new element in society — quite the contrary; but the development of large-scale capitalism on the one hand, and of the wage-earning classes on the other, has evoked a body of regulations and institutions which too often disregard an essential segment of the citizenry of each country. This embraces those who generally contribute to production through their work and personal capi-tal: craftsmen, independent trades-people, owners of small and medium-sized businesses, the majority of farmers, professional men, certain categories of civil servants and mili-tary men, and most persons who live on independent means.

Australian Hierarchy, Socialization, 1948

In the economic sphere, it is there-fore a most important task of govern-ment to encourage that type of eco-nomic organization in which the family and the home may prosper. The normal economic order — that order which is best adapted to the real needs of mankind — is one in which the majority of men are work-ing proprietors; that is to say, where they earn a living for themselves and their families by working their own property, whether that property is a farm, a shop, a workshop, or a fac-tory. This is the best economic order precisely because the institution of the family is strongest where this system prevails. This type of economic order may be adapted to enterprises which require more capital than one family can contribute. Where the amount of capital actually needed for the con-duct of the business is greater than one man can supply, the necessary capital is best made up in the form of a partnership in which each of the partners has an effective share of control.

THE RIGHT TO PRIVATE PROPERTY

PROPERTY is of necessity one of the foundations of economic life. Its accumulation makes men of wealth. Its widespread distribution normally brings about a stable society. Men risk their lives to acquire or to con-serve it, while others, fearing the passion for wealth, take solemn vows relinquishing the right of ownership. To many, it is a bastion of security and a guarantee of freedom. It is no wonder, then, that the concept of property rights normally determines the entirety of a social philosophy. The rights of man and of the state are so closely correlated with those of property that often the one can be deduced from the other.

Disputes over the rights of property were among the major factors occasioning the social encyclicals. The socialists reacted to the abuse of property by calling for state ownership of all productive wealth. Proudhon said: "Property is theft." To which Bishop von Ketteler replied: "The notorious dictum, 'property is theft,' is something more than a mere lie; besides a great lie, it contains a terrible truth. Scorn and derision will not dispose of it. . . . As deep calleth unto deep, so one sin against nature

calls forth another. Out of the distorted right of ownership, the false doctrine of communism was begotten."[1] Then came *Rerum Novarum*, which
vindicated the right of property against socialism, but also denounced
abuses by property owners. Even within the Church, controversy continued, with some holding that the right of property was contingent upon
its proper use. But, when *Quadragesimo Anno* was issued, it clearly
upheld the right of property, defined its individual and social character,
noted the powers of the state in regard to it, and even more strongly
denounced abuses connected with it. Finally, the repeated discourses and
encyclicals of Pope Pius XII stressed both the need for more equitable
distribution of property and the ideal that most men become owners of
property.

The Right to Ownership. The classical treatment of property is found
in the *Summa Theologiae* of St. Thomas Aquinas. The arguments of St.
Thomas for private property have lost none of their luster through the
centuries. His position may be quoted in full:

> Two things are competent to man in respect to exterior things. One is
> the power to procure and dispense them, and in this regard it is lawful for
> man to possess property. Moreover, this is necessary for human life for
> three reasons. First, because every man is more careful to procure what is
> for himself alone than that which is common to many or to all; since each
> one would shirk the labor and leave to another that which concerns the
> community, as happens when there are a great number of servants. Secondly,
> because human affairs are conducted in a more orderly fashion if each man
> is charged with taking care of some particular thing himself, whereas there
> would be confusion if everyone had to look after any one thing indeter-
> minately. Thirdly, because a more peaceful state is ensured to man if each
> is contented with his own. Hence it is to be observed that quarrels arise
> more frequently where there is no division of things possessed.
>   The second thing that is competent to man with regard to external things
> is their use. In this respect man ought to possess external things, not as
> his own, but as common, so that, to wit, he is ready to communicate them
> to others in their need.[2]

These arguments are based on such enduring qualities of human nature
that they possess the virtue of timelessness.

The first argument is that private property fosters initiative, whereas
common ownership leads to slovenly neglect. This element of human
interest in one's own is so obvious that proof is unnecessary. Even chil-

---

[1] Sermon on "The Christian Idea of the Rights of Property," cited in J. J. Laux,
Ketteler's Social Reform (Philadelphia: Dolphin Press, 1912), pp. 38–39.

[2] *Summa*, II, II, 66, 2; cf. W. J. McDonald, *The Social Value of Property According
to St. Thomas Aquinas* (Washington: Catholic University, 1939), and Suarez, *De
Legibus*, II, 17–19.

dren tend to treasure their own toys. A businessman will slave to make his firm a success, whereas the hired manager (unless a personal incentive is present) tends to be careless and timeserving. In colleges and like communities, common property is often neglected. The community car often lacks gas, gets infrequent oil changes, and receives much more abuse than usually happens when an auto is privately owned. People generally take care of their own lawns and yet are careless in littering public parks. Government-owned business is often unimaginative and routine, whereas private business tends to be enterprising and resourceful. There are exceptions to these statements, but usually only where some equivalent motive substitutes for pride of ownership. A manager may be ambitious for success, feeling that his record will bring promotion. He may fear the penalties of failure. The instinct of self-seeking is deep. It may be modified by Christian altruism, but only in a few persons is altruism so dominant that they take care of common goods as if they were their own. So long as human nature remains in this pattern, and fallen nature is prone to evil, private ownership will be more successful than common possessions.

Second, private ownership leads to an orderly handling of human affairs. The distinction of ownership leads to a division of duties. The man who owns a farm will cultivate it. The proprietor of a store will order goods and sell them. If ownership were indeterminate, men would follow their impulses and instincts in a most haphazard fashion. In pleasant weather, there would be an inordinate number taking care of the fishing needs of the community. If snow blocked the streets, most men would prefer to meet their indoor duties, rather than clear off the snow. The alternative to this chaos would be central organization of life by the state. But if all economic power were centered in the state, freedom would be lost. In the absence of universal altruism, the normal method of getting men to work is the use of fear and compulsion. Experiences in the Soviet Union bear this out. The communists first tried the ideal of "from each according to his ability, to each according to his needs." But the system soon degenerated into a cruel incentive system for labor, with a reign of absolute terror superimposed.

Finally, private possessions tend to promote a peaceful society. If goods were held in common, there would be frequent quarrels over the most desirable things. Farmers would fight to cultivate the best land. Workers would want the most pleasant jobs. Each would seek a share of distribution more favorable to himself. The result would be mob rule, with the strongest or the most cunning holding the best positions. Even in religious communities, under a vow of poverty and practicing the virtue of charity, there are strains and tensions because of common possessions. With only one morning newspaper in the common room, some may be unhappy because a colleague persists in reading every word. Not all will agree on the programs to be seen on the community television. These sacrifices are endured and sublimated through religious ideals, but they would be occasions of quarrels outside the monastery walls. Hence, common ownership does not readily accord with fallen nature, except in cases where people voluntarily embrace a life involving the counsels of perfection.

The Thomistic arguments for private property are based upon an analysis of certain enduring traits of human nature. They should be supplemented, however, by the pronouncements of the "social popes," especially those which emphasize property as necessary both for the freedom of the individual and the stability of the family. Pope Pius XII particularly noted that property widely distributed affords an economic basis for political and other freedoms. Pope Leo XIII stressed the value of property ownership as an economic foundation for family stability.

If the right of property is upheld, then it follows logically that the property owner must receive the normal return from his possessions. Where these possessions consist of capital goods, this return is called profit. Money, considered as the equivalent of capital, is productive of interest. Both these types of return were treated in Chapter VIII. There remains one further method of realizing upon property, namely, rent.

Rent is a return based on the value of land, whether this value derives from fertility of soil or location of property. In strict economic usage, rent applies only to land, not to buildings that rest on the land or even to improvements, such as irrigation, that enhance its usefulness. By contrast, in the ordinary "rent" that an apartment dweller pays, an economist finds not only a charge for land, but also interest on capital investment, payment for the costs of management, and normal maintenance and depreciation charges.

Some persons have questioned the moral right of landowners to collect rent. These objectors argue that the special worth that constitutes a basis for rent (as defined above) depends upon natural fertility and artificial location values and not upon any contribution by the owner. Accordingly, he has no moral right to appropriate what is a result of divine bounty or of the enterprise of others. Fertility is a God-given attribute of soil, and location is dependent upon community developments.

Two answers can be offered to the attacks upon economic rent. First, any validity in the arguments cited applies only to the original occupant of the land who held it until it acquired substantial value. Any subsequent purchaser presumably has paid the full value of the land and hence is entitled to a return on his investment. Second, if the so-called unearned increment were to be taxed away or otherwise denied owners, all land would lose its value to an owner. This would have the practical effect of denying private property in land. Such a drastic limitation of property rights can hardly be reconciled with the powerful natural-law arguments in favor of private ownership. It is better to permit unearned gains to property owners, if the alternative is the limitation of the institution of private property in such a drastic manner.

Individual and Social Aspects of Property. St. Thomas stated that while ownership may be private, use should be common, so that an owner is ready to communicate his goods to others in their need. Pope Pius XI made this point more exact by distinguishing between the individual and the social aspects of property. While individual ownership is a right, social obligations also attach to property. These social duties may be evident from the nature of the common good or they may be specified by positive law, whether divine or human. The state normally determines, in the absence of natural or divine law, what should be the duties of owners. Thus, it directs property into its proper place in the universal pattern of the common good. In so acting, government should be careful not to destroy the right of ownership in the guise of regulation or taxation.

That property has a social aspect is evident from even casual consideration. When a man buys an automobile, he acquires a personal possession. It is his to use or to leave idle, to sell or to give. But the ownership and use of a car also involves clear social responsibilities. The owner, in most states, must register his title and acquire license tags. Before he is allowed to drive, he normally must have a permit and this usually involves an examination on his ability to drive and his knowledge of traffic laws. In using the car, he is bound by traffic regulations. He must drive on the right side of the street, at proper speed, and observe signal lights and signs. His brakes and headlights must be in order. In some states, he must secure periodic inspections of the car. All these requirements exist because the common good demands such regulation of private property in automobiles. If people drive haphazardly, lives are endangered and traffic is hopelessly entangled. Social obligations here are clear and binding.

As a general rule, it might be stated that the social aspect of property increases insofar as it affects persons other than its owners. Things which are close to the individual and do not normally affect others do not have important social connotations. Ordinarily such items as personal clothing, furniture in the home, or a tractor on the farm have little social import. But improper clothing offends public decency. A television set in the home should not blare loudly at night. If a tractor is driven on the public highways, its driver must observe traffic rules.

There are types of property which necessarily involve social obligations. Thus, a large factory may employ thousands of workers. It can be a major influence in the community. Its products may be used throughout the nation or even the world. Even if this factory were owned by a single individual, he could not be blind to the many duties implied by the type of ownership he enjoys. This is all the more true where a corporation owns such property, since corporation law gives shareholders the rights of ownership, but exempts them from many of its duties. Stockholders are not legally liable for the debts of the company (except that its property, their equity, may be sold to pay debts) nor are they legally responsible for the actions of their officers. Indeed, courts have upheld boards of directors that refused information requested by stockholders, when the divulging of such information would be contrary to the company's interests. Thus, we have in the large corporation ownership shorn of much of the right of control. The "property" of the stockholder is more a contingent claim upon profits than a title of effective ownership.

Two conclusions follow from this situation. First, the personal responsibility of the stockholder in regard to the large corporation is generally minimal. If he lacks power to control decisions, he can hardly be blamed for such decisions. The most that moralists could realistically expect in such situations is that, when a corporation is acting unjustly, good men do not profit from such injustice by buying or retaining stock in such a company. Second, there are special grounds for government action to specify and enforce social obligations, when property ownership and responsibility are divorced. Here more than ever the social aspects of property must be considered.

Regulation must not be carried to such an extreme that it degenerates into collectivism. This would be a denial of the individual aspect of property rights, a threat to human liberty, and hence a false interpretation of the common good. The community exists to serve its members, not to dominate over them or absorb them. But restraint does not mean a passive, *laissez-faire* attitude by the state, since this would be an abdication to individualism and a denial of the common good. A careful balance between the extremes of individualism and collectivism must be kept at all times. Naturally the emphasis on state intervention will vary according to circumstances of time and place. A small, self-sufficient country with a good balance between agriculture and industry needs less public stress on social duties than does a larger nation with difficult social problems. Again, the impact of social obligations is usually greater in times of war or emergency than in periods of peace and normal times. In a period of war, both the social aspect of property and the right of the state to direct its use for the common good are intensified.

We should not emphasize the function of the state in specifying the social aspects of property to the neglect of obligations springing from natural and divine law. Certain natural rights which are possessed by individuals involve limitations on the use of property. Even in the absence of law, an owner is obligated to consider these social implications of property use. Thus, labor's right to organize and to seek a living wage is bound to affect the employer's use of his productive property. A farmer who cultivates his land in such a way as to cause erosion on other farms is acting unsocially. A mining firm that endangers lives or property by its methods of extraction is doing wrong. Owners likewise have a duty to avoid unnecessary work on Sunday, so that their employees can attend divine worship. While the state may enforce such obligations in view of the common good, they also oblige individual consciences under social justice and other virtues, even in the absence of public law.

Taxation. Papal treatment of taxation is not extensive. Pope Leo XIII warns against confiscatory taxes which destroy property rights in the guise of collecting public funds. Pope Pius XI notes that this warning does not preclude progressive taxation, bearing heavily on the wealthy. Sharing the common burdens in accord with ability to pay, far from destroying property, safeguards it against the possibility of violent revolution. Finally, Pope Pius XII emphasizes the need for preserving economic incentive and directing taxes in terms of an efficient economic organization that provides the material basis for cultural and spiritual values.

The complexity of modern life and the heavy cost of war and preparation against war necessarily involve a high cost of government. Thus, in the United States today about 30 per cent of the national income goes for taxation and in other countries the amount is even higher. Most of these costs are necessary, although savings would be possible through greater efficiency in some phases of government. Accordingly, a high level of taxation seems inevitable. The only method of relieving the relative burden would be a continuing increase in the general national income. An eighty-billion-dollar federal budget would be less troublesome if the national income were five hundred billion instead of three hundred.

It happens that taxation is in turn one of the important determinants of the level of national income. If taxes were so directed as to absorb practically all the savings of the community, there would be no investment and no economic expansion. The economy would be stagnant and unemployment would rise, since industry could not provide for a growing working population. Hence two factors must be balanced in working out a just system of taxation. The tests of equality of sacrifice and payment according to ability would dictate progressive income taxes, which naturally bear most heavily upon the wealthier classes. Yet the need for retaining the profit incentive and of stimulating investment is also vital, if the economic system is to expand and provide more jobs. Hence taxation should not preclude all saving in the group which is prone to invest, nor should it make investment impossible by so taxing gains that the risk becomes prohibitive.

Practically all taxes have social aspects. Thus, sales taxes bear most heavily on low-income groups and so discourage consumption and bring about lower living standards. Taxes on a commodity or service tend to lessen the use of the goods or services. Sometimes this restriction may be deliberate, as with liquor or tobacco. At other times, imposts of this kind may have been enacted for emergency reasons (as with wartime "luxury taxes") and retained merely because of revenue needs. The entire pattern of an industry can be changed by taxation. When some states adopted chain-store taxes which rose progressively with the number of stores owned by a single firm, they practically broke up chain ownership. The relative positions of butter and oleomargarine are largely determined by tax laws. Tariffs and export taxes have great economic effects. Unfortunately, it often happens that such laws are enacted without full consideration of their effect upon the common good.

Since taxation is of far-reaching importance, the United States should re-examine its entire fiscal policy. Even if there were not known abuses, the sheer size of federal, state, and local budgets would make this imperative. Methods which worked well when government costs were less than 10 per cent of national income might not be feasible today. We rightly had a Hoover Commission to study the most efficient way of reorganizing the federal government. An equally distinguished and representative group could well consider our entire fiscal program. Present taxes discourage equity financing and small business, channel economic expansion into the form of enlarging existing corporations, reward debt financing in preference to the more socially desirable equity financing, and place heavy burdens on industries which already find survival difficult. The tremendous impact of government cash collections on the ups and downs of business has received inadequate study. Under any system, the burden of present-day government is bound to be great. But wise tax laws can so distribute and regulate this burden that business incentive will be retained and unnecessary shocks avoided.

Another moral aspect of taxation concerns the duty in conscience of the individual taxpayer in regard to tax laws. Should he consider such laws as being merely "penal," not binding in conscience, but subjecting him to the hazard of prosecution if he is caught evading taxes? Or should he consider taxes in general as moral obligations?

Theologians differ in answering the questions just raised. It would not be feasible here to go into all the complex arguments used on both sides. But it may be useful to comment upon a psychological attitude that runs through many of the discussions. Those who hold that tax laws do not bind in conscience often reflect the views of older theologians who faced a different political situation from that of the modern world. In older times taxes might rightly have been considered as impositions of a sovereign often used to finance his luxuries, wars of conquest, and so forth. In modern democratic societies, taxes should be more nearly tied to the needs of the common good and hence involve the virtue of social justice. If the citizen feels that his contributions are being misused, he can use political means for correcting the abuses. Accordingly, it follows that social (contributive) justice demands that citizens pay taxes as a matter of conscience. The contrary view, practiced in many countries, leads to many injustices and unfair distribution of tax burdens. A democratic political society can hardly thrive if large groups of citizens fail to contribute to the needs of a nation.

Duties of Owners. In addition to the general responsibility for using property in accord with the common good, owners have certain specific obligations in respect to their wealth. Pope Pius XI notes that the wealthy are bound to use their superfluous income in the practice of almsgiving, beneficence, and munificence. His language in this passage is strong:

gravissimo teneantur divites praecepto. The Latin terms *praeceptum* and *grave* are both normally used only for the most serious obligations, although the Latin superlative is sometimes weaker than the positive. Thus, all moralists use the phrase *praeceptum sub gravi* as connoting a duty obliging under pain of mortal sin. This obligation is not in justice but under other virtues, such as charity.

Superfluous income has been defined as the excess over an amount needed to live becomingly in accord with one's state in life. At the same time, moralists have not refined this definition by precise rules as to what is "becoming" in various states. Nor have they clarified the moral conditions involved in advancing to a state of great wealth. In this somewhat inadequately explored field, certain conclusions might be offered. A man with ability and enterprise might, through the use of morally acceptable means, advance to a state of wealth. As he progresses, it would be legitimate to reinvest his savings in the business so as to promote its expansion, at the same time meeting the normal demands of charity appropriate to his income level.

His personal motivation should not be evil. Thus, he should avoid disordered pride, ambition, or avarice. He might be inspired by satisfaction in achievement, desire to help his family, and interest in the community. The building of an enterprise which produces useful goods or services and furnishes needed employment is morally sound. If this process brings great wealth, the owner might then live in accord with healthy community standards for persons in his position. While lavish display, motivated by pride or vanity, would be wrong, yet such luxuries as a large house, servants, two cars, and a winter trip to a warm climate would not necessarily be inappropriate. He might give his children the best of education and protect his family by large insurance policies.

At all times, however, such a wealthy man should be concerned over the needs of charity in his community and nation. Superfluous wealth, above the customary needs of his station, should be considered as money held in trust, to be used in accord with the virtues of almsgiving, beneficence, and munificence. Two of these virtues were treated earlier in Chapter IV. Beneficence implies the Christian virtue of charity, giving help not merely because it is a duty, but rather in terms of love of neighbor. St. Thomas and the popes insist that the helping of the needy out of one's superfluous income is a strict obligation, which could oblige under pain of mortal sin if the need were great and the wealthy man the only source of relief. But it is much more desirable to have a spirit of generous giving, springing from a compassionate heart. This is the true Christian ideal.

A WIDER DIFFUSION OF OWNERSHIP

The Ideal of Distributed Ownership.   While the popes have defended the institution of private property, they have not supported past and present practices of distribution of both income and wealth. Each of the three great social popes has solemnly pronounced the need for a better diffusion of ownership. Pope Leo XIII made the advantages of actual ownership the major arguments for private property. Pope Pius XI reiterated the need for more equitable distribution of wealth and income and attacked existing abuses in this regard. It remained for Pope Pius XII to carry this argument further and to apply it to small business and other forms of distributed productive property. He likewise attacked directly the concentration of economic life into giant cities and huge industrial enterprises.

The central argument for property diffusion is freedom. Long ago, St. Thomas Aquinas noted that the difference between freedom and slavery lies in property ownership. He said that the despot rules over slaves, who cannot resist his rule, since they own nothing. But government over free men is different, since, "although they are subjected to the rule of their president, nevertheless they have something of thir own, whereby they are able to resist the power of the ruler."[3] When the state owns all productive wealth, as under communism, the subject is of necessity a slave. Likewise, when the most important kind of wealth in a community is owned by a few, the many suffer a real limitation of their freedom. Thus, in the United States, to apply the words of *Quadragesimo Anno*, immense power and despotic economic domination have been concentrated in the hands of a few, and these few are not the owners, but the managers of invested wealth.

There have been adequate studies to prove that less than a thousand large corporations own most of the corporate business wealth in the United States. Their strategic control of vital raw materials and essential industries gives them great power over the hundreds of thousands of smaller corporations and the millions of unincorporated businesses and farms. Moreover, such firms have showed great ability to maintain profits

---

[3] *Summa*, I, 81, 3, ad 2.

during recession periods. Hence they survive, while smaller companies may go bankrupt. While ownership of corporations is technically vested in the hands of their stockholders (about ten million), actual control in large firms rests with self-perpetuating boards of directors, powerful minority stockholders, large investment banking houses, and giant insurance companies. By way of reaction, there have arisen giant labor unions, farmers organizations, and government regulatory agencies. Thus, the individual is lost sight of in battles between mammoths.

A very real problem in regard to concentration of property and economic power stems from the enormous resources of pension funds. Already private retirement funds account for over 30 billion dollars in investments, and the total figure is growing at an amazing pace. Since a substantial portion of these funds is invested in common stocks, the relatively few banks and insurance companies that control these investments may soon control the bulk of productive property in the United States. When our private pension funds reach the 100-billion-dollar level, a goal which many think they will attain by 1975, we may have a degree of concentration of economic power that would make the older trusts and combines seem puny by comparison. Paradoxically, this concentration largely resulted from union-sponsored efforts to give the worker additional security in his old age. The worker has his security, but the price he has paid for these gains could be high. Not only has the process led to enormous centralization of funds, but it has also made the worker highly dependent upon both the company and the union for the collection of his benefits. He is no longer free to quit the job or defy the union, unless he wishes to jeopardize the equity he has built up in retirement funds.

There is no intention in the analysis just concluded to leave the impression that scheming financial interests are trying to reduce America to slavery. On the contrary, each step in this drama is compatible with a benign interpretation. The efficiency of large-scale business is often enough to explain its predominance in industry. The fact that stock ownership is widely scattered is the basis for concentration of control in the hands of corporate insiders or holders of large blocks of stock. And the desire to have the best investment advice possible underlies the funneling of billions of pension funds into a small number of New York banks. Nevertheless, whatever may be the motives, the basic fact is that enormous concentrations of power characterize our present economic system.

The fact that the great abuses of the 1920's are now past does not alter the fundamental situation. Business has a far greater sense of public responsibility. Government regulation has been salutary and effective. Labor and the farmers have made great gains. Even the small businessman has been able to hold his own in many fields. But we must consider how many workers are employed by large corporations where of necessity it is difficult to treat them as individuals. Many executives, drawing large salaries, are essentially employees of great chains or sprawling industries. Even the top management of billion-dollar corporations may be subject to the control of absentee financial ownership, more interested in assured profits than in the welfare of its workers or even executives. We cannot honestly say that these men have lost their freedom, but it has been minimized to an unhealthy degree.

Moreover giantism has aggravated concentration into large cities, in which the obstacles to a normal family life are greater. It is difficult for many to own or rent homes suitable for several growing children, where they would have wholesome opportunities for play and association with other children. On the farms, there are the migrants and the sharecroppers who often live in poverty with little hope of owning the land they till. All this is not to deny the real advantages of mechanization and mass production. But we have grown far beyond the optimum size needed for economic efficiency and have ended up with unsocial power concentrations. More recently, both economic reasons and the fear of atomic war have prompted some decentralization and diffusion of industry. But a complex and far-reaching problem remains.

Distribution of Wealth and Income in America. It is difficult to obtain figures on the actual distribution of wealth in the United States. It is even more of a problem to interpret facts and to put them in proper perspective. Available information indicates some trends toward greater economic concentration, especially in cases where corporate mergers are involved. The Department of Justice may act to prevent a merger, or to dissolve merged companies, if this action is necessary to prevent restraint of trade. However, there is a considerable difference between concentration that brings legal inference of monopoly and a trend that diminishes small holdings of property, even though it may be legal under the Clayton Act, as amended in 1950 to restrict mergers in restraint of trade.

Special attention should be paid to the impact of tax laws upon business concentration. Tax policies may stimulate mergers for many reasons. One is the possibility that profits can be "plowed back" into the firm and later realized as capital gains (at lower rates) rather than as income, when a firm is merged with another. Even the existence of losses may make a firm attractive to a prospective buyer, who can use such deficits to offset earnings of more prosperous companies in the merger. Something is fundamentally wrong when our tax policies so control business that normal considerations of profit or loss become secondary in weighing the usefulness of a firm.

In judging trends toward concentration of ownership in productive property, we must at all times keep a proper perspective. It would be a mistake to be so obsessed by the real or imagined efficiency of big business that we failed to see the social values of small firms and distributed ownership. We can concede the real merits of big business and yet also realize the value of smaller firms. Likewise, we should not always feel that smaller companies need special assistance lest they collapse. There is a considerable degree of vitality in this sector of our economy. It is troubled with high mortality rates, yet we should distinguish between normal business failures and a long-term trend away from small enterprise. We may have the former without being plagued with the latter.

The time is ripe for a careful and objective reconsideration of the structure of our economy. We must evaluate the factors that have produced bigness and economic concentration. Then we must decide whether or not we wish to pay this price for the economic gains of large enterprise.

When we come to the question of income distribution, however, an entirely different picture presents itself. Here there are definite indications of a trend toward equalization. This started as a result of tax laws that make it extremely difficult to retain income, once a fairly modest level is reached. (Under the law, federal personal income taxes take over 50 per cent of taxable income, once the $16,000 level is reached. After $200,000, 91 per cent goes to the government.) More important than the cutoff at the top is the increase in the middle levels. More and more families are getting into the $5,000 and over bracket. But fewer are found in the poverty levels, however one may define them.

In the effort to give an accurate picture, two different types of income statistics are presented in the tables below. Table 1, National Income by Distributive Shares, shows the relative returns to various classes in selected postwar years. Figures are given in billions of dollars, with percentages of total income given at the right of each figure. In this way, gains or losses of the different groups can be noted.

Table 1

NATIONAL INCOME BY DISTRIBUTIVE SHARES

	1948 Billions of dollars	1948 Per cent of total	1953 Billions of dollars	1953 Per cent of total	1957 Billions of dollars	1957 Per cent of total
Total national income	221.6	100.0	302.1	100.0	358.2	100.0
Compensation of employees	140.9	63.6	208.1	68.8	254.4	71.0
Business and professional	21.6	9.8	25.9	8.6	28.7	8.0
Farm	16.7	7.5	13.3	4.4	12.1	3.4
Rental income of persons	7.2	3.3	10.2	3.4	10.4	2.9
Corporate profits before taxes; adjusted for inventory gains or losses	30.6	13.8	36.0	11.9	39.7	11.1
Net interest	4.5	2.0	8.7	2.9	12.8	3.6

Another useful study is the material presented in Table 2, showing the upward shift in family incomes during the ten years, 1947–1957. Allowing both for increase in prices and increase in the number of families, there is nonetheless a gain of 20 per cent in average real income and a notable shift of families into higher income brackets. Income, as used in this table, is total income before taxes, including imputed income and income in kind. Families include unattached individuals maintaining a separate household.

Table 2

CHANGES IN FAMILY INCOME: 1947–1957

	Per cent of families in each income bracket 1947	Per cent of families in each income bracket 1957	Per cent of total income received 1947	Per cent of total income received 1957
Under $2,000	25	14	7	3
$2,000–3,999	38	23	28	11
$4,000–5,999	20	25	24	21
$6,000–7,999	9	18	14	20
$8,000–9,999	3	9	7	13
$10,000–14,999	3	7	8	14
$15,000 and over	2	4	12	18

Of the two subjects studied in this section, the matter of wealth distribution is currently more important than that of income distribution. Concentration of control over vital productive wealth means enormous centralization of power and diminution of effective freedom. By contrast, the degree of income concentration under present tax laws is not clearly excessive. Social problems derived from low incomes exist, but the remedy is not generally redistribution of the present income total. As noted in Chapter X, higher incomes ultimately come from increased production, achieved through better economic organization, higher investment levels, and labor-management co-operation. Accordingly, emphasis in the section to follow will be on better distribution of productive wealth, not income.

Remedies for Concentration of Productive Wealth. A glance through the quotations from the writings and addresses of Pope Pius XII indicates the preoccupation of this great Pontiff with the problem of diffusion of ownership. Indeed, this emphasis on widespread ownership of productive wealth is the great social contribution made by Pope Pius XII. Facing this problem in terms of American conditions, a social scientist usually comes up with two broad lines of solution. The first consists of preventing further concentration and of endeavoring to break up existing giants. The second is the more positive and constructive approach of trying to foster small business and individual ownership, without necessarily attacking present-day giants. Both techniques have their merits and difficulties. Indeed, this is a difficult social problem.

In some fields, bigness is essential. Until recent technological developments made small firms possible, steel was basically a large industry. The capital investment and equipment needed was such that only large corporations could enter the field. Mass production of automobiles is likewise, by its very nature, a large industry. But even in the mass-production fields, there is often greater centralization than is required by the economics of the situation. The technical nature of production usually involves an optimum size. When a firm expands beyond that size, it is merely duplicating efficient producing units. Often the same output can be produced by a number of smaller firms at optimum size. This is the evil of the merger movement, which absorbs such efficient companies. But they may have no choice, currently, since they are presented with attractive offers of purchase on the one hand and the threat of destructive and unfair competition on the other. Vigorous enforcement of antitrust and antimerger acts can help to slow down or possibly even reverse movements toward unsocial concentration.

Careful study should be made of the trend toward concentration made possible by the accumulation of pension funds. There have been no charges that banks or insurance companies abuse the powers that their position of trusteeship confers. Nevertheless a potential for abuse remains present. One possible remedy, to be considered when conditions make it necessary, would be the neutralizing of the voting power conferred by pension funds invested in common stocks. Trustees would be compelled by law to secure a court order to permit such voting, when they must take action in order to safeguard their investments.

On the more positive plane of aiding small business, government purchasing policies can be effective. In some fields, government is one of the greatest buyers in the country. A broad policy of favoring small business can be laid down to all departments, with a certain area of discretion permitted on bids. Thus, instead of rigidly adhering to the policy of awarding contracts to the lowest bidder, it may be possible to purchase supplies by prorating orders among the lowest third of the bidders, with a certain priority to small industries and suppliers. Long-range military programs can fit into this pattern, the more so since modern bombing methods make dispersal advisable. Moreover, government research and advisory services for business can give special emphasis to the needs of small business, since such firms do not often have the funds for research.

Much more needs to be done to enable small firms to obtain initial financing, especially through the sale of stock. It is difficult for such firms to find investors. Often the cost of floating securities is prohibitive when small amounts (less than $100,000) are involved (nearly 30 per cent, as compared with a general average of 10 per cent). Investors understandably gravitate toward offerings by established companies. Two devices may be used to make funds more available for small business. One is tax exemption (from surtax but not regular rates) for investors who gain income by investing in such small firms. The other is the encouragement of development corporations founded to lend risk capital to promising ventures, meanwhile exercising supervision over the fledgling companies. Once such development corporations showed evidence of stability and good management, they might be considered suitable investments for pension funds, thus promoting distribution rather than concentration of wealth.

Two promising steps were taken in 1958 to aid small business. One involved tax concessions. Now money invested in "small business stock" is placed in a special category. If the investment goes sour, the loss may be used to offset ordinary income up to $25,000 ($50,000 on a joint return). Small corporations may elect to be taxed like partnerships. Heirs can spread estate taxes over ten years. The second step is the setting up of development banks, such as the corporations urged above. These banks will specialize in risk capital for small business. The banks will have some government financial aid, but will be privately controlled. Initial response to these ventures indicates that, at last, really substantial help for small business will become available. Thus we can continue and even expand the gratifying growth of small business which, in spite of obstacles, increased by one-third since 1941.

Regardless of the techniques adopted, it is essential that we always keep in mind the values produced by widespread ownership of productive property. Ownership leads to economic independence, and this in turn is an important foundation of political democracy. The modern world has suffered too much already from the erosion of freedoms. For the sake of human dignity and the rights that all hold sacred, it is urgent that we do all within our power to protect and enhance the liberty we cherish.

READINGS*

J. Messner, Social Ethics, pp. 202-206, 634-637, 785-800, 823-843.
B. W. Dempsey, The Functional Economy, Chaps. 9–10.
J. A. Ryan, Distributive Justice, Chaps. 1–8, 20–21.
O. von Nell-Breuning, Reorganization of Social Economy, Chap. 6.
J. Villain, L'Enseignement social de l'Église, Vol. II, pp. 19–55.
H. Johnston, Business Ethics, Chap. 3.
Social Order: James V. Schall, S.J., "Liberty and Property," December, 1953; Philip S. Land, S.J., "Evading Taxes Can't Be Justified in Conscience," March, 1955; Philip S. Land, S.J., "A Note on Tax Obligations," June, 1955; Gladys W. Gruenberg, "U. S. Income Distribution, Recent Trends," October, 1955; Paul P. Harbrecht, S.J., "Property in Transition," February, 1958; Edward Duff, S.J., "Property in the American Environment," January, 1959.

---

* For further readings, consult List No. 9 in the Appendix.

Chapter XIII

THE STATE IN ECONOMIC LIFE

PUBLIC AUTHORITY

Leo XIII, Immortale Dei

2. Man's natural instinct moves him to live in civil society. Isolated, he cannot provide himself with the necessary requirements of life, nor procure the means of developing his mental and moral faculties. It is, therefore, divinely ordained that he should lead his life — be it domestic, social, or civil — in contact with his fellow men, where alone his several wants can be adequately supplied. But no society can remain united without someone in command, directing all to strive earnestly for the common good. Hence, every civilized community must have a ruling authority, and this authority, no less than society itself, has its source in nature, and consequently has God for its author. It follows, then, that all public power must proceed from God: for God alone is the true and supreme Lord of the world.

*　　*　　*

Furthermore, the civil power must not be subservient to the advantage of any one individual, or of some few persons, inasmuch as it was established for the common good of all.

Leo XIII, Diuturnum Illud

3. Indeed, very many men of more recent times, walking in the footsteps of those who in a former age assumed to themselves the name of philosophers, say that all power comes from the people: so that those who exercise it in the state do so not as their own, but as delegated to them by the people, and that, by this rule, it can be revoked by the will of the very people by whom it was delegated. But from these, Catholics dissent, who affirm that the right to rule is from God, as from a natural and necessary principle.

4. It is of importance, however, to remark in this place that those who may be placed over the state may in certain cases be chosen by the will and decision of the multitude, without opposition to or impugning of the Catholic doctrine. And by this choice, in truth, the ruler is designated, but the rights of ruling are not thereby conferred. Nor is the authority delegated to him, but the person by whom it is to be exercised is determined upon.

There is no question here respecting forms of government, for there is no reason why the Church should not approve of the chief power being held by one man or by more, provided only it be just, and that it tend to the common advantage. Wherefore, so long as justice be respected, the people are not hindered from choosing for themselves that form of govern-

ment which suits best either their own disposition, or the institutions and customs of their ancestors.

Leo XIII, Libertas Praestantissimum

32. Of the various forms of government, the Church does not reject any that are fitted to procure the welfare of the subject; she wishes only — and this nature itself requires — that

they should be constituted without involving wrong to anyone, and especially without violating the rights of the Church.

Leo XIII, In the Midst of Solicitudes

In this order of speculative ideas, Catholics, like all other citizens, are free to prefer one form of government to another precisely because no

one of these social forms is, in itself, opposed to the principle of sound reason nor to the maxims of Christian doctrine.

Leo XIII, Rerum Novarum*

48. Therefore, those governing the state ought primarily to devote themselves to the service of individual groups and of the whole commonwealth, and through the entire scheme of laws and institutions to cause both public and individual well-being to develop spontaneously out of the very structure and administration of the state. For this is the duty of wise statesmanship and the essential office of those in charge of the state. Now, states are made prosperous especially by wholesome morality, properly ordered family life, protection of religion and justice, moderate imposition and equitable distribution of public burdens, progressive development of industry and trade, thriving agriculture, and by all other things of this nature, which the more actively they are promoted, the better and happier the life of the citizens is destined to be. Therefore, by virtue of these things, it is within the competence of the rulers of the state that, as they benefit other groups, they also

improve in particular the condition of the workers. Furthermore, they do this with full right and without laying themselves open to any charge of unwarranted interference. For the state is bound by the very law of its office to serve the common interest. And the richer the benefits which come from this general providence on the part of the state, the less necessary it will be to experiment with other measures for the well-being of workers.

52. Nevertheless, those who govern must see to it that they protect the community and its constituent parts: the community, because nature has entrusted its safeguarding to the sovereign power in the state to such an extent that the protection of the public welfare is not only the supreme law, but is the entire cause and reason for sovereignty; and the constituent parts, because philosophy and Christian faith agree that the administration of the state has from nature as its purpose, not the benefit of those

* See also quotations on subsidiarity, Chapter VII.

to whom it has been entrusted, but the benefit of those who have been entrusted to it. If, therefore, any injury has been done to or threatens either the common good or the interests of individual groups, which injury cannot in any other way be repaired or prevented, it is necessary for public authority to intervene.

75. Let the state protect these lawfully associated bodies of citizens; let it not, however, interfere with their private concerns and order of life; for vital activity is set in motion by an inner principle, and it is very easily destroyed, as We know, by intrusion from without.

Pius XI, Quadragesimo Anno

78. When we speak of the reform of institutions, the state comes chiefly to mind, not as if universal well-being were to be expected from its activity, but because things have come to such a pass through the evil of what we have termed "individualism," that, following upon the overthrow and near extinction of that rich social life which was once highly developed through associations of various kinds, there remain virtually only individuals and the state. This is to the great harm of the state itself; for, with a structure of social governance lost, and with the taking over of all the burdens which the wrecked associations once bore, the state has been overwhelmed and crushed by almost infinite tasks and duties.

110. The public institutions themselves, of peoples, moreover, ought to make all human society conform to the needs of the common good, that is, to the norm of social justice. If this is done, that most important division of social life, namely, economic activity, cannot fail likewise to return to right and sound order.

Pius XI, On Atheistic Communism

30. Man cannot be exempted from his divinely imposed obligations toward civil society, and the representatives of authority have the right to coerce him when he refuses without reason to do his duty. Society, on the other hand, cannot defraud man of his God-granted rights. . . . Nor can society systematically void these rights by making their use impossible.

32. The genuine and chief function of public and civil authority consists precisely in the efficacious furthering of this harmony and coordination of all social forces.

33. Both man and civil society derive their origin from the Creator, who has mutually ordained them one to the other. Hence neither can be exempted from their correlative obligations, nor deny or diminish each other's rights. The Creator Himself has regulated this mutual relationship in its fundamental lines. . . .

75. It must likewise be the special care of the state to create those material conditions of life without which an orderly society cannot exist.

76. The state itself, mindful of its responsibility before God and society, should be a model of prudence and sobriety in the administration of the commonwealth. Today more than ever the acute world crisis demands that those who dispose of immense funds, built upon the sweat and toil of millions, keep constantly and singly in mind the common good. State

functionaries and all employees are obliged in conscience to perform their duties faithfully and unselfishly, imitating the brilliant example of distinguished men of the past and of our own day, who with unremitting labor sacrificed their all for the good of their country.

Pius XII, Summi Pontificatus, October 20, 1939*

1419. . . . it is the noble prerogative and function of the state to control, aid, and direct the private and individual activities of national life that they converge harmoniously toward the common good.

Pius XII, Christmas Broadcast, 1942

1833. The whole political and economic activity of the state is directed to the permanent realization of the common good, that is to say, those external conditions necessary for the development of their qualities, their functions, and their material, intellectual, and religious life. . . .

1834. That social life, as God willed it, may attain its scope, it needs a juridical order to support it from without, to defend it and protect it. The function of this juridical order is not to dominate, but to serve, to help the development and the increase of society's vitality in the rich multiplicity of ends, leading all individual energies to their perfection in peaceful competition, and defending them with appropriate and honest means against all that may militate against their full evolution. Such an order, that it may safeguard the equilibrium, the safety, and the harmony of society, has also the power of coercion against those, who only by this means can be held within the noble discipline of social life.

Pius XII, Christmas Message, 1944

If then, we consider the extent and nature of the sacrifices demanded of all the citizens, especially in our day when the activity of the state is so vast and decisive, the democratic form of government appears to many as a postulate of nature imposed by reason itself.

Code of Social Principles

64. The authority of the state should also set itself to encourage the growth of material, intellectual, and moral good in the whole body of the members of the community.

65. It does not follow from this that the state ought to make provision for everything in every branch of human activity. It has no totalitarian power. It is even more dangerous for the state to usurp the functions of private persons and private groups than it is to leave them without any control. It is essential to the well-being of the community that an equilibrium should exist between social forces, so that each element of social life, including the state, should be obliged to allow a reasonable liberty to the others. Already for this reason alone the powers of the state ought to be limited.

---

* See also Nos. 1420, 1429, quoted in Chapter V.

PROBLEMS OF THE MODERN STATE — DUTIES OF CITIZENS

Pius XII, To International Union of Leagues of Catholic Women, September 12, 1947

Consequently, heavy is the responsibility of anyone, man or woman, who has the right of voting, especially when religious interests are at stake. As they well know, abstention in such case would of itself be a grave and deadly sin of omission. On the contrary, to use, and to make good use of, this right is to work effectively for the true good of the people and to act as loyal defenders of the cause of God and of the Church.

Pius XII, Congress on Private Law, July 15, 1950

That is why the Church, rejecting the juridical positivism of the extremists, which attributes to law a "sanctity" and quasi-independence all its own, crowns it with a halo of sanctity more sublime and more real, making fidelity to the law, in the final analysis, an obligation for every Catholic, as also for every man who is convinced of the existence and sovereignty of a personal God.

Pius XII, Christmas Message, December 24, 1952

No wonder, then, if in this impersonal atmosphere, which tends to penetrate and pervade all human life, respect for the common good becomes dormant in the conscience of individuals, and the state loses more and more its primary character of a community of morally responsible citizens.

Pius XII, Letter to Semaines Sociales, July 14, 1954

Notwithstanding the fact that civic life in a democratic state imposes rigid demands upon the moral maturity of each citizen, we must not fear to acknowledge that a great many among even those individuals who call themselves Christians share the blame for the present-day confusion of society. The truth of this statement is borne out by facts which we must take positive action to correct. Among these, to cite only the most outstanding examples, are a lack of interest in public affairs, which manifests itself among other ways in a refusal to participate in elections of grave consequence; fiscal fraud, which affects the moral life, the social equilibrium, and the economy of a country; and, finally, sterile criticism of authority and self-centered defense of privileges in contempt of the general interest.

*   *   *

Individual lack of civic consciousness soon acquires however, collective force, and the formation of powerful and active pressure groups is perhaps the most serious aspect of the crisis which you are analyzing. Whether it is a question of syndicates constituted by management or by labor, of economic trusts, of professional or social bodies — certain of which serve the state directly — these organizations have acquired a power which permits them to influence the government and the life of a nation. At grips with these organized forces, which often remain anonymous and, for one reason or another, sometimes extend their authority beyond the boundaries of a country — as equally well beyond the limits of their competence — the democratic state which was born of the liberal norms of the nineteenth century finds it difficult to surmount tasks which each day become more vast and more complex.

Pius XII, To Christian Union of Executives and Businessmen, March 7, 1957

Now undoubtedly, the social doctrine of the Church clearly states that the state has a role of its own in bringing right order into social affairs. And if it is to carry out this role, it must be strong and have authority. But those who continually invoke it and who throw all responsibility onto it are leading it in the direction of ruin and serving the cause of powerful groups with interests of their own. The end-result is that there is no longer any personal responsibility in public affairs, and when someone speaks of the duties or negligence of the state, he means duties or faults of anonymous groups (among which he naturally would not dream of including himself).

John XXIII, To Italian Catholic Jurists, December 11, 1958

. . . since the center of gravity of a democracy normally constituted resides in this popular representation, from which the currents radiate out into every field of public life — for good as well as for evil — the question of the moral nobility, practical competence, of intellectual capacity of deputies of parliament, is for every people in a democratic rule a question of life or death, of prosperity or decadence, of improvement or perpetual misery.

American Hierarchy, God's Law: The Measure of Man's Conduct, November, 1951

In politics, the principle that "anything goes" simply because people are thought not to expect any high degree of honor in politicians is grossly wrong. We have to recover that sense of personal obligation on the part of the voter and that sense of public trust on the part of the elected official which give meaning and dignity to political life. Those who are selected for office by their fellow men are entrusted with grave responsibilities. They have been selected not for self-enrichment but for conscientious public service. In their speech and in their actions they are bound by the same laws of justice and charity which bind private individuals in every other sphere of human activity. Dishonesty, slander, detraction, and defamation of character are as truly transgressions of God's commandments when resorted to by men in political life as they are for all other men.

PUBLIC OWNERSHIP AND NATIONALIZATION

Pius XI, Quadragesimo Anno

114. For certain kinds of property, it is rightly contended, ought to be reserved to the state, since they carry with them a dominating power so great that they cannot without danger to the general welfare be entrusted to private individuals.

115. Such just demands and desires have nothing in them now which is inconsistent with Christian truth, and much less are they special to socialism. Those who work solely toward such ends have, therefore, no reason to become Socialists.

Pius XII, To Catholic Employers, May 7, 1949

Meanwhile feverish attempts are under way to work out other juridical types of organization for the social economy, and at the moment preference favors state enterprise and the nationalization of industry. There can be no question that the Church also admits — within certain just limits — state ownership and management, judging that "certain forms of property may legitimately be reserved to the public authority: those which represent a dominating power so great that it cannot without danger to the general welfare be entrusted to private

individuals" (Quadragesimo Anno). But to make of this state enterprise the normal rule for public economic organization would mean reversing the order of things. Actually it is the mission of public law to serve private rights, not to absorb them. The economy is not of its nature — not more, for that matter, than any other human activity — a state institution. It is, on the contrary, the living product of the free initiative of individuals and of their freely established associations.

Pius XII, To Christian Employers' Association of Italy, June 5, 1955

One of the essential points of Christian social doctrine has always been the affirmation of the primary importance of private enterprise as compared to the subsidiary function of state enterprise. This is not to deny the usefulness and the necessity, in

some cases, of government intervention, but rather to bring out this truth: that the human person represents not only the purpose of the economy, but is its most important element.

Pius XII, To the Italian Federation of Commerce, February 17, 1956

We may hope, then, that the state will be able to remain within the limits of its function of meeting the needs of private enterprise, by keeping a watchful eye upon its progress, and by lending a helping hand, should the need arise. But the state ought not to try to take the place of private enterprise, so long as the

latter functions usefully and successfully. An equilibrium must be maintained between these two component parts of the economic movement, namely the forces of progress and the element of organization; otherwise economic life will fall either into anarchy or stagnation.

SOCIAL LEGISLATION

Leo XIII, Rerum Novarum

53. . . . the law ought not undertake more, nor should it go farther, than the remedy of evils or the removal of danger requires.

54. Rights indeed, by whomsoever possessed, must be religiously protected; and public authority, in warding off injuries and punishing wrongs, ought to see to it that individuals may have and hold what belongs to them. In protecting the rights of private individuals, however, special consideration must be given to the weak and the poor. For the nation, as it were, of the rich, is guarded by its own defenses and is in less need of governmental protection, whereas the suffering multitude, without the means to protect itself, relies especially on the protection of the state. Wherefore, since wage workers are numbered among the great mass of the needy, the state must include them under its special care and foresight.

Pius XI, Quadragesimo Anno

28. A new branch of law, wholly unknown to the earlier time, has arisen from the continuous and unwearied labor to protect vigorously the sacred rights of the workers that flow from their dignity as men and as Christians. These laws undertake the protection of life, health, strength, family, homes, workshops, wages, and labor hazards, in fine, everything which pertains to the condition of wage workers, with special concern for women and children. Even though these laws do not conform exactly everywhere and in all respects to Leo's recommendations, still it is undeniable that much in them savors of the Encyclical, On the Condition of Workers, to which great credit must be given for whatever improvement has been achieved in the workers' conditions.

Pius XI, Casti Connubii

127. Wherefore, those who have the care of the state and of the public good cannot neglect the needs of married people and their families, without bringing great harm upon the state and the common welfare. Hence, in making laws and disposing of public funds, they must do their utmost to relieve the needs of the poor, considering such a task as one of the most important of their administrative duties.

Pius XII, To Catholic International Congresses for Social Study and Social Action, June 3, 1950

For several decades now, in the majority of these countries and often under the decisive influence of the Catholic social movement, social policy has been taking the form of a progressive evolution in labor legislation, with a corresponding subjection of the private owner of the means of production to juridical obligations in favor of the workingman. The desire to see social policy further developed along these lines encounters a limit, and that limit is reached where the danger arises that the working class may follow in its turn the mistaken course of capital. That course involved the withdrawing of personal responsibility, chiefly in big business, from the private owner (individual or partnership) and handing it over to the responsibility of anonymous corporate groups.

Such a development would suit a socialist mentality to perfection. It could not but prove disturbing to anyone who is aware of the fundamental importance of the right to private property in stimulating initiative and fixing responsibility in economic matters.

Pius XII, Address to the Society for the Construction of Waterworks, April 13, 1956

. . . the Church . . . opposes, on the basis of moral principles, everyone who would attribute to the state excessive control over the economic life of its citizens.

Where this interference is not restrained, there can be no adequate solution of the social question. Where this interference is extended to "total planning," certain aims are realized, but only at the cost of inestimable losses brought about by an insane and destructive urge. The just liberties of the individual are destroyed. The serenity of labor is disturbed. The sacred character of the family is violated. The love of country is corrupted. The precious patrimony of religion is obliterated.

We hope, therefore, that responsible men will not yield to the easy temptation of inviting, on the part of the state, an excessive interference which would embarrass, discourage, and suffocate the independent action of men who, while they work, of course, for their own legitimate interests, still are making an essential contribution to the welfare of all their fellow-citizens as well as to the prosperity of their native land.

We must, however, add another word with the same pastoral frankness. One sometimes hears understandable but scarcely justifiable complaints about certain interventions of the state, which are directed, not towards hindering the productive impulse, but rather towards regulating in a more equitable manner distribution of the goods produced by human industry.

Such interventions cannot be called unlawful without some qualifications. Our rejection of totalitarian planning which destroys all individual enterprise does not imply that a regime of absolute freedom in the economic field is acceptable. This would in fact set a premium on indifference to the welfare of others, and would engender contempt for certain indispensable principles dictated by considerations of human and Christian brotherhood.

THE function of the state in economic life has been the subject of frequent allusions throughout the course of this book. From the beginning, man's social nature has been stressed, with political action noted as one of the major manifestations of social life. The virtues of social and distributive justice involve the state. Again, the unsound philosophies of economic life, condemned earlier, showed their major symptoms in their attitudes toward the state. By contrast, the Catholic ideal of economic life assigned an important though limited function to civil authority. Moreover, when the concrete problems of capital, labor, and property were treated, questions of public policy and social legislation arose frequently. Accordingly, it is quite appropriate at this point to offer an explicit and orderly treatment of civil power, especially with reference to economic affairs.

Civil Authority. The Church has steadily affirmed the divine origin and the pre-eminent authority, in its sphere, of the civil state. This must seem remarkable to those not familiar with Catholic dogma, since it would appear that throughout history the Church has been more often in conflict than in alliance with various governments. From the persecutions of early Rome, through the uneasy struggles of the Middle Ages and the sharp conflicts with nascent nationalism at the time of the Protestant Revolt, to the decisive opposition to modern statism, the Church, one, holy, catholic, and apostolic, has found occasion to fulminate against civil powers. Yet it has stood equally firm against those who would deny or unduly limit the authority of civil rulers. Anarchism and nihilism were rejected by Pope Pius IX in the same syllabus that condemned communism. The social contract of Rousseau, and the doctrine that the ultimate and only source of civil power is the people, have been rejected with the same firmness as that displayed toward the nazi and communist teaching that the state is absolute in its powers, with the individual merely a creature of the state.

Man is by nature both a social and a political animal. And, since God made human nature, it can be stated that societies deeply rooted in that nature, such as the family and the state, have their origin in God. Even external religious ceremonies have stressed the sacred character of public power. The ancient kings of Israel were anointed by the high priest, a custom which still prevails with modifications in many Christian states. Our liturgy carries prayers for kings, emperors, and rulers. They are permitted within the sanctuary at solemn services and accorded special honors. True, some may understandably find it difficult to discern the aura of sacredness about civil power in a day when political machines choose rulers, when graft and corruption are not uncommon, and when many laws are passed for private advantage rather than the common good and hence may not be just laws. But the Church, in defending civil power, has not thereby sanctioned the personal character of rulers. Moreover, in a democracy there is little excuse for a purely negative attitude toward government. If it is not good, it is within our power and among our duties to make it good. At any rate, the presumption is always in favor of government and law, with the burden of proof on him who decides to disregard authority.

As noted earlier, the doctrine of the divine origin of civil authority does not preclude the democratic selection of rulers. Indeed, the great Christian writers, Aquinas, Suarez, and Bellarmine, have stressed the importance of the consent of the governed in making laws and choosing rulers. The widespread American impression that the Middle Ages were times of autocracy does not allow for the immense power of customary law, based on the will of the people, in that period.

The notion of the divine origin of civil power flatly contradicts the theory of the "social contract," popularized by Rousseau and widely held today. The modern world swings between two extremes: statism, which makes society a law unto itself, independent of divine law and political control by its citizens; and political individualism, which considers society as the temporary depository of powers surrendered for a time by the citizens. One extreme exaggerates civil power; the other so minimizes it as to lead to the danger of anarchy. The middle position upholds the authority of government, at the same time maintaining the right of citizens to choose their rulers and to instruct them in their policies. Whatever the form of government, it must rule justly, for the common good, and in conformity with natural law and divine positive law.

While Catholics abhor statism and American Catholics are strongly prodemocratic, we are not always so careful to avoid political individualism. Too often we share the common attitude that government is something apart from us which imposes unwelcome restrictions which we evade when we can. We stress the corruption and inefficiency of government, as if we were not responsible for the condition of democratic government. Many times our moral theology texts teach a casuistry in regard to law, taxes, and the social obligations of citizens which is ill-suited for modern times. Possibly such casuistry was applicable in other circumstances to nondemocratic governments, where evasion and passive resistance were often the citizen's only recourse against state tyranny. But in modern times, where the citizen has the right to participate in lawmaking and where social obligations are so diverse and vital, casuistry and negativism are out of place. Likewise, where citizens can pick their rulers, it is unseemly to be carping against political corruption and inefficiency. We have a duty to do something about it, and not merely to withdraw by way of purely negative criticism.

Finally, we should note that the concept of society is broader than that of the state. National society includes the organized people of a region, with their government, their families, and their various social groups in diverse spheres of life. In this society, civil government is supreme in its sphere. Its main function is to promote the common good in the material and cultural orders. While it is supreme, it is not to be all-absorbing. It must foster and stimulate lesser social groups, not swallow them up. It may govern and direct their activities in the light of the general welfare, but control should not be usurpation. Its august authority in matters within its competence does not give it the power to invade fields reserved to lesser or equal social groups. There are sacred individual rights which the state must respect. It must be even more reserved in dealing with the family. In purely religious matters, the Church is an independent society not subject to civil control.

Dictatorship, Democracy, and Nationalism. References to government thus far have been in terms of function rather than form. A ruler is to govern justly under law. This applies alike to presidents and prime ministers, to kings and emperors, to dictators and commissars. Traditionally the Church has not concerned itself with the type of rule, provided it was indeed a rule of justice and law. Even in the case of totalitarian governments, the objections raised have been on the basis of the denial of fundamental rights of the individual, the family, and the Church, rather than in terms of voting rights or political forms.

The historical and philosophical reasons for this attitude are not difficult to understand. It is a simple matter of history that mankind often has been ruled by tribal chiefs, kings, emperors, or dictators. As we glance over the entirety of man's span upon earth, there seems to be little doubt that the democratic pattern, as we know it today, has been the exception rather than the rule. This is certainly the case, if we place emphasis upon the free choice of rulers as a prime element of democracy. Even if we consider consent to law as more basic in the democratic process, it is still doubtful that the bulk of mankind has often been in a position to control its political destiny.

Unquestionably, deficiencies in education, communications, and economic development may explain many of the limitations that encompassed political life in earlier centuries. Generally speaking, a certain degree of education is needed for intelligent participation in the choosing and guidance of rulers. Those who cannot read and write may find themselves unable to know what issues are at stake and what the views of candidates are on major matters. Even with the help of radio and television — aids not available everywhere even today — there is no substitute for the ability to read and understand arguments, since the influence of the spoken word is fleeting. Printing itself is a relatively modern invention. Moreover, even when problems of education and communication are solved, there remains the need for an economic basis for political freedom. If the great majority of people are completely dependent upon a very few for their livelihood, it is not likely that this majority will enjoy a high degree of liberty. He who furnishes the where-withal to eat is likely to determine the political destiny of a people.

These points are stressed, not to play down the value of democracy, but rather to indicate some of its necessary prerequisites. Democracy is to political life what maturity is to the lives of individuals. There is nothing reprehensible in parental guidance of children. On the contrary, parents would be derelict if they did not furnish such guidance. Nonetheless, an individual may rightly rejoice when he has reached a stage of maturity and can enjoy independence and freedom from parental control. Likewise, it is understandable that at certain times and places, men were unable to rule themselves. But it is desirable that they should be prepared for this broader freedom, so that they may have in political affairs the maturity and fullness of decision that they as adults enjoy in their personal affairs.

Two types of government, in particular, come to mind in connection with the observations just made. One is political dictatorship as noted in Chapter V. There was some hesitation on the part of the Church in condemning outright such dictatorships, mainly because of the wide variety of backgrounds involved and certain questions about the earlier effectiveness of the democratic process in such nations. Whatever may have been the initial justifications for a dictatorship, little excuse can be found for its indefinite prolongation in a culturally advanced nation. If such a state were truly seeking the common good of its citizens, it would strive to prepare them so that they would be ready to assume the maturity of full political responsibility.

The second type of government of special interest is the nation newly emerged or seeking to emerge from colonial control. Throughout the extensive areas often characterized as "underdeveloped," there is today "a revolution of rising expectations." Even where such peoples often lack the literacy, communication facilities, and economic independence that form such useful foundations for political democracy, they are nonetheless determined to break with the patterns of the past and to share in the bounty that the Creator intended for all mankind. Caught in the rising tide of nationalism, they demand both political independence from colonial powers and also their rightful place in the world of commerce and industry. There is no point at this late stage in emphasizing for them the need to prepare for both political democracy and economic growth. These nations are not inclined to move slowly. They are seeking quick action and workable short cuts. If the democratic world does not offer effective aid to such peoples, they know that they can turn to communist nations that are eager to help. The precise form of aid needed will be discussed later, in connection with international economic life. Our immediate concern is to note that these nations demand material achievement, and they will choose the political forms that seem most likely to promote such achievement.

In both these situations, free men have an important stake in promoting and safeguarding democracy. Whatever may have been the justifications for other forms of government in earlier times, there is one primary reason why democracy is virtually essential today. This reason is that, under a democracy, mistakes in government can be corrected. By contrast, the techniques of dictatorship have been so refined today that it is most difficult to overthrow a tyrant. In older times, the armed citizen was the equal of a soldier. Today an army under dictatorial control can crush a citizen uprising. The shortcomings in communications of earlier years were not unmixed evils. While they may have made it more difficult for men to unite for political action, they also prevented the monopoly of information such as that held by the modern totalitarian state. Once a dictator gains control over radio, television, the press, and the schools, it is difficult to get the truth that alone can make men free. The power of the modern state is too pervasive for anything but a democracy.

Dangers to Democracy. Even the most casual observation should suffice to make clear the fact that free men may not rest content with the externals of the democratic process. Freedom can be lost in fact even when men are still permitted to vote and go through the motions of choosing their rulers. Three evils in particular should be considered particularly dangerous. These are apathy, self-seeking, and impatience with the rule of law.

Apathy is the failure to participate actively and appropriately in the democratic process. It is contrary to the demand of social justice that all citizens join in seeking the common good of the community. It is essentially a process of dodging responsibility by unwillingness to assume one's civic obligations. The duty of a citizen is not primarily one of voting for top officials at general elections. While a general election is a dramatic stage of the process of choosing rulers, it is often a relatively minor part of the political process. Far more important in the long run are the early electoral stages at which candidates for office are considered and nominated. At these stages the many possibilities are narrowed down to one candidate per party for each office. The building up of a candidate within a political party is the really critical stage of democracy. Equally important is the effort to communicate with an elected official so as to influence his decisions along lines considered sound and equitable. Only by such a continuous process of influencing political decision can democracy be fully effective.

When a citizen endeavors to influence the conduct of government, his actions should be motivated by desire for the general welfare, not by concern with his own selfish interests. The desire for privilege and the setting up of dual standards in regard to law are among the more corrosive forces that democracy must face. When respected citizens use their contacts to "fix" traffic tickets or to obtain special services from government, it is difficult to convince others that law is the embodiment of even-handed justice. This is especially the case when, as sometimes happens, crime may be involved. When a person of standing is exonerated in a drunken-driving homicide case, whereas some poor person spends years in jail for a relatively small theft, respect for law and government is the ultimate victim.

Equally dangerous is impatience with law and the tedious processes often needed to secure justice. Undoubtedly it can be argued that we in America go too far in erecting legal protections for accused persons. Justice is not served when the guilty evade punishment as a result of minor technicalities. But, when we condemn possible abuse of due process, we must always be prepared to defend the rule of law as the ultimate test of democracy and liberty. In recent years the communist problem has posed a serious temptation to seek short cuts that may in the long run lessen our liberties. One danger, for example, is the use of congressional committees for functions of questionable legality. One might question the legislative purpose, for example, of a congressional inquiry that had the effect of uncovering communists in a local school system. Since Congress has no control over local education, how does it have the right to inquire about communist affiliations of teachers in such schools? Emotionally we sympathize with any steps that lead to investigation, exposure, and "neutralization" of such communists. But is this a function of a committee of our *national* legislature?

A somewhat related problem concerns the use of our Bill of Rights, and specifically the Fifth Amendment, by persons connected with communist causes. Much nonsense has been written on both sides of this issue. Some would leave the impression that "invocation of the Fifth" is a minor matter, comparable to brushing of one's teeth. This school of thought apparently would permit no inferences whatever from the use of the amendment. At the other extreme are those who consider "taking the Fifth" as the equivalent to a plea of guilty to the most atrocious crimes that may have been raised at a hearing.

Two simple points of law should clear up some of the worst misunderstandings about the Fifth Amendment. First, it may legally be used only when a witness fears that testimony may incriminate him in a subsequent action. It may not be used to protect friends or to cover up any shameful behavior that is not legally incriminating to the person testifying. Hence the use of this amendment automatically indicates the existence of incriminating evidence. On the other hand, the fear of incriminating evidence is not the same as the admission of a crime. Incriminating evidence simply is evidence that could be used to convict a person of a crime. But such a person may be innocent! To cite an example, a husband may have had a particularly violent quarrel with his wife. In anger he leaves home and wanders the streets aimlessly. He returns home and finds his wife dead from a knife wound, apparently a suicide. The police view it otherwise, and he is charged with murder. In these circumstances, any admission of the quarrel would be incriminating, even though actually no crime was committed by the accused.

A second point of law is that a witness is considered to have waived his immunity if he freely gives testimony on any essential aspect of the subject under investigation. Thus, a witness might not be permitted to deny espionage activity and later "take the Fifth" in regard to membership in the communist party. He must use the amendment in all matters related to communism if he uses it at all. If membership in the communist party could be incriminating in his case, his lawyer might also advise him to use the amendment in regard to questions about espionage, sabotage, or treason, even though testimony about these matters would not be directly incriminating. Hence it does not follow that there is incriminating evidence, even as defined above, in regard to each question where the defendant uses the Fifth Amendment.

If it is true that "eternal vigilance is the price of freedom," then all free men must be prepared at all times to work at home to retain our liberties, just as they willingly fight abroad when a foreign enemy threatens these freedoms. Sensitive concern for all the processes of democracy is of the utmost importance. The surest and safest way to prove devotion to the ideals of our nation is seek justice for all and privilege for none. It is for this reason that many persons who have no sympathy for communism nevertheless fight for the civil rights of communists. Once freedom is threatened in any sector, we surrender hardwon rights.

Government in Economic Life. When *Rerum Novarum* was written, the philosophy of individualism and *laissez faire* was still strong in the world. It was only natural that in this document Pope Leo XIII should stress the duty of government to intervene in the interests of the common good. The Pope insisted upon the power and obligation of the state to protect poor and defenseless workers. This teaching was reiterated in *Quadragesimo Anno*, with words of praise for the social legislation enacted in the intervening years, some of it inspired by Leonine doctrine. In the meantime, however, the ugly specter of statism had appeared, so that Pope Pius XI considered it opportune to give more detailed treatment to the economic function of government. Further clarification in important matters has been added by Pope Pius XII.

The power of the state to intervene in economic life springs directly from its supreme concern over the common good and is controlled and regulated by that principle. This authority might be considered under both negative and positive aspects. Negatively, the state has the right and duty to intervene when any situation threatens the common good. Among the illustrations given in *Rerum Novarum* are the limitations of the hours of work, protection of working women and children, safeguarding the health of workers when it is threatened by bad working conditions, and the prevention of disorders due to strikes. In *Casti Connubii*, Pope Pius XI mentions problems connected with family life, such as housing, medical care, adequate food, and decent wages. Pope Pius XII, in his 1945 address to Italian workers, gives social insurance as an illustration of proper state action. In all these cases, "the law ought not to undertake more, nor should it go farther, than the remedy of evils or the removal of danger requires" (R.N., No. 53).

The controlling principle is the common good, or the welfare of society as a whole and of its constituent parts as members of the social group. When the rights of any group are threatened or the human dignity of persons violated, the state should intervene. In the light of history, it was only natural that the emphasis should have been on protecting the rights of workers. They were the victims of abuses in the economic society which developed after the industrial revolution. Now that labor has acquired considerable power, however, it in turn may need regulation. The state may be required to protect small or large business. In principle, apart from the wisdom of its provisions or the timeliness of its enactment, the Taft-Hartley Act is as justifiable as the Social Security Act or the Employment Act of 1946.

In acting to prevent abuses the state should follow the principles of subsidiarity and minimum intervention. It is not the function of government to procure all good or prevent all evil, but only to deal with matters affecting the general welfare. Hence, a higher authority should not step in where a lesser group is able and willing to meet the needs of the moment. The federal government should not act where the states are doing an efficient job in handling a given situation. Nor should it impose a pattern upon private activities such as labor-management relations, when collective bargaining or like private arrangements are securing results consonant with the common good. Furthermore, when intervention is necessary, it should be at the minimum level required by conditions. An abuse which could be remedied by public control measures would not justify nationalization of an industry. The misuse of a power would not normally justify its abolition, unless this was the only possible method of preventing serious harm.

Changing conditions affect the scope of state authority. In times of peace and stable prosperity, government has less occasion to exercise its power than it would in a period of war or a major depression. The concept of reserve and emergency powers, so deeply imbedded in our laws, is basically sound. But government intervention is not a normal or desirable condition. One might go further and assert that many of the negative state functions should be considered in the light of lesser evils. It would be more desirable that various social groups, under the supreme co-ordinating power of the state, would themselves establish conditions which make remedial legislation unnecessary. This is the positive function of public authority.

As noted in Chapter VII, the primary and positive duty of government is to promote an organic social order which by its nature tends to procure the public economic good. The modern state is the victim of centuries of individualism. Society has been atomized into thousands of conflicting groups, each seeking its own interest, with few concerned with the general welfare. As a result, the state has been forced to step into countless situations and remedy conditions which were hurting society. This burdening of modern government has injured the state itself, through loading it down with innumerable tasks, and has hindered it from exercising its primary mission of aiding lesser groups to govern themselves. Furthermore, it has contributed to the giantism of modern life, which is endangering the freedom of individuals. The fact that such actions have been necessary in the circumstances does not make them more desirable in the light of Christian ideals. Until organic reform is achieved, we may legitimately continue to promote suitable social legislation, but our first emphasis should be upon a fundamental change in our social structure in favor of smaller, self-governing societies.

The direction taken by many modern governments, particularly the socialist regimes in Europe, should be reversed. Instead of taking powers from lesser groups, they should be seeking to restore, as prudence dictates, authority previously assumed. "Thereby the state will more freely, powerfully, and effectively do those things that belong to it alone because it alone can do them: directing, watching, urging, restraining, as occasion requires and necessity demands" (Q.A., No. 80). Society should be organic, based on interrelationship of subordinate and co-ordinate groups working for the common good, and not mechanical, based on power forcing together scattered and hostile groups. This is why Pope Pius XII constantly warned against the trend toward nationalization, which was making society more rather than less mechanical.

Church teaching is not blindly opposed to all nationalization of property. When private ownership would be contrary to the public interest, the state must protect the common good by nationalizing (with compensation) the property in question. An obvious example is the central bank of a nation, controlling as it does the money supply of the economy. Likewise, the state may, under certain circumstances, supply protection or services which private industry fails to provide. If such actions bring the label of the "welfare state," they are nonetheless within the legitimate demands of the common good. Where the real danger arises is when state actions of this nature are considered as desirable in themselves, rather than as reluctant alternatives accepted because the private sector of the economy was unable or unwilling to do its duty.

Facing the situation in the United States, we find two rough trends, neither of which is completely satisfactory in the light of Christian principles. The liberals and reformers are so obsessed by the negative function of the state, the power to remedy abuses, that they are calling for more and more laws and increasing use by the federal government of its reserve authority. Conservatives see the evil in this trend and decry it, but their approach is likewise negative. They would return to a condition of *laissez faire* without taking positive action to remedy abuses which occasion state intervention. We need badly a middle-of-the-road position which will frankly recognize social problems and work out methods for their removal by means of self-governing economic groups. And not the least of these social problems is the very absence of such groups working together organically for the common good.

In this light, the primary duty of our federal government, in the years to come, is to promote co-operation in economic life and to decentralize power to such collaborative groups. Such a statement should not prejudice us against needed social reforms which call for legislation in the interval. But the main emphasis should be upon such ideals as fostering labor-management co-operation; establishing a consultative council, representing all economic groups, to deal with depressions and full employment; the increase of consultation and self-regulation in administering existing laws; and the gradual promotion of self-regulation, under federal direction for the common good, by organized groups of labor, business, industry, finance, farmers, and the professions. Thus, the state would be restored to its true and rightful position as the supreme guardian of the common good, aiding and stimulating lesser groups in this direction, fostering their growth rather than absorbing them, and contributing to a maximum of individual freedom and national well-being.

READINGS*

J. Messner, *Social Ethics*, pp. 140–212, 373–669, 674–678, 922–927, 951–980
(see especially pp. 196–200, 207–212, 573–579, 593–601, 922–927).
H. R. Rommen, *The State in Catholic Thought.*

---

* For further readings, consult List No. 10 in the Appendix.

J. Villain, *L'Enseignement social de l'Eglise*, Vol. II, pp. 313–346.
H. J. Schmandt and P. G. Steinbicker, *Fundamentals of Government*.
G. Clune, *Christian Social Reorganization*, Chap. 12.
H. Johnston, *Business Ethics*, Chap. 12.
Social Order: William F. Drummond, S.J., "Liberty and Authority," June, 1951; Kurt von Schuschnigg, "Philosophy of Democratic Government," January, 1952; Francis J. Marien, S.J., "Social and Political Wisdom of Maritain," November, 1955; Eugene J. McCarthy, M.C., "Politics and the Good Citizen," September, 1956; Mary Holmes, "Censorship and Civil Rights," June, 1957.

Part III

SOCIAL PRINCIPLES AND SELECTED SOCIAL AND POLITICAL PROBLEMS

Chapter XIV

INTERNATIONAL POLITICAL AND ECONOMIC LIFE

INTERNATIONAL POLITICAL LIFE

Pius XI, Ubi Arcano Dei

20. For the love of country and of race, though a spur to many deeds of virtue and of heroism when guided by Christianity, may become also the seed of widespread injustice and iniquity when it transgresses the bounds of right and justice, developing into a spirit of excessive nationalism. They who fall into this error surely forget that all peoples, as members of the universal Christian family, are linked together by the common ties of brotherhood; that other nations also have a right to live and seek prosperity. . . .

Pius XI, Caritate Christi Compulsi

4. Right order of Christian charity does not disapprove of lawful love of country and a sentiment of justifiable nationalism. . . . If however, egoism, abusing this love of country and exaggerating this sentiment of nationalism, insinuates itself into the relations between people and people, there is no excess that will not seem justified.

Pius XII, Summi Pontificatus, October 20, 1939

1429. A disposition, in fact, of the divinely sanctioned natural order divides the human race into social groups, nations or states, which are mutually independent in organization and in the direction of their internal life. But for all that, the human race is bound together by reciprocal ties, moral and juridical, into a great commonwealth directed to the good of all nations and ruled by special laws which protect its unity and promote its prosperity. Now no one can fail to see how the claim to absolute autonomy for the state stands in open opposition to this natural law that is inherent in man — nay, denies it utterly — and, therefore, leaves the stability of international relations at the mercy of the will of rulers, while it destroys the possibility of true union and fruitful collaboration directed to the general good.

Pius XII, Nell' Alba, Christmas, 1941

1758. First: within the limits of a new order founded on moral principles there is no room for violation of the freedom, integrity, and security of other states, no matter what may be their territorial extension or their capacity for defense. If it is inevitable that the powerful states should, by reason of their greater potentialities and their power, play leading roles in the formation of economic groups, comprising not only themselves but smaller and weaker states as well, it is nevertheless indispensable that in the interests of the common good they, and all others, respect the rights of those smaller states to political freedom, to economic development, and to the adequate protection, in the case of conflicts between nations, of that neutrality which is theirs according to the natural as well as international law. In this way, and in this way only, shall they be able to obtain a fitting share of the common good and assure the material and spiritual welfare of the peoples concerned.

Pius XII, To Sacred College of Cardinals, June 2, 1945

It is essential that the hate, the diffidence, the stimuli of an extreme nationalism should give way to the growth of wise counsels, to the flowering of peaceful designs, to serenity in the exchange of views, and to mutual brotherly comprehension.

Pius XII, Christmas Message, 1948

The Catholic doctrine on the state and civil society has always been based on the principle that, in keeping with the will of God, the nations form together a community with a common aim and common duties. Even when the proclamation of this principle gave rise to violent reactions, the Church denied her assent to the erroneous concept of an absolutely autonomous sovereignty divested of all social obligations.

The Catholic Christian, persuaded that every man is his neighbor and that every nation is a member, with equal rights, of the family of nations, co-operates wholeheartedly in those generous efforts whose beginnings might be meager and which frequently encounter strong opposition and obstacles, but which aim at saving individual states from the narrowness of a self-centered mentality.

Pius XII, To Italian Catholic Jurists, December 8, 1953

The clear fact that relations between individuals of various nations, and between nations themselves, are growing in multiplicity and intensity makes daily more urgent a right ordering of international relations, both private and public; all the more so since this mutual drawing together is caused not only by vastly improved technological progress and by free choice, but also by the more profound action of an intrinsic law of development. This movement then is not to be repressed, but fostered and promoted. . . .

In this community of nations, then, every state becomes a part of the system of international law, and hence of natural law, which is both foundation and crown of the whole. Thus the individual nation no longer is — nor in fact was it ever — "sovereign," in the sense of being entirely without restrictions. "Sovereignty" in the true sense means self-rule and exclusive competence concerning what has to be done and how it is to be done in regard to the affairs of a definite territory, always within the framework of international law, without however becoming dependent on the juridical system of any other state. Every state is immediately subject to international law. States which would lack this fullness of power, or whose independence of the power of any other state would not be guaranteed by international law, would not be sovereign. But no state could complain about a limitation of its sovereignty if it were denied the power of acting arbitrarily and without regard for other states. Sovereignty is not a divinization of the state, or omnipotence of the state in the Hegelian sense, or after the manner of absolute juridical positivism.

Pius XII, To Assembly of the International Movement of Catholic Intellectuals, April 25, 1957

A Christian, consequently, cannot remain unmoved by international developments. As he sees the pressure of events giving rise to a more and more strictly defined world-community, he knows that this divinely willed unification should result in a union of hearts and minds in a single faith and love.

He not only may, but must work for the accomplishment of this growing community, because he has at hand an incomparable light and strength, the example and command of the Divine Master. All men are his brothers, not merely because of their common origin and participation in the same nature, but in a way which is yet more striking — in their common vocation to the supernatural life.

Pius XII, To Atlantic Treaty Association, June 27, 1957

Let them drink in the invigorating air of universal charity, purified by a faith, that teaches that in God's plan every man is his neighbor's brother, every people a member in the family of nations, which forms a single community destined for a common end and with solemn, social obligations resting on all.

INTERNATIONAL SOCIAL PROBLEMS

Pius XII, La Solennità della Pentecoste, June 1, 1941

1693. When this happens, emigration attains its natural scope, as experience often shows; We mean the more favorable distribution of men on the earth's surface suitable to colonies of agricultural workers; that surface which God created and prepared for the use of all. If the two parties, those who agree to leave their native land, and those who agree to admit the newcomers, remain anxious to eliminate as far as possible all obstacles to the birth and growth of real confidence between the country of emigration and that of immigration, all those affected by such a transference of people and places will profit by the transaction: the families will receive a plot of ground which will be native land for them in the true sense of the word; the thickly inhabited countries will be relieved, and their peoples will acquire new friends in foreign countries; and the states which receive the emigrants will acquire industrious citizens. In this way the nations which give and those which receive will both contribute to the increased welfare of man and the progress of human culture.

Pius XII, Christmas Broadcast, 1942

1852. The progress and the extent of urgent social reforms depend on the economic possibilities of single nations. It is only through an intelligent and generous sharing of forces between the strong and the weak that it will be possible to effect a universal pacification in such wise as not to leave behind centers of conflagration and infection from which new disasters may come.

Pius XII, Christmas Message, 1948

The Christian will for peace is practical and realistic. Its immediate aim is to remove, or at least to mitigate, the causes of tension which aggravate the danger of war morally and materially. These causes are, among others, chiefly the comparative scantiness of national territory and the lack of raw materials. So instead of sending foodstuffs, at enormous expense, to refugee groups, crowded into the best place available, why not facilitate the immigration and emigration of families, directing them to countries where they will find more readily the food they need?

And instead of restricting production, often for no just reason, why not allow the people to produce to the limit of their normal capacity and so gain their daily bread as the reward of their own labor, rather than receive it as a gift? Finally, instead of setting up barriers to prevent one another's access to raw materials, why not make their use and exchange free of all unnecessary restrictions, especially of those which create a harmful situation of economic disparity?

Pius XII, Christmas Message, 1952

. . . the natural right of the individual to be unhampered in immigration or emigration is not recognized or, in practice, is nullified under the pretext of a common good which is falsely understood or falsely applied, but sanctioned and made mandatory by legislative or administrative measures.

Pius XII, To United Nations Food and Agriculture Organization, December 8, 1953

It is a fact, in spite of recent improvements, that the problem of food remains a crucial one for a large part of mankind. As you state in your report, the present situation of the world from an agricultural point of view is characterized by a marked imbalance between developed areas and countries which are still insufficiently developed. In the first case, production is increasing rapidly, the level of consumption is rising again and exports are mounting; in the other — particularly in the Far East — production remains inadequate, food insufficient, and imports limited. The possibility of famine, with its frightful consequences, unceasingly haunts millions of men, a period of drought being enough to bring about that terrible calamity. Moreover, it is necessary to take account of the continuous growth of the population, which demands, at the risk of making the evil worse, a parallel increase in the goods to be consumed.

* * *

In fact, it is useless to send out experts to teach new methods and improve mechanical equipment when the human conditions in which a man lives keep him from drawing from his efforts the profit he has a right to expect. To stimulate interest and personal initiative, to show that the good of the community will not be achieved at the expense of the welfare of individuals, but to their profit, and to see to it that this is really the case are certainly elements of primary importance for your success. Thus to your economic task is added a no less decisive social one, whose value We should like to emphasize.

* * *

The civilized world always looks with great sadness at the pitiful picture of hunger victims at a time when the earth is capable of feeding all men. To abolish such an evil once and for all is certainly worth sacrifices and justifies great devotion.

Pius XII, To the Associations of Large Families, January 19, 1958

So overpopulation is not a valid reason for spreading illicit birth-control practices. It is simply a pretext used by those who would justify avarice and selfishness — by those nations, for instance, who fear that the expansion of others will pose a danger to their own political position and cause a lowering of the general standard of living, or by individuals, especially those who are better off, who prefer the greatest possible enjoyment of earthly goods to the praise and merit of bringing new lives into existence. The final result is that they break the fixed and certain laws of the Creator under the pretext of correcting supposed errors on the part of His Providence.

It would be more reasonable and useful if modern society would make a more determined, universal effort to correct its own conduct, by removing the causes of hunger in the overpopulated or "depressed areas," through a more active use of modern discoveries for peaceful aims, a more open political policy of collaboration and exchange, a more far-seeing and less nationalistic economy; above all, by reacting to all suggestions of selfishness with charity, to those of avarice with a more concrete application of justice.

Pius XII, To the Catholic World Health Congress, July 27, 1958

No one possesses the spirit of Christ without sharing the worries of all his brothers, wherever they may live or whatever their race may be nor without ardently desiring to provide them with advantages still reserved to certain privileged countries.

Code of Social Principles

48. The phenomenon of emigration, so widespread today, imposes duties on states. They relate both to the country which the emigrants leave and that to which they go. The country of origin should look after the material, moral, and religious welfare of emigrants, and help them to acclimatize themselves. The country of destination should strive to establish peaceful and cordial relations between its nationals and the immigrants on the same soil. The spiritual life of the immigrants is a far from negligible factor, even from an economic point of view, since religion is the highest social good. The country of destination, if it limits the number of immigrants, must not overlook the higher interests of the whole human race, and the need for maintaining a world-wide equilibrium of population.

INTERNATIONAL ECONOMIC PROBLEMS

Pius XI, Quadragesimo Anno

89. Furthermore, since the various nations largely depend on one another in economic matters and need one another's help, they should strive with a united purpose and effort to promote by wisely conceived pacts and institutions a prosperous and happy international co-operation in economic life.

Pius XI, On Atheistic Communism

76. In international trade relations let all means be sedulously employed for the removal of those artificial barriers to economic life which are the effects of distrust and hatred. All must remember that the peoples of the earth form but one family in God.

Pius XII, Nell' Alba, Christmas, 1941

1760. Thirdly: within the limits of a new order founded on moral principles there is no place for that cold and calculating egoism which tends to hoard economic resources and materials destined for the use of all, to such an extent that the nations less favored by nature are not permitted access to them. In this regard, it is a source of great consolation to see admitted the necessity of a participation of all in the natural riches of the earth even on the part of those nations which, in the fulfillment of this principle, belong to the category of givers and not to that of receivers. It is, however, in conformity with the principles of equity that a solution to a question so vital to the world economy should be arrived at methodically, and in easy stages with a necessary guarantee, always drawing useful lessons from the omissions and mistakes of the past. If, in the future peace, this point were not to be courageously dealt with, there would remain in the relations between people a deep and far-reaching root blossoming forth into bitter dissensions and burning jealousies, which would lead eventually to new conflicts.

Pius XII, To Congress of International Exchange, March 7, 1948

(Summarized.) International exchange, instead of fostering economic balance among nations, has often degenerated into political maneuvering and even a source of exploitation. Men are confused as to the remedies. Some favor nineteenth-century internationalism, with others supporting regional trade pacts. Some want the mechanism of free markets to rule, while others demand central direction of all economic life. Christian principles offer four lines of solution.

1. Economic life means social life. To seek the material basis of cultural and spiritual life, there must be an external order and social norms. "An appeal to an automatic and magic law is a mirage, no less vain in the economic order than in any other sphere of human activity."

2. Economic life means social life — the life of human beings. It cannot be conceived of without liberty. This will come neither from *laissez faire* nor from submission to mighty organizations. Men should rather demand that their economies be so directed toward social ends that liberty is guaranteed and protected.

3. National economy is itself a natural unity. "Accordingly, international economic relations have a function which, although positive and necessary, is only subsidiary. . . . At this juncture, it would perhaps be opportune to examine whether or not a regional union of national economies would render possible a more efficacious development of the forces of production."

4. There must be victory over the principles that egoism and utility should be the main basis of economic life. Rather there must be solidarity and co-operation among free and autonomous nations.

Some inconsistent nations demand free trade for their own goods, but deny it to other peoples. Likewise, certain champions of the rights of private property "so interpret and use the relationships of private property that they succeed — even better than their adversaries — in overturning this very institution, so natural and indispensable to human life, and especially to the family."

Pius XII, To French Government Officials, April 13, 1958

. . . in the modern world economic interdependence has become such that an underdeveloped country cannot enjoy complete freedom.

The unequal division of the gifts and treasures of nature gives to men the moral obligation to aid each other, each according to the understanding and strength he has received. This obligation constantly increases in proportion to the increase in the power at the disposal of the social or national group.

CONSIDERATION of the major institutions of socioeconomic life does not exhaust the obligations imposed by justice and charity in the modern world. Problems connected with international political and economic life, the racial crisis of our times, and issues revolving around rural life are all vitally important. Likewise it is essential to discuss the application of social principles to social action, in the context of Catholic life in the United States.

All these subjects are urgent. Nor are they as unconnected as they may appear at first glance. While racial and rural problems are treated in the domestic context, they have vital international implications. Finally, it is logical to raise as a concluding question: What are we as Catholics to do about the problems discussed throughout the book? This question is answered in terms of principles and general forms of social action, rather than in detail, since movements and organizations tend both to differ from place to place and also to change with the passage of time.

As Catholics, we should have no doubts about our concern with international problems. The very term "catholic" means universal and the interest of the Church knows no boundaries of nation or race. In recent years, however, the problems of world peace and world economic development have intensified this concern, as is evident from the quotations taken from addresses of Pope Pius XII. Social justice is a world-wide problem.

A World Society.   One of the most difficult concepts for many persons to grasp is that of a world society and the consequent demand for a juridical order to deal with the various relationships among nations. One reason for this difficulty is the failure to note the distinction between society and state, as noted in Chapter XIII. We can recognize the existence of a world society and still admit the obstacles that surround any attempt to secure a world government to supplement the sovereign nations of today. A world society is a fact; one-world government is but a dream at this time.

The world is truly a community, in the first place, because of the unity of mankind under the fatherhood of God. We are all brothers, one to another. Over and above differences in race, culture, and national origin is the common humanity of all men. This unity is far more evident today because progress in communications has broken down the barriers of distance that once made isolation possible. Moreover, there are common problems to challenge every nation of the world. Among these, the most urgent are those connected with world peace and prosperity.

World peace is more critically needed than ever before in the history of the world, since war has become unbelievably cruel and devastating. With hydrogen weapons likely to be delivered by intercontinental missiles, any war could cause the death of tens of millions and the destruction of entire nations. Indeed, a prolonged and all-out nuclear attack might so poison the atmosphere with radioactive dust that the survival of the entire human race could be threatened. Certainly dangers of this magnitude emphasize the unqualified necessity for peaceful solutions of disputes among nations.

Economic problems of the world are almost as acute as its political problems. In Chapter XIII, a reference was made to the "revolution of rising expectations." On the one hand, millions whose lands have known centuries of poverty have suddenly awakened to the possibilities of economic progress. They desire not only the necessities of life, but some of the comforts and even luxuries that others enjoy. Concurrent with this rise in expectations there has been a population explosion of considerable magnitude. This has largely been the result of dramatic increases of life expectancy caused by new developments in medicine. Hence in many areas, economic gains have been canceled out by the sharp pressure of population upon resources.

To meet these problems, we must apply upon an international scale many of the principles of justice and charity that we have studied in relation to national economies. First we note that, since mankind forms a world society, we must expect relationships within that society to conform to the moral law. Justice, in its many forms, and charity should be the basis of a juridical order that governs the conduct of nations in world affairs. The alternatives that confront us are clear: we have a choice between order and law, on the one hand, and force on the other.

If the relations among the peoples of the world are to be settled by law rather than force, we must expect that no nation will claim a sovereignty so absolute that it considers all its decisions as beyond review or question. Just as the basic freedom of individuals is not lost when they submit to the rule of law within a nation, so the sovereignty of nations is not compromised by the establishment of some lawful means for handling international problems. Experience of mankind has shown that these problems usually fall into either of two categories: matters of interest and matters of right. Where claims and interests are involved, the normal procedures for settlements of difficulties or disputes involve the use of negotiation and conciliation. Since these are not matters of right, we do not use arbitration or courts of law. But when matters of strict right do arise, there should be a court for the determination of such rights.

At the present moment, the world does have machinery, however imperfect, to meet the needs outlined above. The United Nations, with its

General Assembly and its Security Council, and the various international groups either subsidiary to it or at least in relationship to it, do make an attempt to handle problems in a peaceful fashion. Political disputes and those dealing with claims and interests are usually referred to the General Assembly and the Security Council. Legal problems are handled by the International Court of Justice.

Some persons have been highly critical of the work of the United Nations because it has not been able to solve such difficult problems as East-West disputes or Arab-Israeli tensions. It is not logical, however, to abandon world efforts to promote peace just because they have failed to solve these extraordinarily complex challenges that have confronted the UN. We do not give up marriage counseling efforts just because some attempts fail and the parties end up in divorce courts. The United Nations did not create East-West tensions, nor would the dissolution of the UN contribute to their solution.

Nevertheless, realism compels us to confess that we are just beginning to erect the framework of a juridical order to govern international affairs. Power relationships rather than justice too often dictate settlements of disputes. On the more hopeful side, we are slowly building a corps of international civil servants and a body of legal precedents, that can be considered as the beginnings of the rule of justice in world relationships.

International Economic Problems. A wide variety of economic problems confront the world today. Among the more important are population and migration problems, productivity and economic growth in "developing" nations, financial and technical assistance to such nations, and the promotion of international trade. To help in meeting these needs there exist such an enormous number of agencies and programs that it would take almost an entire book to describe them adequately. In the international sphere we have, in addition to the Economic and Social Council of the United Nations, various related groups such as the International Labor Organization, the Food and Agriculture Organization, and the World Health Organization. UNESCO and the International Refugee Organization also have their economic aspects. Then there are regional groupings, such as the European Iron and Coal Organization, Euratom, and the European Economic Community (European Common Market). Even individual nations have their programs. Thus, the United States has its own technical assistance and foreign-aid activities.

Since the number of organizations and programs is so great, it is better in this limited space to deal only in terms of the problems involved and the principles invoked for their solution. There will be no attempt to pinpoint the precise contribution of any given nation or international organization.

To mention first one of the most difficult of all problems, there is the question of the explosive pressure of population upon resources. Such a pressure exists here and now because world health measures have lowered the death rate far more rapidly than economic measures have increased the production of food and fibers. This problem is most acute in Asia. It can be met by any of a combination of four measures: (1) bringing food and fibers to the people from surpluses elsewhere; (2) moving people to idle land areas so they can cultivate their own food; (3) increasing productivity of these peoples in their present home areas; and (4) using morally acceptable measures to adjust the birth rate so that population growth will remain within limits set by resources.

Meeting the Population Problem. Bringing of food and fibers from nations with surplus stocks to peoples in need is not always easy. Even if the exporting nation were willing to give its products, there would still be obstacles of transportation and processing. Sometimes the surplus material is not acceptable because of local customs. It may be difficult, for example, to get some Asian peoples to use wheat instead of rice. Southern Europeans may not like potatoes. Since milk and egg products must be shipped in dried form, they too may not be acceptable. Thus, we may continue to be faced with a paradox of surplus foods in Canada and the United States, while people elsewhere may be in desperate need. Certainly we should be ready to contribute from our abundance, but we must also realize that such contributions may not solve the long-range problems of poverty in some parts of the world.

Emigration poses serious political problems when it involves huge numbers of potential migrants. When surplus population is calculated in tens or hundreds of millions, as may well be the case with India and China, emigration is hardly a feasible solution. It would call for the availability of enormous tracts of fertile but unused land, a fantastically involved shipping operation, willingness on the part of host nations to receive millions completely alien in language and customs, and the availability of funds to finance the operation. This type of solution is understandable when relatively small numbers are concerned, such as the surplus population from Italy or the refugees from Iron Curtain countries. But it is hardly a solution for Asian population pressures.

Another solution that seems very simple at first glance may involve its own share of problems. Reference is made to the suggestion that we step up productivity in the nations now troubled by population pressures upon food resources. This is being done, to some degree, by programs of technical assistance. Often, however, the obstacle to increased production is not so much technical as economic. Land may be owned by a wealthy few who may not be willing to have it cultivated or who may not wish to change social and economic conditions of tenants. Usurious rates for loans may pose effective obstacles to the purchase of land or even of simple tools needed for more efficient production. Hence political and social changes of a type that cannot be imposed by international bodies may often be prerequisites for important gains in economic life in many parts of the world.

The practical difficulties that other proposed solutions involve explain why many population experts favor measures to control the birth rate, so that children will not be brought into the world only to face misery and starvation. When propositions of this sort are advocated, the instinct among many Catholics is to oppose them, since there is every likelihood that they will be conjoined with proposals for the use of contraceptive means for family limitation. Yet we must distinguish between the principle of family limitation or population control and the means used to achieve these ends. The principle that economic, social, or eugenic indications might counsel family planning or population control is not contrary to Catholic teaching. On the contrary, it has been explicitly accepted by Pope Pius XII. It is nothing more than using reason to control instinct in a very important phase of life. Only the use of wrong methods, such as contraception, is per se forbidden in this area. Nevertheless, the difficulties surrounding the use of morally acceptable methods of family planning, under our present state of scientific knowledge, will lead many population experts to favor contraception as the only acceptable means to be used. This in turn forces Catholics into what many outsiders consider a purely negative position, opposing the "only feasible" means of population control, and not offering any acceptable alternative.

In view of the dogmatically necessary stand on contraception and the difficulties this raises, Catholics should redouble their efforts to remove obstacles to other methods for meeting this problem. In particular, continuing interest in bringing surplus products to needy peoples, support for technical-assistance programs, and efforts to secure land reform can all help in raising the economic level of peasants now confronted with the grim threat of undernourishment or even starvation.

In this connection, the highest tribute should be paid to two Catholic organizations in the United States, the Catholic Association for International Peace and the National Catholic Rural Life Conference. Both groups have been indefatigable, not only in educating their members and the general public, but also in keeping in close touch with government agencies interested in problems of developing nations. Special attention should be drawn to the 1951 International Catholic Congress on Problems of Rural Life, sponsored by the NCRLC. Its findings are available in an outstanding document, "Christianity and the Land." Also notable were the First Latin American Catholic Congress on Rural Life Problems, in 1953, and the Caribbean Area Catholic Congress on Rural Life Problems, in 1955. "Conclusions" from these conferences were also published by the NCRLC. Nor should we overlook the splendid work of the American Catholic missionary societies and the Mission Secretariat of the Society for the Propagation of the Faith. All these groups are interested in every phase of economic development: migration, technical assistance, health, and education, in addition to strictly rural problems.

Economic Development. Population presents only one of the many social and economic problems of "developing" nations. A score or more of nations, newly released from the bonds of colonialism, now desire economic development as well as political independence. They wish their equitable share in the riches that modern technology can produce. The achievement of this goal calls for a variety of steps, depending in part on the history and resources of a nation. In general, however, such peoples want native manufacturing to supplement agricultural production or extractive industries. They prefer not to depend upon one commodity, no matter how much it is in demand. They have seen the fate of nations that depended upon such commodities as natural rubber, tin, copper, and coffee. Because of the uncertainties of such markets, these new nations wish a more varied output and some approach to self-sufficiency.

The achievement of these goals is to a considerable degree dependent upon both the natural and human resources of a country. In general, a nation needs to have or secure adequate transportation facilities, power resources, some industrial raw materials, and natives trained in technology, engineering, and business management. These in turn pose problems of financing and training. If the first need is for public facilities, such as ports, roads, schools, and medical clinics, then outside funds are not normally available on a business basis. Long-term loans can often be secured, however, on a combined economic and political foundation.

Thus the Soviet Union or the United States may offer such loans primarily to secure or keep the political allegiance of a nation. In such cases, interest rates may be artificially low and repayment may be accepted in commodities produced by the borrowing nation, even though the lender may not readily find an outlet for the items it receives in payment. Of course, it would be desirable to keep Cold War politics out of the picture and to make such loans available merely as a human duty of the "have" nations toward the "have-nots." Such altruism is not the controlling factor at the present moment.[1]

Likewise, the availability of technical training, especially in the form of scholarships for technicians, engineers, and business students, is also bound up with the world political situation. In many areas, the critical problem is to determine who teaches the chemists, engineers, and scientists of tomorrow. Training at home in the form of technical assistance is to some degree divorced from world tensions. Important programs of technical assistance are being carried out under the supervision of United Nations bodies, such as the Food and Agriculture Organization or the International Labor Organization. At the same time, the United States and the Soviet Union have their own programs, somewhat more oriented to the contest for the allegiance of mankind.

When a nation wishes to develop manufacturing and extractive industries, it may face a choice between domestic and foreign sources for funds and guidance. If the decision is to have locally controlled development, there may be a further choice between private industry and nationalized industry. The argument for domestic financing of industry is that it precludes the economic imperialism that characterized industrial developments of colonial times. In addition, there may be pressure for nationalization of basic industries in the interests of centralized economic planning and short cuts toward economic growth. Those who favor outside capital argue that industry is no longer shortsighted, as it was in the nineteenth century, and that outside firms will bring "know-how" as well as money. Proponents of this latter view tend also to favor the Western World in the Cold War. Those who reject foreign firms, or even local private business, are more likely to be "neutralist" with procommunist leanings.

---

[1] See M. F. Millikan and W. W. Rostow, *A Proposal: Key to an Effective Foreign Policy* (New York: Harper, 1957). A more conservative view is given by P. T. Bauer, *Economic Analysis and Policy in Underdeveloped Countries* (Durham, N. C.: University of North Carolina Press, 1957).

It would be a mistake to look at these problems from oversimplified and doctrinaire points of view. On the one hand, the need is great. Half of humanity receives less than 10 per cent of the world income. Less than one third has enough food for minimum caloric needs. Life expectancy in the less developed regions is less than half that of industrial Europe and North America. Yet, on the other hand, a poorly planned program often does more harm than good. Forced industrialization, rapid changes in age-old habits, imposition of foreign standards rather than development of native wants, all these create dislocations rather than cure evils. The best forms of growth accelerate and intensify sound native patterns, at the same time providing adequate opportunity for readjustment when innovations are truly necessary.

Whatever decisions are made, they are likely to determine the course of history for the next century in great areas of the world. For this reason, self-interest reinforces the demand of Christian principles that we seek to help these developing nations. It is not merely a matter of keeping them from the clutches of communism. Even if this were not a threat, we would have legitimate grounds for concern over the type of government and economy that would control the lives of hundreds of millions in Asia and Africa. At the least, we would want forms that were compatible with democracy in the political sphere and socially oriented free enterprise in the economic sphere.

International Trade. Thus far, our emphasis has been primarily upon the economic problems of developing nations. We should not overlook, however, the trade needs of countries that have already reached a degree of economic maturity. Trade among nations is normal. Varieties of climate, resources, aptitudes, and skills make some exchange among different peoples essential. Even great and richly endowed nations and empires have not achieved economic self-sufficiency. From the broader viewpoint of the common good of peoples, there is a still stronger case for reasonable freedom of trade relations. Some nations lack resources, so that their only hope for a decent standard of living is the exchange of products made with their labor for the goods of more fortunate peoples. Richer nations have an obligation in charity and social justice to consider the needs of poorer countries. In this way, the great riches of the world will accrue fairly to all.

From an ethical viewpoint, it is necessary to adopt a middle ground between extreme nationalism and excessive internationalism. The love of one's country is normal and laudable. But this should not be carried to the point where it becomes a worship of the nation, to the derogation of the rights and claims of other sovereign peoples. At the other extreme, those who deride national independence as outmoded are unrealistic. Culture, tradition, race, customs, and language often form a strong bond uniting people into a single nation. It would be expecting the unusual from human nature to think that these bonds can be ignored.

A similar approach to the economic aspect of international life is needed. Here the extremes are complete free trade and autarky. As noted in the March 7, 1948, address of Pope Pius XII, the nineteenth-century ideal was absolute freedom of trade. This followed from the philosophy of individualism and the teachings of the classical school of economics. The mechanism for such trade was the international gold standard, which was used to settle balances not covered by equal exchange of goods. If a nation were buying more than it sold, it would lose gold. This would cause internal credit contraction, unemployment, and lower prices. At the lower prices, its goods would be more attractive and balance would be achieved. Conversely, the nation selling more than it bought would receive gold. This would cause credit expansion, higher prices, and thus make its goods less attractive in comparison with other countries. Balance again would be had. Such was the simple, automatic mechanism of international trade. But, in practice, this device had serious drawbacks. It left the internal economy of a nation subject to influences not under the control of a people. Any international crisis or upset in foreign exchange markets would mean domestic depression or inflation. Thus, the already difficult problem of achieving economic security and full employment was further intensified. It was only natural, as a result, that nations tended more in the direction of nationalism.

The move toward nationalism often degenerated into a race for autarky or a selfish and excessive policy of protectionism. Before World War II, international trade was often bogged down in a welter of quotas, blocked currency, bilateral negotiations, barter agreements, and similar efforts to build one nation's economy at the expense of others. Germany was the great offender in the race for autarky. The United States was notorious for unreasonable tariff barriers. Undoubtedly the economic tension generated in this struggle contributed to international unrest and was a factor in developing warlike attitudes.

Principles for World Trade. Sound international economic relations must respect two major principles: first, it must be acknowledged that each nation has a right to internal security and stability; and, second, each nation must be ready to co-operate with others for the common good of all. The first principle rejects nineteenth-century automatism, while the second is contrary to twentieth-century autarky. If these principles are applied to economic life, a sound program can be developed.

National security demands that international trade, although necessary, should take a subsidiary position. Insofar as this is possible, the internal economy of a nation should not be subject to the vagaries of world trade. Certainly, the domestic monetary and price systems should be immunized from serious shocks resulting from short-range and random fluctuations in foreign exchange or trade. In principle, the present arrangements under the International Monetary Fund are sound. They provide for reasonable controls over currency fluctuations, instead of a purely automatic system. A further degree of immunity obtains in the United States, where we have a managed currency, quite independent of gold. An additional factor in giving us stability is the relatively small proportion of our trade consisting in imports and exports. Other nations, more dependent on foreign trade, must calculate more carefully the relative value of their currencies in comparison with those of customers, suppliers, or competitors. But, at least, we have a mechanism today for careful consultation on foreign exchange matters instead of either automatism or irresponsible nationalism.

It is also legitimate to seek some measure of protection for domestic industries through tariffs and quotas. But these must not be abused to the extent of stifling all trade. If nations wish to sell abroad, they must also buy. It is economic folly to be pushing sales in other nations and yet erecting barriers so that they will be unable to sell to us so as to pay for what they bought. Protection of domestic industry should be reasonable. It should conserve heavy capital investment and safeguard against unfair foreign competition. But it should not foster domestic monopoly or penalize the consumers of a nation in the interests of a favored few producers.

As a general rule, when a domestic industry is efficient and capable of meeting most national needs, it should receive protection. When it is small and inefficient, it is unwise to try to remove competition and thus subsidize high-cost production. Should this latter course be necessary for military reasons, in the light of national security, it is better to subsidize the domestic industry directly instead of making all consumers pay more because of tariffs. This is simple arithmetic. If we can produce 130,000 long tons of manganese ore at a cost of forty dollars a ton and can import a million tons at thirty dollars a ton, it would be cheaper to pay a ten-dollar subsidy on the smaller amount than to make the steel industry pay forty dollars for the entire amount. Of course, subsidies raise taxes, whereas tariffs bring income. But it is better to have lower prices, with slightly higher taxes, than higher prices brought on by tariffs.

An important step toward freedom of trade was taken in 1958 when six nations of Western Europe signed a pact for the ultimate abolition of custom barriers and any other economic obstacles within their boundaries. Under this agreement, after a period of ten years goods and workers alike can move freely with no concern over national barriers. The purpose of this program is to secure for Europe a market of sufficient size to warrant the economies of mass production. In addition, it will tend to force industries to modernize, since they will no longer be cushioned against the effects of competition.

Another move in the direction of normal free trade is the projected International Trade Organization, sponsored by the United Nations and submitted to the member nations in 1948. The I.T.O. would have five main objectives: (1) maintaining full employment and economic growth within each member nation; (2) encouraging economic development and reconstruction throughout the world; (3) modification of trade barriers and commercial restrictions; (4) prevention of restrictive business practices; and (5) the control of intergovernment commodity agreements through mutual understandings, consultation, and co-operation. These principles can be accepted as sound and in harmony with the ideals of international common good. Such an organization, together with the International Monetary Fund and the International Bank for Reconstruction and Development, would promote the welfare of peoples and lay an economic foundation for world peace.

Whether we like it or not, the world today is on the threshhold of major changes. Patterns that were accepted without question a few decades back are now rejected with contempt. People do not ask whether the road ahead will be easy or difficult. They have simply decided to move ahead, without calculation of price. From one end of the world to another, mankind seems to have discovered or rediscovered human dignity and the rights that accrue to all men. The challenge to us who enjoy the long tradition of Christian thought, and in addition the privileges of a democratic way of life, is to give of our treasure and experience alike to those who need and seek guidance. If we do this, mankind can look forward to a golden era of peace and prosperity. Should we fail, we and our children may pay a bitter price in a world torn by dissension and possibly gripped by the awful tyranny of communism.

READINGS*

J. Messner, *Social Ethics*, pp. 641–692, 951–980.
G. Gonella, *Papacy and World Peace*.
J. Eppstein, ed., *Code of International Ethics*.
W. Gurian and M. A. Fitzsimons, eds., *The Catholic Church in World Affairs*.
Social Order: Francis J. Corrigan, "Trade, Not Aid — and Fast," October, 1953; John S. Coleman, "Let's Free Trade," October, 1953; Michael H. Jordan, S.J., "Our Bishops Speak . . . On International Relations," October, 1954; Harry W. Flannery, "Foreign Aid; a 'New Look,'" June, 1957; James V. Schall, S.J., "UN Scrutinized," October, 1957; James L. Vizzard, S.J., "Foreign Trade: Challenge to Americans," April, 1958; "Foreign Aid," May, 1958; Sister Frances Jerome Woods, C.D., "The Pope on Minority Rights," December, 1958; Neil H. Jacoby, "Economic Aspects of the Cold War," January, 1959; John L. Thomas, S.J., "The Population Problem," March and April, 1959; John F. Cronin, S.S., "The International Common Good," June, 1959.

---

* For further readings, consult List No. 11 in the Appendix.

Chapter XV

RACIAL DISCRIMINATION AND RACIAL JUSTICE

Pius XII, Sertum Laetitiae, November 1, 1939

We confess that we feel a special paternal affection which is certainly inspired of heaven for the Negro people dwelling among you; for in the field of religion and education we know that they need special care and comfort and are very deserving of it. We, therefore, invoke an abundance of heavenly blessing and we pray fruitful success for those whose generous zeal is devoted to their welfare.

Pius XII, Summi Pontificatus, October 20, 1939

1404–6. . . . that law of human solidarity and charity which is dictated and imposed by our common origin and by the equality of rational nature in all men, to whatever people they belong. . . . A marvelous vision, which makes us see the human race in the unity of one common origin in God, "one God and Father of all, Who is above all, and through all and in us all"; in the unity of nature which is every man is equally composed of material body and spiritual, immortal soul; in the unity of dwelling place, the earth, of whose resources all men can by natural right avail themselves, to sustain and develop life; in the unity of the supernatural end, God Himself, to Whom all should tend, in the unity of means to secure that end.

1410. Those who enter the Church, whatever be their origin or their speech, must know that they have equal rights as children in the Lord's House, where the law and peace of Christ prevail.

Pius XII, Mystici Corporis, June 29, 1943

73. How can we claim to love the divine Redeemer, if we hate those whom He has redeemed with His precious blood, so that He might make them members of His Mystical Body? For that reason the beloved disciple warns us: "If any man say: I love God, and hateth his brother, he is a liar. For he that loveth not his brother whom he seeth, how can he love God whom he seeth not? And this commandment we have from God, that he who loveth God love also his brother." Rather one should say that the more we become "members one of another," "mutually one for another," the closer we shall be united with God, with Christ; as on the other hand the more ardent the love that binds us to God and our divine Head, the closer we shall be united to each other in the bonds of charity.

Pius XII, To Negro Publishers, May 27, 1946

In this you have the key to the solution of the problem that vexes you. All men are brothered in Jesus Christ; for He, though God, became also man, became a member of the human family, a brother of all.

This fact, the expression of infinite, universal love, is the true bond of fraternal charity which should unite men and nations. May it be welded ever more firmly through the efforts of all men of good will.

With this prayer in our heart and with deep, fatherly affection we invoke on you, on all who are dear to you, and on all who labor with you in charity to further the cause of interracial justice, the blessing of Almighty God.

Pius XII, To Belgian Pilgrims, April 12, 1952

[At Holy Mass] There is no longer distinction of race or color, of social background or of culture: a common Faith creates a most profound unity.

Pius XII, To Delegates of Italian Catholic Action, July 16, 1952

Catholics likewise are educated from childhood to consider all men of whatever area, nation or color as creatures and images of God, redeemed by Christ and called to an eternal destiny, to pray for and to love them.

Pius XII, To Delegates of Apostolate of the Sea, September 7, 1956

God did not create a human family made up of segregated, dissociated, mutually independent members. No; He would have them all united by the bond of total love of Him and consequent self-dedication to assisting each other to maintain that bond intact. How better could you show your love for your neighbor than by striving to procure for him what is his greatest boon, love of His Lord and Creator.

Pius XII, To Hematological Congress, September 5, 1958

It is only too well known, alas, to what excesses pride of race and racial hate can lead. The Church has always been energetically opposed to attempts of genocide or practices arising from what is called the "color bar."

John XXIII, Christmas Message, 1958

. . . why could not this unity of the Catholic Church, heeded directly and through the divine call to the interests of social peace, why could it not be applied also to the recomposition of racial differences and the differences between nations mutually attentive to the purposes of living together in society, confirmed by laws of justice and by fraternity?

American Hierarchy, Essentials of a Good Peace, November, 1943

In the Providence of God there are among us millions of fellow citizens of the Negro race. We owe to these fellow citizens, who have contributed so largely to the development of our country, and for whose welfare history imposes on us a special obligation of justice, to see that they have in fact the rights which are given them in our Constitution. This means not only political equality, but also fair economic and educational opportunities, a just share in public welfare projects, good housing without exploitation, and a full chance for the social advancement of their race. When given their rights in fact as in law, they will prize with us our national heritage and not lend ear to agitators whose real objective is not to improve but to destroy our way of living.

American Hierarchy, Discrimination and the Christian Conscience, November, 1958

*   *   *

Our nation now stands divided by the problem of compulsory segregation of the races and the opposing demand for racial justice. No region of our land is immune from strife and division resulting from this problem. In one area, the key issue may concern the schools. In another it may be conflicts over housing. Job discrimination may be the focal point in still other sectors. But all these issues have one main point in common. They reflect the determination of our Negro people, and we hope the overwhelming majority of our white citizens, to see that our colored citizens obtain their full rights as given to them by God, the Creator of all, and guaranteed by the democratic traditions of our nation.

There are many facets to the problems raised by the quest for racial justice. There are issues of law, of history, of economics, and of sociology. There are questions of procedure and technique. There are conflicts in cultures. Volumes have been written on each of these phases. Their importance we do not deny. But the time has come, in our considered and prayerful judgment, to cut through the maze of secondary or less essential issues and to come to the heart of the problem.

The heart of the race question is moral and religious. It concerns the rights of man and our attitude toward our fellow man. If our attitude is governed by the great Christian law of love of neighbor and respect for his rights, then we can work out harmoniously the techniques for making legal, educational, economic, and social adjustments. But if our hearts are poisoned by hatred, or even by indifference toward the welfare and rights of our fellow men, then our nation faces a grave internal crisis.

No one who bears the name of Christian can deny the universal love of God for all mankind. When Our Lord and Savior, Jesus Christ, "took on the form of man" (Phil. 2, 7) and walked among men, He taught as the first two laws of life the love of God and the love of fellow man. "By this shall all men know that you are my disciples, that you have love, one for the other." (Jn. 13, 35) He offered His life in sacrifice for all mankind. His parting mandate to His followers was to "teach all nations." (Mt. 28, 19)

Our Christian faith is of its nature universal. It knows not the distinctions of race, color, or nationhood. The missionaries of the Church have spread throughout the world, visiting with equal impartiality nations such as China and India, whose ancient cultures antedate the coming of the Savior, and the primitive tribes of the Americas. The love of Christ, and the love of the Christian, knows no bounds.

*   *   *

Even those who do not accept our Christian tradition should at least acknowledge that God has implanted in the souls of all men some knowledge of the natural moral law and a respect for its teachings. Reason alone taught philosophers through the ages respect for the sacred dignity of each human being and the fundamental rights of man. Every man has an equal right to life, to justice before the law, to marry and rear a family under human conditions, and to an equitable opportunity to use the goods of this earth for his needs and those of his family.

From these solemn truths, there follow certain conclusions vital for a proper approach to the problems that trouble us today. First, we must repeat the principle — embodied in our Declaration of Independence — that all men are equal in the sight of God. By equal we mean that they are created by God and redeemed by His Divine Son, that they are bound by His Law, and that God desires them as His friends in the eternity of Heaven. This fact confers upon all men human dignity and human rights.

Men are unequal in talent and achievement. They differ in culture and personal characteristics. Some are saintly, some seem to be evil, most are men of good will, though beset with human frailty. On the basis of personal differences we may distinguish among our fellow men, remembering always the admonition: "Let him who is without sin . . . cast the first stone . . . " (Jn. 8, 7). But discrimination based on the accidental fact of race or color, and as such injurious to human rights regardless of personal qualities or achievements, cannot be reconciled with the truth that God has created all men with equal rights and equal dignity.

Secondly, we are bound to love our fellow man. The Christian love we bespeak is not a matter of emotional likes or dislikes. It is a firm purpose to do good to all men, to the extent that ability and opportunity permit.

Among all races and national groups, class distinctions are inevitably made on the basis of like-mindedness or a community of interests. Such distinctions are normal and constitute a universal social phenomenon. They are accidental, however, and are subject to change as conditions change. It is unreasonable and injurious to the rights of others that a factor such as race, by and of itself, should be made a cause of discrimination and a basis for unequal treatment in our mutual relations.

The question then arises: Can enforced segregation be reconciled with the Christian view of our fellow man? In our judgment it cannot, and this for two fundamental reasons.

1) Legal segregation, or any form of compulsory segregation, in itself and by its very nature imposes a stigma of inferiority upon the segregated people. Even if the now obsolete Court doctrine of "separate but equal" had been carried out to the fullest extent, so that all public and semipublic facilities were in fact equal, there is nonetheless the judgment that an entire race, by the sole fact of race and regardless of individual qualities, is not fit to associate on equal terms with members of another race. We cannot reconcile such a judgment with the Christian view of man's nature and rights.

*   *   *

2) It is a matter of historical fact that segregation in our country has led to oppressive conditions and the denial of basic human rights for the Negro. This is evident in the fundamental fields of education, job opportunity, and housing. Flowing from these areas of neglect and discrimination are problems of health and the sordid train of evils so often associated with the consequent slum conditions.

* * *

One of the tragedies of racial oppression is that the evils we have cited are being used as excuses to continue the very conditions that so strongly fostered such evils. Today we are told that Negroes, Indians, and also some Spanish-speaking Americans differ too much in culture and achievements to be assimilated into our schools, factories, and neighborhoods. Some decades back the same charge was made against the immigrant, Irish, Jewish, Italian, Polish, Hungarian, German, Russian. In both instances differences were used by some as a basis for discrimination and even for bigoted ill-treatment. The immigrant, fortunately, has achieved his rightful status in the American community. Economic opportunity was wide open and educational equality was not denied to him.

Negro citizens seek these same opportunities. They wish an education that does not carry with it any stigma of inferiority. They wish economic advancement based on merit and skill. They wish their civil rights as American citizens. They wish acceptance based upon proved ability and achievement. No one who truly loves God's children will deny them this opportunity.

To work for this principle amid passions and misunderstandings will not be easy. It will take courage. But quiet and persevering courage has al-

ways been the mark of a true follower of Christ.

We urge that concrete plans in this field be based on prudence. Prudence may be called a virtue that inclines us to view problems in their proper perspective. It aids us to use the proper means to secure our aim.

The problems we inherit today are rooted in decades, even centuries, of custom and cultural patterns. Changes in deep-rooted attitudes are not made overnight. When we are confronted with complex and far-reaching evils, it is not a sign of weakness or timidity to distinguish among remedies and reforms. Some changes are more necessary that others. Some are relatively easy to achieve. Others seem impossible at this time. What may succeed in one area may fail in another.

It is a sign of wisdom, rather than weakness, to study carefully the problems we face, to prepare for advances, and to bypass the non-essential if it interferes with essential progress. We may well deplore a gradualism that is merely a cloak for inaction. But we equally deplore rash impetuosity that would sacrifice the achievements of decades in ill-timed and ill-considered ventures. In concrete matters we distinguish between prudence and inaction by asking the question: Are we sincerely and earnestly acting to solve these problems? We distinguish between prudence and rashness by seeking the prayerful and considered judgment of experienced counselors who have achieved success in meeting similar problems.

For this reason we hope and earnestly pray that responsible and sober-minded Americans of all religious faiths, in all areas of our land, will seize the mantle of leadership from the agitator and the racist. It is vital that we act now and act decisively. All must act quietly, courageously, and prayerfully before it is too late.

For the welfare of our nation we call upon all to root out from their hearts bitterness and hatred. The tasks we face are indeed difficult. But hearts inspired by Christian love will surmount these difficulties.

Clearly, then, these problems are vital and urgent. May God give this nation the grace to meet the challenge it faces. For the sake of generations of future Americans, and indeed of all humanity, we cannot fail.

South African Hierarchy, Race Relations, June, 1952

The choice of a proper course of action in the solution of the racial problem can never be easy. It is particularly difficult for persons imbued with a strong prejudice; it is, if anything, more difficult for those who feel they suffer the privation of legitimate rights. These strong feelings can only be controlled by the exercise of charity and justice.

Archbishop Rummel, The Morality of Racial Segregation, February, 1956

1. Racial segregation as such is morally wrong and sinful because it is a denial of the unity and solidarity of the human race as conceived by God in the creation of man in Adam and Eve. Male and female He created them and breathed into them the spirit of life and commanded them to increase and multiply and fill the earth. Throughout the pages of the Old Testament and the New there is constant recurrence of this truth, that all mankind has in Adam and Eve one common father and mother and one common destiny, namely to serve God in this world and find eternal happiness with Him in the world to come.

2. Racial segregation is morally wrong and sinful because it is a denial of the unity and universality of the Redemption. The Eternal Son of God, Christ Jesus our Lord, came into the world to redeem and save all men, to die for all men on the cross, to make the life of grace available through the Church and the Sacraments for all men, to embrace all men in His Mystical Body on earth and in the life of glory in heaven. Racial segregation would draw the color line across the inspiring plan of the Redemption and thus sin against the Divine Providence, the love and the mercy that conceived and carried out the wonderful Mystery.

3. Racial segregation is morally wrong and sinful because it is basically a violation of the dictates of justice and the mandate of love, which in obedience to God's will must regulate the relations between all men. To deny to members of a certain race, just because they are members of that race, certain rights and opportunities, civic or economic, educational or religious, recreational or social, imposes upon them definite hardships and humiliations, frustrations and impediments to progress which condemn them to perpetual degradation which is only a step removed from slavery. Such indignities are grievous violations of Christian justice and charity, which cannot be justified in this modern age of enlightenment and loudly proclaimed democracy.

4. Because the emancipation during the War between the States involved certain physical and economic hardships, racial segregation was regarded with toleration but never justi-

fiable as a permanent racial adjustment. Even the Catholic Church considered it wise and necessary to give separate church and school facilities to Negroes to afford them the opportunity to practice their faith more freely and educate their children more fully than was often possible in mixed congregations, but this arrangement was never intended to be permanent.

South African Hierarchy, Race Relations, July, 1957

To our beloved Catholic people of the white race, we have a special word to say. The practice of segregation, though officially not recognized in our churches, characterizes, nevertheless, many of our church societies, our schools, seminaries, convents, hospitals and the social life of our people. In the light of Christ's teaching this cannot be tolerated forever. The time has come to pursue more vigorously the change of heart and practice that the law of Christ demands.

*   *   *

. . . the Christian duty remains of seeking to unite rather than separate, to dissolve differences rather than perpetuate them. A different color can be no reason for separation when culture, custom, social condition and, above all, a common faith and common love of Christ impel towards unity.

Code of International Ethics

5. Men are descended from a single couple, their first parents; they are children of the same Father, who is in heaven; they have been redeemed by the blood of the God-Man and are invited to incorporate themselves in His Mystical Body. Mankind therefore constitutes a single family, and no differences of race, color, language or nationality can hide the indestructible unity of that family.

ONE of the most difficult problems of practical application of justice and charity is found in race relations. The securing of racial justice has always been troublesome. Its difficulty has been increased enormously by reactions to the 1954 Supreme Court decision, outlawing segregated public education as contrary to the American Constitution. The result of this decree has been an exacerbating of feelings and a virtual destruction of moderate, positive approaches to racial matters, particularly in the Southern white community. Thus, the use of federalized National Guard troops in Little Rock, Arkansas, in 1957 was but one phase of a conflict that has caused most serious internal cleavages in the United States. The Little Rock situation showed not only the bitterness that attends upon efforts to bring about certain forms of racial justice, but also the narrow dividing line between success and failure in such matters. At least there was a widespread conviction among observers that, had the situation been handled differently by state and federal authorities, integration in Little Rock might well have been accomplished without difficulty.

Exploded Myths. While irreparable harm has often been the result of the extreme racial tensions of the late 1950's, the evil has not been unmixed. One result of the many explosive situations has been to disprove many of the myths surrounding racial issues, and thus to throw the probing spotlight of realism upon the vital problems that must be faced. Several examples may be cited to illustrate this point.

One myth that has been discredited is that the racial problem is the exclusive property of the Southern part of the United States. It is now recognized that there are areas of potential serious tension in many of the large Northern cities of the United States. Racial discrimination of the most appalling type is being practiced in the Union of South Africa. India and Japan have their own type of untouchables. Civilized France is confining Algerians to slum areas in its mainland cities. Even citizens of West Germany and England are beginning to talk of what is called the "color problem." It is indeed regrettable that such situations exist. But it will be far easier to remedy them if we recognize the pervasiveness of prejudice and discrimination, and not deal with the problem only in terms of Dixie and Uncle Tom.

Another lost myth is the view that the Negro has been content with his lot and that outside agitators alone are responsible for the headlines of recent years. Perhaps the best answer to that illusion is to cite the large migration of Negroes from the South. We may also note the case of the 1957 bus boycott in Montgomery, Alabama. There an entire Negro community, at considerable cost both in terms of money and hardship, boycotted a segregated bus system until finally Negroes were able to secure fair treatment. This action, and dozens like it, show the true temper of the American Negro. Given even the semblance of leadership and opportunity, Negroes will fight for equality and justice. What was mistaken for docility and acquiescence was simply the prudent restraint that captive and conquered peoples show until the time is ripe for liberation. The communists were surprised when the workers of East Berlin, of Poland, and of Hungary revolted. They too were supposed to have been resigned to their lot.

A final myth that is a casualty of racial tensions is the thought that these problems can be easily solved by a few laws or committees. It is now abundantly clear that racial feelings in the Southern United States are deep and pervasive. They are too rooted in history to be removed overnight. Likewise, the Northern cities that permit a ghetto pattern of Negro housing segregation are building problems far more serious than many seem to realize. This is especially true where there is large-scale migration from Southern farms to Northern cities. This involves serious cultural adjustments, and potential clashes, quite independently of any specific racial elements. Assimilation is always difficult when large groups and sharp differences in education, cultural background, and work habits are involved.

What we face in the United States now is a many-sided problem. The forward movement of the Negro people is irreversible. Even under the best of circumstances, it would be a difficult path. As it is, a century or more of inferior education, housing, job opportunities, and social status have left their marks in terms of cultural differences. In the South, these factors will be emphasized by those who favor the *status quo*. In the North, they may provoke disillusionment on the part of the naïve who feel that the problems of a New York, a Detroit, or a Chicago can be met by methods adapted to simpler problems of a few decades back, when the Negro minority was a relatively small group that assimilated with no difficulty. In this connection, we must also note that these cities have troubles with many low-income white migrants from the South.

Now that the picture is presented in clearer focus, it is possible to examine the principles and problems involved. This in turn will permit a realistic program for seeking racial justice. Once such a program is formulated, our Christian conscience can seek its full implementation.

Racial Justice.   In one sense, there should be no special principles to apply to racial matters. It should be self-evident that all men are equal in the sight of Almighty God. There is one Father of all mankind, and under Him we are brothers, one to another. Christ died to redeem all men. We are all called to be members of His Mystical Body. To a true Christian, anything that would deny or even qualify the unity of the human race is utterly inadmissible.

What the believer holds as a tenet flowing from his Christian faith, the anthropologist affirms as a scientific fact. Generally accepted tests for intelligence and learning ability indicate that there are no basic differences along racial lines. To be blunt, Negroes are quite as intelligent, basically, as whites. "Proofs" to the contrary, based on problems arising when schools are integrated or when a rural Negro is suddenly introduced into an urban, industrial community, are simply failures to distinguish between inherent abilities and acquired cultural patterns.

It is obvious that a person, no matter what his color, who is illiterate and who has the slow reactions of the untutored is going to appear to some disadvantage when compared with an educated, sophisticated urban type. Likewise, when a whole people has been submerged and given a second-class status, they are not likely to come up with all the virtues (such as they were) of the Court of Versailles, simply because the Supreme Court has stricken down certain legal barriers to equality. These limitations are cultural traits that can be changed in time. They are not fundamental disabilities.

Too often we tend to judge differences in the context of a particular problem, and forget that equal or greater differences exist elsewhere. Thus, with the focus upon the racial problem in the United States, presumably we are sensitive to any facts indicating cultural differences between Negro and white. But it would be most helpful, and illuminating, were we to carry the study further and note differences within nations that do not have the Negro as a substantial minority. The traveler in Ireland will note sharp contrasts when he moves from Dublin, to Cork, to Galway. The tourist in Germany may not find too much in common, in terms of certain cultural patterns, among the inhabitants of Berlin, Cologne, and Munich. The "typical" Italian is quite different, oftentimes, depending upon his native city, whether it be Milan, Rome, or Naples. Those who like or dislike Chinese cooking should realize that most of the time they are served Cantonese foods, and that these are quite different from the cooking of the Shanghai or Peiping regions.

It is not necessarily wrong to distinguish among persons on the basis of such individual qualities. An excellent card player, for example, is not being unjust or unkind when he seeks partners of equal ability. Indeed, he might be less than kind were he not to discriminate. But if he were to pass up an excellent Negro partner in favor of an indifferent white player, then it is likely that he is rejecting the Negro because of color only. Such a decision certainly is contrary to the Christian concept of his relations with his fellow man. At the least, it is a violation of the law of charity. It can well, under certain circumstances, be a violation of justice.

Today, in the United States, segregation is discrimination and hence unjust. Many persons object to a flat statement of this nature, implying that it in effect reflects moral relativism. They argue that "separate but equal" was both law and custom for many decades, accepted in practice by Church and state alike. It is amazing, they assert, that suddenly what was common practice in a great part of the nation should become a sin.

How could the Catholic churches, for example, enforce segregated seating but a few decades back and now declare that this same practice is contrary to God's will?

The objection thus raised is more plausible than solid. It has always been a sin to mistreat, degrade, and abuse one's fellow man. When a man is denied vital opportunities and basic rights because of the accident of color, an injustice is done to that man. However, it is not always clear that a given pattern of action is contrary to justice and charity. This is the more true when available alternatives might lead to much worse violation of essential rights. When the American Negro was freed from slavery, he was ill prepared to exercise the rights that suddenly were accorded to him. He was, through no fault of his own, the symbol of a bitter defeat accorded the Southern states in the War Between the States. It is arguable, at least, that under such conditions a segregated pattern of life was a lesser evil. He was protected from a pattern of bitter strife such as we see today, at a time when he was much less prepared to fight for his rights. Actually, however, many "Jim Crow" laws are relatively recent and were resisted by the more educated white citizens. Discrimination is strongest in the "poor-white" groups.

Regardless of these arguments, today the evidence is clear that segregation is the greater, not the lesser, evil. It leads to inferior education, housing, job opportunities, and medical care. Indirectly, at least, it is responsible for much ignorance, crime, and vice, since people who live under degrading conditions are likely to be affected by their surroundings. Every argument that is used against integration, based on cultural clashes between colored and white, is actually an indictment of the segregation that produced such patterns. Separate but equal facilities are in fact a myth; if they are separate, they are almost inevitably unequal. For this reason, we now say that it would be wrong to tolerate any longer a pattern that has proved to be harmful.

It is not moral relativism to change judgments as experience makes clear that certain assumptions are no longer valid. For example, both St. Thomas Aquinas and Suarez listed slavery among the basic human institutions. Indeed, the practice was considered a comparative act of mercy, in contrast to the alternative sometimes practiced of slaying prisoners of war. Today it is doubtful that even the strongest defenders of segregation would come out in favor of slavery. What they fail to realize, however, is that the moral conscience of mankind has now come to realize that segregation is also an evil practice, little better than slavery.

Implications of Justice. When we assert that the Negro must be accorded the same human rights as are recognized in others, we must accept certain practical implications, such as the seven points which follow:

1. He has full and unqualified rights to any facilities furnished from public tax money, including access to all schools and libraries. These must be available on the same reasonable conditions afforded to others, on a nonsegregated basis.

2. He must be accorded full civil rights, with specific emphasis upon the right to vote and to participate in juries.

3. Public policy should protect his right to secure a job on a nondiscriminatory basis, with full opportunity to join a union, advance in the job, receive necessary in-service training, and even reach supervisory and executive levels, if qualified. A contrary public policy would be adverse to the common good and hence unjust.

4. Public policy should protect his right to nondiscriminatory access to housing, either on a rental or purchase basis. This applies to private as well as public housing.

5. The doctrine of equality implies nondiscriminatory access to any other facility available to the general white public on the basis of willingness to pay the costs involved. Examples would be department stores, restaurants, motion picture houses, and hotels.

6. No minority group has the right to complain if selective admission is practiced according to reasonable rules which are impartially administered to everyone. A school, for example, might limit admissions to pupils resident in the school district. Unless there were injustice in drawing up the district lines, pupils might not reasonably complain of such a limitation.

7. No minority or other group has the right to complain when strictly private and primarily social groups restrict membership or invitations to congenial persons. This applies to private homes, clubs, and private societies. It does not apply to labor unions. In all likelihood, it should not apply to school fraternities or sororities, since these are — like labor unions — not entirely private groups today.

The connection between the statements made above and the principle of racial equality may not always be self-evident. For this reason, it is helpful to examine each of the major areas involved, to see how discrimination and injustice have been practiced, and what must be done to remedy them.

Schooling and Civil Rights. It should be self-evident that tax-supported facilities and civil rights should be available to all citizens without discrimination. Unfortunately, this has not always been the case. Public facilities have often been segregated. And basic civil rights, especially the rights to vote, to serve on juries, and to receive equal justice before the law, have been shamefully disregarded.

In practice, segregated facilities often meant that Negroes received inferior quality of treatment. Generally, their schools were poorer, their teachers less prepared, and their libraries inadequate. In Washington, D. C., for example, it was found upon integration that the average Negro student at a given grade level was, in effect, two to three grades behind white students at the same level. Surprisingly, segregationists used this fact to prove that integration does not work. It should be patent that it is rather an argument that separate is in fact unequal. This is true even, as occasionally happens, when the Negro is actually given better facilities from a physical standpoint than are accorded to white students in the area. Beautiful surroundings cannot erase the stigma of inferiority.

Inferior education is the first step in perpetuating a practice of discrimination. Obviously if the Negro is not so well educated as the white, he is handicapped in seeking suitable jobs and other opportunities to advance. His cultural inferiority, a product of inferior schooling, is then used to justify further discrimination and thus a continuation of the vicious circle. Undoubtedly this was the reason that impelled the Supreme Court in 1954 to rule that segregated schooling violated the Fourteenth Amendment.

While there were certain arguments for tolerating segregation in education, few persons of any prominence have tried publicly to justify denial of Negro rights in the matter of voting, jury service, and the receipt of a fair trial. Arguments of this nature would be such an obvious contravention of the Bill of Rights that even the most prejudiced could hardly be expected to uphold them publicly. In practice, however, conditions have been quite contrary to the standards set by our Constitution. Negroes have been widely disfranchised in many Southern states, sometimes by arbitrary application of literacy and competence tests, often by sheer economic pressure against Negroes who registered and voted. In addition, there is frequently a double standard of law for crimes committed by Negroes and by whites. Lynching has ceased to be a problem, but white judges and juries are far more lenient, as a rule, with "their own" than with colored defendants. Unfortunately, the Negro criminal is often regarded as lacking in basic human qualities and rights.

It need hardly be noted that the Fifteenth Amendment and our basic concept of democracy are completely incompatible with the conditions just described. Moreover, as a practical matter, it may be most difficult for the Negro to secure his rights in other areas, if he does not have an effective right to vote. If the governor of Arkansas, for example, had to face a sizable Negro vote at the polls, he would hardly have disgraced himself, his state, his nation, and his race before the entire world in 1957. It is evident that the right to vote is one of the key rights that will spell the difference between success and failure in our effort to win justice for the Negro.

Job Discrimination. No less important is the right of the colored worker to get a suitable job. Education will benefit him little, for example, if he is relegated to the most menial and poorest-paying jobs. He may be a skilled mechanic, but can only find work as a porter or unskilled manual laborer. Obviously under such conditions he cannot earn the income that will make possible good housing, medical care, and educational opportunities for his children. He will be condemned to poverty, no matter what his abilities and training.

Clearly such a situation is contrary to public policy, even when private employers are involved. It is a generally accepted principle of law that private actions that are contrary to the public interest may be enjoined by statute. For example, a contract entered into by a minor may not be enforceable, since the government wishes to protect the young against any abuse of their tender years. A gambling debt generally is no basis for a court action, since the state does not wish to encourage gambling. Traffic fines are not deductible expenses in operating a car, even though the car is used exclusively for business. On a similar basis, the government has a right, and often a duty, to see that private employment practices do not perpetuate racial discrimination.

Full job rights mean the opportunity to prepare for a job, including a chance to get the training needed; equal access to job openings on a nondiscriminatory basis; right to join a union, when this is helpful; unqualified freedom to apply for on-job training; and unrestricted opportunities for advancement. More simply, ability should be recognized, regardless of race.

A sizable number of states and cities now have antidiscrimination laws. Most of them are based on the principle that education and persuasion should be used at first, with penal provisions available in case of persistent and flagrant noncompliance. As a result of the wise use of these laws, barriers of discrimination have been more and more breached and the areas of job opportunity have been extended.

Of equal value is the practice of using the enormous buying power of the federal government as a weapon against discrimination. The Committee on Government Contracts, for example, holds hearings and endeavors to persuade employers holding government contracts to give out all jobs, and job opportunities, without any element of partiality or unfairness. This Committee can be of particular value in areas, such as the South, where it is most unlikely that local legislation will be available to enjoin job discrimination.

Sometimes it is objected that the legal approach to job discrimination is a mistake, since one cannot eradicate prejudice by law. It is true, of course, that laws cannot control anyone's feelings, but they can make quite a difference when actions are involved. Laws cannot make a communist feel more loyal to the United States than he does to the U.S.S.R. They cannot compel a thief to respect in his mind the rights of property owners. They have no power to force the lustful man to control his thoughts. But in each of these cases, they can and should enjoin actions that are contrary to the common good. So it is with racial prejudice. Laws cannot control how people feel. That is a matter for education and religious training. But laws should keep these feelings from overflowing into practices that do harm to millions of Americans.

What the law commands should be reinforced by the demands of a Christian conscience.

On the level of principle, it would seem that job discrimination for racial and religious reasons is clearly against the virtue of charity and very probably against justice. That any group of citizens should be relegated to an inferior position because of color or cultural background is obviously contrary to the Christian principle of brotherhood. More than this, widespread denial of job opportunity is definitely unjust. Men have in justice a right to a job consonant with their ability and human dignity. If a skilled Negro mechanic is forced to work as a common laborer, he is being denied his rights. Likewise, if he is paid less for the same kind of work performed by equally trained whites in his locality, he is being defrauded. It is difficult to see how such discrimination does not involve justice.

The question as to which type of justice is involved is more obscure. Earlier it was stated that a worker does not normally have a claim in strict justice to be hired for any particular job. His right to a job obtains in regard to the economic system as a whole rather than any given employer. If such is the case, then an employer does not sin against strict justice in denying a job to a properly qualified worker because of race, religion, or national origin. But social justice requires that all concerned work as circumstances permit to change the institutions which bring about the evil of discrimination. Social justice applies here, in that rights are being denied under circumstances definitely contrary to the common good. When a group is being deprived of basic rights, the common good demands that steps be taken to remedy the evil. The appropriate steps are matters of technique and prudential judgment. Such steps would include education and fair-employment practice legislation. At the same time, we should not overlook the serious personal obligation of employers and workers, at least in charity, to avoid discrimination in employment patterns. Personal example, as well as education and legislation to change faulty institutions, can be a means of achieving social justice in this field.

Housing for Minorities. Many Negroes, and to some degree other groups such as the Spanish-speaking or Asians, find that even a good job may not give them and their families adequate opportunities. This is particularly the case when they are denied access to good housing. Here is where the North is often more gravely at fault than is the South. In New York and Chicago, for example, Negroes have found extreme difficulties in getting private rental housing, except in certain ghetto areas. The result is that families that can afford good housing are often forced to live in hovels and slums. In these areas, families often pay higher rents for a few broken-down rooms than a white family would pay for a comfortable apartment.

The evils of discrimination in housing are many. In the first place, this is an important factor in creating or preserving slum conditions in many cities. This practice makes it extraordinarily difficult for a talented Negro family to advance culturally and socially. Incentive is killed, so that only the strongest-willed persist in the upward path. Others fall back into a "what's the use" attitude, and accordingly try to get the most enjoyment out of the present, since it is hopeless to plan for the future. The Negro family that dares to move to white neighborhoods is often snubbed, if not actually mobbed. This leaves lifelong scars. Although "restricted covenants" are no longer enforceable at law, many ways are still found to enforce segregation in housing.

Two arguments are sometimes used to condone or even support present practices. One is the argument that people have a right to choose their neighbors. The other is the allegation that racial groups moving into an area depress property values.

As a matter of general principle, there may be nothing wrong with the argument that people should have the right to choose their neighbors. What is wrong in this context is that the basis of choice be color alone, without any regard to personal qualities or abilities. It is incongruous, for example, when a university trained Chinese couple, who have thousands of years of culture as their national inheritance, is refused housing in an area where any white persons, no matter how low their cultural backgrounds, can automatically qualify. If people want to form communities composed exclusively of couples addicted to square dancing, or of families of atomic physicists, or of devotees of "Charlie Brown," these may be acceptable, if somewhat bizarre, reasons for picking one's neighbors. But race is not acceptable, either on a basis of moral principle or of public policy.

Likewise, families have a right to protect the value of their property, even to the point of trying to avoid having "undesirable" neighbors. Again, the problem remains of what in fact should be considered undesirable. If what is feared is overcrowding and similar slum conditions, proper zoning laws can handle the problem. Zoning can also handle any danger that sharp cultural changes will be imposed upon a neighborhood. This is true because, as a rule, economic and cultural levels are related. If the economic pattern of a neighborhood is maintained — for example, no boardinghouses, no apartments, and so forth — it is quite likely that its cultural level will not be changed, regardless of the race of the groups entering that neighborhood.

Neighborhoods deteriorate because of inadequate zoning protection, plus panic selling by former owners. The pattern is rather simple. The first house for Negroes is bought, almost regardless of price. Then white owners panic and try to sell their houses immediately. Obviously their bargaining power is almost nil, so they get little for their houses (hence the charge that Negroes cause value to decline). Then the real-estate groups sell the houses at huge profits to Negro tenants. Often the prices they charge are so exorbitant that overcrowding is forced, and slum conditions ensue. All this seems to prove that Negro in-migration deteriorates a neighborhood. Yet, if nobody panicked in the first place, none of these events would have occurred. Any Negro in-migration would be confined to those whose economic and cultural backgrounds would make them quite acceptable, save to the prejudiced, in their new neighborhood.

Housing problems can be handled in either of two ways. The first and better method is one of voluntary adjustment to neighborhoods that are mixed racially. This can be done, with proper preparation. As noted before, proper zoning standards can help. But the really important point is that people in the neighborhood agree that they will accept racially mixed housing, and that they will continue the same neighborhood patterns as before, with their new neighbors accepted as full equals. This may be an ambitious program, but it is not impossible. It has proved a success where it has been tried.

The other alternative is the use of law to make housing sale and rental a matter of public policy, just as jobs are today in some jurisdictions. New York City was the pioneer in regulatory legislation, but its pattern will undoubtedly be adopted elsewhere. In New York, it is no longer legal to discriminate on the basis of race even in private rental housing. Because of this, it is possible for well-paid Negroes and Puerto Ricans to break from the ghettos that formerly confined them. They not only have the physical comforts of better housing, but they also have the psychic satisfaction of being freed from the confines of racially segregated living.

Public Facilities. Once a break-through has been made in the really essential areas of education, civil rights, jobs, and housing, there will be comparatively little difficulty in securing equal access to other public facilities. In fact, under the more moderate and gradual integration policies of earlier years, these were among the first all-white outposts to fall. Reference is made here to transportation facilities, parks, libraries, hospitals, camps, restaurants, stores, motion-picture houses, and hotels. In the list just given, both public and privately owned facilities are listed indiscriminately. This was done because the type of ownership makes little difference in regard to segregation and discrimination. In areas where segregation is the law, it is applied to almost any facility open to the public, regardless of ownership. The reverse is true when segregation is being broken down. Privately owned department stores may change, for example, before public swimming pools will be desegregated. The important factor in determining the degree of resistance to integration is the extent that the proposed step leads to full racial equality, with emphasis upon social equality. In the South, there is no physical objection to the Negro in the capacity of cook, servant, or waiter. But the very fact of physical closeness seems to demand strong social barriers. Hence a private facility that has social aspects, such as a restaurant, would be more strongly taboo than would a public library or lecture hall. Resentment regarding school integration confirms rather than disproves this observation, since there is much social life connected with the schools in many Southern areas.

In spite of these feelings, the trend of court decisions indicates that the reversal of segregation patterns will extend to practically all facilities supported by taxes and open without discrimination to the white public. The same will be true for private facilities available to all (white) comers who are willing to pay the price. Presumably, this can be done by law, but it is now unlikely that in most cases laws will be necessary. If segregation dies in the more important areas, it is not likely to survive in peripheral public facilities. Its sole stronghold will be purely private and purely social activities. Normally the law is reluctant to enter into these fields, since there is so little of a public aspect involved.

Social Equality. Surprisingly, the one area in which integration may not legally be enforced is the area which most segregationists use as an argument for their practices. They argue that integration, once commenced, will lead to a complete fusion of the races. Yet it is not true that "once you break down the barriers, there is no telling where they will stop." The barriers of overt discrimination have long since disappeared for Irish, Italians, and Poles, for example, but very few of them belong to the Union Club or appear in social registers or blue books. There are certain clubs to which no amount of money would be sufficient to buy admission. Birds of a feather can always find effective ways to flock together, without the intrusion of other varieties.

There is even less weight to the argument that equal access to public facilities will lead to mixed marriages and dilution of "racial purity." Racial purity is being diluted with sufficient regularity as it is, without benefit of clergy. The fact that the father is nearly always white may have Mendelian significance, but to the average observer the offspring appear the same. But all this is incidental; the main point is that in our culture marriages are arranged almost exclusively by the potential bride and groom. The man proposes, the woman consents, and the wedding date is fixed. If the parties are of sufficient age to give presumptively valid consent, neither the law nor the general public should generally have any further interest in the matter. The Supreme Court is not in a position to force interracial marriages — only the consenting parties make a marriage. On the other hand, the law should not interpose barriers to marriage because of color.

If there is no legal interest in social equality (except for borderline cases, such as resort hotels, that may be considered public facilities), the question may arise as to the moral implication of discrimination in social matters. This question is difficult to answer categorically, since much depends upon motive and circumstances. There is nothing wrong per se in seeking congenial company for social relationships. One person may prefer a quiet club, another wants a young and gay set. There are Beethoven clubs, Mozart clubs, and French clubs. Some persons gather to improve the breed of horses. Others, like the mythical Ferdinand, would rather be alone to enjoy the beauty of the flowers.

In a world that is not doing too well in keeping existing moral obligations, there is little point in trying to find new ones for people to evade. Since there are no grounds to claim any *right* to the social companionship of another, the most we can demand is that we try not to be unkind or offensive if we choose one companion, or group of companions, in preference to another. We would act from wrong motives if we rejected the social companionship of a person, otherwise quite acceptable, purely on the basis of color. But the motivation (other than fear of flouting public opinion) that prompts such a decision undoubtedly leads to dozens of other wrong decisions in vital areas where clear rights are involved. The place to attack evils of this sort is where they are clear and unmistakable, not in borderline situations. Otherwise we would be fighting the wrong war in the wrong place at the wrong time.

Racial Tensions. In view of the fact that the present chapter has advocated strong steps toward racial equality, some thought should be given to the racial tensions this would provoke. This problem is not readily solved by leaning from the ivory tower and proclaiming: "Let justice be done, though the heavens fall." Such an approach can be very comforting to righteous folk who already have adequate bomb shelters, but consideration must be given to the less fortunate persons on the firing line. Unquestionably, in applying the principles given here, we must give proper thought to the ensuing community reactions. It is not merely a matter of *what* is to be done, but also *how* it is to be done most effectively. Prudence is also among the cardinal virtues.

The fact that correction of an evil will provoke unrest and possible violence is not necessarily a reason for inaction. At times we are impelled to tolerate one evil, lest by seeking to correct it, far greater evils be unleashed. But there are other times when we must fight the fight for justice, regardless of consequences. When *Catholic Social Action* was written ten years ago, it was possible to counsel "a moderate and gradual approach," noting that "moderation is not inertia or passivity," and yet say: "only in rare and exceptional cases is it permissible to acquiesce in a major evil on the ground that action against it may bring even greater evils."[1] The world has changed enormously in the intervening decade. The Cold War is as cold as chilly levels of Sputnik-filled outer space, and racial discrimination is a weapon in this war. The Supreme Court has put the prestige of the Constitution itself in the battle against discrimination. When the stakes are this high, we cannot listen to the counsels of the timorous. On the threefold grounds of moral right, the world struggle against communism, and internal respect for law within our borders, the only answer today is "God wills it," as the crusade against prejudice and discrimination marches on.

Moreover, the matter of tension today is not one-sided. It is not just a matter of not disturbing "Massa" lest he "get riled up" — today "Uncle Tom" is equally likely to become disturbed. It is no accident that many elements in the nation smiled wistfully when a group of Southern Indians "shot up" a Klan rally in 1958 and dispersed the "hooded terrors" in ridiculous confusion. But the next outbreak may not have its ludicrous aspects; it may be bloody race war in New York, Detroit, or Chicago. It may be a desperate revolt by the Southern Negro. Passivity today will not alleviate tension, even in the short run. Over a longer period, it is inviting the most serious type of revolt.

Racial tension is a fact, but it is not a one-sided fact. For every advocate of the *status quo* who is unhappy over possible change, there are as many if not more persons who hold that race relations must be patterned upon justice. If there is a clash between these points of view, it is more likely that those who are thoroughly convinced of the justice of their cause will win out.

Reform Procedures. Even though we are convinced that a sense of urgency must attend racial-reform programs today, it does not mean that we can ignore the question of seeking the best and most peaceful techniques. In the matter of school integration, for example, the experience of Louisville and a number of other cities can be enlightening. Experiments were most successful when both teachers and students were prepared in advance, and public authorities were firmly determined to enforce the law. Haphazard approaches and timorous attitudes by authorities invite violence and mob action.

Priority might well be given to steps toward job equality, especially

---

[1] *Op. cit.,* p. 171.

when this can be secured through the medium of government contracts. A sizable number of national corporations have established branch plants in Southern states in recent years. This not only increases the demand for labor, but it often places hiring control in the hands of officials who have no particular prejudices against the colored. Judicious pressures by federal agencies upon such firms can mean an important economic breakthrough for the Southern Negro. This in turn may lessen some of the housing problems in the North, since massive migrations of unskilled workers are bound to cause difficulties, independently of any racial aspects of the problem.

It is most important that consistent pressures be set up in the area of civil rights, and especially voting rights. If the Negro vote becomes important politically in many areas, there is every likelihood that different attitudes will prevail in regard to schooling, justice before the courts, and equal use of public facilities.

All the steps emphasized thus far belong in the category of rights, to be honored as a result of the practice of justice. Considerable emphasis has also been placed upon governmental action, much of it federal. Such an approach is necessary, but it does suffer from two inherent limitations. One is the point that justice gives people their rights, but it does not make them friends. The second is that federal action, while necessary, involves undesirable elements of coercion and centralization of power. It would be more satisfactory were it possible to achieve good results by voluntary, local action.

On the basis of these observations, it is incumbent upon the moderate elements in local communities, especially those under strong religious inspiration and leadership, to try once again to initiate programs of harmony and conciliation. The bitterness caused by reforms forced upon an unwilling community is a corrosive influence. Of course, even worse is the bitterness of a race that is made the consistent victim of injustice. Both feelings can be moderated or even removed by kindly and intelligent efforts to recruit men of good will in both camps. It would be a mistake to underestimate the difficulty that such an approach faces. The flow of recent history has been in the direction of extremism, not moderation. Demagogues have seized upon any incidents that have occurred and have used them to stir up more trouble, the while promoting their own political fortunes. Undoubtedly those who foment violence represent only a minority just as, regrettably, those who work for racial justice also represent a minority. The majority, so far as Southern whites are concerned, does not favor integration, but it also does not favor violence and demagoguery. This is the group that must be won over, first to the insistence that law and the courts shall prevail, and ultimately to a recognition that segregation must go, and that it is better that the change be made graciously and constructively.

The problems of our day, critical as they are, can also be considered as opportunities. They are opportunities for the American people to purge from the national conscience the sin of oppression. They are opportunities for the moral and religious leaders of our nation to give a type of leadership that will truly reflect their deep conviction of the equality of all men under God. If our nation fails this test, the foes of democracy throughout the world can say that we preach freedom and practice discrimination. If our religious leaders fail to lead in this crisis, they too will be charged as failing to practice what they preach, of being selective in condemning evil and promoting good, and of seeking the easy way out and not the stern path of the Cross. No greater peacetime challenge has ever confronted the United States. Our stature in history may well be judged by our manner of meeting it.

READINGS*

D. M. Cantwell, *Catholics Speak on Race Relations.*
J. LaFarge, *The Catholic Viewpoint on Race Relations.*
G. Myrdal, *An American Dilemma.*
E. F. Frazier, *The Negro in the United States.*
M. E. Walsh and P. H. Furfey, *Social Problems and Social Action,* Chap. 7.
Social Order: John LaFarge, S.J., "Psychologists Study Group Relations," March, 1951; Trafford P. Maher, S.J., "Human Relations Workshops," March, 1953; H. K. Cooper, S.J., "Questions and Answers on Segregation," November, 1956; William J. Kenealy, S.J., "The Lawyer and Segregation," December, 1956; Raymond Bernard, S.J., "Calm Voices Rise in the South," February, 1958.

----
* For further readings, consult List No. 12 in the Appendix.

Chapter XVI

CATHOLIC RURAL PHILOSOPHY

Pius XI, Quadragesimo Anno

59. . . . the huge army of rural workers, pushed to the lowest level of existence and deprived of all hope of ever acquiring some property in land, and therefore permanently bound to the status of nonowning worker unless suitable and effective remedies are applied.

75. A right proportion among wages and salaries also contributes directly to the same result; and with this is closely connected a right proportion in the prices at which the goods are sold that are produced by the various occupations, such as agriculture, manufacturing, and others.

102. Even today this is not, it is true, the only economic system in force everywhere; for there is another system also, which still embraces a huge mass of humanity, significant in numbers and importance, as for example, agriculture, wherein the greater portion of mankind honorably and honestly procures its livelihood. This group, too, is being crushed with hardships and with difficulties, to which Our Predecessor devotes attention in several places in his Encyclical, and which We Ourselves have touched upon more than once in Our present Letter.

Pius XII, La Solennità della Pentecoste, June 1, 1941

1692. Of all the goods that can be the object of private property, none is more conformable to nature, according to the teaching of Rerum Novarum, than the land, the holding on which the family lives, and from the products of which it draws all or part of its subsistence. And it is in the spirit of Rerum Novarum to state that, as a rule, only that stability which is rooted in one's own holdings, makes of the family the vital and most perfect and fecund cell of society, joining up in a brilliant manner in its progressive cohesion the present and future generations. If today the concept

and the creation of vital spaces is at the center of social and political aims, should not one, before all else, think of the vital space of the family and free it of the fetters of conditions which do not permit one even to formulate the idea of a homestead of one's own?

1693. Our planet, with all its extent of oceans and seas and lakes, with mountains and plains covered with eternal snows and ice, with great deserts and tractless lands, is not, all the same, without habitable regions and vital spaces, now abandoned to wild natural vegetation, and well suited to be cultivated by man to satisfy his needs and civil activities; and more than once it is inevitable that some families, migrating from one spot or another, should go elsewhere in search of a new homeland.

Pius XII, To Italian Farmers, November 15, 1946

(Summarized.) Labor on farms "still reflects the natural order willed by God, namely, that man, with his own labor, ought to rule material things, and not that material things rule man." Farmers are rooted in nature. They are producers as well as consumers. This gives them economic force and power of resistance in critical times. They gain simple virtues, which they should conserve at all costs.

Farmers have a right to a decent reward for their work, but they should not be lured into seeking quick profits at the expense of human need. "Show yourselves to be honest sellers, not greedy calculators to the damage of the people. . . ." They should beware of the vices so often found in city economic life. ". . . it happens too often that human needs no longer regulate, according to their natural and objective importance, economic life and the employment of capital, but, on the contrary, capital and its desire for gain determine those needs and in what measure they ought to be satisfied. In this way, it is not human labor destined for the common good that attracts to itself capital and places it at its service, but, instead, it is capital that moves the work, and man himself, here and there like balls in a game. If now the city dweller suffers from this unnatural state, how much more is it contrary to the intimate essence of the farmer's life."

Farmers should seek principal help from their own co-operative effort. They should also unite with laboring groups into a great community of workers. Thus we would have an organic society, instead of one ruled by great power groups.

Pius XII, To International Catholic Congress on Rural Problems, July 2, 1951

Everyone of good will must recognize that the system of industrial capitalism has helped render possible, and has even stimulated an increase in agricultural production; that it has permitted, in many regions of the world, higher levels of physical and spiritual life for rural people. It is not, then, the system itself which is to be opposed, but rather the danger it would run if its influence were to succeed in altering the specific character of rural living, by assimilating it to the life of urban and industrial centers, by making of the "country," as we understand it here, a simple extension of the "city."

Such a program, with the theory which supports it, is false and harmful. As is well known, Marxism professes just such a theory. It has fallen into the idolatrous worship of technology and industrialization to an extreme degree. The "collectivization" of agricultural labor, after the manner of a factory, the degradation of the countryside, reduced to nothing more than a reserve of manpower for industrial production — this is where Marxism leads. But this is where the principles of economic liberalism also lead, once the pursuit of gain, on the part of finance capitalism, bears with all its weight upon economic life;

once the interrelations of the national economy are considered exclusively from the point of view of the market as a price mechanism. And note that the consequences are identical for rural populations abused by industrial capitalism: either they become mere reservoirs of manpower, or they remain lethargic in the midst of a miserable existence, subject to the most dangerous tensions.

*   *   *

. . . in permanent contact with nature, as God created and governs it, the worker in the fields knows by daily experience that human life is in the hands of its Author. No other working group is so suited as his to the life of the family, viewed as a spiritual, economic, and juridical unit,

and also in the matter of production and consumption. However hard this work may be, man finds himself still master of his world through action at the heart of the community: of the family, of the neighborhood, and also, secondarily, of various economic co-operatives, provided, nevertheless, that these remain in all truth, and not merely as a matter of form, grounded on the responsibility of the entire membership. As regards modern technology, in the full measure in which it should place itself at the service of the individual farm enterprise, it will adapt itself naturally to the concrete situation in each particular case. Thus it will leave intact the individual character of agricultural labor.

Pius XII, To International Federation of Agricultural Producers, June 10, 1953

In full accord with your organizations and all men of good will, the Church has always deplored the present abnormal situation. On the one hand, agricultural production is being menaced by lack of profit, while on the other hand one can see entire peoples gravely undernourished and even in acute want. A remedy must be sought in an increase in, and in a rational stabilization of economic re-

lations between peoples, and this is valid not only for the field of agriculture. But, keeping within the spirit of social doctrine of the Church, one can also deplore an essential error in economic development since the appearance of modern industrialization. Agriculture has become, in a most abnormal way, only an appendage to industry and particularly to commerce.

Pius XII, To the Italian National Federation of Farmers, May 18, 1955

In thus making the family the foundation of your economy you will be able to overcome the great temptation of our time, to which so many yield. That is the temptation to regard a higher living standard and constantly increasing productivity as the fulfillment of man's desire for prosperity. For even in the economic field the family stands for what is lasting,

for what assures the continuance of future generations. Mere abundance of goods at low prices, the mere lightening and lessening of the strain of work are doubtful benefits, as they do not remove anxiety for the future; rather they increase it, in as much as they arouse inordinate desires, and never satisfy man.

Pius XII, Problems of Rural Life, September 18, 1957

We eagerly desire to see Catholics continue to move forward courageously toward the goals set by Catholic social doctrine, carefully seeing to it that the agricultural unit in each of its forms corresponds to the demands of human personality while remaining in harmony with the service of all. Most of all, wherever possible you should favor the wider spread of an economically efficient family unit among countrypeople. When it is set into the framework of a co-operative union and defended by a professional association, this unit constitutes a bulwark of sound liberty, a protective dike against the danger of urbanism, and an effective contribution to the continuation of the sound traditions of the people.

Code of Social Principles

106. In certain countries in particular there has arisen a rural problem, under circumstances detailed below: (1) the existence of estates, untilled or undertilled, whose use and improvement are indispensable to the common good; (2) cultivation which, though technically satisfactory, has by its mass production led to the use and growth of a rural proletariat in great poverty, who are forced to leave the land, to emigration, or to some other alternative hurtful to the common good.

In all such cases the state has the right, when less radical means have failed, to decree the division of cultivation and, if need be, of properties. The exercise of the right is always subject to the granting of a just and well-considered indemnity to all those whose legitimate rights would be injured by the measures taken toward division.

JUST as the racial problem is more than an American domestic problem, since it has world-wide ramifications, so likewise the study of United States farm problems fittingly follows the treatment of international political, social, and economic issues. Farmers throughout the world face difficulties because of the impact of changing technology. Hungry people in many areas cast longing eyes upon the surpluses piled up in American granaries. Understandably, then, the great Catholic farm group of the United States, the National Catholic Rural Life Conference, has, as was noted in Chapter XIV, a world-wide perspective.[1]

The Church has shown an abiding interest in problems connected with the land. Numerous popes have testified to their special affection for the farmer. Moreover, in many countries, Catholic rural organizations are among the most flourishing forms of Catholic life. The United States is no exception in this regard. While the Church is not generally strong

---

[1] For a graphic description of world rural problems, see "Christianity and the Land" (Des Moines: NCRLC, 1951), pp. 9–12.

in rural areas, it is nonetheless disproportionately active in these regions. The National Catholic Rural Life Conference has shown a vigor and comprehensiveness in its programs unexcelled by any urban Catholic group. It has also worked out a thorough philosophy of rural life, as well as varied methods for putting this into practice.

Some of the most carefully prepared literature on United States rural problems to appear anywhere has been published by the NCRLC. Its fundamental position was stated in the 1939 *Manifesto on Rural Life*. These views have been amplified and kept up to date by frequent policy statements. The interests of the Conference are not confined to social and economic problems of the farm. It has offered help in every phase of family living, including the preparation of a unique prayer book, with prayers and blessings for many occasions.[2]

MORAL VALUES IN RURAL LIFE

One of the main reasons for extensive Catholic interest in rural problems derives from the moral values inherent in farm life. Many phases of country living contribute to Christian culture. It fosters family life. It contributes to the character of those living on farms. There is a stability and sound conservatism about rural life which is favorable to religious ideals. For all these reasons, we can truly say that the farm is the cradle of many of the best elements in a nation's culture.

The Family. Farm life is family life. Practically every phase of rural activity tends to strengthen family bonds, whereas city living imposes many obstacles and difficulties in the way of the family. This can be seen from the nature of work on the farm. The whole family participates in the common task. As soon as children are old enough to work, they have their share of the chores. They may be given charge of some particular animal or allowed to cultivate their own plot of land. This gives them a sense of independence and self-reliance. But they also have a portion of common duties. They may milk the cows or turn them out to graze. They help bring in firewood or assist in the kitchen. Thus, their independence is tempered by a sense of social solidarity. This social sense is closely tied up with the family, thereby deepening and reinforcing the ties which bind all together. By contrast, city labor is often divisive. The

---

[2] An annotated selection of NCRLC literature is given at the end of this chapter. At the time that these pages are being written, the *Manifesto on Rural Life* (Milwaukee: Bruce, 1939) is being revised.

family does not often have a natural interest in the work done by its various members, except insofar as it contributes to total family income. Children in the city are not normally integrated into a family productive unit. They may aid in small duties around the home, but most of their activity and recreation is done outside the home. Thus, one form of life is cohesive and centripetal, whereas the other is divisive and centrifugal.

The farm family is particularly well adapted for children's needs. They have space to live, to play, and to work. From the economic viewpoint, they are assets to the family, instead of liabilities as often happens in city life. Today they have practically all the advantages of city children — education, companionship, and recreation — without the disadvantages of crowded conditions, immoral influences, and excessive strain and tension. The country child faces more constructive challenges than is often the case with his city cousin. He must be resourceful and quick thinking, but he learns this constructively from meeting farm economic problems. The city child is also usually resourceful, but he often gains these qualities in contests with his fellows or by surmounting the hazards of the streets. It is this ingenuity which has so often distinguished Americans: both the positive and useful form of achieving marvels of production, and the less desirable form of mere cleverness sometimes associated with antisocial practices. The former quality is more likely to be derived from the farm, whereas the latter is more a product of urban living.

In the light of Church interest in the family, it is not surprising that Pope Pius XII said that "the tiller of the soil still reflects the natural order of things willed by God."[3] The Pontiff goes on to say:

> This, then, is the deep-seated cause of the modern conflict between city and country: each viewpoint produces altogether different men. The difference of viewpoints becomes all the more pronounced the more capital, having abdicated its noble mission to promote the good of all groups in society, penetrates the farmer's world or otherwise involves it in its evils. It glitters its gold and a life of pleasure before the dazzled eyes of the farm-worker to lure him from his land to the city where he may squander his hard-won savings. The city usually holds nothing for him but disillusionment; often he loses his health, his strength, his happiness, his honor, and his very soul there.[4]

At the same time, there are disadvantages in rural living. They are not inherent or inevitable; indeed, they should be removed if families are to remain on farms. Farm families still suffer at times from isolation, scarcity

---

[3] Pope Pius XII *To Italian Farmers*, November 15, 1946, in *The Pope Speaks on Rural Life* (NCRLC), p. 10.
[4] *Ibid.*, pp. 10–11.

of social and cultural contacts, and lack of educational and religious facilities. Their health and hospital care is often inadequate. Sometimes, there is a cultural barrenness in the country, caused by overconservatism and excessive individualism. Too many farmers are blind traditionalists, unwilling to adopt new methods and processes. All this makes rural life less attractive, particularly for children who learn from motion pictures and radio some of the surface glamour and excitement of the city. This makes them less content with their way of living. Poor economic practices tend to lower living standards, thereby further accentuating the contrasts between farm and factory. Unless farmers living on the estimated two million marginal farms can get more land, capital, and better methods of operation, they are condemned to poverty and insecurity.

Farmers too often fail to realize the values inherent in education and cultural development. It is true that low per-capita incomes have frequently stifled the growth of rural schools, but even when income is available it is not always willingly used for such aims. The same is true in regard to beautifying the home and the use of laborsaving machinery. Thus, farm children today want electric lighting and inside plumbing. The lack of such comforts is sometimes caused by conservatism as much as by economic stringency. Church and other groups should take an interest in these matters, since they influence the choice of young farmers as to their future way of life. There is no inherent reason why the farm should not offer all the real advantages of city life, together with its own special attractions.[5]

Family Farms. Because the farm is the natural cradle of the family, it is understandable that the NCRLC should favor family farms instead of farm corporations. The ideal is a farm owned or securely held by its operator.

A formal definition of the family farm, offered by the NCRLC, is "a socioeconomic institution in which the capital, labor, and management of the family is organized toward the production of food and fiber for the benefit of the family and society."[6] Among the necessary characteristics are ownership or security of tenure, management by the family, the bulk of labor contributed by the family, a full-time occupation for

---

[5] These points are stated in the *Manifesto*, Chap. 1. For a more recent expression of the advantages and problems of farm life, see the 1957 NCRLC policy statement, "A Program for the Rural Community," pp. 7–9, 16–17.

[6] "A Program for the Family Farm," 1956 NCRLC policy statement, p. 4. See also the statements issued in January and June, 1958, as well as "Christianity and the Land," cited earlier.

the family, and income fully adequate for the support of the family. Its size will vary according to the economics of the crop. It could be a ten-acre truck farm in Delaware or a five-thousand-acre ranch in Texas. The family farm is not to be confused with small farms, subsistence farms, or part-time farms.

In contrast to the family farm are the very large commercial farms, sometimes called "corporations in the fields." These latter depend upon large numbers of hired workers, often migrants. Many of these workers are poorly paid. Often they are immigrants from Mexico, either illegal (wetbacks) or legal (braceros) who are willing to work for 50 cents an hour or less. It is alleged that such farms profit disproportionately from government aid programs, since they can simply release workers when land is retired from cultivation. On the other hand, family farms that meet the definition used above (adequate size, capital, and management) have been more efficient than corporation farms, either in terms of output per acre or return per dollar of investment. Understandably, the family farm is far superior in terms of noneconomic values. It is for this reason, and not because of fear of economic competition, that the NCLRC wants government policy to work in favor of family farms and against the oversized commercial farm.

The city dweller may be astonished to know of the capital investment in the average family farm. A sum of $100,000 is not unusual. This is the key problem in regard to the two million marginal farms in the United States. Their owners will need credit if they are to secure sufficient land and machinery to make productive use of their labor and management. The alternative, as will be noted later in this chapter, is (preferably) part-time industrial work for added income or (less desirable) programs to help farmers move to the city and obtain industrial work.

Even were family farms less efficient economically, there would be social reasons to encourage them. Pope Pius XII is very clear on this point: "During the last century and even at the present time, there have been discouraging examples of attempts to sacrifice farming to other ends. If one is looking for the highest and most rapidly increasing national economy, or for the cheapest possible provisioning of the nation with farm products, there will be in either case a temptation to sacrifice the farming enterprise."[7] In another section of the address, he attacks speculative ownership or unwise proposals for nationalization or collective farming. He concludes: "The Church teaches that the whole economy of

---

[7] Ibid., p. 4.

a people is organic and that the productive capacities of a national territory should be developed in healthy proportion. The conflict between country and city would never have become so great if this fundamental truth had been observed."[8] Any program which subordinates agriculture, with its family values, to considerations of productive efficiency alone would be contrary to the common good and to the organic nature of economic life.

To facilitate family ownership of farms, the NCRLC favors private and governmental measures which definitely foster family farms. It would have tax and aid programs graduated in such a way that a differential exists in favor of the smaller group. In addition, it is considered most important to have fair arrangements for transferring title to the farm to a son, without the problems involved in the payment of estate taxes and the division of property among heirs. With this in mind, the NCRLC favors the "father-son agreement." The son who is to take title to the farm could build up an equity over the years by payments to compensate for his labor and managerial services. Moreover, under our tax laws, gifts of under $3,000 a year are not taxable. Thus, a timely program of purchase and gift would permit the orderly and intact transfer of the property, with no problems of estate taxes or buying out other heirs.

The NCRLC has many other programs to aid family farmers. It encourages land-placement service in rural parishes. In this way, Catholic farmers can learn about land for sale or rent. The Conference is especially concerned about developing the full potentialities of farm youth. It wishes to help those who belong on the farm to hold to this way of life. Conference priests also emphasize the integration of the liturgy with farm family life. By making the sacraments, family prayer, and special blessings a basic part of farm living, these priests bring a richness of life to farm families and thus encourage them in their chosen path.

While the Conference favors family farms, it also sees distinct benefits in what is sometimes called "rurban living." The factory worker who owns and tills an acre or two of land is raising his family in a more wholesome environment. He has added security in that his food needs are not dependent upon his factory job. He may even get some additional income from the sale of surplus farm products. But he is primarily an industrial worker living on the land, not a farmer.

Rural Culture. In addition to family values, rural life affects individual character. Indeed, it has produced its own definite psychological

[8] *Ibid.*, pp. 10–11.

traits in farm dwellers. Thus, Emerson Hynes, in the June, 1948, issue of the *American Catholic Sociological Review*, enumerates seven quantitative and five qualitative differences between farm and city life. Rural occupations are more diversified; they are influenced more directly by nature; population density is less; mobility is also less; fertility is higher; costs are lower; and social statistics vary sharply, sometimes in favor of the country (as with crime, divorce) and sometimes in favor of the city (standards of living, medical care). Qualitative differences include a different philosophy of life; distinct psychological traits, such as conservatism; self-contained family life; deeper but more limited social contacts; and varying types of arts and skills.

Rural attitudes differ clearly, although often intangibly, from those of most city dwellers. There is definite meaning to the phrase: close to nature. The farmer is constantly engrossed in such deep realities as birth, growth, and death. He lives in a world of biology. His environment is organic in the original sense of the term. By contrast, the city dweller often lives in a mechanical world. His work concerns machines and inanimate products, and often such abstractions as buying and selling, finance, statistics and calculations, and other impersonal things. Of course, urban residents deal with other human beings. They have their families, with the basic human problems and contacts implied in this. But this is often a different world from that in which they work. By contrast, the farmer is close to life in all his work. He is engrossed with elemental nature and hence may find it easier to think of nature's God. It may be more than a coincidence that the religious literature of the Old and New Testaments is full of references to various forms of living things and to nature in its elemental form of sea and sky. It is at least possible that the preoccupation with the mechanical and the works of man leads city people more easily into a humanistic and secularistic mentality, forgetting God and His works. At any rate, religion and religious values are held with greater tenacity by farm families than is often the case with urban families.[9]

The versatile nature of farm life tends to develop a well-rounded human being. A farmer's life is varied. Today he must have skills ranging from making simple repairs to a tractor to some knowledge of soil chemistry. He nurses injured animals and builds houses and barns. He must adapt his plans to the varied pattern of weather and season. Since he sells for

---

[9] See "Christianity and the Land," pp. 8–9, and "A Program for the Rural Community," p. 14.

a market, he must know something of business and economics. Thus, he has a chance to develop many aspects of his nature, much more than is the case with the assembly-line worker. This in turn affects personality and character. There is a stability and self-assurance which goes with the known possession of skill and the conquest of obstacles and difficulties. This is evident in the skilled city craftsman, and it is even more true with the versatile and competent farmer.

These qualities are further accentuated when the farmer owns his land. He then has the added stability which goes with ownership and relative independence. He has more control than is normally the case with urban workers of such essentials as food, clothing, and housing. For the essentials of life, at least, he is not so subject to the vagaries of an economic system. Moreover, he is his own boss. He does not get detailed orders in regard to every phase of his activity. This is why he becomes restive under government controls. It is noticeable that the tremendous extension of federal power in recent years softened its impact considerably when it reached farm areas. The administration of farm legislation is normally less bureaucratic and more decentralized than has been the case for most social legislation. In the past, rural independence had been carried too far. The farmer was too conservative in the matter of adopting new techniques, particularly in such matters as soil conservation and increasing soil fertility. But at least, this was an antidote to the pragmatism and experimentalism which too often prevailed among urban groups.

The self-reliance of the farmer has now extended into useful forms of social co-operation. Thus, in the United States there are over ten thousand organizations for co-operative marketing or purchasing. About one fifth of the farm products sold commercially are marketed through such groups. Farmers often buy such items as fertilizer, seed, cattle feed, and gasoline through their own purchasing groups. In addition, they have credit organizations, co-operative insurance, and irrigation, telephone, and electrification projects achieved through common action. As an illustration, over 90 per cent of farms are now electrified, whereas the use of electricity on farms was relatively rare two decades ago. Understandably, the NCRLC favors co-operative action:

> Farm co-operatives are necessary. Were it not for co-operative enterprise, the family-type farmer would be at the mercy of the economically powerful in society. Unorganized, he would find himself pitted as an individual against the organized forces of concentrated wealth. The farmer cannot allow himself to become a slave either of a domineering state or of the

economic dictatorship of the mighty of the earth. The farmer will be free only insofar as he is organized.[10]

Thus, the principle of self-help, stressed by Pope Pius XII, has been vital and fruitful in our farm life. The isolation fostered by scattered homesteads, in contrast to the village community where farmers live and drive to their outlying holdings, has been largely broken down both by new forms of transportation and by community projects. Today farm life is in many ways more social and more effectively organized than is the case with city life. The cities are intensively organized from one aspect, but the individual participates less in actual community work. He delegates such actions to civic or union officials and remains content to pay taxes or dues. Thus city dwellers are generally farther removed from an organic social life, whereas our rural population is now participating richly in such organic activities.

Farm Labor. Many of the social problems connected with rural life exist where the family-type farm is not the norm. Farm workers, for example, are often underpaid and insecure. This is particularly the case with migratory workers, although it also obtains for stable workers on large commercialized farms. The institutions of tenancy and share cropping are likewise fraught with social evils which could be removed by long-term plans for fostering ownership. In other cases, social ills can be traced to a long history of low income for farmers. This is especially true of educational and medical facilities. Since it happens that whole states are affected by low-average incomes this becomes a national rather than a local problem. As a result, there is considerable pressure for federal aid both in the educational and the medical fields.

Many crops require little care during the ripening season, but need a large labor force for harvesting when they are ripe. Such is obviously the case with cotton, sugar beets, fruit, vineyards, and even truck crops. Some of these crops are highly perishable, so that the farmers must have assistance for the short period of harvesting. Much of this help is furnished by migratory workers, who move north with the ripening of crops, particularly on the East and West coasts. Usually entire families move, living in shacks or barracks for the period of employment in a region. Often the whole family, including very small children, works. As a result of this migration, children do not receive much education and have little oppor-

---

[10] *Manifesto*, p. 56. For more specific pronouncements on the function of co-operatives, see "A Program for the Rural Community," p. 18; "The Land: God's Gift to Man," pp. 21–22; and "Christianity and the Land," pp. 18–20.

tunity for normal social contacts. Furthermore, employment methods are casual, so that at times families may travel to a region only to find all jobs filled. The same situation often obtains in canning industries, which are equally seasonal adjuncts to agricultural work.

The number of migratory farm workers is not known with certainty. The low figure cited for domestic workers, excluding *braceros* and non-working family members, is 500,000. Many church and civic groups, however, estimate that the total volume of migrants is over a million and may approach two million, counting families traveling with male workers. Average annual cash earnings, in 1956, were estimated as less than $1,400 for male workers and at $500 for women workers.[11] This includes a small amount of nonfarm earnings. As many as 15 per cent of the children never go to school, and education for the rest is often a hit-or-miss proposition. Families often live in shacks of unbelievable squalor. They have no social security and are covered by workmen's compensation in only five states. Because hiring practices are casual, Mexican labor is imported even where there is unemployment among American migrant workers.[12]

For the sake of clarity, it is necessary to distinguish among three different types of farm labor that should be classified in the problem group. These are: Mexican farm labor, native migratory workers, and seasonal farm workers. Mexicans may be admitted for temporary work at not less than 50 cents an hour, under suitable working conditions. About 400,000 such workers have entered in recent years. They are called *braceros*. Illegal Mexican workers, wetbacks, can be more easily exploited because they are subject to deportation. But even legal workers may get lower pay and poorer working conditions than specified in their contracts, partly because they are often not able to assert their rights, and partly because of poor enforcement. Low wages and poor conditions affecting the Mexicans tend to drive down standards for native migratory workers (including Puerto Ricans). Seasonal farm workers do not suffer the disabilities connected with being on the move, but their wages are quite low in many areas. About half of farm hired workers are employed in the South. Most of these (over 80 per cent) were seasonal, having less

---

[11] United States Department of Agriculture, Bulletin 187, April, 1958, "The Hired Farm Worker Force of 1956." See also material available from the President's Commission on Migratory Labor.

[12] For further data, see *Migratory Labor in American Agriculture* (Washington: Superintendent of Documents, 1951). See also "A Program for the Rural Community," pp. 18–19; and "The Land: God's Gift to Man," pp. 25–26.

than one hundred and fifty days' work per year. Most hourly workers get less than eighty-five cents an hour. The average daily wage, for those paid by the day, was less than five dollars. Those paid by the week or month might get around thirty dollars a week or one hundred and ten dollars a month. These figures are based upon the 1954 Census of Agriculture.

It is easier to outline the problems of migratory workers than to offer a feasible solution for these problems. Unquestionably, many farm crops are such that temporary heavy labor demand is inevitable. These farms could not possibly support such a labor force during the entire year. Given this fact, three types of approach may be considered. First, the condition of migratory workers could be improved through public and private efforts to obtain suitable housing and a steady flow of employment. Enforcement of child labor regulations could prevent deprivation of schooling to children of migrants. Second, increased mechanization might lessen the labor needs for some crops and hence reduce the number of migrants. This has been done successfully for some field crops, such as wheat, where huge combines do the work of many men. It may also be found feasible for other crops, if suitable research were undertaken. Finally, it may be possible to recruit casual labor locally through the use of college students or even more mature high school students in their summer vacations. All this would assume adequate safeguards and more attractive conditions than are currently available.

Since the problem of migratory work is regional or even national, it is clear that the handling of it should be on a large scale. One possible approach is through unionization of workers to demand better wages and more regular conditions of employment. By this method, a labor union would act as a stabilizing force, just as it has been in the clothing industry. Another approach would be through action by the federal government, after a thorough study of the entire issue, including the agricultural economics involved. From the political viewpoint the union approach is preferable. If workers organized to demand better conditions, farmers would be forced to make the necessary adjustments or do without labor at a critical time. They might then welcome any help which the federal government might give. But if the government were to act first, there would be tremendous political opposition from the highly organized and effective farm lobby. A parallel case would be the condition of domestic servants. Evils in this field seemed impervious to legislative remedy, but when economic conditions gave workers more attractive alternate conditions of employment, the shortage of servants quickly led to raised standards. In many cities, this form of work is now on an organized basis, sometimes handled by teams working from a central office. Thus, necessity forced the overcoming of inertia and lethargy and led to greatly improved conditions. A similar approach may be the more feasible answer to the problem of migratory and casual labor.

It should not be assumed that farm labor is the only form of migratory labor. In addition to canneries previously mentioned, there are elements of casualness in logging, construction, shipping, and resort occupations. As a rule, however, these occupations do not pose the serious social problem associated with migratory farm labor, since techniques have been found for stabilizing employment and income. In all likelihood, similar gains can be made in connection with farm labor, provided sufficient incentives are present. Apathy and neglect tend to perpetuate the *status quo*. If government, labor, farm organizations, and various reform groups can keep up constant pressure for higher standards, it is likely that this most exploited group of workers in the United States can begin to move up the economic ladder.

ECONOMIC PROBLEMS OF AGRICULTURE

Few issues in public life are so complex and controversial as the so-called "farm problem." Actually, the title is a misnomer. There are many farm problems. If we approach the situation from the viewpoint of average farm income, we find that nearly three million farms are generally profitable, whereas two million or more are considered marginal. If the approach is in terms of product, again there are wide variations. Hogs may be very profitable one year and two years later they may cause a glut in the market. Cotton may be grown profitably in Texas and at a loss in Georgia. A region that is prosperous for five years may then face five years of drought. Because of this complexity, it is not easy to make generalizations about farm economics. Likewise, any single method of solution is likely to be uneven in result.

Some sources of farm difficulties are inherent in the very process of farming. Weather conditions, crop and animal diseases, and varying fertility of the soil primarily reflect natural conditions. Man is learning ever new techniques to control these conditions. but they still remain to some degree beyond prediction and control. Other problems spring from revolutionary improvements in agriculture. In almost every area of farming, there has been startling progress in the quality of seeds and animals, the use of machinery, and the general application of science to rural problems. The typical American farm today is a small or medium-sized business, involving very substantial amounts of capital and demanding specialized managerial ability. The result of these trends has been fewer but larger and more efficient farms. This in turn has meant a steady displacement of farm population. A century ago, the majority of Americans derived their living from farming. Today less than 12 per cent of our population is supported by farm income.

An important event in recent years has been the trend toward "vertical integration" in many crops. Here a processor or food dealer contracts for the entire output of a farm. Contracts vary, with some merely guaranteeing a price with the farmer furnishing his own resources, while others may involve the furnishing of capital, feed, and facilities. These guarantees help take some of the risk out of farming, and may furnish capital to some who could not otherwise obtain it, but they also pose the serious danger of lessening or destroying the independence of the farmer. Unless such farmers strengthen their economic position by collective bargaining with processors or other integrators, they may lose their freedom and become mere adjuncts to supermarkets and similar purchasers.

The market for farm products is constantly changing. On the plus side, population growth and higher living standards have expanded the domestic market. High-income conditions particularly favor meats, fruits, and vegetables. Proportionate direct consumption of cereals tends to go down. Foreign markets are more capricious. War periods tend to heighten demand. In times of peace, American products often lose out to competition from low-cost areas elsewhere. The expansion and contraction caused by this factor alone has been seriously disruptive for many farm areas. In addition, some crops, such as cotton, have felt the inroads of competition by synthetic fibers.

Surpluses. As production expanded more rapidly than markets, the problem of surpluses arose. A surplus is created when a crop cannot be sold at a price that will pay farmers' costs and give them a fair return on their investment, management, and labor. The federal government, through various laws, has tried to meet this problem by agreeing either to purchase and store certain crops at a support price, or to lend money to the farmer to perform this storage. Security for such loans is the stored crop; a farmer's capital is not subject to assessment should he default on this type of loan. Concomitant with price supports have been programs to retire land from production, either of the crop supported or of all crops. Such programs have not been very successful in reducing surpluses, since greater efficiency and intensive use of the remaining land kept total output at high levels.

Some farm problems are more easily solved than others. As was noted earlier, tremendous progress has been made in controlling the vagaries of nature. Irrigation, erosion control, better fertilizers, resistant strains of seeds, new insecticides, special breeds of animals — all these have lessened the element of risk attributable to natural causes. It is even feasible to insure certain crops against losses caused by weather. There are facilities for teaching most farmers the specialized knowledge needed by modern farming, although more aids are needed. Federal and private credit of various types is also available, yet many of the marginal farmers who need credit most cannot obtain the amounts they need.

The problem of price-depressing food surpluses is thornier. The NCRLC has repeatedly urged more imaginative disposal of surplus crops to needy persons abroad and at home. Such programs of shared abundance must be managed carefully, so as not to compete with normal markets and thus cause international or domestic tensions. But the piling up of unused surpluses, when millions are hungry, is a moral problem. It is also an economic problem both because of its direct cost and because of the impact that such surpluses have upon farm prices and income.

As these pages are being written, there is almost universal agreement among farm economists that a price-support program that leads to constantly increasing surpluses cannot be defended. It has received political support as a means of bolstering farm income, but even such support is waning. Current thinking is divided along many lines, but two lines of approach are frequently mentioned. One would guarantee farm incomes and let prices seek their free-market level. This might be less costly than storage and would mean lower prices to consumers. The second approach is to lower the level of support prices so that they, in effect, become a form of disaster insurance. Farmers would be freed of controls and left to produce the crop that they can produce most efficiently. It is maintained that efficient farmers could make good incomes under this system. Less efficient farmers would need to seek other forms of income. In effect, this would further cut down the number of American farms.

If this second program prevails, it is essential that Americans learn more about the Rural Development Program of the federal government. This program is aimed at giving direct assistance to the marginal farmer who is the greatest sufferer from the present farm crisis and who contributes heavily to the class whose incomes are below two thousand dollars a year. It is estimated that over two million farmers belong in this class. Rural Development is a complex pilot program to stimulate local initiative in helping marginal farmers. Help is along two broad lines: either aid in securing capital and knowledge for better farming, or aid in securing some other form of income. For example, a food-processing company might be persuaded to open a plant in an area where many farmers are underemployed. These farmers could continue to have the advantages of farm living, but they could supplement their incomes and thus achieve higher living standards. Some farmers even could be given training for full-time work in the cities or towns.

Much can be said in favor of a combined program of removing controls from more efficient farmers and aiding their marginal brothers. It is socially desirable to minimize the area of government control over farming. This should not mean a return to *laissez faire*, with farming as one of the few purely competitive groups in a highly organized economy. But government aid should involve a minimum interference with the normal function of the market in fixing prices and allocating resources. A controlled economy rarely, if ever, functions efficiently.

The farm is a bastion of family life and political stability. It should be maintained as a cradle of independence. Outside aid, when it is needed because of the complexities of farm economics, should be of a nature that contributes to, rather than weakens, this independence. Our entire society will be stronger as a result.

READINGS*

Manifesto on Rural Life.
M. R. Benedict, *Can We Solve the Farm Problem?*
R. L. Mighell, *American Agriculture: Its Structure and Place in the Economy.*
L. Soth, *Farm Trouble.*
T. W. Schultz, *Economic Organization of Agriculture.*
W. W. Cochrane, *Farm Prices: Myth and Reality.*
Reports and Publications of the National Catholic Rural Life Conference.
    The following are relatively recent and of special value in the fields indicated.
"Policy Statement, June 18, 1958." For statements on agricultural revolution, vertical integration, and efficiency of family farms.
"Policy Statement, January, 1958." Vertical integration, large versus small farms, low-income problems, migratory labor.

---
* For further readings, consult List No. 13 in the Appendix.

"A Program for the Rural Community," 1957 Policy Statement. Wide range of issues, with excerpts from earlier statements; valuable as a brief but broad presentation of NCRLC policies.

"Start Where You Are" (1957). Jocist-type brochure for young people, giving them elements of Christian social action.

"A Program for the Family Farm" (1956). Defines the family farm, indicates its importance, and notes how it may be strengthened.

"Our Thirty-Fourth Year" (1956). Brochure describing organization and work of the Conference.

"A Program for Shared Abundance." Abundance for the farmer and for the world.

"Conclusiones de Panama" (1955) and "Conclusiones de Manizales" (1953). Primarily Latin-American problems, with principles that apply more widely to world problems of population and food.

"The Land: God's Gift to Man" (1952). Another broad statement on farm problems, with suitable reference material.

"Christianity and the Land" (1951). World conference report; excellent primer on Catholic rural philosophy, as well as statements on international food problems; contains papal address on farming, July 2, 1951.

Rural Life Prayer Book (1956). A 410-page prayer book, containing the Ordinary of the Mass, prayers for the country family, occasional prayers, blessings from the Roman Ritual, prayers and devotions, liturgical devotions for country living, and selected psalms.

Social Order: "The Farm Problem," October, 1958.

Chapter XVII

SOCIAL PRINCIPLES AND SOCIAL ACTION

SPIRITUAL NATURE OF MODERN CRISIS

Leo XIII, Graves de Communi

10. For it is the opinion of some, which is caught up by the masses, that the social question, as they call it, is merely economic. The precise opposite is the truth. It is first of all moral and religious, and for that reason its solution is to be expected mainly from the moral law and the pronouncements of religion.

Leo XIII, Rerum Novarum

42. For when Christian morals are completely observed, they yield of themselves a certain measure of prosperity to material existence, because they win the favor of God, the source and fountain of all goods; because they restrain the twin plagues of life — excessive desire for wealth and thirst for pleasure — which too often make man wretched amidst the very abundance of riches; and because finally, Christian morals make men content with a moderate livelihood and make them supplement income by thrift, removing them far from the vices which swallow up both modest sums and huge fortunes, and dissipate splendid inheritances.

Pius XI, Quadragesimo Anno

98. The first and most necessary remedy is a reform of morals.

127. Yet, if we look into the matter more carefully and more thoroughly, we shall clearly perceive that, preceding this ardently desired social restoration, there must be a renewal of the Christian spirit, from which so many immersed in economic life have, far and wide, unhappily fallen away, lest all our efforts be wasted and our house be built not on a rock but on shifting sand.

129. "Wherefore," to use the words of Our Predecessor, "if human society is to be healed, only a return to Christian life and institutions will heal it." For this alone can provide effective remedy for that excessive care for passing things that is the origin of all vices; and this alone can draw away men's eyes, fascinated by and wholly fixed on the changing things of the world, and raise them toward Heaven. Who would deny that human society is in most urgent need of this cure now?

136. No genuine cure can be furnished for this lamentable ruin of souls, which, so long as it continues, will frustrate all efforts to regenerate society, unless men return openly and sincerely to the teaching of the Gospel, to the precepts of Him who alone has the words of everlasting life, words which will never pass away, even if Heaven and earth will pass away. All experts in social problems are seeking eagerly a structure so fashioned in accordance with the norms of reason that it can lead economic life back to sound and right order. But this order, which We Ourselves ardently long for and with all Our efforts promote, will be wholly defective and incomplete unless all the activities of men harmoniously unite to imitate and attain, insofar as it lies within human strength, the marvelous unity of the divine plan. We mean that perfect order which the Church with great force and power preaches and which right human reason itself demands, that all things be directed to God as the first and supreme end of all created activity, and that all created goods under God be considered as mere instruments to be used only insofar as they conduce to the attainment of the supreme end. Nor is it to be thought that gainful occupations are thereby belittled or judged less consonant with human dignity; on the contrary, we are taught to recognize in them with reverence the manifest will of the divine Creator who placed man upon the earth to work it and use it in a multitude of ways for his needs. If these principles are observed by everyone, everywhere, and always, not only the production and acquisition of goods but also the use of wealth, which now is seen to be so often contrary to right order, will be brought back soon within the bounds of equity and just distribution. The sordid love of wealth, which is the shame and great sin of our age, will be opposed in actual fact by the gentle yet effective law of Christian moderation which commands man to seek first the Kingdom of God and His Justice, with the assurance that by virtue of God's kindness and unfailing promise, temporal goods also, insofar as he has need of them, shall be given him besides.

143. But above all, let them hold in high esteem and assiduously employ for the good of their disciples that most valuable means of both personal and social restoration which, as We taught in Our Encyclical, Mens Nostra, is to be found in the Spiritual Exercises for all the laity, but also the highly beneficial Workers' Retreats. For in that school of the spirit, not only are the best of Christians developed, but true apostles also are trained for every condition of life and are enkindled with the fire of the heart of Christ. From this school they will go forth as did the Apostles from the Upper Room of Jerusalem, strong in faith, endowed with an invincible steadfastness in persecution, burning with zeal, interested solely in spreading everywhere the Kingdom of Christ.

Pius XI, On Atheistic Communism

41. As in all the stormy periods of the history of the Church, the fundamental remedy today lies in a sincere renewal of private and public life according to the principles of the Gospel by all those who belong to the Fold of Christ, that they may be in truth the salt of the earth to preserve human society from total corruption.

44. And here We wish, Venerable Brethren, to insist more particularly on two teachings of our Lord which have special bearing on the present condition of the human race; detachment from earthly goods and the precept of charity. "Blessed are the poor in spirit" were the first words that fell from the lips of the divine Master in His sermon on the mount. This lesson is more than ever necessary in these days of materialism athirst for the goods and pleasures of this earth. All Christians, rich or poor, must keep their eyes fixed on heaven, remembering that "we have not here a lasting city, but we seek one that is to come." The rich should not place their happiness in things of earth nor spend their best efforts in the acquisition of them. Rather, considering themselves only as stewards of their earthly goods, let them be mindful of the account they must render of them to their Lord and Master, and value them as precious means that God has put into their hands for doing good; let them not fail, besides, to distribute of their abundance to the poor, according to the evangelical precept.

45. But the poor, too, in their turn, while engaged, according to the laws of charity and justice, in acquiring the necessities of life and also in bettering their condition, should always remain "poor in spirit," and hold spiritual goods in higher esteem than earthly property and pleasures. Let them remember that the world will never be able to rid itself of misery, sorrow, and tribulation, which are the portion even of those who seem most prosperous. Patience, therefore, is the need of all, that Christian patience which comforts the heart with the divine assurance of eternal happiness.

59. But "unless the Lord keep the city, he watcheth in vain that keepeth it." And so, as a final and most efficacious remedy, We recommend, Venerable Brethren, that in your dioceses you use the most practical means to foster and intensify the spirit of prayer joined with Christian penance. When the Apostles asked the Saviour why they had been unable to drive the evil spirit from a demoniac, our Lord answered: "This kind is not cast out but by prayer and fasting." So, too, the evil which today torments humanity can be conquered only by a world-wide holy crusade of prayer and penance. We ask especially the contemplative orders, men and women, to redouble their prayers and sacrifices to obtain from Heaven efficacious aid for the Church in the present struggle. Let them implore also the powerful intercession of the Immaculate Virgin who, having crushed the head of the serpent of old, remains the sure protectress and invincible "Help of Christians."

77. Everywhere today there is an anxious appeal to moral and spiritual forces; and rightly so, for the evil we must combat is at its origin primarily an evil of the spiritual order.

Pius XI, Caritate Christi Compulsi, May 3, 1932

13. For God or against God — this once more is the alternative that shall decide the destinies of all mankind, in politics, in finance, in morals, in the sciences and arts, in the state, in civil and domestic society.

25. But to prayer we must also join penance, the spirit of penance and the practice of Christian penance.

27. Penance is of its very nature a recognition and re-establishment of the moral order in the world that is founded on the eternal law, that is, on the living God. He who makes

satisfaction to God for sin recognizes thereby the sanctity of the highest principles of morality, their internal binding power, the need of a sanction against their violation.

29. It is a weapon that strikes right at the root of all evil, that is, at the lust for material wealth and the wanton pleasures of life. By means of voluntary sacrifices, by means of practical and even painful acts of self-denial, by means of various works of penance, the noblehearted Christian subdues the base passions that tend to make him violate the moral order.

30. No leader in public economy, no power of organization will ever be able to bring social conditions to a peaceful solution, unless first in the very field of economics there triumphs moral law based on God and conscience.

Pius XII, Summi Pontificatus, October 20, 1939

1398. The radical and ultimate cause of the evils which We deplore in modern society is the denial and rejection of a universal norm of morality as well for individual and social life as for international relations; We mean that disregard, so common nowadays, and the forgetfulness of the natural law itself, which has its foundation in God. . . . When God is denied, every basis of morality is undermined; the voice of conscience is stilled or, at any rate, grows very faint. . . .

1400. The consequence is that the moral values by which, in other times, public and private conduct was gauged have fallen into disuse; and the much vaunted laicization of society, which had made ever more rapid progress, withdrawing man, the family, and the state from the beneficent and regenerating effects of the idea of God and the teaching of the Church, has caused to reappear . . . the signs of a corrupt paganism.

1402. With the weakening of faith in God and in Jesus Christ, and the darkening in men's minds of the light of moral principles, there disappeared the indispensable foundation of the stability and quiet of that internal, and external, private and public order which alone can support and safeguard the stability of states. . . . Dissensions come not only from the surge of rebellious passion, but also from a deep spiritual crisis which has overthrown the sound principles of private and public morality.

1437. For true though it is that the evils from which mankind suffers today come in part from economic instability and from the struggle of interests regarding a more equal distribution of the goods which God has given man as a means of sustenance and progress, it is not less true that their root is deeper and more intrinsic, belonging to the sphere of religious belief and moral convictions. . . . The re-education of mankind if it is to have any effect, must be, above all things, spiritual and religious. Hence it must proceed from Christ as from its indispensable foundation; must be actuated by justice and crowned by charity.

1444. There is no opposition between the laws that govern the life of faithful Christians and the postulates of a genuine brotherly humanitarianism, but rather unity and mutual support.

Pius XII, Christmas Message, 1948

A convinced Christian cannot confine himself within an easy and egotistical isolationism when he witnesses the needs and miseries of his brothers; when pleas for help come to him from those in economic distress; when he knows the aspirations of the working classes for more normal and just conditions of life; when he is aware of the abuses of an economic system which puts money above social obligations; when he is not ignorant of the aberrations of an intransigent nationalism which denies or spurns the common bonds linking the separate nations together, and imposing on each one of them many and varied duties toward the great family of nations.

Pius XII, To Members of Pax Christi, September 13, 1952

A supernaturalism that withdraws itself from economic and political needs and duties as if they did not concern the Christian and Catholic is something unhealthy, something alien to the thinking of the Church.

Pius XII, To Italian Catholic Workers' Association, May 14, 1953

Certain Catholics, promoters of a new social order, are in error when they maintain that social reform must come first of all and that afterwards care will be taken of the religious and moral life of the individual and of society. The first cannot, in fact, be separated from the second, because this world cannot be disjoined from the other, nor can man, who is a living whole, be broken up into two parts.

Pius XII, Easter Message, April 6, 1958

. . . only through Christ and in Christ will man achieve his personal perfection; through Him his works will be truly alive, his relations with his fellowmen and with creatures well-ordered, his worthy aspirations satisfied.

American Hierarchy, Secularism, November, 1947

Secularism takes God out of economic thinking and thereby minimizes the dignity of the human person endowed by God with inalienable rights and made responsible to Him for corresponding individual and social duties. Thus, to the detriment of man and society, the divinely established balance in economic relations is lost.

When disregard of his responsibility to God makes the owner forget his stewardship and the social function of private property, there comes that irrational economic individualism which brings misery to millions. Helpless workers are exploited; cutthroat competition and antisocial marketing practices follow. When men in labor organizations lose the right social perspective, which a sense of responsibility to God gives, they are prone to seek merely the victory of their own group, in disregard of personal and property rights.

THE WORK OF THE CLERGY

Leo XIII, Letter to Italian Bishops, December 8, 1902

For this purpose We desire that the aspirants to the priesthood, while abstaining . . . from all participation in actual movements outside, should, toward the end of their seminary course, be duly instructed in the papal documents which have to do with the social question and Christian democracy. Later on, when advanced to the priesthood, let them employ themselves with the people who at every period have been the special object of the Church's most affectionate care. . . . To defend the principles of justice and Christian charity in which all the rights and duties of civil society find a fair and equitable balance, such in its outstanding characteristics is the grand duty and object of social activities.

St. Pius X, Il Fermo Proposito, June 11, 1905

The priest, raised higher than other men to fulfill the mission he has received from God, ought to keep himself equally above all human interest, all classes of society. His proper field of action is the Church where, as ambassador of God, he preaches the truth, and inculcates along with respect for the rights of God, respect also for the rights of every creature. Acting thus, he does not expose himself to opposition; he does not appear as a party man, supporting one side and going against another; nor for the sake of avoiding collision with certain tendencies, and of not irritating by argument minds already embittered, does he put himself in danger of disguising the truth, or of suppressing it, which in both cases would be to fail in his duty; nor is it necessary to remark that having very often to treat of material things, he might find himself involved in responsible liabilities, hurtful alike to his person and to the dignity of his ministry.

Benedict XV, Letter to Bishop of Bergamo, March 11, 1920

Let no member of the clergy suppose that activity of this kind is something foreign to his priestly ministry because the field in which it is exercised is economic. *It is precisely in this field that the salvation of souls is imperiled. Therefore it is Our will that priests consider it as one of their duties to give as much of their life as possible to social science and social action,* by study, observation, and work, and to support in all ways those who, in this sphere, exercise a wholesome influence for the good of Catholics.*

Pius XI, Ad Catholici Sacerdotii

8. The priest contributes most effectively to the solution, or at least the mitigation, of social conflicts, since he preaches Christian brotherhood, declares to all their mutual obligations of justice and charity, brings

* In this and the following sections of the quotations, many passages are italicized by the author. The purpose of this is to emphasize teachings which form the doctrinal basis of Catholic social action.

peace to hearts embittered by moral and economic hardship, and alike to rich and poor points out the only true

riches to which all men both can and should aspire.

Pius XI, Quadragesimo Anno

27. Sacred ministers of the Church, thoroughly imbued with Leo's teaching, have, in fact, often proposed to the votes of the people's representatives the very social legislation that has been enacted in recent years and have resolutely demanded and promoted its enforcement.

142. A difficult task, certainly, is thus imposed on priests, and to meet it, all who are growing up as the hope of the Church, must be duly prepared by an intensive study of the social question. Especially is it necessary that those whom you intend to assign in particular to this work should demonstrate that they are men possessed of the keenest sense of justice, who will resist with truly manly courage the dishonest demands or the unjust acts of anyone, who will excel

in the prudence and judgment which avoids every extreme, and, above all, who will be deeply permeated by the charity of Christ, which alone has the power to subdue firmly but gently the hearts and wills of men to the laws of justice and equity. Upon this road so often tried by happy experience, there is no reason why we should hesitate to go forward with all speed.

143. These Our Beloved Sons who are chosen for so great a work, We earnestly exhort in the Lord to give themselves wholly to the training of the men committed to their care, and in the discharge of this eminently priestly and apostolic duty to make proper use of the resources of Christian education by teaching youth, forming Christian organizations, and founding study groups guided by principles in harmony with the Faith.

Pius XI, On Atheistic Communism

61. To priests in a special way We recommend anew the oft-repeated counsel of Our Predecessor, Leo XIII, to go to the workingman. We make this advice Our own, and faithful to the teaching of Jesus Christ and His Church, We thus complete it: "Go to the workingman, especially where he is poor; and in general, go to the poor. . . ."

62. Indisputably much has been done in this direction, especially after the publication of the Encyclicals Rerum Novarum and Quadragesimo Anno. We are happy to voice Our paternal approval of the zealous pastoral activity manifested by so many bishops and priests who have with due prudence and caution been plan-

ning and applying new methods of apostolate more adapted to modern needs. But for the solution of our present problem all this effort is still inadequate. When our country is in danger, everything not strictly necessary, everything not bearing directly on the urgent matter of unified defense, takes second place. So we must act in today's crisis. Every other enterprise, however attractive and helpful, must yield before the vital need of protecting the very foundation of the Faith and of Christian civilization. Let our parish priests, therefore, while providing of course for the normal needs of the Faithful, dedicate the better part of their endeavors and their zeal to winning back the laboring masses to Christ and to His Church. Let them work to infuse the Christian spirit into quarters where it is least at home. The willing response of the masses, and results far exceeding their expectations, will not fail to reward them for their strenuous pioneer labor.

63. But the most efficacious means of apostolate among the poor and lowly is the priest's example, the practice of all those sacerdotal virtues which We have described in Our Encyclical Ad Catholici Sacerdotii. Especially needful, however, for the present situation is the shining example of a life which is humble, poor, and disinterested, in imitation of a divine Master who could say to the world with divine simplicity: "The foxes have holes and the birds of the air nests, but the Son of Man hath not where to lay His head." A priest who is really poor and disinterested in the Gospel sense may work among his flock marvels recalling a St. Vincent de Paul, a Curé of Ars, a Cottolengo, a Don Bosco, and so many others; while an avaricious and selfish priest, as We have noted in the above-mentioned Encyclical, even though he should not plunge with Judas to the abyss of treason, will never be more than empty "sounding brass" and useless "tinkling cymbal." Too often, indeed, he will be a hindrance rather than an instrument of grace in the midst of his people. Furthermore, *where a secular priest or religious is obliged by his office to administer temporal property, let him remember that he is not only to observe scrupulously all that charity and justice prescribe, but that he has a special obligation to conduct himself in very truth as a father of the poor.*

Pius XI, Firmissimam Constantiam, November 23, 1939

23. If you truly love the laborer (and you must love him because his conditions of life approach nearer to those of the divine Master), you must assist him materially and religiously. Materially, bringing about in his favor the practice not only of commutative justice but also of social justice, that is, all those provisions which aim at relieving the condition of the proletarian; and then religiously, giving him again the religious comforts without which he will struggle in a materialism that brutalizes him and degrades him.

APOSTOLATE OF THE LAITY

St. Pius X, Il Fermo Proposito, June 11, 1905

Our Predecessor Leo XIII, of holy memory, fully perceived this, and pointed out, notably in the famous Encyclical Rerum Novarum, and in later documents, the object to which Catholic Action should be specially devoted, namely, the practical solution of the social question according to Christian principles.

Further, in order that Catholic Action may be effectual on all points, it is not enough that it be adapted to actual social needs only; it ought also to be invigorated by all the practical methods furnished at the present day by progress in social and economic studies, by experience already gained elsewhere, by the condition of civil society, and even by the public life of states. Otherwise there will be a risk of groping for a long time for new and hazardous things, while good and safe ones are ready to hand, and have been already well tried; or again, there will be the danger of proposing institutions and methods suitable, perhaps, in former times, but not understood by people of the present day; or finally, there will be the danger of stopping halfway by not using, in the measure in which they are granted, those rights of citizenship which modern constitutions offer to all, and therefore also to Catholics.

Pius XI, Firmissimam Constantiam, November 23, 1937

19. Catholic Action should never take responsibility in matters that are purely technical, financial, or economic because such matters lie outside the scope and purpose of Catholic Action.

Pius XI, Quadragesimo Anno

19. It is not surprising, therefore, that many scholars, both priests and laymen, led especially by the desire that the unchanged and unchangeable teaching of the Church should meet new demands and needs more effectively, have zealously undertaken to develop, with the Church as their guide and teacher, a social and economic science in accord with the conditions of our time.

20. And so, with Leo's Encyclical pointing the way and furnishing the light, a true Catholic social science has arisen, which is daily fostered and enriched by the tireless efforts of those chosen men whom We have termed auxiliaries of the Church. They do not, indeed, allow their science to lie hidden behind learned walls. As the useful and well-attended courses instituted in Catholic universities, colleges, and seminaries, the social congresses and "weeks" that are held at frequent intervals with most successful results, the study groups that are promoted, and finally the timely and sound publications that are disseminated everywhere and in every possible way, clearly show, these men bring their science out into the full light and stress of life.

141. For We are now confronted, as more than once before in the history of the Church, with a world that in large part has almost fallen back into paganism. That these whole classes of men may be brought back to Christ whom they have denied, we must recruit and train from among them, themselves, auxiliary soldiers of the Church who know them well and their minds and wishes, and can reach their hearts with a tender brotherly love. *The first and immediate apostles to the workers ought to be workers; the apostles to those who follow industry and trade ought to be from among them themselves.*

142. *It is chiefly your duty, Venerable Brethren, and of your clergy, to search diligently for these lay apostles both of workers and of employers, to select them with prudence, and to train and instruct them properly.*

Pius XI, On Atheistic Communism

55. To give to this social activity a greater efficacy, it is necessary to promote a wider study of social problems in the light of the doctrine of the Church and under the aegis of her constituted authority. If the manner

of acting of some Catholics in the social-economic field has left much to be desired, this has often come about because they have not known and pondered sufficiently the teachings of the Sovereign Pontiffs on these questions. *Therefore, it is of the utmost importance to foster in all classes of society an intensive program of social education adapted to the varying degrees of intellectual culture.* It is necessary with all care and diligence to procure the widest possible diffusion of the teachings of the Church, even among the working classes. The minds of men must be illuminated with the sure light of Catholic teaching, and their wills must be drawn to follow and apply it as the norm of right living in the conscientious fulfillment of their manifold social duties. Thus they will oppose that incoherence and discontinuity in Christian life which We have many times lamented. *For there are some who, while exteriorly faithful to the practice of their religion, yet in the field of labor and industry, in the professions, trade, and business, permit a deplorable cleavage in their conscience, and live a life too little in conformity with the clear principles of justice and Christian charity.* Such lives are a scandal to the weak, and to the malicious a pretext to discredit the Church.

56. In this renewal the Catholic press can play a prominent part. Its foremost duty is to foster in various attractive ways an ever better understanding of social doctrine. It should, too, supply accurate and complete information on the activity of the enemy and the means of resistance which have been found most effective in various quarters. It should offer useful suggestions and warn against the insidious deceits with which Communists endeavor, all too successfully, to attract even men of good faith.

64. *Catholic Action is in effect a social apostolate also,* inasmuch as its object is to spread the Kingdom of Jesus Christ not only among individuals, but also in families and in society. It must, therefore, make it a chief aim to train its members with special care and to prepare them to fight the battles of the Lord. This task of formation now more urgent and indispensable than ever, which must always precede direct action in the field, will assuredly be served by *study circles, conferences, lecture courses, and the various other activities undertaken with a view to making known the Christian solution of the social problem.*

65. The militant leaders of Catholic Action, thus properly prepared and armed, will be the first and immediate apostles of their fellow workmen. They will be an invaluable aid to the priest in carrying the torch of truth, and in relieving grave spiritual and material suffering, in many sectors where inveterate anticlerical prejudice or deplorable religious indifference has proved a constant obstacle to the pastoral activity of God's ministers. In this way they will collaborate, under *the direction of especially qualified priests,* in that work of spiritual aid to the laboring classes on which We set so much store, because it is the means best calculated to save these Our beloved children, from the snares of communism.

66. In addition to this individual apostolate which, however useful and efficacious, often goes unheralded, *Catholic Action must organize propaganda, on a large scale, to disseminate knowledge of the fundamental principles on which, according to the pontifical documents, a Christian Social Order must build.*

68. We are thinking likewise of those associations of workmen, farm-

ers, technicians, doctors, employers, students, and others of like character, groups of men and women who live in the same cultural atmosphere and share the same way of life. Precisely these groups and organizations are des-

tined to introduce into society that order which We have envisaged in our Encyclical Quadragesimo Anno, and thus to spread in the vast and various fields of culture and labor the recognition of the Kingdom of Christ.

Pius XII, Letter to Semaines Sociales, July 18, 1947

The present hour, from whatever standpoint it is viewed, summons the faithful to exert their every energy to render to the social teaching of the Church its maximum of efficiency and of practical results. It is an illusion to imagine, as some people do, that anticlericalism and anti-Catholic fanaticism can be disarmed by confining the principles of Catholicism

within the domain of private life. This "minimalist" attitude would, on the contrary, merely afford new pretexts to the enemies of the Church. Catholics will maintain and improve their positions in proportion to the courage they display in converting their intimate convictions into action over the entire range of life, public as well as private.

Pius XII, To World Congress of the Lay Apostolate, October 14, 1951

The apostolate of the laity, in its proper sense, is without doubt to a large extent organized in Catholic Action and in other forms of apostolic activity approved by the Church; but, apart from these, there can be, and

actually are, lay apostles, those men and women who see all the good to be done and the possibilities and means of doing it; and they do it with only one desire; the winning of souls to truth and grace.

Pius XII, To World Union of Catholic Women's Organizations, September 29, 1957

Individual initiative has its place along with action that is organized and applied through various associations. This initiative of the lay apostolate is perfectly justified even without a prior explicit "mission" from

the hierarchy. The mother of a family who devotes herself to charitable works, the one who shows courageous fidelity in guarding her dignity or the moral climate of her environment, all practice a real apostolate.

WORK WITH NON-CATHOLICS

Pius XI, On Atheistic Communism

72. But in this battle joined by the powers of darkness against the very idea of Divinity, it is Our fond hope that, besides the host which glories in the name of Christ, all those —

and they comprise the overwhelming majority of mankind — who still believe in God and pay Him homage may take a decisive part.

Pius XII, To Sacred College of Cardinals, June 2, 1948

Only on the principles of Christianity and in accord with its spirit can social reforms, called for imperatively by the necessities and aspirations of our times, be carried out. They demand from some the spirit of renunciation and sacrifice, from others the sense of responsibility and endurance, from everybody hard and strenuous work.

Wherefore we turn to the Catholics of the whole world, exhorting them not to be satisfied with good intentions and fine projects, but to proceed courageously to put them into practice. *Neither should they hesitate to join forces with those who, remaining outside their ranks, are nonetheless in agreement with the social teaching of the Catholic Church and are disposed to follow the road she has marked out, which is not the* road of violent revolution but of experience that has stood the test, and of energetic resolution.

Pius XII, To the International Movement of Catholic Intellectuals, April 25, 1957

It is desirable, therefore, that Catholics co-operate in any undertaking which bases its activity on a theoretical and practical respect for the data of the Natural Law.

In any group which aspires to a humanitarian goal, they will find men of generosity and superior character, who can rise above material considerations and understand that any truly collective destiny for mankind presupposes the absolute value of the persons who compose it and the existence, outside of time, of that true society of which a world community can only be a reflection and resemblance.

Pius XII, Christmas Message, 1957

There are no territories that are out of bounds, no directions forbidden for a Christian's activity. No field of endeavor, no institution, no exercise of power can be excluded for those who are co-operating with God in maintaining the divine order and the harmony of the world.

This intervention that We have been discussing does not mean or imply an activity cut off from that of others or jealous of the contributions made by others. We have often before said that Catholics can and must work with others as long as the activity of these people and the understanding reached with them is really benefiting the order and harmony of the world. Before undertaking work of this kind though, Catholics should be definite about their own capacities and aims; this means that they should be prepared spiritually and professionally for the work they are undertaking. Otherwise they will be of no positive help to the common cause, and much less will they bring it the precious gift of eternal truth; the results will obviously be to the detriment of the honor due to Christ and to the detriment of their own souls.

Granted all this, it is not right for anyone to see a supposed spirit of "intolerance" or separatism, the "ghetto" mentality as it is often called, in the desire of Catholics to have schools, education, and the formation of youth on a Christian basis, or in their desire to set up Catholic professional organizations and to favor an organized influence of Christian principles in the fields of politics and labor, in cases where tradition and circumstances make it desirable.

THIS concluding chapter is more than a summary of the chapters preceding. The purpose rather is to integrate Catholic social principles and Catholic social action. We seek to present our beliefs about the proper goals of society, and our views as to the proper steps to be taken toward these goals.

THE GOAL SOUGHT

Economic Society. In the most general terms, we seek an economic society which ministers to the needs of man. It should serve as the material basis for the protection of individual freedom and dignity, a sound family life, and properly organized civic society. Negatively, we should root out evils and abuses which threaten human values. Positively, we should strive for such economic balance that social institutions will of their own nature tend to promote the general welfare. These positive and negative aspects are rarely separated in practice, any more than moral reform is likely in the concrete to be distinct from institutional reform. We should remove evils by replacing them with healthy social institutions. We replace, not merely displace.

In a proper social order, the institutions of economic life should promote both the immediate interests of the affected parties and the common good of all. This means a society organized along lines of collaboration and co-operation, rather than conflict and strife. Against individualism, we bespeak the need for organization in labor, business, industry, finance, trades, professions, and farming. Well organized groups must, above all, seek the common interests of all concerned in the several occupations, subordinating such concerns, however, to the general welfare of the body public. In practice, this means labor-management co-operation in industry, organized action in business and the professions to place proper limits upon competition, and collaborative action by all economic groups to handle on the highest level common problems such as depressions and unemployment. In such a society, there will be a legitimate place for special-interest groups, such as labor unions or employer associations. But their activities will likewise be subject to the demands of the common good, and should be ultimately subordinate in importance to the common-interest groups.

As a foundation for a collaborative society, there should be diffusion of economic power. This is to be sought by three main methods: encouragement of widespread ownership of productive property; the development of a partnership atmosphere between labor and management; and the transferences of many functions, now assumed by government as a result of default by private groups, into the hands of quasi-public common-interest groups in business, industry, finance, trade, the professions, and farming. Diffusion of power will check collectivist trends which threaten individual freedom. Collaborative action for the general welfare means exercise of social responsibility by free individuals and groups, thus avoiding the danger of individualism and selfish atomization of society. In this social order the first duty of government will be to promote the aims outlined above. Then the state, freed from complex problems of detailed regulation, will more efficiently perform those duties which belong to it alone, encouraging, directing, or restraining the actions of lesser groups in the interests of the community.

Through common action, the various economic groups will seek the most efficient use of natural resources and, as a result, a national standard of living adequate to meet human needs. Production will be organized in a rational fashion, so that labor productivity will be enhanced and workers can earn a family living wage. Sound methods of distribution and other devices should keep the level of production reasonably constant, with a long-range trend toward higher output, thus avoiding depressions and unemployment. Many men will then have the independence which comes with the ownership of productive wealth. Millions more, who are wage earners, will have security in employment and dignity in work. Such a well-organized society could gradually clear up social problems in regard to housing, medical care, unsuitable employment of women and children, and even the economic factors entering into racial and other forms of discrimination. With material needs thus taken care of, man would have the opportunity to devote more time to the cultural and spiritual side of his nature.

Means Used. The fundamental means for achieving this goal involve a combination of moral reform and institutional change. We use the phrase moral reform in the broader sense, including a replacement of secularism by the restoration of God to His proper place in society; by **working against selfishness, greed, avarice, and unsound ambition for**

power, with the aim of making social justice and social charity dominant forces in economic life; and by using all the resources of the Church in raising man to God, so that thereby he may be truly human. But at the same time we seek to infuse the social virtues into the institutions of economic society, so that organized groups will collaborate for the common interests of their occupation and the general good of all. This means that men of good will should strive to influence their economic environment, even aspiring to positions of leadership, so that the truth of Christ will permeate these groups. "The kingdom of heaven is like unto a leaven."

In carrying out this program, the Church has a great duty of education and inspiration. In the first place, it must train and inspire its own sons to think clearly and soundly in social matters. More than this, they should be given the flaming zeal of apostles, so that they will influence others according to their stations in life. Nor should the Church overlook the opportunity of direct influence on those who do not accept its discipline. Men of good will are looking for the truth. They will not reject our message, if it is properly presented to them.

It may be necessary to distinguish between long-range and short-term objectives in working out a program of social reform. Once the desired goal is seen clearly, we must appraise the existing social order and evaluate it in terms of the ideal. Undoubtedly the result of such study will be mixed. Areas of injustice and selfish individualism will be found. Here stern measures must be taken to secure justice for workers, farmers, small businessmen, or others who are victims of economic aggression. In other regions we will find much good will and high aspiration. This must be encouraged, nurtured, guided, and integrated into a sound pattern of common welfare. Much of the economy will be found in an intermediate position — confused, uncertain, and groping. Here we can offer an outlook which some will eagerly accept and others will at least examine, sometimes skeptically, sometimes with a feeling of desperate hope. We will have enemies in our crusade. Some will be from the reactionary right, seeking to go back to nineteenth-century *laissez faire*. Others will be liberals or even radicals of the left, who seek a collectivist or at least an excessively centralized economy. Fortunately, the influence of extremists is usually slight, if only the great intermediate mass can be given a sense of unity and direction. The Church can meet this challenge, if we have the zeal and energy to put our own ideals into effect.

THE TASK OF THE CHURCH

Social Education Needs. The first task of the Church must include an intensified study of the social problem and the training of its members in sound Christian ideals in relation to economic life. In general, education must be the prelude to action. This does not of necessity involve chronological priority, in the sense that social action must remain dormant for twenty years until we have finished our task of education. There is such a thing as education through action. Again, we can use our present trained resources, while seeking a broader program of indoctrination. But, generally speaking, we will not have much influence until our own thinking is clarified, a large body of clergy trained in the social field, our laity in turn instructed in schools and through adult-education devices, and all groups inspired with the zeal to permeate social life with justice and charity.

We need more study in the social field. The goal should be a large corps of priests and laymen, trained to high scientific excellence in the fields of economics or sociology, and equally conversant with the social ethics of the Church. It would be tragic if the social encyclicals were misapplied through shoddy economic thinking. It would be equally calamitous, were our experts in social science to ignore the place of ethics and religion in setting goals and determining values in this field. There is need for further clarification in matters of social ethics. Obligations and objectives should be made as precise as possible in terms of modern conditions. But sound principles must be applied with exactitude and with full knowledge of the scientific and practical problems involved. We stultify ourselves if we give, as an application of Catholic social theory, a program based on unsound economic analysis. Nor is it a practical solution of this difficulty to say: Let the theologians and economists consult. Men trained exclusively in either discipline find it difficult to understand the problems of the other science. The only feasible approach is to have a sufficient number of men who are experts in both fields. Such men can write for theologians in their language and for economists or sociologists in terms which carry meaning and conviction.

The training of these experts should be primarily the duty of our colleges and universities and of the religious communities or other authorities who direct them. This is not an advocacy of inbreeding. On the contrary, it would be desirable that some priests get their Ph.D. in economics at a high-class secular university and then an S.T.D. at some Catholic university. But Catholic schools might well require for their degrees in the social sciences a knowledge of social ethics as well as technical competence in the specific discipline involved. The idea of theology courses for laymen, now happily taking root, might furnish an opportunity for our lay professors to acquire a high degree of competence in both fields. Our schools might subsidize such courses and consider this training in offering academic advancement in the social sciences. The Catholic Economic Association, the Catholic Theological Society, and the American Catholic Sociological Society could be important factors in stimulating these programs.

Training the Clergy. The next step, again logically rather than chronologically, is the training of the clergy. What is needed here, more than anything else, is to capture the sense of urgency contained in papal writings on the subject. It is difficult to reconcile the quotations given at the head of this chapter and elsewhere in this book with the uneven and haphazard courses offered in many seminaries. Too often the only training offered is in connection with the moral theology course in justice. The textbooks used are frequently antiquated in regard to social problems and, at times, the professors do not have the technical competence to supplement them. Regardless of this fact, it is doubtful that any incidental training in connection with the treatise on justice meets adequately the needs of the times and the commands of the popes.

For a priest to speak with even minimum assurance in this field, it would seem that at least four courses are necessary, dealing with economics, sociology, Catholic social principles, and Catholic social action. The first two could be offered in the philosophy section and the latter two given at the theology levels, with social action studied at the same time that pastoral theology is taken. Such a program would not interfere with adequate training in philosophy, dogmatic and moral theology, Sacred Scripture, canon law, and church history. Few seminaries confine their students only to these last-named courses. Most of them offer other subjects, suitable in another age, but less vital today than a careful training in social problems. Secondary studies of this nature might well yield place in these days to the social sciences. The need is equally great for religious as for diocesan priests. Even students for the foreign missions find that in most mission regions social problems are pressing concerns. If present professors are not trained to handle social subjects, there are abundant opportunities for summer courses in the field.

We cannot wait for a new generation of priests adequately trained by the seminaries. There is need for courses to be given to men already ordained. Larger dioceses, particularly in industrial areas, could spare one or two priests to get an M.A. or Ph.D. in economics or sociology. Both large and small dioceses could give interested priests the opportunity for six weeks at the Institute of Catholic Social Studies, at the Catholic University Summer School. If 3 per cent of the clergy had such training, a vigorous program of social action would be feasible. Finally, there is need for some instruction for priests who will not have the opportunity to leave the diocese for study. This would call for social action schools, lasting from two weeks to a month, held in one or more large cities of a diocese.

Priests could attend such schools without leaving their parishes overnight. They would receive a minimum training, enabling them to co-operate more readily with diocesan social action programs staffed by men who had a more extensive preparation. Teachers in these diocesan courses could be obtained from local colleges and universities, from religious orders, or from nationally recruited staffs who would tour the country. If held during the summer, they could command a wider variety of trained teachers from other regions, but it may often be feasible to have such schools throughout the year, with experts who are not confined to teaching duties. A large-scale program of this nature would call for sacrifices on the part of all concerned, but the results would be worth the effort. Diocesan schools or even one-day meetings also serve as recruiting agencies for priests who desire more thorough training in these subjects.

Training the Laity. A trained clergy could give moral instructions to the laity in social matters. The task of social education of the laity must be carried out on many levels. In the first place, there should be a social emphasis in our schools. The task of preparing a curriculum for this purpose has been brilliantly achieved for elementary schools by the Commission on American Citizenship, at the Catholic University. The Commission is currently proceeding with the high school curriculum. Moreover, many of the more recent Catholic textbooks in social sciences and in religion bring the Church teaching on social questions to high school students. Indeed, the problem now is to train teachers to use the newer texts in an adequate manner. Social institutes for teachers as well as for the clergy are a pressing need.

On the other hand, our social program has been quite uneven in colleges, universities, and professional schools. Many Catholic colleges require

all students to study ethics, but not all offer courses in social ethics and
the papal encyclicals. The ideal would be a required course in Catholic
social principles to be taken by all students in Catholic colleges. This
should be supplemented in professional schools by a special course applying these principles to the needs of doctors, lawyers, businessmen, teachers,
and even chemists and engineers. It often happens that engineers or similar technicians advance to managerial positions in industry. Accordingly,
they should receive the same social training offered (if the ideal were
realized) in schools of business and commerce. Quite apart from future
business or professional opportunities, our Catholic college graduates normally attain to some position of leadership or civic responsibility. They
need commensurate social training.

Once again, however, we cannot wait for a new generation to emerge
from the schools. The social problem is with us today. Hence there is need
for general and specialized adult social education. This involves use of all
the media for adult education, such as lectures, forums, schools, discussion
and study clubs, the radio, the press, sermons, and similar devices. Nearly
all the techniques named have been mentioned explicitly in papal encyclicals in connection with the social training of the laity. Moreover, there
is an important place for specialized forms of adult education. These
would include labor schools and forums for employers. Likewise, farmers
and all the various professions should be reached, preferably through Catholic organizations in each field. In this way, Catholic laymen would be
trained and inspired to the work of the apostolate, so vitally needed if we
are to permeate our society with justice and charity. This training could
be given by parish priests, by diocesan social action groups, and by various
specialized groups of Catholic action. Whether the work be done by older
groups, such as the Confraternity of Christian Doctrine and various Catholic societies, or by newer groups such as the Young Christian Workers
and similar Jocist-inspired movements or the Christopher movement, the
important point is that it be done. Experience will determine which techniques insure the best results. In all likelihood, it will be found that any
of several approaches may be equally successful. The main point is to
keep the goal clear: the thorough training of the laity in the social teaching of the Church, so that they will be apostles in their respective fields
of work.

As the work progresses, the need will be felt for various teaching aids,
such as simple books, pamphlets, specialized studies, films, radio scripts,
and the like. We have adequate resources in the way of trained personnel

to meet these needs. Here the main problem will be one of co-ordination and direction of activity. This should be a challenge to national Catholic groups, such as learned societies in the social field and the various departments and affiliated organizations of the National Catholic Welfare Conference. These national groups could visualize needs and map out a suitable program. The execution of these writings and related projects could then be entrusted to teachers, specialists in religious orders, and lay experts in various walks of life. For current applications, Catholic periodicals and newspapers would be of service. Ultimately it would be desirable to set up a national research and information service, as has already been done in the social field by several Protestant groups. We would then be doing a full job of teaching and applying the social principles of the Church in the light of current problems.

INFLUENCE ON AMERICAN ECONOMIC LIFE

Principles. Since Catholics are a minority in this country, the question might legitimately be asked: Could our social program affect American economic life? In reply to this query, there are solid reasons to feel that we may be influential. Some may be prejudiced against our ideas in view of their source, but those ideas, properly presented, should carry considerable appeal on the basis of intrinsic merit. Here is a middle ground between statism and individualism which should be acceptable to those who are groping for sound solutions. Moreover, Catholics are not seeking their own selfish interests in promoting these ideals. We would gain by their adoption only to the extent that we participate in the public economic good and share the common benefits accruing to everyone.

We should not meet opposition from Jewish or Protestant religious groups, since we have often discussed social questions with such groups in a friendly and harmonious atmosphere. There will be, of course, objections to any Church organization's mingling in the economic field, but this type of prejudice is now lessening among businessmen. Many are more receptive than formerly to the notion that religion can offer a positive contribution to the world of affairs. Accordingly, there is no inherent reason why the Catholic social program would not be of service to the general American public. Our task is to present our views in the proper language and with arguments designed to convince those not of our faith. We ask them to accept our principles, not because they are Catholic, but because they are true.

In the action field, Catholic lay apostles and priests engaged in social action will be working side by side with businessmen, industrialists, workers, professional men, and farmers — all men of varying principles and religious convictions. Our task will be to use the diverse techniques of influence and persuasion, adapted to concrete situations, to bring about a more social attitude in particular environments. In doing this, it is necessary to have both a clear view of long-range aims and sound ideas as to immediate objectives. The latter will normally be controlled by the former. Short-range programs should lead to the ultimate goal, although at times the course may be indirect and devious. Thus, justice may call for social legislation as the means for meeting a particular problem, although in the long run we may aim to decentralize economic authority and remove many regulatory burdens from government. Prudence and good sense will dictate the answers in this field.

Concrete Steps.   One of the first problems to be met is the establishment of justice where injustice prevails today. It may sometimes happen that good results may be secured by relatively direct and isolated action. This is the case where the evil in question is likewise isolated. An example would be exploitation of workers by a single employer, motivated by selfishness rather than driven to such an extreme by unfair competition. Here the unionization of workers would be the obvious answer. But, in other cases, a wage problem may be industry-wide. The remedies may range from extensive organization and minimum-wage legislation to even drastic measures in the case of sick industries. In most cases, it is necessary for economic groups to organize so as to meet their common problems and needs. Such organization in the United States is fairly well advanced, even though there are areas where labor, business, or similar groups are not adequately united. Without overlooking the need for promoting unions or business or professional associations, the major task ahead is the encouragement of common-interest in contrast to special-interest groups.

Here we face a choice between creating new organizations or transforming existing ones. As a rule, the latter approach is preferable. It is usually easier to adapt and modify what already exists than to promote something entirely new. Hence the immediate task is to minimize selfishness and stimulate concern for the common good in present-day trade unions, employers' associations, professional groups, and farmers' organizations. This is a task of education and persuasion. Thus, to promote labor-management co-operation, case histories of successful plans should be studied with great care. An effort should be made to draw general principles from these cases and to apply the principles to immediate problems in particular plants or industries. Both groups should be persuaded that it is to their common interest to find means of working together on mutual problems. In such instances, it is often helpful to work from the problem to the solution, rather than to propose ready-made solutions at the beginning. Here the clergy and trained laymen can perform valuable functions, not only as teachers of these ideals, but also as mediators in the effort to restore trust where hostility has prevailed.

The methods used on the local level may also be applied nationally. To the extent that we can influence national organizations of economic groups, directly as a Church, through our trained laity, or merely by the force of sound ideas, we can promote the cause of unity and collaboration. Here likewise, the problem approach is preferable to the blueprint technique. All economic groups are interested in higher standards of living, steady and full employment, maintenance of individual freedom, and avoidance of depressions. Unceasing efforts should be made to promote common discussion of common problems, in the hope of gradually enlarging the area of agreement. Many will still seek selfish, short-term interests, but the overwhelming importance of the problems listed should conduce to sober thought and concern over long-range results. On this level likewise, the Church can exercise an important mission of mediation and conciliation. This is best done when our representatives gain the confidence of all groups because they recognize our competence, integrity, and sincere interest in the general welfare. The mediation approach is particularly valuable for toning down hostility based on past conflicts and securing the abandonment of positions held through stubborn adherence to previous stands.

What began as conferences or discussions of immediate problems on local, industrial, regional, or national levels could, with the passage of time, develop into firm institutions designed to seek the common good in each area. Successful handling of particular issues leads to increased confidence and a broadening of the area of mutuality. All would work toward the common objective of steadily increasing production and employment. There might still be special-interest conflicts over the distribution of the national product. Even here, however, the degree of strife might well be minimized. Workers' interest in higher wages is often paralleled by employers' concern for mass consumption. Employers' desire for adequate profits and opportunities for investment and expansion meets the workers' need for more jobs for an expanding population. There might be gradual agreement upon a body of sound economic principles which all groups would accept.

It is to be expected that some problems will not admit of solution in terms of mutual interest. Thus, the promotion of small business in contrast to large business, or of family farms in preference to huge commercial farms, is a matter of general national welfare rather than of mutual interest of the affected parties. This would be an appropriate field for government action, since the state is primarily concerned with the common good of the entire nation. The role of the state would not be limited merely to conflict situations. It may need to intervene so as to protect the interests of groups which are not able to defend themselves. Present reform legislation may need modification or even extension. Illustrations of this would be an upward revision of minimum-wage levels and social-security payments, with broadening of the coverage of both laws. But the general trend of government action should be in the direction of promoting self-government by the affected parties, always subject to the superior claims of the common good of all.

The promotion of collaboration will not automatically solve our problems. It is a means to an end, not an all-sufficient goal. Definite technical and economic obstacles must be removed, if we are to have full employment and increasing living standards. Some industries must increase efficiency drastically in order to pay a living wage to their workers. Farm problems will continue to be difficult. We must make many changes to encourage small business, investment, and job expansion. But these problems will be solved much more readily by collaborative effort than by conflict.

The work of the Church in encouraging a sound reorganization of society will not be easy. We face a tremendous problem of scholarship in bridging the gap between sound principles and detailed applications which will gain wide acceptance. Once this is done, the educational task of spreading these ideas will reach considerable proportions. If we are to perform the duty of mediation, we must gain influence and respect in business and professional groups comparable to that which we already have with organized labor. At the same time, we must use all available media to promote a concept of government which is neither statist nor individualist. The magnitude of these aims might well be considered overwhelming and discouraging. But we can gain courage and resolution from the powerful teachings of the popes. We might also look around the world and consider the alternatives to success in our task. With the threat of communism or statism hovering before our eyes, and knowing the fearful price in terms of souls paid for a faulty organization of society and material life, we simply cannot acknowledge the possibility of failure. Time and again the popes have called for courage and resolution in the face of the present crisis. They consider those who isolate themselves from the fray or who minimize the social duties of Christians as virtual traitors in the face of the enemy. They call us to a crusade more urgent and vital than those of old. To such a task we must give our all.

A SUMMARY

What We Seek. Justice and charity, where injustice and strife now exist. Justice sought through education, organization, and, where necessary, legislation — these are the goals.

An organic society, based on collaboration and co-operation among the social and economic groups. The common good at all levels of economic and political life, to replace class struggle and ruthless competition.

Diffusion of economic power, through widespread ownership of productive property, as the best guarantee of freedom. At the same time, co-operative action of owners and workers for the highest possible level of production and the soundest methods of distribution.

Education of Social Apostles: Information and attitudes given in both grammar and high schools, in courses based on curricula prepared by the Commission on American Citizenship. Integrally Catholic approach to a problems-of-democracy course. More specialized training for those who go to college, university, and professional schools. Intensive training for students for priesthood. Continuing education through reading of good Catholic periodicals in social field. Membership in appropriate organizations and conferences, such as Catholic Interracial Councils or National Catholic Social Action Conference. Learning through action.

Formation and Motivation: Special efforts by clergy to train lay leaders and to inspire them to zeal in doing the work of God and in helping their fellow man. Retreats and spiritual conferences for such workers. While primary work of priest is to train and inspire the laity, direct action by clergy in appropriate fields is not precluded; examples: labor mediation, guidance in race-relations problems, and Cana conferences and other family-life work. Even though motivation is supplied by principles of our Faith, it does not follow that all activities must be specifically Catholic.

Prudence should indicate which fields are better served by "neutral" or interfaith activities.

Fields of Action: Family and related problems, such as housing, slum clearance, and urban rehabilitation. Labor-management relations. Internal democracy in trade unions and seeking proper leadership for such unions. Race problems. Perfection of political life and the democratic process. International peace and international relations. The farm problem. Areas of avoidable poverty. In each case, try to study the problem locally and firsthand. Know existing efforts and organizations. Aim to be positive and constructive. Consult and co-ordinate action.

How to Influence American Life.   Develop lay apostles to work in their own fields, promoting a middle ground between statism and anarchic individualism. Give special stress to encouragement of common-interest, in contrast to special-interest, social groups. Foster harmony between capital and labor. Develop a sense of common problems and needs, to be met by joint action. Permeate existing groups with this new spirit, rather than seek to create entirely new organizations.

Stress the importance of such problems as depressions. Promote discussions with the hope that the need for common action will be felt. Advocate government intervention where necessary, but seek self-governing mutual-interest groups where possible.

Realize that attitudes and approaches are more important than techniques. Men working together for common goals will find the technical means for securing the best results. Divided they will fail. When they fail, government must step in, thus increasing the trend toward statism. The middle way is the only hope. Properly presented, it will be accepted by all but the most extreme Americans.

READINGS*

J. Messner, *Social Ethics*, pp. 262–280.
J. A. Ryan, *Social Doctrine in Action*.
O. von Nell-Breuning, *Christian Social Reorganization*, Chap. 18.
Social Order: John J. O'Connor, "Industrial-Age Apostles," November, 1952; Raymond Bernard, S.J., "The American Apostolate," March, 1953; Gerald J. Schnepp, S.M., and Thomas J. Bain, S.J., "Social Encyclicals Today," February, 1954; Cornelius A. Eller, S.J., "Social Justice and Reform," May, 1956; John L. Vessels, S.J., "The Movement for a Better World," February, 1957; Richard Arès, S.J., "Catholic Employers Meet," November, 1957; William J. Smith, S.J., "Are Labor Schools Passé?" December, 1957; "Catholic Social Action," September, 1958.

* For further readings, consult List No. 14 in the Appendix.

ANNOTATED READING LISTS

IN GENERAL, the reading lists herein presented follow the same pattern as those in *Catholic Social Principles.* A large portion of the titles is new. Those retained are given in a slightly different pattern. Except for List No. 3, the compilations follow exactly the chapter order of the book. In addition, there are more subheadings, so that specific types of books can be found more easily. Unless a subheading contains more than one distinct subject, books are listed alphabetically by author. This will simplify the task of finding a book after the reader has consulted the index.

As a rule, preference is given to more recent works. Out-of-print titles are included, for library consultation, when volumes are considered to be uniquely valuable. Every effort has been made to ascertain which books are no longer in print.

Understandably, the listing of any book is not necessarily meant as an endorsement of its contents. This is obvious in the case of works approving communism, socialism, or extreme individualism. But even in the case of authors following a Catholic or natural-law point of view, there may be interpretations or applications not accepted by the author. The principle of *libertas* for stimulating adult thinking is too important to permit spoon-feeding in bibliographies. Omissions of titles may have no significance other than to warn scholars against becoming entangled with administrative work (even though there are compensating values in overcoming any tendency toward an ivory-tower mentality).

A few select periodicals are given at the end of List No. 1. They can be helpful in supplementing and updating the compilations given here.

List No. 1.   THE SOCIAL QUESTION

This list primarily covers material treated in Chapter I, with some general source material included at the end.

Medieval Social Problems

Fanfani, A., *Catholicism, Protestantism, and Capitalism* (New York: Sheed and Ward, 1955). Traces individualist spirit to the eleventh century and shows how it led to rise of modern capitalism.

Pirenne, H., *Economic and Social History of Medieval Europe* (New York: Harcourt, 1956). Balanced in treatment. Generally favorable picture of medieval society.

Tawney, R. H., *Religion and the Rise of Capitalism* (New York: Harcourt, 1926). Brilliant in style and incisive in thought. Studies breakdown of medieval ethical controls and the rise of individualism.

Industrial Revolution and the Rise of the Modern Social Question

Cochran, T. C., *The American Business System: Historical Perspective, 1900–1955* (Cambridge: Harvard University Press, 1958). A well-written history of modern industrial America.

Dietz, F. C., *The Industrial Revolution* (New York: Holt, 1927). Brief but clear. Bibliographical note at end.

Mantoux, P., *The Industrial Revolution in the Eighteenth Century* (New York: Macmillan, 1947). Scholarly treatment of this important period.

Packard, L. B., *The Commercial Revolution* (New York: Holt, 1927). Brief but intelligent survey of the expansion of commerce prior to the Industrial Revolution.

The Social Problem in the United States

Allen, F. L., *Lords of Creation* (New York: Harper, 1935). Interesting study of business mispractice during the years of 1901–1935. Out of print.

———— *The Big Change* (New York: Harper, 1952). A survey of the radical transformation of American economic society since the time of the New Deal.

Goldman, E. F., *Rendezvous with Destiny: A History of Modern American Reform* (New York: Knopf, 1956). History of social reform in the United States, with analyses of the various "liberal" camps.

Josephson, M., *The Robber Barons* (New York: Harcourt, 1934). Studies the great American capitalists during the period of 1861–1901. An exposé of various evils which characterized this period.

Myers, G., *History of the Great American Fortunes* (New York: Modern Library, 1936). A reprint of a classic depiction of the greed and corruption attendant upon the rise of industrialism in the United States.

Schlesinger, A. M., *The Age of Roosevelt* (New York: Houghton Mifflin, 1958). Account of the background crisis that led to President Roosevelt and the New Deal.

Steffens, Lincoln, *The Autobiography of Lincoln Steffens* (New York: Harcourt, 1931). The period from Cleveland to Wilson, seen through the eyes of an acute reporter.

Wecter, D., *The Age of the Great Depression* (New York: Macmillan, 1948). A survey of the period 1929–1941. Valuable for background of the New Deal.

Current Social Issues

Burnham, J., *The Managerial Revolution* (New York: John Day, 1941). Upholds the thesis that business and government administrators are main centers of power today, displacing stockholders, labor, and voters.

Carskadon, T. R., and Soule, G., *U. S. A. in New Dimensions: The Measure and Promise of America's Resources* (New York: Macmillan, 1957). Digest of the Dewhurst study on the growth prospects of the American economy.

Clark, J. M., *Economic Institutions and Human Welfare* (New York: Knopf, 1957). In the fight for the allegiance of the uncommitted peoples of the world, we must introduce moral considerations rather than undiluted self-interest in governing our economic activities. Professor Clark's views seem to be harmonious with Catholic social teaching, although he does not always think through his ethical positions.

Dewhurst, J. F., *America's Needs and Resources: a New Survey* (New York: Twentieth Century Fund, 1955). A major study of the possibilities for raising our standards through full use of resources.

Drucker, P. F., *The New Society: The Anatomy of Industrial Order* (New York: Harper, 1950). Advocates a collaborative industrial society based on recognition of workers' dignity. Similar to the teaching of the popes on vocational order.

Fromm, E., *The Sane Society* (New York: Rinehart, 1955). Society will be sane when man becomes an end, rather than a creature of his own economic system.

Galbraith, J. K., *The Affluent Society* (Boston: Houghton Mifflin, 1958). A sharp challenge to the thesis that indefinite growth in wealth is an unmixed blessing. We need a new look at the real goals of our society. Much of this book reads like passages from Pope Pius XII.

Kirk, R., *A Program for Conservatives* (Chicago: Regnery, 1954). True conservatism should be based on spiritual values, with great respect for human rights and liberties. Centralized power may endanger these liberties.

———— *The Intelligent Woman's Guide to Conservatism* (New York: Devin-Adair, 1957). True conservatism, as distinguished from reaction, appealingly presented by one of its best apologists.

Lerner, M., *America as a Civilization* (New York: Simon & Schuster, 1958). Massive study of American culture, with a number of chapters devoted to economic and social problems.

Mayo, E., *The Social Problems of an Industrial Civilization* (Boston: Harvard Graduate School of Business Administration, 1945). Argues that our social organization has lagged behind technological progress. A very important book.

Mumford, L., *In the Name of Sanity* (New York: Harcourt, 1954). Impassioned appeal to control technological development, so that it serves man and does not act as his master.

Pieper, J., *Leisure: The Basis of Culture* (New York: Pantheon Books, 1952). Proper use of leisure can save man from being fettered to his work.

Polanyi, K., *The Great Transformation* (New York: Farrar & Rinehart, 1944). An evaluation of modern capitalism in terms of its effect on human welfare. Extensive bibliographical note.

Riesman, D., *The Lonely Crowd* (New Haven: Yale, 1950). We have become a crowd rather than a society because we lack the stabilizing force of either tradition or deep inner convictions.

———— *Faces in the Crowd* (New Haven: Yale, 1952). Series of interviews aimed to determine influence of our political structure upon the average individual.

———— *Individualism Reconsidered* (Glencoe, Ill.: Free Press, 1954). Illuminating insights into the institutions and ideas of the American people, and the reasons why we so often flounder without any strong sense of direction.

Roepke, W., *Civitas Humana* (London: William Hodge, 1948). This book criticizes collectivism and extreme individualism, proposing instead a humanism based on proper ownership and use of property. Critics differ on "Catholic" nature of this work.

────── *The Social Crisis of our Times* (Chicago: University of Chicago Press, 1950). An earlier work, with more emphasis upon criticism of capitalism and collectivism, and less elaboration upon economic humanism.

Rossiter, C., *Conservatism in America* (New York: Knopf, 1955). A plea for enlightened conservatism, combining the spiritual values of older traditions with liberal views on social reform.

Schumpeter, J. A., *Capitalism, Socialism, and Democracy* (New York: Harper, 1950). The author is pessimistic as to the possibility of capitalist survival. Discusses various forms of socialism which may succeed present-day capitalism.

Whyte, W. H., Jr., *The Organization Man* (New York: Simon and Schuster, 1956). Conformity and consistency are the main values in our society, with discussion and group action the way to get things done. An angry protest against the stifling of individuality and initiative.

Church Reaction to the Social Problem

Carlyle, R. W. and A. J., *A History of Medieval Political Theory in the West* (New York: Barnes & Noble, 1903–1936). Two non-Catholic authors devote six volumes to a documented study of medieval institutions.

Fogarty, M. P., *Christian Democracy in Western Europe* (Notre Dame, Ind.: University of Notre Dame Press, 1957). The origins and development of a movement that has contributed so much to the stability of Europe after World War II.

Hales, E. E., *The Catholic Church in the Modern World: A Survey From the French Revolution to the Present* (New York: Doubleday, 1958). Background material on Church's reaction to modern problems, with emphasis upon the political.

McEntee, G. T., *The Social Catholic Movement in Great Britain* (New York: Macmillan, 1927). English social Catholicism up to the end of World War I. Out of print.

Moody, J. N., ed., *Church and Society; Catholic Social and Political Thought and Movements, 1789–1950* (New York: Arts, Inc., 1953). A monumental study of the evolution of Catholic social and political thought in various countries. Treatment is divided according to country and region. No previous book in English has the scope and depth of this study.

Moon, P. T., *The Labor Problem and the Social Catholic Movement in France* (New York: Macmillan, 1926). Well-documented study of French social Catholicism, with reference to related movements elsewhere. Out of print.

O'Brien, G. A., *Essay on Mediaeval Economic Teaching* (New York: Longmans, 1920). The social ethics of great medieval theologians, applied to economic problems. Valuable, but out of print.

Troeltsch, E., *The Social Teaching of the Christian Churches* (New York: Macmillan, 1949). A monumental two-volume study covering the period from the Gospels to the nineteenth century.

Weber, M., *The Protestant Ethic and the Spirit of Capitalism* (New York: Scribner's, 1930). Holds that ethical teachings of Protestantism contributed to the rise of modern capitalism.

Social Ethics From Non-Catholic Sources

Boulding, K. E., *Principles of Economic Policy* (Englewood Cliffs, N. J.: Prentice-Hall, 1958). Economic policy involves moral and political as well as economic considerations. Seeks means to assure progress, stability, justice, and freedom.

Duff, E., S.J., *The Social Thought of the World Council of Churches* (New York: Association Press, 1956). Penetrating and sympathetic study by a Catholic priest of the development of social principles in various meetings of the World Council and its subordinate organs.

Mumby, D. L., *Christianity and Economic Problems* (New York: St. Martin's Press, 1958). An Anglican Scottish layman shows considerable skill in relating his religious principles to major economic problems.

National Council of Churches of Christ, series on "Ethics and Economics of Society." This series comprises ten volumes, issued from 1953 to 1958, dealing with various phases of American economic life, as seen from a religious aspect. More detailed information available from the National Council or from Harper & Brothers.

Vorspan, A., and Lipman, E. J., *Justice and Judaism* (New York: Union of American Hebrew Congregations, 1956). The authors cover a wide range of social problems, with special emphasis upon civil liberties.

Economic Source Material

Colm, G., and Geiger, T., *The Economy of the American People* (Washington: National Planning Association, 1958). A nontechnical and inexpensive study of the working of our economic system.

Coman, E. T., *Sources of Business Information* (New York: Prentice-Hall, 1949). Lists and evaluates sources of information on broad business problems. Several chapters highly useful for students of social questions.

The Economic Almanac (New York: National Industrial Conference Board, anually). Contains privately gathered statistics in addition to government figures. Glossary at end.

The Economic Report to the President (Washington: Government Printing Office, annually). These reports contain, in addition to the analyses of the Council of Economic Advisers, selected statistics on national production and income. Statistics kept current by monthly publication, *Economic Indicators*.

Harriss, C. L., *The American Economy* (Homewood, Ill.: Irwin, 1953). Economic principles and a description of the American economy, in a well-written textbook.

Samuelson, P. A., *Economics, An Introductory Analysis* (New York: McGraw-Hill, 1955). A readable text with full emphasis upon modern theories.

Statistical Abstract of the United States (Washington: Government Printing Office, annually). Basic compilation of government statistics.

Wright, D. M., *A Key to Modern Economics* (New York: Macmillan, 1954). Mature and sophisticated text on our economic system, with emphasis upon the broad forces that dominate our economy.

In addition to the books and periodicals listed above, *Social Order* is recommended as the best Catholic periodical for keeping up to date on general problems. *America, Commonweal, Ave Maria,* and *Sign* often have worthwhile material. General publications of value include *U. S. News and World Report, Business Week, Fortune, Annals of the American Academy of Political and Social Science,* and the *Industrial and Labor Relations Review. The Pope Speaks* is unique as a source of papal documents, although *The Catholic Mind* carries some addresses, in addition to other useful articles.

List No. 2.   THE CHURCH AND THE SOCIAL PROBLEM

This list consists of primary source material on Catholic Social Teaching.

Papal Social Teaching

Chinigo, M., *The Pope Speaks: the Teachings of Pope Pius XII* (New York: Pantheon, 1957). This compilation of the selected excerpts from the writings of Pope Pius XII is arranged in topical order. There is a good table of contents, but the index is only fair.

Discorsi e Radiomessagi di sua Santità Pio XII (Rome: Tipographia Poliglotta Vaticana, 1939–1959). The best single source for the complete utterances of Pope Pius XII. All documents are given in the language of the authentic original document.

Harte, T. J., *Papal Social Principles* (Milwaukee: Bruce, 1956). Summary of major papal social pronouncements of the past seventy-five years.

Husslein, J., S.J., ed., *Social Wellsprings* (Milwaukee: Bruce, 1940–1942). These two volumes contain the main social encyclicals of Popes Leo XIII and Pius XI. Paragraph numbering differs from that used in many N.C.W.C. and Paulist Press pamphlet editions of the same encyclicals.

Koenig, H. C., ed., *Principles for Peace* (Milwaukee: Bruce, 1943). Selections from papal documents dealing with peace, arranged chronologically from 1878 to 1942. Excerpts are generous and include many documents dealing with socioeconomic problems. Out of print.

Kothen, R., *L'Enseignement social de l'Église* (Louvain: Warny, 1949). A topical arrangement of excerpts from social writings of the popes, from 1878 to 1948. Introductory and explanatory material is brief but valuable.

Pollock, R. C., ed., *The Mind of Pius XII* (New York: Crown, 1955). Topically arranged excerpts from the writings of Pope Pius XII. Good selections, but sources are difficult to trace because of the method of editing.

Powers, F. J., ed., *Papal Pronouncements on the Political Order* (Westminster, Md.: Newman, 1952). A well-organized collection of crucial passages from papal documents from Leo XIII to Pius XII, covering the nature and purpose of the state, relations of Church and state, liberty and law, war and peace. Out of print.

Two Basic Social Encyclicals (New York: Benziger, 1943). Contains the Latin text and the newest English translation of *Rerum Novarum* and *Quadragesimo Anno.*

Utz, A., O.P., and Groner, J. F., O.P., *Summe Soziale Pius XII* (Fribourg, Switzerland: Paulusverlag, 1954). Comprehensive compilation of social statements by Pope Pius XII. Available also in a French translation.

Werth, A., and Mihanovich, C., *Papal Pronouncements on Marriage and the Family from Leo XIII to Pius XII (1878-1954)* (Milwaukee: Bruce, 1955). This compilation gives valuable excerpts from papal writings on the important topic of marriage and the family. Useful for students seeking accurate information without the necessity of lengthy study of original papal sources.

Other Sources

Giordani, I., *The Social Message of Jesus* (Paterson, N. J.: St. Anthony Guild Press, 1943). A volume of a trilogy dealing with origins of Catholic social thought. Out of print.

———— *The Social Message of the Early Christian Fathers* (Paterson, N. J.: St. Anthony Guild Press, 1944). A volume of a trilogy dealing with origins of Catholic social thought.

Huber, R. M., O.F.M., ed., *Our Bishops Speak* (Milwaukee: Bruce, 1952). Pastorals, statements, and occasional messages of the national hierarchy of the United States, 1919-1951.

International Union of Social Studies, *A Code of Social Principles* (Oxford, England: Catholic Social Guild, 1952). Latest edition of the well-known Malines Code, quoted freely in these pages.

List No. 3. SOCIAL ETHICS

Included here are commentaries on Catholic social principles and books dealing with social ethics and special problems in this area. Pertinent to Chapters III, IV, and VII.

General Works

Bruehl, C., *The Pope's Plan for Social Reconstruction* (New York: Devin-Adair, 1939). A somewhat philosophical discussion of the social teaching of Pope Pius XI.

Cirillo, R. R., ed., *Catholic Social Thought* (Malta: A. C. Aquilina, 1956). Various essays on social problems, written by authorities of many nations.

Clune, G., *Christian Social Reorganization* (Dublin: Browne & Nolan, 1940). A careful study of Christian social ethics as applied to economic and political life. While written for Irish readers, it has a much broader field of usefulness. Out of print.

Dempsey, B. W., *The Functional Economy* (Englewood Cliffs, N. J.: Prentice-Hall, 1958). An advanced and highly useful study of social order in the light of the American economy. The author has exceptional insight into both the social teaching of the Church and the workings of economic life.

Ford, J. C., S.J., and Kelly, G., S.J., *Contemporary Moral Theology* (Westminster, Md.: Newman, 1958). Essays on current problems in moral theology. Chapters 1-3 of Volume I deal with problems of social economics.

Lubac, H., ed., *Catholicism* (New York: Longmans, 1950). Dogmatic basis for social Catholicism. Profound doctrinal study of the solidarity of the Church.

Messner, J., *Social Ethics* (St. Louis: Herder, 1949). A learned study of social ethics with emphasis on political and economic problems. More profound than most English studies on the subject.

Mulcahy, R. E., *Readings in Economics* (Westminster, Md.: Newman, 1959). Father Mulcahy has compiled a set of readings which reflect, or are compatible with, the social teachings of the Church. Stresses Scholastic economic doctrine and the vocational order.

Nell-Breuning, O., *Reorganization of Social Economy* (Milwaukee: Bruce, 1936). A careful commentary on the general principles of *Quadragesimo Anno.* The translator, Rev. Bernard Dempsey, S.J., has given an English bibliography. Out of print.

O'Connor, D. A., *Catholic Social Doctrine* (Westminster, Md.: Newman, 1956). Largely theological and ethical in content and only partly original. Much of the work is adapted from the works of Father Gestel. No effort was made to apply the doctrine to current problems.

Pesch, H., *Lehrbuch der Nationalökonomie* (Freiburg: Herder, 1905–1924). This five-volume study is considered a definitive presentation of Catholic socioeconomic philosophy as embodied in papal encyclicals.

Sheed, F. J., *Society and Sanity* (New York: Sheed and Ward, 1953). Principles of human behavior in terms of the individual, the family, and the state. Reverence and respect for man's dignity are leading ideas in this book.

Smith, W. J., S.J., *Spotlight on Social Order* (Rochester, N. Y.: Christopher Press, 1954). The Catholic viewpoint on industrial and labor relations, with emphasis upon the Industry Council Plan.

Villain, J., S.J., *l'Enseignement social de l'Église* (Paris: Spes, 1954). Late and authoritative French commentary on Catholic social teaching.

Williams, M. J., *Catholic Social Thought* (New York: Ronald Press, 1950). Dr. Williams, a non-Catholic, tells the story of Catholic sociology, history, anthropology, economics, political science, law, and social work. The author centers his attention on the contributions of American Catholics, but does not exclude the work of Catholics in other countries.

Special Problems

Drummond, W. F., S.J., *Social Justice* (Milwaukee: Bruce, 1955). An effort to expand the concept of social justice as distinct from legal justice. Emphasis upon proper use of material goods.

Ferree, W., *The Act of Social Justice* (Dayton, Ohio: Marianist Publications, 1951). An excellent doctoral study on the nature of social justice.

Gearty, P. W., *The Economic Thought of Monsignor John A. Ryan* (Washington: Catholic University Press, 1953). Msgr. Ryan, a pioneer in American Catholic social thought, holds eclectic economic views considered most suitable for implementing ethical ideals.

Maritain, J., *The Person and the Common Good* (New York: Scribner's, 1947). The eminent French philosopher shows that society should serve the individual person and that the common good is not a totalitarian concept.

Mueller, F., *Heinrich Pesch and His Theory of Christian Solidarism* (St. Paul: College of St. Thomas, 1941). A pamphlet study of this important but little-known philosopher.

Mulcahy, R. E., S.J., *The Economics of Heinrich Pesch* (New York: Holt, 1952). Profound and sometimes abstruse, this is the first full-sized study of Pesch in English. Since many students consider him to be the father of modern Catholic social thought and the forerunner of recent papal encyclicals, the work will be valuable to scholars.

Rommen, H. A., *The Natural Law* (St. Louis: Herder, 1947). The history of natural-law ethics.

Textbooks

Brown, L. C., S.J., et al., *Social Orientations* (Chicago: Loyola University Press, 1954). Useful text on social problems connected with the family, work, and political life. Handy reference work for readers with broad social interests.

Haas, F. J., *Man and Society* (New York: Appleton-Century-Crofts, 1952). While this text deals mainly with sociology, there is considerable socio-economic emphasis. A new and completely revised edition of a standard work.

Johnston, H., *Business Ethics* (New York: Pitman, 1956). Quite valuable for its insight into current social problems and their ethical implications. Case histories are stimulating.

Kilzer, E., and Ross, E. J., *Western Social Thought* (Milwaukee: Bruce, 1954). Biographical data, works, and theories of about 200 social thinkers, starting with the early Greeks and coming down to modern times.

Mihanovich, C. S., and Schuyler, J. B., S.J., *Current Social Problems* (Milwaukee: Bruce, 1950). Economic and social problems, carefully selected, factually treated, and clearly analyzed.

Ryan, J. A., *A Living Wage; Distributive Justice; A Better Economic Order;* and *Social Doctrine in Action*. Principal works of Monsignor Ryan. All out of print.

List No. 4. INDIVIDUALISM, CAPITALISM, SOCIALISM, AND STATISM

A selected list of materials pertinent to Chapter V.

Individualism

Devane, R. S., *The Failure of Individualism* (Dublin: Browne & Nolan, 1948). Treats of religious, political, and economic individualism as the roots of modern life.

Hayek, F. A., *The Road to Serfdom* (Chicago: University of Chicago Press, 1944). This much-quoted and challenging book argues that economic planning leads of necessity to totalitarianism.

Mises, L. von, *Omnipotent Government* (New Haven: Yale, 1944). Holds that statism leads to war and destruction of liberty.

—— *Human Action* (New Haven: Yale, 1949). A plea for a free economy in contrast to a controlled system.

Neill, T. P., *The Rise and Decline of Liberalism* (Milwaukee: Bruce, 1953). In a scholarly fashion, the author traces the development of the broad movement of classical liberalism, and shows the forces which led to its current eclipse.

Sennholz, M., *On Freedom and Free Enterprise* (Princeton, N. J.: Van Nostrand, 1956). The extreme right, economic liberalism as condemned by the popes, presented in a collection of essays.

Capitalism

Griffin, C. E., *Enterprise in a Free Society* (Homewood, Ill.: Irwin, 1949). A defense of free enterprise in contrast to the welfare state.

Kelso, L. O. and Adler, M. J., *The Capitalist Manifesto* (New York: Random House, 1958). Striking defense of capitalism, with emphasis upon wide distribution of wealth. Somewhat impractical in suggesting means toward this end.

Sombart, W., *Quintessence of Capitalism* (New York: Dutton, 1915). One of the pioneer studies in the field. Authoritative. Out of print.

Sutton, F. X., et al., *The American Business Creed* (Cambridge: Harvard University Press, 1956). The ideology of American business, as revealed in public statements by national organizations representing this community.

Wright, D. M., *Capitalism* (New York: McGraw-Hill, 1951). Capitalism is dynamic and hence is likely to produce a better economic society than any alternative. An effective defense.

Socialism

Beckwith, B. P., *The Economic Theory of a Socialist Economy* (Stanford, Calif.: Stanford University Press, 1949). An effort by an advocate of socialism to spell out how a socialist economy could work.

Eastman, M., *Reflections on the Failure of Socialism* (New York: Devin-Adair, 1955). An account of how a leading American socialist gave up Marxism and embraced a conservative point of view.

Egbert, D. D., and Persons, S., eds.; Bassett, T. D. S., bibliographer, *Socialism and American Life* (Princeton, N. J.: Princeton University Press, 1952). An encyclopedia of American socialism, with various competent authors, plus a volume of bibliographical study of the movement.

Gray, A., *The Socialist Tradition* (New York: Longmans, 1946). Socialist ideas traced from Old Testament days to modern times.

Jewkes, J., *Ordeal by Planning* (New York: Macmillan, 1948). Opposes all centralism, whether by business or by government. Moderately liberal.

Lange, O., and Taylor, F. M., *On the Economic Theory of Socialism* (Minneapolis: University of Minnesota Press, 1938). Argues that economic calculation and free consumer choice are possible under socialism.

Statism

Florence, P. S., *Industry and the State* (New York: Rinehart, 1957). British experience of state controls, showing dangers of government interference in areas best left to private initiative.

Friedrich, C. J., ed., *Totalitarianism* (Cambridge: Harvard University Press, 1954). Twenty-one papers on seven major aspects of totalitarianism. Many of the authors have had firsthand experience with the evil.

Friedrich, C. J., and Brzezinski, Z. K., *Totalitarian Dictatorship and Autocracy* (Cambridge: Harvard University Press, 1957). Penetrating study of dictatorship, based primarily upon communist techniques.

Metz, H. W., and Thomson, C. A. H., *Authoritarianism and the Individual* (Washington: Brookings Institution, 1950). The impact of authority upon the freedom of the individual is studied, with special reference to historical background as well as modern statism.

List No. 5.   COMMUNISM

Reading list for Chapter VI.

Sources Favorable to Communism

Lenin, V. I., *Left Wing Communism: An Infantile Disorder* (New York: International Publishers) and *Religion* (New York: International Publishers, 1933). Two brochures by the major modern theoretician of communism.

Marx, K., *Capital* (New York: Modern Library reprint). An inexpensive edition of the first authentic exposition of communism.

Marx, K., and Engels, F., *Communist Manifesto* (New York: Appleton-Century-Crofts, 1955). The classic statement of communist aims, written over a century ago.

Peters, J., *The Communist Party: A Manual on Organization* (New York: Workers' Library, 1936). A basic document by a Comintern agent, telling communists how to organize most effectively. Out of print.

Stalin, J., *Foundations of Leninism* (New York: International Publishers, 1939). The Stalinist interpretation of Leninism. One of the basic texts for communists.

General and Historical Works

Almond, G., et al., *The Appeals of Communism* (Princeton, N. J.: Princeton University Press, 1954). Sociological study of 221 former communists from four countries. Suggests emotional problems as important factors in adherence to this movement.

D'Arcy, M. C., *Communism and Christianity* (Harmondsworth, Middlesex: Penguin Books, 1956). The contrast between communism and Christianity is noted. The author stresses their different philosophies of life and the resultant codes of conduct.

Djilas, M., *The New Class* (New York: Praeger, 1957). Masterful dissection of communism, showing that its failures are inherent in the system.

Hunt, R. N. C., *The Theory and Practice of Communism* (New York: Macmillan, 1957). A well-written and orderly study of communist theory and its practical working.

Hyde, D., *One Front Across the World* (Westminster, Md.: Newman, 1956). Account of the conflict between Christianity and communism in the Far East. The author is a Catholic who formerly had lapsed into communism.

La Pira, G., et al., *The Philosophy of Communism* (New York: Fordham University Press, 1952). Twenty-two papers on various aspects of communist philosophy and also upon the practical carrying out of the system.

Orwell, G., *Animal Farm* (New York: Harcourt, 1946). Satire describing the transformation of communism into an exploitive system, in terms of a fable of animal life. A highly superior treatment.

——— *Nineteen Eighty-Four* (New York: Harcourt, 1949). The impact of statism on human personality is discussed in novel form.

Overstreet, H., and Overstreet, B., *What We Must Know About Communism* (New York: Norton, 1958). Written primarily for the liberal who is sceptical about the agitation against communism. Shows the menace of this system both in its international and domestic aspects.

Possony, S., *Century of Conflict* (Chicago: Regnery, 1953). A scholarly study of the various forces which led to the communist rise to power in the modern world.

Selznick, P., *The Organizational Weapon* (New York: McGraw-Hill, 1952). Emphasizes seizure of power at all levels as a basic tactic of communism. An unusually valuable work.

Seton-Watson, H., *From Lenin to Malenkov* (New York: Praeger, 1953). A comparative analysis of world communist movements and their interrelationships, one with the other. His analysis of different developments shows unusual insight into the movement.

Sheed, F. J., *Communism and Man* (New York: Sheed and Ward, 1939). The nature of communism and the nature of man are compared, showing that they do not harmonize. Out of print.

Shub, D., *Lenin, A Biography* (New York: Doubleday, 1948). Penetrating study, revealing much of the psychology and tactics of communism. Abridged edition, New American Library.

Soviet Communism

Bauer, R. A., Inkeles, A., and Kluckhohn, C., *How the Soviet System Works: Cultural, Psychological, and Social Themes* (Cambridge: Harvard University Press, 1956). Social relationships in a communist society, as told by hundreds of refugees interviewed. Especially enlightening in classifying causes of unrest.

Bauer, R. A. and Wasiolek, E., *Nine Soviet Portraits* (New York: Wiley, 1955). Conclusions from mass interviews with Russian refugees. Valuable as a corrective to stereotypes often given in our press.

Berliner, J. S., *Soviet Economic Aid to Underdeveloped Countries* (New York: Praeger, 1958). Factual information on a vital aspect of Soviet foreign policy.

Counts, G. S., *The Challenge of Soviet Education* (New York: McGraw-Hill, 1957). Critical survey of strength and weaknesses of Soviet education.

Dallin, D., *The Changing World of Soviet Russia* (New Haven: Yale, 1956). Background information on internal conditions in the U.S.S.R. up to 1955.

Fainsod, M., *How Russia is Ruled* (Cambridge: Harvard University Press, 1953). Sociological-historical study of the power system in the Soviet Union. Explains necessity for centralization and the glorification of rulers.

Gunther, J., *Inside Russia* (New York: Harper, 1958). Reasonably accurate account of Russia as of 1957.

Gurian, W., et al., eds., *Soviet Imperialism, its Origins and Tactics: a Symposium* (Notre Dame, Ind.: University of Notre Dame Press, 1953). Seven distinguished authors present facets of the Soviet problems. They try to differentiate between communist and Russian elements in Soviet policy, and they discuss the difficult nationality problem in the U.S.S.R.

Hazard, J. N., *The Soviet System of Government* (Chicago: University of Chicago Press, 1957). Discussion of Soviet government as it actually operates, with due recognition of possible instability because of army or intelligentsia dissatisfaction.

Kelsen, H., *The Communist Theory of Law* (New York: Praeger, 1954). Since there is little law in a dictatorship, there seems to be no need for a book such as this. But the author shows up the poverty of Soviet jurists and thus strengthens the case against the regime.

Korol, A., *Soviet Education for Science and Technology* (New York: Wiley, 1957). Balanced and critical examination of Soviet educational system, noting its narrow aims as well as its impressive gains.

Kulski, W. W., *The Soviet Regime: Communism in Practice* (Syracuse: Syracuse University Press, 1956). This monumental study can serve as a one-volume encyclopedia of communist practice in the Soviet Union. It does not cover such changes as followed the death of Stalin, but it remains a uniquely valuable work.

Levine, I. R., *Main Street, U.S.S.R.* (Garden City, N. Y.: Doubleday, 1959). A well-known radio correspondent offers a lively and informative story of life in the Soviet Union. Replete with telling anecdotes.

Meissner, B., *The Communist Party of the Soviet Union: Party Leadership, Organization and Ideology* (New York: Praeger, 1956). Since the Communist Party rules the Soviet Union, under the control of its leaders, it is important to have this careful study of its functioning.

Schwartz, H., *Russia's Soviet Economy* (New York: Prentice-Hall, 1954). An objective and scholarly analysis of industry, agriculture, and finance in the Soviet Union, supplemented by the historical background of the Russian economy.

Communism in Europe and Asia

Borkenau, F., *European Communism* (New York: 1953). One of Europe's leading authorities examines the state of communism in the principal countries of Europe.

Dallin, D. J., *The Rise of Russia in Asia* (New Haven: Yale, 1949). Emphasis upon traditional Russian interest in Far East. Useful insights into fall of China.

Kolarz, W., *Russia and Her Colonies* (New York: Praeger, 1952). All colonies and nationality groups, except those in Asia, are discussed in this comprehensive treatment.

Rossi, A., *A Communist Party in Action* (New Haven: Yale, 1949). A profound study of the workings of a communist party, based on French experience. Applies equally well to the United States.

Rostow, W. W., et al., *The Prospects for Communist China* (New York: Wiley, 1954). A team survey of Communist China, offering considerable insight into the functioning of this monolithic state.

Tang, P. S. H., *Communist China Today: Domestic and Foreign Policies* (New York: Praeger, 1957–1958). Factual, unemotional analysis of Chinese communist leadership, politics, propaganda, social policies, and governmental machinery. Volume II contains documents pertinent to this thesis.

Walker, R. L., *China Under Communism: The First Five Years* (New Haven: Yale University Press, 1955). One of the most detailed studies ever made of the communist regime in China, showing its utter ruthlessness.

Wu, Y., *An Economic Survey of Communist China* (New York: Bookman Associates, 1956). Careful and unbiased study of the Chinese economy and the programs designed to make the People's Republic a major economic power.

Biographical and Autobiographical Material

Chambers, W., *Witness* (New York: Random House, 1952). Widely considered as the greatest American work on the communist movement. It is written with great feeling and deep insight.

Dodd, B., *School of Darkness* (New York: Kenedy, 1954). Dr. Dodd was a top educational leader for the Communist Party. Her autobiography is powerfully written and quite revealing.

Fast, H., *The Naked God* (New York: Praeger, 1957). World-renowned writer explains why he left the Communist Party.

Hicks, G., *Where We Came Out* (New York: Viking, 1954). Should be read in conjunction with *Witness*, since both books cover the same period, but with different emphasis and interpretation.

Kravchenko, V., *I Chose Freedom* (New York: Scribner's, 1946). A diplomat and industrial official describes Russian life and tells why he fled Soviet tyranny.

Leonhard, W., *Child of the Revolution* (Chicago: Regnery, 1958). Clinical autobiography of a German communist who reached high levels in the East German Party and defected in 1949. He studied in the Soviet Union and hence can give a forceful picture of how communism affected his generation.

Communism and Religion

Galter, A., *The Red Book of the Persecuted Church* (Westminster, Md.: Newman, 1957). A complete study, country by country, of the communist war on religion. Essential documentation for any extended discussion of this persecution.

Gsovski, V., et al., *Church and State Behind the Iron Curtain* (New York: Praeger, 1955). Detailed study of Church problems in Eastern European communist satellites.

Shuster, G. N., *Religion Behind the Iron Curtain* (New York: Macmillan, 1954). The author, a prominent Catholic, examines persecution of all religious faiths under communism.

Communism in America

Alexander, R. J., *Communism in Latin America* (New Brunswick, N. J.: Rutgers University Press, 1957). Excellent study of trends of communism in the nations of Latin America.

Bouscaren, A. F., *A Guide to Anti-Communist Action* (Chicago: Regnery, 1958). Suggested techniques for handling both external and internal communist threats. Seven chapters were written by well-known experts other than the author.

Budenz, L. F., *The Techniques of Communism* (Chicago: Regnery, 1954). An analytical study of the aims and methods of the Communist Party, suitable for general reading or classroom use.

Burnham, J., *The Web of Subversion* (New York: John Day, 1954). The story of communist penetration into our government, based on Senate hearings on the subject.

De Toledano, R., and Lasky, V., *Seeds of Treason* (New York: Funk & Wagnalls, 1950). A gripping account of the Hiss-Chambers episode, with an analysis of the motivation of both principals.

Hoover, J. E., *Masters of Deceit* (New York: Holt, 1958). Complete and accurate study of the communist movement in the United States in the late 1950's.

Howe, I., and Coser, L., *The American Communist Party: A Critical History, 1919–1957* (Boston: Beacon Press, 1958). Balanced and judicious study of the workings of the Communist Party in the United States.

Nolan, W. A., *Communism Versus the Negro* (Chicago: Regnery, 1951). Father Nolan tells of the unsuccessful efforts of the communists to win the allegiance of the American Negro.

Reports, Internal Security Subcommittee, Senate Judiciary Committee. Well-documented and balanced studies of American subversion.

Reports, House Committee on Un-American Activities. This controversial organization has improved the quality of its various reports starting with 1948. Actually, the earlier reports were of more value than has been generally realized. In evaluating the earlier work, a distinction should be made between full hearings and the offhand political statements which caused so much adverse reaction.

Stouffer, S. A., *Communism, Conformity, and Civil Liberties: a Cross-section of the Nation Speaks Its Mind* (Garden City, N. Y.: Doubleday, 1955). Results of an extensive survey of American public opinion regarding communism and civil liberties. Reveals that opposition to communism is often uninformed and emotional.

List No. 6 CAPITAL AND FREE ENTERPRISE

Reading list for Chapter VIII.

Special Problems

Kaplan, A. D. H., et al., *Pricing in Big Business* (Washington: Brookings Institution, 1958). The authors conclude that a variety of factors influence so-called administered prices. Attitudes range from sensitivity to competition to virtual disregard of market considerations.

Moore, W. E., *Industrial Relations and the Social Order* (New York: Macmillan, 1951). Social organization of industry and relationship of industry to society. Labor relations also discussed.

Noonan, J. T., Jr., *The Scholastic Analysis of Usury* (Cambridge: Harvard University Press, 1957). Well-written and challenging analysis of the attitudes of the medieval Churchmen. Author upsets, with proof, many theories that have become part of the literature on interest-taking.

Osborn, R. C., *Corporate Profits: War and Postwar* (Urbana: University of Illinois, 1954). Valuable facts on this controversial subject. Author concludes that profits have not risen excessively since 1940.

Business Leadership

Barnard, C. I., *The Function of the Executive* (Cambridge: Harvard University Press, 1938). Studies the techniques of business organization, with stress on the ability to develop co-operation.

Black, J. M., and Piccoli, J. G., *Successful Labor Relations for Small Business* (New York: McGraw-Hill, 1953). Useful as a reference manual both for employers and teachers in labor schools.

Planty, E. G., et al., *Training Employees and Managers for Production and Teamwork* (New York: Ronald Press, 1948). One of the most comprehensive and enthusiastic books in the field. Gives detailed suggestions for building teamwork in a plant.

Roethlisberger, F. J., *Management and Morale* (Cambridge: Harvard University Press, 1941). One of the pioneer studies in human relations, calling for co-operation between management and workers.

Ross, M. G., and Hendry, C. E., *New Understanding of Leadership* (New York: Association Press, 1957). Summary of recent research on the nature and meaning of leadership. Useful for all organizations, as well as business groups.

Tead, O., *The Art of Leadership* (New York: McGraw-Hill, 1935). Still considered a classic in its field of defining the functions of a leader.

Terry, G. R., *Principles of Management* (Homewood, Ill.: Irwin, 1956). Well-written suggestions on industrial management, with emphasis upon the human-relations approach.

Industrial Psychology and Sociology

Blum, M. L., *Industrial Psychology and Its Social Foundations* (New York Harper, 1949). The human dignity of workers and method of co-operatior. studied from a psychological aspect.

Heron, A. R., *Sharing Information with Employees* (Stanford, Calif.: Stanford University Press, 1942). First volume of a valuable trilogy on making workers effective partners in industry.

——— *Beyond Collective Bargaining* (Stanford, Calif.: Stanford University Press, 1948). Emphasizes the scores of common interests between workers and employers. Good material for industry-council study.

——— *Why Men Work* (Stanford, Calif.: Stanford University Press, 1948). Argues that workers must be given some share in managerial functions, if they are to do their best work.

Knox, J. B., *The Sociology of Industrial Relations* (New York: Random House, 1956). A simple and clear analysis of the problems posed by modern industrial relations. This textbook can be very useful to students in the labor field.

Walker, C. R., and Guest, R. H., *The Man on the Assembly Line* (Cambridge: Harvard University Press, 1952). The authors conclude, from case studies, that monotony is unavoidable in mass production, but that higher wages induce men to take such jobs.

Yoder, D., *Handbook of Personnel Management and Labor Relations* (New York: McGraw-Hill, 1958). An experienced writer condenses the main problems and offers constructive solutions.

Human Relations

Barnard, C. I., *Organization and Management* (Cambridge: Harvard University Press, 1948). A selection of papers dealing with good human relationships in industry.

Bursk, E. C., ed., *Human Relations for Management, the Newer Perspective* (New York: Harper, 1956). A selection of articles having religious implications. One was written from a Catholic viewpoint.

Davis, K., *Human Relations in Business* (New York: McGraw-Hill, 1957).

Excellent study of the main approaches to the human problems of industrial relations.

Gardner, B. B., and Moore, D. C., *Human Relations in Industry* (Homewood, Ill.: Irwin, 1955). New edition of a management-oriented study of the human factor in industry. The place of unions is fairly presented.

Hoslett, S. D., ed., revised edition, *Human Factors in Management* (New York: Harper, 1951). Revised edition of a valuable text dealing with many important factors faced by management in directing the operations of its employees.

Human Relations in Modern Business (New York: Prentice-Hall, 1950). A blending of social ethics with business practice. Developed by a representative committee and signed by seven corporation executives. Useful for social action work with employers. Bibliography.

Profit Sharing

Meier, J. B., ed., *Profit Sharing Manual* (Chicago: Council of Profit Sharing Industries, 1957). Up-to-date information on profit sharing presented in a balanced and comprehensive fashion.

Nunn, H. L., *The Whole Man Goes to Work* (New York: Harper, 1953). An autobiography of an employer who pioneered in promoting labor-management harmony, profit-sharing, and guaranteed wages, motivated by a sense of justice and charity.

Profit Sharing: Key to Industrial Teamwork (Chicago, Ill.: Council of Profit Sharing Industries, 1956). An effort to meet many of the practical problems connected with profit-sharing. Realistic appraisal of its limitations.

Thompson, K. M., *Profit Sharing* (New York: Harper, 1949). An authoritative study of this important problem. Concrete and informative. Bibliography, references, and appendix material. Out of print.

Codetermination

Blumenthal, W. M., *Codetermination in the German Steel Industry* (Princeton: Industrial Relations Section, Princeton University, 1956). Excellent study based on intensive field investigation of this important experiment in labor-management partnership enforced by law.

Newman, J., *Co-responsibility in Industry* (Westminster, Md.: Newman, 1956). The problems of labor-management relations as seen by an eminent Irish scholar. Emphasis is largely European, with special stress upon the German experiment in codetermination.

Shuchman, A., *Codetermination: Labor's Middle Way in Germany* (Washington: Public Affairs Press, 1957). History and present trends in the German experiment. Author's sympathies lie with union demands for extension of comanagement.

List No. 7.   LABOR PROBLEMS

Material herein contained refers mainly to matters covered in Chapters IX and X.

General Works

Chamberlain, N. W., *Labor* (New York: McGraw-Hill, 1958). How business and labor organize for collective bargaining, and the impact of union policies upon the general economy.

Labor's Library (Washington: Workers Education Bureau, A. F. of L., 1952). Annotated and topically divided reading list on labor problems and related topics.

Myers, J., and Laidler, H. W., What do You Know About Labor? (New York: John Day, 1956). A very useful handbook, giving the highlights of all the important problems in the labor field. Would be very useful for discussion groups or even for labor-school classes.

Reder, M. W., Labor in a Growing Economy (New York: Wiley, 1957). Sound, well-written, and interesting textbook on labor problems.

Reynolds, L. G., Labor Economics and Labor Relations (New York: Prentice-Hall, 1954). A textbook in labor economics, with considerable emphasis upon the history of the labor movement.

Taft, P., Economics and Problems of Labor (Harrisburg, Pa.: Stackpole & Heck, 1955). One of the better labor textbooks.

Tannenbaum, F., A Philosophy of Labor (New York: Knopf, 1950). A non-Catholic Columbia University professor elaborates a philosophy of labor which is quite similar to that of the encyclicals.

Year Book of Labor Statistics (Geneva: International Labor Office). Valuable for international figures on employment, price levels, and other items connected with labor problems.

Union Structure and Policy

Bakke, E. W., and Kerr, C., Unions, Management and the Public (New York: Harcourt, 1948). Uses many sources to show impact of trade unionism on workers, management, and the public.

Barbash, J., The Practice of Unionism (New York: Harper, 1956). A former union official writes with penetration and insight about the internal operations and problems of the American trade union.

Ginzberg, E., The Labor Leader (New York: Macmillan, 1948). The psychology of labor leadership, based on a study of leaders in ten national unions.

Goldberg, A. J., AFL-CIO: Labor United (New York: McGraw-Hill, 1956). An architect of labor unity tells the story of the amalgamation. A good history of this dramatic development in the labor scene.

Hardman, J. B. S., and Neufeld, M. F., eds., The House of Labor (New York: Prentice-Hall, 1951). An unusual symposium, with top labor leaders as contributors, showing the internal functioning of our complex trade-union system.

LeRoy, A., The Dignity of Labor (Westminster, Md.: Newman, 1957). Part played by Catholics in the International Labor Organization, written by a priest long associated with this important organization.

Liveright, A. A., Union Leadership Training: A Handbook of Tools and Techniques (New York: Harper, 1951). Suggestions, based on wide experience, for labor education.

Lorwin, L. L., The International Labor Movement (New York: Harper, 1953). In addition to a competent historical treatment of the problem, the author analyzes and discusses current trends in international labor organizations and related problems.

Mire, J., *Labor Education: A Study on Needs, Programs, and Approaches* (Madison: Inter-University Labor Education Committee, 1956). An effort to make workers' education more effective by studying gaps in the present system and making recommendations for expansion and improvement.

Purcell, T. V., *The Worker Speaks His Mind on Company and Union* (Cambridge: Harvard University Press, 1954). On the basis of case history, Father Purcell reports on labor-management relationships in the packinghouse industry. He finds no essential conflict between worker loyalty to the company and worker loyalty to the union.

Sayles, L. R., and Strauss, G., *The Local Union: Its Place in the Industrial Plant* (New York: Harper, 1953). Students of union democracy can find abundant source material in this careful study of internal policies in twenty selected local unions.

Seidman, J., *The Worker Views His Union* (Chicago: University of Chicago Press, 1958). Documents the thesis of rank-and-file apathy.

Taft, P., *The Structure and Government of Labor Unions* (Cambridge: Harvard University Press, 1954). Various papers on internal union problems, written from a viewpoint sympathetic to the labor movement. Somewhat less realistic than Barbash's study.

Criticism of Unions

Chamberlin, E. H., *The Economic Analysis of Labor Union Power* (Washington: American Enterprise Association, 1958). The public interest requires major restrictions upon the monopoly power of labor. Favors smaller bargaining units.

Keller, E. A., *The Case for Right-to-Work Laws: a Defense of Voluntary Unionism* (Chicago: Heritage Foundation, 1956). Father Keller defends laws which restrict the union shop and other forms of "unionism by contract." A moderately good defense of the conservative viewpoint on this problem.

Lindblom, C. E., *Unions and Capitalism* (New Haven: Yale, 1949). The author sees the vices as well as the virtues of unionism. Fears monopoly tendencies and interference with essential freedom of enterprise.

Pound, R., *Legal Immunities of Trade Unions* (Washington: American Enterprise Association, 1957). One of our greatest jurists contends that labor enjoys exemption from laws enacted to prevent monopoly and exploitation.

Richberg, D. R., *Labor Union Monopoly: A Clear and Present Danger* (Chicago: Regnery, 1957). A sample of the most extreme and all-out attacks upon the labor movement and its economic policies.

Collective Bargaining

Braun, K., *Labor Disputes and Their Settlement* (Baltimore: Johns Hopkins Press, 1955). Methods used here and abroad to achieve peaceful rather than forced settlements of labor-management disputes.

Carpenter, W. H., *Case Studies in Collective Bargaining* (New York: Prentice-Hall, 1953). A discriminating and sophisticated touch is shown in the selection and organization of these case histories.

Chamberlain, N. W., *Collective Bargaining* (New York: McGraw-Hill, 1951). The author does not hesitate to express strong viewpoints, thus producing a valuable and provocative study of this basic problem.

Davey, H. W., *Contemporary Collective Bargaining* (New York: Prentice-Hall, 1951). Unusually realistic and comprehensive study of the realities of labor-management relations. Emphasizes the value of free collective bargaining.

Dunlop, J. T., and Healy, J. J., *Collective Bargaining: Principles and Cases* (Homewood, Ill.: Irwin, 1953). The social process of collective bargaining, illustrated by fresh case studies.

Peters, E., *Strategy and Tactics in Labor Negotiations* (New London: National Foremen's Institute, 1955). A primer in labor negotiations, interestingly written, for executives and others concerned with collective bargaining.

Strikes and Arbitration

Bernstein, I., *Arbitration of Wages* (Berkeley: University of California Press, 1954). Problems faced in wage arbitration. Author holds that such processes should be considered as extensions of collective bargaining.

Chamberlain, N. W., *Social Responsibility and Strikes* (New York: Harper, 1953). Because public opinion and community suffering do not prevent serious strikes, the author advocates strong government action to curb labor disputes.

Chamberlain, N. W., and Schilling, J. M., *The Impact of Strikes* (New York: Harper, 1954). How strikes affect the workers, consumers, and suppliers of firms shut down by industrial disputes.

Gitlow, A. L., *Wage Determination Under National Boards* (New York: Prentice-Hall, 1953). Criteria for wage-fixing, based on study of decisions rendered by various public boards.

Kornhauser, A., Dubin, R., and Ross, A. M., eds., *Industrial Conflict* (New York: McGraw-Hill, 1954). Forty authors contribute to this symposium, exploring every phase of industrial strife. Moderate and realistic in approach.

Taylor, G. W., ed., *Labor Arbitration Series* (Philadelphia: University of Pennsylvania Press, 1952). Nine volumes on various phases of arbitration.

Labor-Management Co-operation

Braun, K., *Union-Management Co-operation* (Washington: Brookings Institution, 1947). A thorough study of co-operation in the clothing industry, with some analysis of implications for other industries.

Golden, C. S., and Parker, V. D., eds., *Causes of Industrial Peace Under Collective Bargaining* (New York: Harper, 1955). Condensation and evaluation of National Planning Association case studies on peaceful labor relations.

Nyman, R. C., *Foundations for Constructive Industrial Relations* (New York: Funk & Wagnalls, 1949). A sociologist works out a pattern of labor-management co-operation.

Partners in Production (New York: Twentieth Century Fund, 1949). Shows how major goals of labor and management can be reconciled in their mutual interest to the furthering of the common good.

Selekman, B. M., *Labor Relations and Human Relations* (New York: McGraw-Hill, 1947). Social changes enforced by collective bargaining analyzed, with special stress on need for leadership on both sides. Excellent.

Whyte, W. F., *Pattern for Industrial Peace* (New York: Harper, 1951). From this detailed study of how industrial peace was achieved in one corporation, useful generalizations can be developed.

Automation

The Challenge of Automation (Washington: Public Affairs Press, 1957). Papers delivered at a national conference, reflecting fears that automation will bring serious unemployment.

Diebold, J., *Automation: The Advent of the Automatic Factor* (New York: Van Nostrand, 1953). Automation will come gradually, thus minimizing the impact upon workers. An optimistic viewpoint.

Einzig, P., *The Economic Consequences of Automation* (New York: Norton, 1957). The author is a facile popularizer of difficult economic problems. In this volume he explains well the implications of automation.

Friedmann, G., *Industrial Society: The Emergence of the Human Problems of Automation* (Glencoe, Ill.: Free Press, 1955). European study of the effect of mechanization upon the personality of workers. Shows excellent insights into this problem.

Macmillan, R. H., *Automation: Friend or Foe?* (New York: Cambridge University Press, 1956). An engineer gives an optimistic appraisal of the effects of automation.

Phillips, A., *Automation, Its Impact on Economic Growth and Stability* (Washington: American Enterprise Association, 1957). Argues that automation will bring undreamed-of prosperity, without causing economic dislocations.

Pollock, F., *Automation: A Study of Its Economic and Social Consequences* (New York: Praeger, 1958). Explains automation, forces accelerating the development, and its consequences.

Wage Determination and Employment Problems

Burns, A. F., *Prosperity Without Inflation* (New York: Fordham University Press, 1957). One of America's best known economists holds that inflation is a major threat to our economic welfare. Especially valuable because of the author's government experience.

Dunlop, J. T., ed., *The Theory of Wage Determination* (New York: St. Martin's Press, 1957). A 1954 symposium of the International Economic Association. A mine of information on the forces behind wages.

Gomberg, W., *Trade Union Analysis of Time Study* (Chicago: Science Research Associates, 1955). A critical but competent survey of time-study methods, written by a former union official.

Haber, W., and Levinson, H. M., *Labor Relations and Productivity in the Building Trades* (Ann Arbor: Bureau of Industrial Relations, University of Michigan, 1956). Contrary to the general view, productivity in the building trades is increasing and unions are co-operating with management in this regard.

Lerner, A. P., *Economics of Employment* (New York: McGraw-Hill, 1951). Clear explanation of Keynesian theories of employment, now widely accepted, at least in part, in devising remedies for the business cycle.

Patton, J. A., and Littlefield, C. L., *Job Evaluation* (Homewood, Ill.: Irwin, 1957). Studies job evaluation and merit rating in the attempt to secure a scientific appraisal of a worker's contribution to the enterprise.

Ross, A. M., *Trade Union Wage Policy* (Berkeley: University of California

Press, 1956). Stimulating study of collective bargaining considered as a political activity.

Taylor, G. W., and Pierson, F. C., eds., *New Concepts in Wage Determination* (New York: McGraw-Hill, 1957). Descriptive approach to wage theory. Not entirely successful in developing new concepts as promised by the title.

Woytinsky, W. S., et al., *Employment and Wages in the United States* (New York: Twentieth Century Fund, 1953). A comprehensive compilation of data regarding wages and employment, with enough history, theory, and analysis to make the data more pertinent.

Labor Law

Gregory, C. O., *Labor and the Law* (New York: Norton, 1958). Gives both the basic laws and the most important judicial decisions affecting labor.

Mathews, R. E., *Labor Relations and the Law* (Boston: Little, Brown, 1953). A textbook on labor law, with emphasis upon constructive attitudes toward collective bargaining.

Millis, H. A., and Brown, E. C., *From the Wagner Act to Taft-Hartley: A Study of National Labor Policy and Labor Relations* (Chicago: University of Chicago Press, 1950). A thorough study of our basic labor laws and their administration.

Werne, B., *The Law of Labor Relations* (New York: Macmillan, 1951). This analysis is nontechnical, and centers heavily on the Taft-Hartley Act as a basic law in the field.

List No. 8. FAMILY ECONOMIC PROBLEMS

Material for Chapter XI.

The Family and Its Economic Problems

Callaghan, H. C., *The Family Allowance Procedure* (Washington: Catholic University Press, 1947). A doctoral dissertation exploring the field with great thoroughness and insight.

Cissell, R., and Cissell, H., *Stretching the Family Income* (New York: Wagner, 1953). Practical suggestions for money management in the home, including tips on purchasing, borrowing, self-help, and insurance.

Clemens, A. H., *Marriage and the Family* (Englewood Cliffs, N. J.: Prentice-Hall, 1957). Textbook with useful hints on family economic problems.

Croteau, J. T., *The Federal Credit Union — Policy and Practice* (New York: Harper, 1956). How credit unions help meet the needs of Americans in all walks of life. The author is a professor at the University of Notre Dame.

Kyrk, H., *The Family in the American Economy* (Chicago: Chicago University Press, 1953). Economic position of the family in our nation. Notes changes both in the family and its economic status.

Mihanovich, C. S., et al., *Marriage and the Family* (Milwaukee: Bruce, 1952). Brother Schnepp has a chapter, with bibliography, on family economics.

Ogburn, W. F., and Nimkoff, M. F., *Technology and the Changing Family* (Boston: Houghton Mifflin, 1955). Modern technology has changed the family from a productive unit to a loosely knit society, more likely to fall apart. Useful, but somewhat oversimplified.

Thomas, J. L., *The American Catholic Family* (New York: Prentice-Hall, 1956). One of our best sociologists studies the Catholic family in an environment which often poses problems of adjustment and conflict. Excellent treatment of the cultural differences which this situation exposes.

Troelstrup, A., *Consumer Problems* (New York: McGraw-Hill, 1957). One of the better texts in treating economic problems as they affect family life.

Health and Housing

Bachman, G. W., and associates, *Health Resources in the United States* (Washington: Brookings Institution, 1952). Factual survey of health resources available. Trends and regional differences noted.

Beyer, C. H., *Housing, a Factual Analysis* (New York: Macmillan, 1958). Represents the result of a seminar and hence reflects many viewpoints regarding the housing problem.

Bloomgarden, H., *Before We Sleep* (New York: Putnam, 1959). A passionate plea for the federal government to step up its program of medical research. Favors federal aid to medicine and attacks the American Medical Association for failure to promote a truly modern medical program.

Davis, M. M., *Medical Care for Tomorrow* (New York: Harper, 1955). Scholarly and courageous presentation of the economics and sociology of medicine. Holds that new methods must be found for paying for medical care.

Means, J. H., M.D., *Doctors, People, and Government* (Boston: Little, Brown, 1953). Medicine is a concern of the community and public opinion should make its wishes known to the medical profession. Co-ordinated services would give better medical care at lower cost.

Rothenberg, R. E., et al., *Group Medicine and Health Insurance in Action* (New York: Crown Publishers, 1949). Stresses advantages of group medical practice within framework of voluntary national health insurance.

Serbein, O. N., *Paying for Medical Care in the United States* (New York: Columbia University Press, 1954). Factual study of medical economics, with a minimum of interpretation.

Winnick, L., and Shilling, N., *American Housing and Its Use* (New York: Wiley, 1957). Factual study of American housing, interpreting data of 1950 census.

Social Security

Becker, J. M., *The Problem of Abuse in Unemployment Benefits* (New York: Columbia University Press, 1953). Careful study of abuses of unemployment compensation, suggesting that legislative reforms would make possible greater benefits to those genuinely unemployed.

Burns, E. M., *Social Security and Public Policy* (New York: McGraw-Hill, 1956). Policy and practice of social security, with its impact on individuals and families assessed.

Gagliardo, D., *American Social Insurance* (New York: Harper, 1955). A concise textbook on social security and related problems, including proposed improvements.

Meriam, L., et al., *The Cost and Financing of Social Security* (Washington: Brookings Institution, 1950). A critical survey, in terms of costs, of the social-security system.

List No. 9.   PROPERTY

Selected works for Chapter XII.

General Works

Belloc, Hilaire, *The Restoration of Property* (New York: Sheed and Ward, 1936). A blueprint for a distributist society. Out of print.
────── *The Servile State* (New York: Holt, 1946). One of the first arguments for distributism. Holds that ownership by the few means a servile state. Out of print.
Berle, A. A., and Means, G. C., *The Modern Corporation and Private Property* (New York: Macmillan, 1933). The authors study the social implications of power concentration through narrow control of corporate wealth. A masterly treatment.
Crofts, A. M., *Property and Poverty* (Dublin: Irish Rosary Office, 1948). Private ownership according to the principles of St. Thomas Aquinas.
Miller, H. P., *Income of the American People* (New York: Wiley, 1955). Study of American incomes and related social and economic factors.
Paul, R. E., *Taxation in the United States* (Boston: Little, Brown, 1954). An expert with wide experience writes well of the history of our tax system and the unfinished task before us.
Schumacher, L. S., *The Philosophy of the Equitable Distribution of Wealth* (Washington: Catholic University Press, 1949). A doctorate applying Thomistic ideals of property to modern wealth distribution.

Monopoly and Related Problems

Berle, A. A., *The Twentieth Century Capitalist Revolution* (New York: Harcourt, 1954). Big business is developing a higher code of morality and concern for the public interest.
Chamberlin, E. H., ed., *Monopoly and Competition and Their Regulation* (New York: St. Martin's Press, 1954). Papers read at a meeting held in France in 1951. Wide and useful variety of opinions on the monopoly question.
Edwards, C. D., *Maintaining Competition: Requisites of a Governmental Policy* (New York: McGraw-Hill, 1949). While rejecting the idea that competition can automatically guide the entire economy, the author explores useful areas where it should be promoted.
Kaplan, A. D. H., *Big Enterprise in a Competitive System* (Washington: Brookings Institution, 1954). Another favorable study that gives the nod to big business in terms of dynamic growth and vigorous competition.
Lilienthal, D. E., *Big Business: a New Era* (New York: Harper, 1952). A New Deal liberal defends modern big business as growing in social responsibility.
Mason, E. S., *Economic Concentration and the Monopoly Problem* (Cambridge: Harvard University Press, 1957). Collection of essays by one of the nation's foremost experts in antitrust problems. Authoritative and inspiring.
Maurer, H., *Great Enterprise: Growth and Behavior of the Big Corporation* (New York: Macmillan, 1955). Effort to gain insight into the over-all rationale of large firms.

Stocking, G. W., and Watkins, M. W., *Monopoly and Free Enterprise* (New York: Twentieth Century Fund, 1951). The authors feel that we have workable competition today, but that we must continue to fight undue concentration if we are to preserve economic vitality.

List No. 10.   THE STATE

Readings for Chapter XIII.

General Works on Government

Davitt, T. E., S.J., *The Nature of Law* (St. Louis: Herder, 1951). Historical survey of the Augustinian and Thomist approaches to law. Brilliant philosophical study.

De Jouvenel, B., *Sovereignty: An Inquiry into the Political Good* (Chicago: University of Chicago Press, 1957). Qualities of political leadership and moral requirements for just rule.

Evans, J. W., and Ward, L. R., eds., *The Social and Political Philosophy of Maritain* (New York: Scribner's, 1955). A compilation of the writings of Jacques Maritain in the field of social and political philosophy. Many important modern problems are covered in these selections.

Gilby, T., O.P., *Between Community and Society; a Philosophy and Theology of the State* (New York: Longmans, 1953). A thorough study of the political writings of St. Thomas Aquinas, presented brilliantly in terms of current problems. The author's knowledge of history adds richness to his presentation.

Keller, J., M.M., *Government Is Your Business* (Garden City, N. Y.: Doubleday, 1951). A primer on the workings of government and suggestions for infusing Christian principles into this important field. Inspiring and practical.

Lippmann, W., *Essays in the Public Philosophy* (Boston: Little, Brown, 1955). The tradition of natural law is considered essential for the proper working of a democracy. Unless people adhere to standards, they cannot hold firm principles when confronting the difficult issues of our time.

Maritain, J., *Man and the State* (Chicago: University of Chicago Press, 1951). An eloquent defense of the moral character of politics and political theory, with excellent chapters on the rights of man, the natural law, and the *jus gentium*.

Rommen, H. A., *The State in Catholic Thought* (St. Louis: Herder, 1945). Applies social ethics to government.

Schmandt, H. J., and Steinbicker, P. G., *Fundamentals of Government* (Milwaukee: Bruce, 1954). Text on the principles and problems of government, written from a Catholic point of view.

Democracy

Blaisdell, D. C., *American Democracy Under Pressure* (New York: Ronald Press, 1957). A thorough study of pressure groups as important factors in our governmental process.

Dahl, R. A., *A Preface to Democratic Theory* (Chicago: University of Chicago Press, 1956). Unusual insight into the underlying philosophy of our democracy and its unanswered problems.

Eby, K., and Greenlief, J., *The Paradoxes of Democracy* (New York: Association Press, 1956). Shortcomings of democracy which must be overcome if we are to realize our full potential.

Einaudi, M., and Goguel, F., *Christian Democracy in Italy and France* (Notre Dame, Ind.: University of Notre Dame Press, 1952). Two great scholars discuss the important developments in the Latin version of Christian democracy.

Grindel, C. W., ed., *Concept of Freedom* (Chicago: Regnery, 1955). A symposium on the subject of freedom. Prepared by the Humanities Research Board of St. John's University in Brooklyn.

Hallowell, J. H., *The Moral Foundation of Democracy* (Chicago: University of Chicago Press, 1954). Emphasizes need for a philosophy of life underlying democratic institutions. Considers democracy a means, not an end.

Maritain, J., *Christianity and Democracy* (New York: Hillary, 1944). A study of the close interrelationship between the two.

Shields, C., *Democracy and Catholicism in America* (New York: McGraw-Hill, 1958). The author examines classic liberalism, democracy, and Catholicism. Holds that Catholicism is compatible with democracy, but that liberalism is incompatible.

Simon, Y. R., *Philosophy of Democratic Government* (Chicago: University of Chicago Press, 1951). A consideration of the advantages, difficulties, and characteristic features of democracy, which does not make the usual mistake of falling into vague generalities and wishful thinking.

Stamps, N. L., *Why Democracies Fail* (Notre Dame, Ind.: University of Notre Dame Press, 1957). The author holds that dictatorship does not arise merely because of the personality of its leaders. There is also a failure on the part of previous democratic regimes.

Stumpf, S. E., *A Democratic Manifesto* (Nashville: Vanderbilt University Press, 1954). Democracy will survive if we keep our faith in the dignity of man. Religious principles should be applied to public life.

Tolerance and the Catholic: A Symposium (New York: Sheed and Ward, 1955). Religious liberty in a pluralist society as seen by leading French and Belgian theologians. Emphasizes theological aspects, but gives adequate consideration to the political problems involved.

Ward, B., *Faith and Freedom* (New York: Norton, 1954). Freedom as developed through the centuries is the main theme of this book. The author concentrates upon the Western world as the finest embodiment of human liberty.

Civil Rights and Liberties

Cushman, R. E., *Civil Liberties in the United States: A Guide to Current Problems and Experience* (Ithaca, N. Y.: Cornell University Press, 1956). Orderly summary of the main challenges to American civil liberties today.

Gardiner, H. C., S.J., *Catholic Viewpoint on Censorship* (Garden City: Hanover House, 1958). Realistic defense of Catholic views and programs in the area of censorship.

Hand, L., *The Bill of Rights* (Cambridge: Harvard University Press, 1958). One of America's greatest jurists takes issue with the thesis that the Supreme Court has the right to overrule the legislature.

Hook, S., *Common Sense and the Fifth Amendment* (New York: Criterion Books, 1957). Dr. Hook holds that the public is right in making reasonable inferences when a witness or defendant uses the Fifth Amendment. He claims that arguments to the contrary are based on fanciful suppositions.

Kirk, R., *Academic Freedom: An Essay in Definition* (Chicago: Regnery, 1955). Strong defense of the thesis that we have freedom to teach the truth, but not license to propagate error.

Taylor, T., *Grand Inquest: the Story of Congressional Investigations* (New York: Simon and Schuster, 1955). Congressional investigations have a long and honored history. Here is the legal and historical background of this important congressional function.

Special Problems

Dimock, M. E., *Business and Government* (New York: Holt, 1957). The mixed economy of private enterprise under some government control analyzed from economic and political aspects.

Douglas, P., *Ethics in Government* (Cambridge: Harvard University Press, 1952). Senator Douglas discusses a much publicized problem of our day. He puts the issue into perspective and offers some sound remedies for corruption in government.

MacIver, R. M., *The Web of Government* (New York: Macmillan, 1947). A sociopolitical study of government. Warns against excessive concentration of power in the state.

MacNeil, N., and Metz, H. W., *The Hoover Commission Report* (New York: Macmillan, 1956). The main outlines of our most recent and most ambitious plan for reforming government.

List No. 11. INTERNATIONAL ECONOMIC AND POLITICAL PROBLEMS

Selected works for Chapter XIV.

General Works

Eppstein, J., *The Catholic Tradition and the Law of Nations* (London: Burns, Oates, 1935). Christian principles on peace. Out of print.

—— ed., *Code of International Ethics* (Westminster, Md.: Newman, 1953). The latest revision of the Malines code, with commentary by a distinguished specialist on international problems. Discusses among other things the morality of atomic bombing.

Gonella, G., *Papacy and World Peace* (Westminster, Md.: Newman, 1950). Explanation of the ethical principles involved in papal peace messages, particularly the Christmas messages of Pope Pius XII.

Gurian, W., and Fitzsimons, M. A., eds., *The Catholic Church in World Affairs* (Notre Dame, Ind.: University of Notre Dame Press, 1954). The Catholic Church's influence on world affairs is evaluated by sixteen authorities in the field of international relations. Out of print.

Woytinsky, W. S., and Woytinsky, E. S., *World Population and Production: Trends and Outlook* (New York: Twentieth Century Fund, 1953). Massive study of world population, resources, and production, with efforts to project trends years ahead.

Pamphlet studies by the Catholic Association for International Peace, 1312

Massachusetts Avenue, N.W., Washington 5, D. C. A series of timely studies on both ethical principles and current problems.

United Nations and Its Agencies

Asher, R. E., Kotschnig, W. M., Brown, W. A., Jr., and associates, *The United Nations and Economic and Social Cooperation* (Washington: Brookings Institution, 1957). Case study of the Economic Commission for Europe, as an example of the broad economic work of the United Nations.

Hambidge, G., *The Story of FAO* (New York: Van Nostrand, 1955). Hunger is one of the greatest problems in the world today. The Food and Agriculture Organization, United Nations, is striving valiantly to conquer this foe of human welfare.

Morgan, M., *Doctors to the World* (New York: Viking, 1958). Programs and policies of the World Health Organization.

Reitzel, W., Kaplan, M. A., and Coblenz, C. G., *United States Foreign Policy* (Washington: Brookings Institution, 1956). Critical examination of our policy during the decade after World War II. Authors feel that there has been too much improvisation.

Statistical Office of the U. N., *Demographic Yearbook* (New York: Columbia University Press). Studies based on annual population statistics.

────── *Statistical Yearbook* (New York: Columbia University Press). Increasingly valuable statistics are found in these annual compilations.

────── *Yearbook of International Trade Statistics* (New York: Columbia University Press). Annual survey of world trade.

Economic Problems

Bauer, P. T., *Economic Analysis and Policy in Underdeveloped Countries* (Durham, N. C.: Duke University Press, 1957). A strong plea for private, as contrasted with statist, development in newly growing economies. Many suggestions closely parallel the warnings of Pope Pius XII.

Buchanan, N. S., and Ellis, H. S., *Approaches to Economic Development* (New York: Twentieth Century Fund, 1955). Argues that developing nations should do more to build up their own capital resources.

The Changing Environment of International Relations (Washington: Brookings Institution, 1956). A symposium of lectures on international problems, with emphasis upon underdeveloped nations.

Clark, C., *The Conditions of Economic Progress* (London: Macmillan, 1957). Comparative study of national economies and their ability to provide economic welfare. Author is an internationally known expert.

Condliffe, J. B., *The Commerce of Nations* (New York: Norton, 1949). Economic history of foreign trade, leading up to current problems.

Enke, S. S., and Salera, V., *International Economics* (Englewood Cliffs, N. J.: Prentice-Hall, 1957). Stresses interrelationship of economic policy and international relations.

Heilperin, M. A., *The Trade of Nations* (New York: Knopf, 1947). A discussion of world trade theory and policies, supporting the ideal of more freedom of trade.

Millikan, M. F., and Rostow, W. W., *A Proposal: Key to an Effective Foreign Policy* (New York: Harper, 1957). Emphasizes the necessity for a long-range program for aiding developing nations.

Wilcox, C., *A Charter for World Trade* (New York: Macmillan, 1949). The author defends the International Trade Organization as the best method for restoring world trade.

Social Problems

Cirtautas, K. C., *The Refugee* (Boston: Meador Publishing Company, 1957). Psychological study of the problems facing a refugee when he migrates here.

Divine, R. A., *American Immigration Policy, 1924–1952* (New Haven: Yale, 1957). Background material on our immigration policy, explaining not only the major laws, but the pressures that influenced legislation and policy.

Higham, J., *Strangers in the Land: Patterns of American Nativism, 1860–1925* (New Brunswick, N. J.: Rutgers University Press, 1955). Fascinating survey of American nativism and its result in restriction of immigration.

Keeny, S. M., *Half the World's Children* (New York: Association Press, 1957). Studies the work of United Nations' Children's Fund (UNICEF). Gripping story of an important program.

Proudfoot, M. J., *European Refugees, 1939–1952* (Evanston, Ill.: Northwestern University Press, 1956). Population movements in Europe after World War II, and the operation of the United Nations Relief and Rehabilitation Administration.

List No. 12. THE RACE QUESTION

Books for Chapter XV.

General Works

Cantwell, D. M., *Catholics Speak on Race Relations* (Chicago: Fides Publishers, 1952). Statements by prominent Church authorities, including two popes, are included in this stimulating booklet.

Cole, S. G., and Cole, M. W., *Minorities and the American Promise* (New York: Harper, 1954). Contrast between professed ideals of equality and realities of prejudice and intolerance in American life.

Dollard, J., *Caste and Class in a Southern Town* (New York: Doubleday, 1937). Intensive and perceptive study of race relations in one community of the Deep South.

Foley, A. S., *God's Men of Color: the Colored Catholic Priests of the United States, 1854–1954* (New York: Farrar, Straus, and Cudahy, 1955). The work of colored Catholic priests in the United States during the past century.

Frazier, E. F., *Black Bourgeoisie* (Glencoe, Ill.: Free Press and Falcon's Wing Press, 1956). Analysis, possibly exaggerated at times, of the Negro middle class and its alleged weakness.

————— *The Negro in the United States* (New York: Macmillan, 1957). Standard text on Negro problems.

LaFarge, J., *The Catholic Viewpoint on Race Relations* (Garden City: Hanover House, 1956). A useful handbook on race relations, by an expert with decades of experience in this important field.

Logan, R. W., *The Negro in the United States: a Brief History* (New York: Van Nostrand, 1957). Scholarly, emphasizes present century.

Myrdal, G., *An American Dilemma* (New York: Harper, 1944). One of the basic works on Negro problems, based on an extensive survey by a Swedish sociologist.

Rose, A., *The Negro in America* (New York: Harper, 1948). A summary of Myrdal's two-volume work.

Warren, R. P., *Segregation* (New York: Random House, 1956). Report on attitudes of Southerners regarding segregation. Finds them uneasy over their prejudices.

Woodward, C. V., *The Strange Career of Jim Crow* (New York: Oxford University Press, 1957). Development of racial segregation in the South from 1877 to the present. Many will be surprised to know that restrictions are often relatively recent.

Special Problems

Abrams, C., *Forbidden Neighbors: A Study of Prejudice in Housing* (New York: Harper, 1955). The broad pattern of xenophobic discrimination, including religion, national origin, and race as reasons for rejection.

Ashmore, H. S., *The Negro and the Schools* (Chapel Hill: University of North Carolina Press, 1954). Good background material for understanding problems arising from integration of schools. Traces the slow progress toward the 1954 Supreme Court decision.

Ginzberg, E., *The Negro Potential* (New York: Columbia University Press, 1956). Emphasizes the tremendous possibilities of Negro advances, given the proper opportunities.

King, M. L., *Stride Toward Freedom. The Montgomery Story* (New York: Harper, 1958). Rev. Martin Luther King tells how the example of Gandhi influenced him in his inspired leadership of his people.

Price, H. D., *The Negro and Southern Politics: A Chapter of Florida History* (New York: New York University Press, 1957). Existing state of Negro voting in Florida. Indications are that the future is brightening in regard to civil and political rights.

Shoemaker, D., ed., *With All Deliberate Speed: Segregation-Desegregation in Southern Schools* (New York: Harper, 1957). Eleven essays on the state of educational desegregation in mid-1957. Should aid in realistic appraisal of the problem.

Wilmer, D. M., *et al.*, *Human Relations in Interracial Housing* (Minneapolis: University of Minnesota Press, 1955). Study of effects of various patterns of interracial housing.

Liberal Southern Viewpoint

Ashmore, H. S., *An Epitaph For Dixie* (New York: Norton, 1958). Little Rock editor discusses problems of integration.

Carmichael, O., and James, W., *The Louisville Story* (New York: Simon and Schuster, 1957). Brief analysis of a successful experiment in school integration.

Cash, W. J., *The Mind of the South* (New York: Knopf, 1941). Classic analysis of basic Southern attitudes on race matters.

Dykeman, W., and Stokely, J., *Neither Black nor White* (New York: Rinehart, 1957). Two Southern newspaper reporters present a careful study of interracial problems and attitudes.

Pope, L., *The Kingdom beyond Caste* (New York: Friendship Press, 1957). Shows that racial barriers can be crossed. Feels Southern churches lag in the struggle.

Rowan, C., *Go South to Sorrow* (New York: Random House, 1957). A Northern Negro reporter visits the South and learns how his people are treated there.

Weatherford, W. D., *American Churches and the Negro* (Boston: Christopher, 1957). Criticizes Southern churches for lagging in the struggle for Negro rights.

Woofter, T. J., *Southern Race Progress* (Washington: Public Affairs Press, 1957). Relatively objective and penetrating study of problems facing the Southern Negro.

List No. 13.   FARM PROBLEMS

Selected works for Chapter XVI.

General Works

Baer, U. J., *Letters to an American Farmer* (Des Moines, Iowa: National Catholic Rural Life Conference, 1956). A rural pastor writes to a friend on the problems of the day. Emphasis upon secularism.

Les valeurs humaines dans le domaine rural (Montreal: L'Oeuvre des Tracts, 1950). A declaration of principles from the Malines International Union of Social Studies (issued September, 1949).

Lindstrom, D. E., *American Rural Life* (New York: Ronald Press, 1948). A study of rural sociology, with emphasis on methods for bettering conditions in the country.

Manifesto on Rural Life (Milwaukee: Bruce, 1939). A co-operative statement by leading Church authorities giving a philosophy of rural life. About to be revised.

Taylor, C. C., et al., *Rural Life in the United States* (New York: Knopf, 1949). Eight U. S. Department of Agriculture experts write an excellent text on rural sociology.

Economic Problems

Benedict, M. R., *Can We Solve the Farm Problem?* (New York: Twentieth Century Fund, 1955). Historical study of farm problems and policies, with some recommendations for future handling of surpluses.

Bowen, E. R., *The Cooperative Road to Abundance* (New York: Abelard, 1953). Balanced treatment of the co-operative movement by an author with more than twenty-five years of experience in this area.

Cochrane, W. W., *Farm Prices: Myth and Reality* (Minneapolis: University of Minnesota Press, 1958). Cogent analysis of the core of the farm problem.

Mighell, R. L., *American Agriculture: Its Structure and Place in the Economy* (New York: Wiley, 1955). Strong plea for family farms, arguing that they are economically efficient as well as socially desirable.

Schoff, L. H., *A National Agricultural Policy: For All the People of the United States* (New York: Harper, 1950). Our agricultural policy should be geared to the needs of the entire nation, not particular groups. Favors flexible price supports and devices for giving away surplus crops.

Schultz, T. W., *Economic Organization of Agriculture* (New York: McGraw-Hill, 1953). Factual and comprehensive survey of new problems and developments in American farming.

Soth, L., *Farm Trouble* (Princeton, N. J.: Princeton University Press, 1957). Considers an excess number of marginal farms as the root of the farm problem. Would solve this problem by government aids to get marginal farmers off the land.

List No. 14. Social Principles in Action

Material for Chapter XVII.

Anderl, S., and Ruth, Sr. M., *The Religious and Catholic Action* (La Crosse, Wis.: St. Rose Convent, 1947). Emphasizes part played by religious in Catholic action. Reprints many papal and episcopal documents.

Cardijn, J., *Challenge to Action* (Chicago: Fides, 1955). The pioneer in the Jocist approach to the apostolate offers a challenge to Catholics everywhere.

Geaney, D. J., O.S.A., *You Are Not Your Own* (London: Chapman, 1958). The lay apostolate of the YCW variety, with emphasis upon penetration of environment with Christian principles.

Marx, P. B., *Virgil Michel and the Liturgical Movement* (Collegeville, Minn.: The Liturgical Press, 1957). Biography of a leader in a still too little understood aspect of social action. Emphasizes religious motivation that must underlie the full practice of justice and charity.

Meyer, B. F., M.M., *Lend Me Your Hands* (Chicago: Fides, 1955). The Christian Family Movement as a means for exercising the social apostolate. Appeal for new techniques to meet modern problems.

Montcheuil, Y. De, *A Guide for Social Action* (Chicago: Fides, 1954). Emphasizes the need for spiritual motivation for any program of social renovation.

Philips, G., *The Role of the Laity in the Church* (Chicago: Fides, 1956). Basic principles on the lay apostolate.

Putz, L. J., C.S.C., *The Modern Apostle* (Chicago: Fides, 1957). On the lay apostolate.

—— ed., *The Catholic Church, U.S.A.* (Chicago: Fides, 1956). Excellent symposium on the problems and challenges facing the Church here.

Saliege, Cardinal, *Who Shall Bear the Flame?* (Chicago: Fides, 1949). Dignity of man in connection with work, the family, and the state.

Suhard, E., *The Church Today* (Chicago: Fides, 1953). The pastoral letters and spiritual diary of the great Cardinal Archbishop of Paris. Although the background is postwar France, the principles and policies have universal application.

Walsh, M. E., and Furfey, P. H., *Social Problems and Social Action* (Englewood Cliffs, N. J.: Prentice-Hall, 1958). Various social, political, and economic problems explained. Authors give both institutional and personalist approaches in their solutions.

Ward, L. R., C.S.C., ed., *The American Apostolate* (Westminster, Md.: Newman, 1952). This symposium contains eighteen chapters covering most major fields of Catholic social action. Family, education, racial problems, and many other important fields are treated by specialists. Emphasis is upon accomplishments and present-day organizations, rather than upon abstract problems.

Wilmes, A. F., and Martin, C. J., eds., *Liturgy and the Social Order* (Elsberry, Mo.: National Liturgical Conference, 1956). These papers represent a major step forward in the efforts to bind the liturgical and social-action movements.

INDEX OF AUTHORITATIVE STATEMENTS

GENERAL INDEX

Abrams, C., on housing prejudice, 414
Adler, M. J., on capitalism, 394
Administered prices, 222
Advertising, fraudulent, 71
Age, of workers, 176
Agriculture, 344 ff; child labor in, 245; and the Church, 344 ff; and cultural values, 349 ff; economic problems of, 355 ff; and the family, 345 ff; federal aid for, 356 ff; and human values, 350 f; labor problems in, 352 ff; markets in, 356 f; migratory labor in, 352 ff; moral values in, 345 ff; prices in, 357; social problems of, 346 ff; Soviet, 111; surpluses in, 356 ff; see also Farms
Alexander, R. J., on Latin American communism, 398
Allen, F. L., on business abuses, 386; on New Deal, 386
Almond, G., on communist appeals, 395
Almsgiving, 78 f, 266 f
America, recommended, 390
A.F.L.-C.I.O., 74
Anderl, S., on Catholic action, 416
Annals of the American Academy of Political and Social Science, recommended, 390
Antitrust, 273 f
Apathy, political, 290
Apostolate, of clergy, 375 ff; lay, 377 ff
Aquinas, St. Thomas, see St. Thomas Aquinas
Arbitration, compulsory, 189 f
Asher, R. E., on UN in Europe, 412
Ashmore, H. S., on integration, 414; on school integration, 414
Association, right of, 52, 56
Autarky, 314 ff
Authoritarianism, 96 ff
Automation, effects of, 215 f; and living wage, 214 ff
Avarice, 59
Ave Maria, recommended, 390

Bachman, G. W., on health resources, 407
Baer, U. J., on farm life, 415
Bakke, E. W., on unions, 402
Barbash, J., on unions, 402

Barnard, C. I., on executive leadership, 399; on human relations, 400
Bassett, T. D. S., on socialism, 394
Bauer, P. T., on economic development, 412
Bauer, R. A., on Soviet life, 396
Becker, J. M., on unemployment insurance, 407
Beckwith, B. P., on socialism, 394
Bellarmine, R., on consent of governed, 286
Belloc, Hilaire, on distributism, 408
Benedict, M. R., on farm problems, 415
Berle, A. A., on capitalist revolution, 408; on modern corporation, 408
Berliner, J. S., on Soviet economic aid, 396
Bernstein, I., on labor arbitration, 404
Beyer, C. H., on housing, 407
Big business, need for, 273; and social justice, 163; trends toward, 269 f; see also Business
Birth control, 310
Black, J. M., on labor relations, 399
Black Death, 13
Blaisdell, D. C., on pressure groups, 409
Bloomgarden, H., on medical needs, 407
Blum, M. L., on industrial psychology, 400
Blumenthal, W. M., on codetermination, 401
Borkenau, F., on European communism, 397
Boulding, K. E., on economic policy, 389
Bouscaren, A., on communist techniques, 398
Bowen, E. R., on co-operatives, 415
Boycott, 190
Braun, K., on collective bargaining, 403; on union-management harmony, 404
Brown, E. C., on labor law, 406
Brown, L. C., on social problems, 393
Brown, W. A., on UN in Europe, 412
Bruehl, C., on papal social teaching, 391
Brzezinski, Z. K., on totalitarianism, 394
Buchanan, N. S., on economic development, 412
Budenz, L. F., on communist techniques, 398